Before Motown

Before Motown

A History of Jazz in Detroit, 1920–60

Lars Bjorn with Jim Gallert

Ann Arbor
The University of Michigan Press

Published in the United States of America by
The University of Michigan Press
Manufactured in the United States of America
⊗ Printed on acid-free paper
Cover & book design by Wesley B. Tanner/Passim Editions

2008 2007 2006 2005 7 6 5 4

A CIP catalog record for this book is available from the British Library.

Library of Congress Cataloging-in-Publication Data

Bjorn, Lars, 1944–
Before Motown : a history of jazz in Detroit, 1920–60 / Lars Bjorn with Jim Gallert.
p. cm.
Includes discography (p.) and index.
ISBN 0-472-09765-2 (cloth : alk. paper) — ISBN 0-472-06765-6 (paper : alk. paper)
1. Jazz—Michigan—Detroit—History and criticism. I. Gallert, Jim, 1950– II. Title.
ML3508.8.D4 B56 2001
781.65'09774'34—dc21 00-012321

To Susan, Mia, Krister,
and the memory of my parents

Preface

I WAS FIRST MOTIVATED to study jazz when I taught a course entitled "Society and the Arts in Detroit" with an interdisciplinary team at the University of Michigan–Dearborn. I had a deep passion for jazz from my early teens in Sweden and was familiar with some Detroit jazzmen, so I jumped at the chance to lecture on the history of jazz in Detroit. I soon discovered there was nothing in print on the topic and that I had to do my own research. I interviewed Dave Wilborn, a veteran of McKinney's Cotton Pickers, and was on my way. I made many connections as a member of the short-lived Jazz Research Institute at the Detroit Jazz Center, with help from John Sinclair and Herb Boyd. After publishing a few articles on Detroit jazz history up to World War II, I began work on the next 20 years with a book in mind.

In the mid-1980s I crossed paths with Jim Gallert, a Detroit jazz disc jockey, and we immediately discovered that we shared the same musical passions. We became friends and decided to collaborate. Jim knew more about jazz history than anyone I knew and also had a lot of personal contacts in the Detroit jazz community. He met and interviewed many musicians through his wonderful *Jazz Yesterday* show on WDET-FM, and in 1985 we started doing interviews together. Jim's contagious enthusiasm and deep insights contributed immeasurably to the final product, and for this I am forever indebted to him. More specifically, Jim shared the job of interviewing, collected all but a few photos, and provided all the captions. He coauthored the chapter on rhythm and blues, wrote the Club Congo Orchestra story, and added passages to and reviewed the other chapters.

One of the great rewards of researching this book has been getting to know many local musicians. Their support for this project has been unflagging, and it has made me all the more aware of the awesome responsibility involved in this attempt to tell their history. Jazz musicians tell stories when they improvise, but they also pass on stories about their playing through oral tradition. I have tried to capture and retell this tradition in a narrative framework; if I have failed, the responsibility falls squarely on my shoulders. I thank all of them for the privilege of getting to know them through conversations about the great music they make. There are simply too many individuals to mention all of them by name here. Please see Appendix A for a list of interviews.

A number of institutions and their staffs have provided invaluable resources for this project. In particular I would like to mention the Campus Grants Committee of the University of Michigan–Dearborn, the Mardigian Library at the Dearborn campus, the Hatcher Graduate and School of Music Libraries at the University of Michigan in Ann Arbor, the Burton Historical Collection and the E. Azalia Hackley Memorial Collection at the Detroit Public Library, and the Institute of Jazz Studies at Rutgers in Newark, New Jersey.

Several individuals volunteered their skills and knowledge at different stages of producing the book. I would like to thank Bill Kenney, Will Milberg, Rick Steiger, R. J. Spangler, Ben Baber, Frank Driggs, Pam Grady, and Virgil Grady for their encouragement; Stan Kuwik, Stan Hester, and Dan Kochakian for sharing their research; Byron X. Taylor and Fred Netting of the Detroit Federation of Musicians for their assistance; Clyde Stringer for help in locating and copying photos; John Willems for scanning and cleaning ads; Clarence (C. J.) Johnson and Randy Leipnik for scanning photos; Arthur LaBrew for providing copies of the *Owl;* Harold Borkin and Adrienne Kaplan for maps; Mary Erwin at the University of Michigan Press for her rapid responses and consistent support; and the late Lou Cramton for prodding me to write faster. I am grateful to those who took the time to read various drafts of the book: Sid Bolkosky, Mike Montgomery, Teddy Harris, Ray McKinney, Frank Driggs, Kenn Cox, Bill Randle, Mike Rowe, Dave Penny, and three anonymous reviewers. Piotr Michalowski has provided me with good advice and encouragement throughout. I want to thank him in particular for the title and a close reading of the manuscript. Most of all I want to thank my most constructive critic, my wife, Susan Wineberg. I thank her for taking on that role and even more for putting up with me during the ups and downs of this lengthy project.

Lars Bjorn

Collaborator's Comments

I have spent most of my spare time in the last 30 years supporting, promoting, and researching Detroit jazz. I began interviewing musicians in 1973 while host of *Jazz Yesterday,* and over the years I was drawn into the jazz community and formed friendships with many musicians and fellow supporters. Some of the information I gleaned from these friendships surfaced in articles, in liner notes, and on various radio programs I hosted. I am grateful and pleased that my research has found a permanent home in *Before Motown.* My research has been greatly aided by the love, support, and understanding of my wife, Dawn Beavon.

Jim Gallert

Acknowledgments

Every effort has been made to locate the holders of copyrighted material. The following have graciously given their permission to reprint the following material.

Bob Douglas for the photos appearing in figures 60, 61, 63, 64, 65, 66, 69, 73, 76, 77, 93. Copyright © 1946, 1947, 1948 by Bob Douglas.

John Lee Hooker/Bernard Besman for reprinting the lyrics of "Boogie Chillen." © 1967 Careers-BMG Music Publishing, Inc. (BMI). All rights reserved. Used by permission.

Oxford University Press for selections from pages 87, 160, 259–62 in *Swing to Bop* by Ira Gitler. Copyright © 1985 by Oxford University Press.

Princeton University Press for maps 2.1, 7.1(b), and 7.1(c), appearing here as figures 43, 78, and 79, from Sugrue, Thomas J.; *The Origins of the Urban Crisis.* Copyright © 1996 by Princeton University Press. Reprinted by permission of Princeton University Press.

James Richardson for the photos appearing in figures 82, 83, 85, 89, 91, 95. Copyright © 2000 by James Richardson.

Simon & Schuster and Miles Davis Properties, LLC, for selections from pages 170, 172–75 in *Miles: The Autobiography* by Miles Davis with Quincy Troupe. © 1989. Miles Davis Properties, LLC. Reprinted by permission of Simon & Schuster and Miles Davis Properties, LLC. Used by Permission/All Rights Reserved.

Rudy Tucich for the photos appearing in figures 88 and 90. Copyright © 2000 by Rudy Tucich.

Contents

Introduction

THERE *WAS* MUSIC IN DETROIT before Motown in the 1960s.

Detroit has a remarkable jazz history, which in fact made contributions to the Motown Sound. Jazz historians have usually passed by Detroit when discussing the development of jazz, and the goal of this book is to fill this gap in scholarship.[1]

Jazz emerged as a distinct type of music at the beginning of this century. Its pioneers were African Americans who drew upon musical traditions within and outside their community: blues, ragtime, Tin Pan Alley popular songs, and brass band music. Once jazz was born it went through rapid stylistic changes. Big band jazz developed around 1923, and some 20 years later bebop was born.

While the best known early jazz pioneers were from New Orleans, the idea that jazz was born in New Orleans and traveled up the Mississippi River to Chicago has been revised by jazz historians. It is now recognized that jazz-like music developed simultaneously in many U.S. cities between 1900 and 1920, but New Orleans had a unique style and was the single most influential city in its early history. Since jazz was the result of the mixing of a number of musical ingredients, the exact mix varied from place to place. For example, the influence of the blues was stronger in New Orleans than it was in New York City, where European musical traditions were more influential. Chicago occupied a midpoint between New Orleans and New York in this regard.

Where does Detroit fit into the development of jazz in the first half of this century? I will examine Detroit's contributions to jazz through three stylistic periods: early jazz (up to 1923), big band jazz, and bebop (up to 1960). In each period I will examine the interaction between local and national developments in jazz.

The Detroit jazz scene will be examined within its immediate social context as I investigate interactions between black and white musicians and audiences. A guiding idea is that the music played was a result of the cultural identities of the musicians and the opportunities they had to express these within a rapidly changing

1. This is the first book-length treatment of Detroit jazz history. I have published a few articles with more limited scope: "Black Men in a White World: The Development of the Black Jazz Community in Detroit, 1917–1940," *Detroit in Perspective* 5, no. 1 (fall 1980): 1–19; "Stompin' at the Graystone: Jazz in Detroit, 1917–1940," in *Detroit Jazz Who's Who*, ed. Herb Boyd and Leni Sinclair (Detroit: Jazz Research Institute, 1984); and "From Hastings Street to the Blue Bird: The Blues and Jazz Traditions in Detroit," *Michigan Quarterly Review* 25, no. 2 (spring 1986): 257–68. Herb Boyd has also published articles on aspects of Detroit jazz history: "The Beginning: Black Music in Detroit, 1850–1920" and "Black Bottom and Beyond," both in Herb Boyd and Leni Sinclair, eds., *Detroit Jazz Who's Who* (Detroit: Jazz Research Institute, 1984); and three newspaper articles entitled "The History of Jazz in Detroit" in *Metro Times* in September and October 1997.

urban society. I will look at the kinds of jobs that were available to jazz musicians as Detroit went through the social changes associated with the auto industry and World War II, when it was known as the Arsenal of Democracy. The market for jazz was also influenced by the state of race relations in the city, which were transformed as Detroit's black community grew at unprecedented rates.

The data on musicians and jazz venues come from a number of sources. Most important were the 93 oral history interviews conducted with musicians and others who were active in the Detroit jazz world. Jim Gallert and I conducted these interviews, alone or together, over the last 20 or more years. (See app. A for a list of interviews.) For some of the more prominent Detroit musicians already published interviews in the jazz press were used. I also searched systematically through several local newspapers and the *Chicago Defender*. Other researchers have found the African-American press an invaluable resource for jazz research and so did I. The *Michigan Chronicle* was the single most important newspaper, since its entertainment pages provided extensive coverage of the local jazz scene for the period. (See app. B for a complete listing of library resources.) Gallert and I also managed to put our hands on, and turn our ears to, virtually every existing recording by a Detroit jazz artist. Reviews of these recordings in jazz periodicals and books were also used to assess Detroit's contributions to jazz.

The book is organized chronologically by decade. The first chapter paints a portrait of the musical spectrum of black Detroit on the eve of big band jazz. The next chapter examines Detroit's important role in the creation of big band jazz with bands like McKinney's Cotton Pickers and Jean Goldkette's orchestra. The third chapter looks at the music and places of an area on the Near East Side called Paradise Valley in the 1930s. Detroit's role in the birth of bebop is covered in the fourth chapter, which is followed by two chapters on the 1950s, because I consider this decade the golden age of jazz in Detroit. This was the decade when Detroit contributed heavily to the further development of bop called hard bop. In the seventh chapter Jim Gallert and I examine Detroit's contributions to rhythm and blues in the 1940s and 1950s from jump blues to Motown. The final chapter summarizes the history of Detroit jazz within its social context.

Before Motown

The Music of Black Detroit before Big Band Jazz

WHEN EDWARD B. DUDLEY visited Chicago in 1919 the *Chicago Defender*, an African-American newspaper, took note.

> *E. B. Dudley, the biggest man in Michigan theatrical circles and one of the leaders in the game, universally speaking, was a visitor to Chicago a couple of days this week. "Dud" was here on a business mission and was all lit up like a million simoleons [dollars]. He is the sole owner of the Vaudette Theatre in Detroit. It is the only theater in the Wolverine metropolis run by our people for our people.*[1]

Dudley had run the Vaudette in downtown Detroit for six years and was just about to become manager of the larger Koppin Theatre, the single most important musical institution in black Detroit in the 1920s. As such it was one of the foundations for the development of jazz in Detroit. The ballrooms built in downtown Detroit during World War I provided further venues for the new music. Dudley and his theaters catered to the new black community that was developing with amazing speed on the Near East Side as southern migrants poured in. The increased pace of social change was part of the dynamics of a city built around a single industry, particularly one as volatile as the auto industry.

The Birth of the Motor City and Race Relations

DETROIT IS THE LARGEST U.S. city dependent upon a single industry. What is less well known about the Motor City is that it also grew faster than other cities in the first three decades of this century.[2] By 1900 Detroit was a midsize city with a population of 286,000 and no unique industrial features.[3] Twenty years later it was the Motor City and the fourth largest city in the country, with a population of almost a million. The growth continued at the same rate in the 1920s, when another half million people moved in. The preeminence of the auto industry also meant that Detroit was a city

Leroy Smith orchestra, Detroit, 1914.

1. "Dudley in Town," *Chicago Defender*, September 27, 1919.

2. A debated issue is why the auto industry became concentrated in Detroit. One side argues that there were a number of economic and social preconditions for the development of the auto industry in the city; the other argues that it was for the most part due to chance.

3. Melvin Holli, ed., *Detroit* (New York: New Viewpoints, 1976), 118–19.

more dominated by manufacturing than any other large city. As in many other northern industrial cities a disproportionate number of the new workers in the city were foreign born. In 1900 about one-third of the population was foreign born, and by 1925 this share had grown to half.[4]

There was also a large influx of migrants from the U.S. South, and what is particularly relevant for our purposes is the growth of the black population. The most common sources of black Detroit migrants were, in order, Georgia, Alabama, Tennessee, South Carolina, and Mississippi. From the end of the Civil War to the beginning of the Great Migration in 1915 Detroit's black population grew at a slower rate than the white population.[5] By 1910 there were about 5,700 blacks in Detroit, or 1.2 percent of the population. By 1915 the black population was 7,000, and hereafter the rates of increase were phenomenal: by 1920 it reached 40,000; by 1925 80,000; and by 1930 120,000, or 7.7 percent of the total population in the city.[6] The dramatic population increase had a number of social consequences.

From the Civil War until World War I the black population was largely confined to the Near East Side of Detroit.[7] The dramatic increase in the minority population in the last part of the second decade of the twentieth century and in the 1920s led to a severe housing shortage, partly due to overt racial discrimination. Black Bottom, as the Near East Side ghetto was called, overflowed as the white population resisted black expansion to the north or the east and the downtown business district expanded from the west. Racial tensions increased throughout the 1920s and reached a high point in September 1925 when a white crowd mobbed the home that Dr. Ossian Sweet had just purchased in a white neighborhood. One person in the crowd was killed, and, in a much-publicized trial the NAACP hired Clarence Darrow, who successfully defended Dr. Sweet and his family against charges of murder.[8]

Other indicators of increased racial tension in Detroit in this period were the political influence of the Ku Klux Klan in the 1925 mayoral election and increased violence between the police and the black community. For example, in 1925 14 black men were killed by the Detroit police, as compared to 3 black men in New York City. This was disproportionate since New York City's black population was more than twice as large as Detroit's.[9]

The Black Community

THE DRAMATIC INCREASE in the black population also changed the class structure of the black community, as an industrial working class replaced low-wage service workers (e.g., domestics) as the most numerous class. By 1920 Detroit could claim to be the premier working-class city in the country for both blacks and whites. This also led to changes in class relations within the black community. In the 1880s a new black middle class started to take the place of a small elite as leaders of the black community.[10] This new middle class was largely made up of small businesspeople and skilled workers. Faced with stiff labor market competition from European immigrants around the turn of the century, the black community turned inward and developed an ideology of racial solidarity and self-help. This was expressed in two types of community efforts: the development of black businesses for the black market and organized efforts at "uplifting" the lower classes. The Great Migration after 1915 presented a massive challenge to both of these efforts at community building.[11]

The black business community expanded in response to the increased demand from migrant farmers turned factory workers. We can see this reflected in the increase in two types of businesses: restaurants and boardinghouses.[12] Racial pride and organizational efforts, such as

4. Ibid., 121.

5. David A. Levine, *Internal Combustion: The Races in Detroit, 1915–1926* (Westport, Conn.: Greenwood, 1976), 50.

6. Ibid., 44; Holli, *Detroit,* 271.

7. Woodward Avenue divides the city into East and West Sides.

8. Levine, *Internal Combustion,* 158–65.

9. Forrester B. Washington, "Police Brutality," *The Negro in Detroit* (Detroit: Research Bureau, Associated Charities of Detroit, 1926), 11.

10. The ties between this integrationist small elite and the Republican Party have been described by David Katzman, *Before the Ghetto: Black Detroit in the Nineteenth Century* (Urbana, Ill.: University of Illinois Press, 1973), 129.

11. Richard Thomas, *Life for Us Is What We Make It: Building Black Community in Detroit, 1915–1945* (Bloomington: Indiana University Press, 1992), 18–19.

12. Richard W. Thomas, "From Peasants to Proletarians: The Formation and Organization of the Black Industrial Working-Class in Detroit, 1915–1945" (Ph.D. diss., University of Michigan, 1976), table 5, 126.

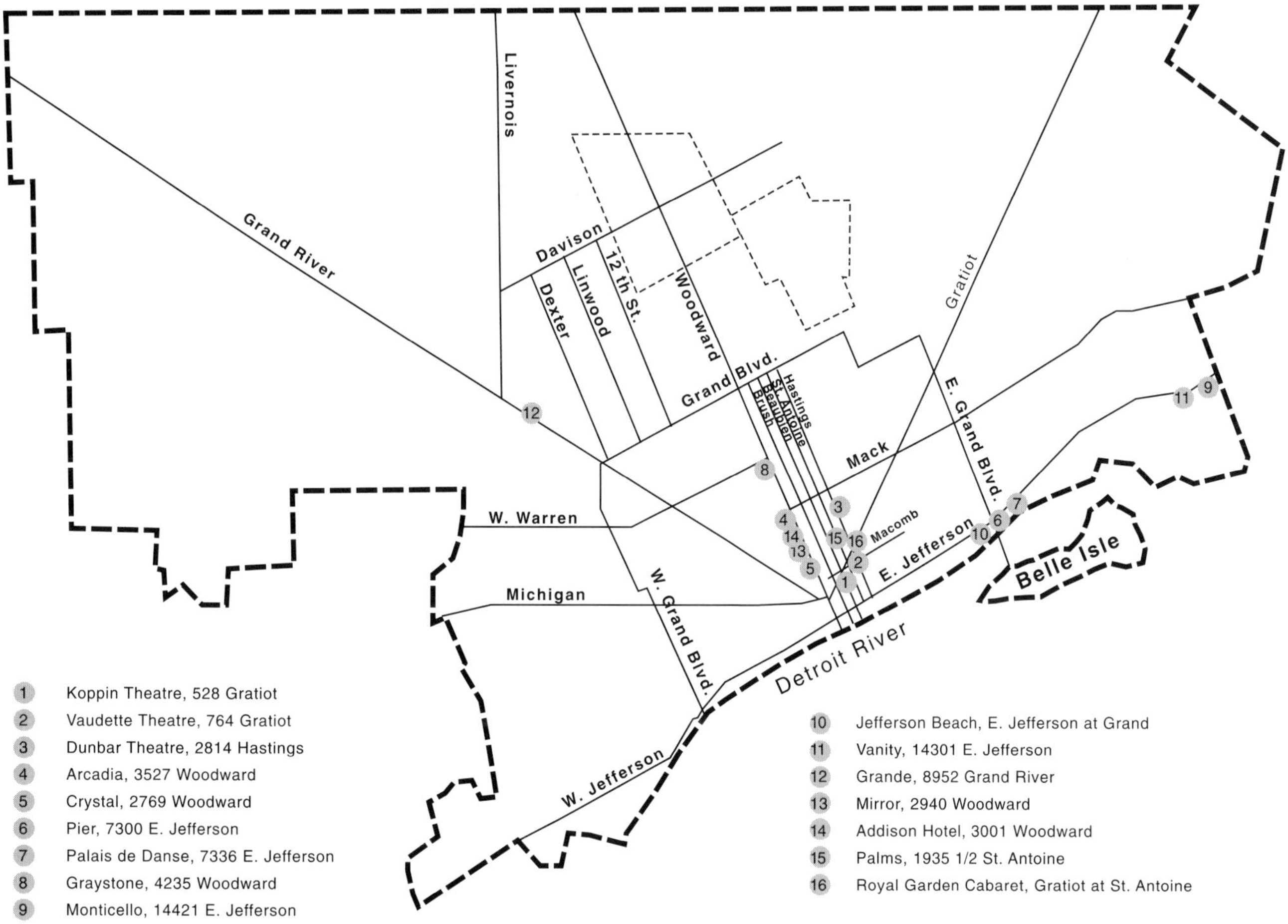

Fig. 1. Detroit ballrooms and cabarets, 1920s.
(Map by Borkin and Kaplan.)

the formation of a chapter of Booker T. Washington's National Negro Business League in 1926, fueled this business expansion.[13]

There was also considerable concern among social reformers that the newcomers would fall victim to unscrupulous employers, landlords, or businesspeople. The Detroit Urban League was formed in 1916 to help migrants adjust to urban life. A *Detroit News* story on July 15, 1917, described the work of the league and also trumpeted the moral mission of "uplift."

> *The provision of wholesome recreation for the immigrant presented one of the most difficult problems. Removed from the restraining influence of family and friends and beset by many vicious attractions entirely new to him, the incoming Negro easily became susceptible to [the] bait of vice and crime in the Negro district. A welcome from the great majority of colored citizens who have had time to establish themselves in Detroit was not generally extended, while the always welcoming hand of the vicious was waiting. There are 23 saloons, 10 pool rooms and three colored cabarets in the district bounded by Rowena, Macomb, Brush and Hastings streets. [Rowena was renamed Mack. See fig. 1.] Added to these there were 12 gambling clubs and countless number of disorderly houses. . . . a program of practical, primitive recreation was resolved upon. This program consists in part of community dances for the newcomers, and a baseball league of four teams.*

The Urban League also carried out sociological surveys of the black community. Of particu-

13. Thomas, *Life for Us Is What We Make It*, 17.

Fig. 2. Advertisement for Pier Ballroom.
(From Detroit Saturday Night, January 18, 1919.)

lar interest are the reports entitled *The Negro in Detroit,* published in 1920 and 1926, prepared by Forrester B. Washington. Washington's surveys give us insight into many areas of community life, including one closely connected with music: leisure activities. Some of the most popular places to spend leisure time were theaters, pool rooms, ballrooms, and baseball parks. The Detroit Stars were part of the American Negro League, and the average black attendance at Mack Park was as large as 4,500.[14]

Theaters

The theaters frequented by the black population were located in the downtown business district or within the black community. While legitimate theaters had been prevented from engaging in racial discrimination in 1890, other theaters catering to the less affluent discriminated in varying degrees.[15] Washington found that many theaters tried to limit black customers to balconies and galleries but that "whenever a colored person insists on being sold a ticket in a certain row and section of the theatre this is generally not denied."[16] These policies were followed at both vaudeville/burlesque theaters and movie theaters.

The number of theaters within the black community expanded dramatically during the 1920s. A 1917 survey found only three compared to the nine Washington found in 1926.[17] Most of these theaters were located on Hastings Street, which by the mid-1920s began to change from a Jewish to an African-American business district.[18]

Only one of the theaters was black owned, but others had black managers. The Vaudette was owned and managed by Edward B. Dudley from 1913 to 1921, and in 1921 he took over the management of the Koppin Theatre for what would prove to be a six year period.[19] Both theaters were located on Gratiot, and since they were part of the black vaudeville circuit they were central to the musical life of the black community. In addition to stage performances they also offered movies.[20]

Having a black manager or owner of these theaters was significant in the eyes of the black community. Black businessmen—often referred to as "Race Men"—were role models, and they were also important as bulwarks against discrimination. Theater owner E. B. Dudley was mentioned earlier in this chapter. The *Chicago Defender* carried articles about Dudley, an "Important Man in Show Business," and his theater in 1919–20.

> *[T]he Vaudette theater . . . is the only theater in the Wolverine metropolis run by our people for our people. . . . One of the most successful men of the race, as far as show business is concerned, is E. B. Dudley. . . . "Dud" is owner and proprietor, manager and treasurer, booker and overseer of the Vaudette. . . . This house . . . seats 650 people, gives three shows a night and turns them away at every performance. Feature pictures of the best sort are a part of the program and the best of the race's acts, only, ever find a place on his vaudeville bills. Four acts are used each week, and the pictures are changed each day. . . . Dud . . . drives $4,500 worth of Haynes 90 Horse Power.*[21]

The *Defender* pointed out that Dudley's background as a musician made him well suited for the job. He had played cornet and violin with the legendary W. C. Handy in Memphis and had traveled with minstrel shows in the South.[22]

Dudley got the job as manager of the Koppin after the Vaudette closed, but he was not the

14. Forrester B. Washington, "Recreation," *The Negro in Detroit* (Detroit: Research Bureau, Associated Charities of Detroit, 1926), 15.

15. Katzman, *Before the Ghetto,* 98.

16. Washington, "Recreation," 12.

17. George Haynes, *Negro Newcomers in Detroit* (New York: Arno Press, 1969), 24.

18. Sidney Bolkosky, *Harmony and Dissonance: Voices of Jewish Identity in Detroit, 1914–1967* (Detroit: Wayne State University Press, 1991), 97.

19. "Dudley in Town," *Chicago Defender,* September 27, 1919; and Russ Cowens, "He's Seen All of Them: Veteran Musician Edward Dudley," *Michigan Chronicle,* May 16, 1959.

20. A less prominent theater with the same offering was the Dunbar at 2814 Hastings. Washington, "Recreation," 13. The Dunbar was also managed by E. B. Dudley. The Castle Theatre at 3412 Hastings was a moving picture house with some live performances. Blues singer Alberta Adams remembered that when she was a young girl, "you could get in free to the Castle if you brought a potato or canned goods or somethin'. I used to sit all day and watch the performers. I really wanted to dance. I used to go back home and try to tap dance." Alberta Adams, interview by Jim Gallert, Detroit, Michigan, July 24, 1996.

21. "Dudley in Town," *Chicago Defender;* and "E. B. Dudley: Short Sketch of Important Man in Show Business," *Chicago Defender,* February 28, 1920. The Vaudette was located at 764–66 Gratiot, between St. Antoine and Hastings.

22. Cowens, "He's Seen All of Them."

Koppin's first black manager. The Koppin was a larger theater seating 1,500, which opened in 1919 on the south side of Gratiot between St. Antoine and Beaubien. It was owned by Henry Koppin, who ran a chain of theaters in Detroit.[23] While Koppin was Jewish he eventually hired black managers, after some prodding. About half a year after the Koppin opened the *Chicago Defender* ran a very critical article: "'Koppin.' That's the Name of a Money Grabber Who 'Fattens' in Detroit."

> *When Henry S. Koppin opened his theater he selected a small group of Race men—musicians—and placed them in his orchestra pit; that was fine, as far as it went, but it didn't go any further, for since the opening day . . . he hasn't employed a member of the Race in any capacity. . . . He has even refused to use one of us as a doorman, so it has settled down to a place where we have to fiddle and fiddle only for representation. . . . There is no excuse for the above conditions, for it is a fact that 90% of his trade . . . is made up of our people.*[24]

After using some anti-Semitic slurs the *Defender* urged Detroiters to stay away from the Koppin. Within a few months Koppin had hired his first black manager, and soon the *Defender* published a conciliatory article in which Koppin defended himself against accusations of prejudice.[25] The *Defender* columnist visited Detroit and "was much gratified upon seeing that virtually the entire crew was Race people and that the show, which was playing to a packed and overflowing house, was composed entirely of our own folks."[26] The whole matter was laid to rest, and the Koppin became the single most important musical venue within the black community in the 1920s.

The "Dance Craze" and Ballroom Building

A DANCE CRAZE SWEPT THE COUNTRY, including Detroit, in the second decade of the twentieth century. The two figures most

Select Dancing Nightly
Palais de Danse
Particular People Prefer
the Palais
Strictly censored. Highest
Standard
Floyd Hickman's Superb Orchestra

Fig. 3. Advertisement for Palais de Danse. (From *Detroit Saturday Night*, March 1, 1919.)

commonly associated with this craze were Vernon and Irene Castle, who popularized the foxtrot. Their musical director was the black society bandleader James Reese Europe, who introduced the Castles to this dance.[27] The foxtrot, the black bottom, and the cakewalk were dances that defined the Jazz Age to the general public. These dances were in the African-American dance tradition; their roots were in the jook (juke) joint dances that developed after Emancipation. The rural jook joint dances were transformed with the Great Migration and took place in the urban honky-tonks and after-hours joints of the northern black community.[28] The Castles and other dance teachers transmitted this African-American tradition to white urbanites in the ballrooms that mushroomed around World War I.

Before the end of World War I at least four ballrooms had opened in downtown Detroit: two along Woodward Avenue (the Arcadia and Crystal Palace) and two along Jefferson (the Pier Ballroom and the Palais de Danse). (See fig. 1).[29] Dancing was also a major attraction on

23. The address of the Koppin was 528–30 Gratiot. 1921–22 *Detroit City Directory*, 1301. See advertisement in *Detroit News*, September 2, 1926, for list of Henry S. Koppin theaters.

24. *Chicago Defender*, March 27, 1920.

25. The first black manager of the Koppin was Tim Owsley, who had a background as a vaudeville manager. The second was Ben Shook, Detroit bandleader and businessman. *Chicago Defender*, July 24, 1920; June 21, 1921.

26. "H. Koppin: Detroit Theater Owner Disproves Many False Ideas," *Chicago Defender*, September 25, 1920.

27. Reid Badger, *A Life in Ragtime: A Biography of James Reese Europe* (New York: Oxford University Press, 1995), 116.

28. Katrina Hazzard-Gordon, *Jookin': The Rise of Social Dance Formations in African-American Culture* (Philadelphia: Temple University Press, 1990), 94.

29. The Arcadia's address was 3527 Woodward, at the corner of Stimson. The Arcadia probably opened in 1913 since it was listed for the first time in the 1913 *Detroit City Directory*. In contrast a *Detroit News* article from August 6, 1961, claims it opened in 1914. The Crystal was on Woodward at Bagley. It opened in May 1919 according to an advertisement in *Detroit Saturday Night*, May 31, 1919, p. 12. The Pier was located on Jefferson at Field, just east of the Belle Isle Bridge. The Palais de Danse was located at 7336 Jefferson. The Pier was listed in the 1914 *Detroit City Directory*, and the Palais de Danse was advertised for the first time in *Detroit Saturday Night*, March 8, 1919.

Fig. 4. Graystone Ballroom, exterior, 1928. (Courtesy Frank Driggs, Gallert Collection.)

the Detroit riverboats. On its maiden voyage in 1911 the *Put-in-Bay* featured George Finzel, "a longtime favorite band leader among pleasure seekers on the river."[30]

The ballroom building boom continued in the 1920s, mainly along Woodward and Jefferson Avenues. The city's largest ballroom, the Graystone, opened its doors on March 7, 1922, on Woodward Avenue, near Canfield.[31] It was billed as "Detroit's Million Dollar Ballroom," and it could handle 3,000 customers on its floors and balconies.[32] Additional space was added in the back of the building in 1928 with the opening of the Graystone Gardens.[33] Before the building boom in Detroit ended with the 1929 stock market crash, five more major ballrooms had appeared: the Monticello, Jefferson Beach, the Vanity, the Mirror, and the Grande.[34] (See fig. 1.)

Detroit ballrooms, like those elsewhere, were largely segregated institutions. Washington's 1926 survey found that

> *There is only one hall in the city, however, owned and operated by colored people, which can always be secured for dancing purposes, namely, the Masonic Hall at 632 East Livingston Street. This hall is too small. . . . its capacity is about 100 couples. Other colored dances of any size must be given at white dance halls whenever these can be obtained. There are three white dance halls that colored people are able to obtain occasionally. They are the Palais de Danse, the Arcadia and the Graystone. The former of these can be obtained for colored dances only on holidays between midnight and five or six o'clock in the morning; the latter two can be obtained whenever they have an open night. This is usually on Monday. There are dancing spaces connected with numerous cafes and cabarets which are conducted by colored people and these are extensively patronized.*[35]

Monday night dances were usually a cooperative effort where a black dance promoter drummed up business for the ballroom from community organizations. The community organizations rented the ballroom and invited the public through flyers and advertisements in the black press. Wilson "Stutz" Anderson was one of the first promoters, who arranged dances at the Graystone for organizations like the Nacirema Club, the NAACP, and various fraternities and sororities.[36] The Scholarship ball in September 1928 was actually organized by Professor J. F. DeWitt but might be representative of Monday nights at the Graystone. The ballroom does come alive in this account by Vivian Dudley in the *Owl*, an African-American weekly.

> *Taxi cabs lined the curb stones for blocks away as each awaited its turn to stop for an instant in front of the beautiful Graystone Ballroom and Gardens to deposit its pleasure bent occupants. A stream of eager, expectant humanity*

30. Don Lochbiler, *Detroit's Coming of Age*, (Detroit: Wayne State University Press, 1973), 239. Lochbiler's reference to George Finzel is the only one found. Otherwise the Finzel orchestra was led by William (Bill) Finzel.

31. The Graystone was located at 4235 Woodward Avenue.

32. *Detroit Free Press*, February 26, 1922.

33. Graystone advertisement in *Owl*, June 15, 1928.

34. The Monticello opened in the late 1920s according to Charles V. Moore, interview by Lars Bjorn, Ecorse, Michigan, July 18, 1978. It was first listed in the 1930–31 *Detroit City Directory* at 14421 Jefferson. Jefferson Beach opened in 1928 at East Jefferson at Grand; the Vanity at 14301 Jefferson opened in 1929;

flowed through the massive doors and past the ticket offices where Professor DeWitt, King of entertainment and sponsor of this colossal affair presided with an efficiency and unhurried haste borne of long experience. The teaming throng swarmed past the ticket takers where many youths were stationed to hand out ballots for the Scholarship contest. Within, strains of Jazz music floated out to the corridors where newcomers hastened with eager steps to check rooms to unburden themselves of wraps that they might join in this surging mob of dancers.

"Le Afro-Americaine" was out in all his splendor. The numerous types of Black American were present in their entirety. Girls tall, dark and queenly with the grace of African water-carriers; others, golden brown of skin and hair, tawny beauty reminiscent of Hawaiian skies; rich cream colored maidens with hair like smooth black silk, calling to mind Spanish haciendas and swarthy youths strumming amorous strains on guitars while his lady, standing on an iron balcony, flashes dark eyes over a fan of lace; Titan beauties with their copper-gold hair fluffed above sea-green eyes; lithe swaying blondes whose fathers might have come over in some Viking ship; every conceivable Negro type was represented within this mighty throng.[37]

Fig. 5. Graystone Ballroom, interior, 1928.
(Courtesy Frank Driggs, Gallert Collection.)

and the Grande at 8952 Grand River (near Joy) opened in 1928 according to *Detroit News*, August 6, 1961. Others were the Majestic at 3116 Woodward and the Arena Gardens at Woodward and Hendrie. Several ballrooms were located in the Detroit suburbs. The largest were Eastwood Park and Westwood Inn.

35. Washington, "Recreation," 16.

36. Wilson "Stutz" Anderson, interview by Lars Bjorn, Belleville, Michigan, August 28, 1978.

37. Vivian B. Dudley, "The Scholarship Ball," *Owl*, September 15, 1928.

Other promoters joined in to meet the growing demand, and within a few years after Washington's survey more ballrooms were willing to allow black dancers at odd hours.[38] Detroit riverboats were also segregated, as only some of them, like the Put-in-Bay and the Tashmoo, seem to have allowed black dancers for organized events.[39]

Thus the dance craze took place within the context of racial segregation. Access to the new ballrooms was severely limited for African Americans. Not until the 1930s were black businesspeople able to make inroads into this corner of the entertainment field as owners and managers of dance venues.

The Music of Black Detroit

JAZZ EMERGED AS A DISTINCT FORM of music within the musical spectrum of the African-American community during the first two decades of the century. This spectrum reached from black folk forms, like the blues, on one end, to European-American art music performed by society bands on the other end. A middle ground of the spectrum was taken up by popular U.S. musical forms with African-American variants, like vaudeville, band music, or ragtime. While we do not have as much information on the music of black Detroit as we do for New Orleans or New York, we can sketch the contours of the musical spectrum of Detroit around the time of the development of early jazz.[40]

Urban Blues

VARIOUS STRAINS OF COUNTRY BLUES developed around the turn of the century in several parts of the Deep South, each with particular characteristics. The Mississippi Delta blues was the most influential of these regional styles. With the Great Migration the blues traveled north, especially to Chicago, where some Delta bluesmen got a chance to record in the late 1920s. In the process of migration the blues was also transformed into a more urban form. While country blues was typically performed by a lone singer-guitarist, the urban blues added a piano and rhythm instruments.[41]

Detroit was an important center for the development of urban blues. Our knowledge about this type of blues music in Detroit is severely limited by the fact that artists who wanted to record were forced to go to Chicago. Not until the late 1940s do we find record companies in Detroit recording local blues artists. Any attempt to stylistically characterize Detroit blues before the 1940s is hazardous. Blues scholar Paul Oliver suggests that one stylistic trait could be the prevalence of blues pianists, especially those with a boogie-woogie style of playing.[42] The most famous Detroit blues artists from the 1920s do, in fact, turn out to be pianists: Speckled Red (Rufus Perryman), Charlie Spand, Will Ezell, and Big Maceo. All hailed from the Deep South and thus are representative of black Detroit migrants as a whole. We will focus our attention on Big Maceo since he is the only one of the four who spent most of his life in Detroit. He is also considered one of the great blues pianists of this period.

Big Maceo (Major Merriweather) was born in Georgia in 1905 and joined the rest of his family in Detroit in 1924. Like many blues players he had a day job and received little formal training. He worked as a handyman and at the Ford Motor Company, the only auto company to hire blacks in large numbers before World War II. Many of his musical jobs in Detroit were at house parties on the Near East Side, and at one of them he met his future wife, Rosell "Hattie Bell" Spruel. She ran a boardinghouse and sold whiskey upstairs on Alfred Street, close to Hastings Street. As she told Mike Rowe: "And that's where I met him. He used to come to my house all the time and I'd give him money and the rest used to give him whiskey. And I told him, don't take no whiskey, don't play yourself cheap."[43] Maceo also had jobs

38. The Temple (*Owl*, December 17, 1927) and Majestic Ballrooms on Woodward (*Owl*, November 17, 1928) and the Campus Ballroom on Fenkell and Livernois (*Owl*, July 27, 1928). Other promoters were E. B. Dudley, Professor J. F. DeWitt, and Andrew "Jap" Sneed.

39. Washington, "Recreation," 10. Also advertisement in *Owl*, August 19, 1927.

40. For recent reviews of the literature on New Orleans, New York, and Chicago see Thomas J. Hennessey, *From Jazz to Swing: African-American Jazz Musicians and Their Music, 1890–1935* (Detroit: Wayne State University Press, 1994); William H. Kenney, *Chicago Jazz: A Cultural History, 1904–1930* (New York: Oxford University Press, 1993); and Burton W. Peretti, *The Creation of Jazz: Music, Race, and Culture in Urban America* (Urbana: University of Illinois Press, 1992).

41. Robert Palmer, *Deep Blues* (New York: Penguin Books, 1982), chap. 4.

42. Paul Oliver, liner notes, Various Artists, *Detroit Blues: The Early 1950s*, Blues Classics 12 (LP).

43. Mike Rowe, liner notes, Big Maceo, *Chicago Breakdown*, RCA AXM2-5506 (LP).

in bars on Hastings, Rivard, and Macomb Streets. Speckled Red was by comparison a more economically successful blues artist. In speaking about his years in Detroit from 1924 to 1928 he told an interviewer: "The best money I ever made was in Detroit. Once I had a car and a chauffeur, I just left because I wanted to see the country."[44]

For many of the bluesmen, Detroit was not the last stop on what was often an itinerant musician's life. A look at blues lyrics from this period shows the migration experience as a common topic. The 1928 recording of "Detroit Bound Blues" by Blind Blake illustrates—in the language of the demographer—the "pull" of Detroit's auto industry as well as the "push" of Southern poverty.

I'm goin' to Detroit, get myself a good job *(twice)*
Tried to stay around here with the starvation mob.

I'm goin' to get me a job, up there in Mr. Ford's place *(twice)*
Stop these eatless days from starin' me in the face.

When I start makin' money, she don't need to come
around *(twice)*
'Cause I don't want her now, Lord, I'm Detroit bound.[45]

Black Bottom and particularly Hastings Street were also mentioned in blues lyrics from the 1920s. A notable example is Charlie Spand and guitarist Blind Blake's recording of "Hastings Street" in the late 1920s.[46] In a talking blues filled with double entendres, Bland teases Spand about how he's "crying when you've been gone from Detroit for three weeks." He cries because he misses his love and Hastings Street "where they are doing the woogie." Later examples of celebrations of Hastings Street are Big Maceo's "Detroit Jump" with guitarist Tampa Red from 1945 and Detroit Count's "Hastings Street Opera" from 1948.[47]

Classic Blues

Another form of blues was the so-called classic blues, sung by women with jazz accompaniment. This music was actually the first type of blues to be recorded on the "race record" labels that were marketed particularly to the black community starting in 1920. In that year Mamie Smith's "Crazy Blues" was the first big hit of the Okeh record company. The classic blues singers were typically women who sang on stage in a more "legitimate" style coming out of the black vaudeville tradition. They were accompanied by small jazz groups and performed as one of the acts in a complete vaudeville show. As the black population migrated north the demand for vaudeville grew, and the black vaudeville circuit expanded. The circuit reached its zenith with the organization of the TOBA circuit in 1920, and it included Detroit.[48] Early the following year the Vaudette became part of TOBA. Even though it was a relatively small theater the Vaudette had a five-piece pit band led by violinists like Clarence Lee and Willie Tyler.[49] The Koppin Theatre took the Vaudette's place on the TOBA circuit by June 1921, when Mamie Smith visited for the first time.[50] The Koppin became the undisputed center of classic blues in Detroit for the next decade.

The Koppin Theatre was located on Gratiot Avenue, on the southern boundary of what by the early 1930s was called "Paradise Valley," the entertainment center of Black Bottom.[51] The center of the Valley was a few blocks north around St. Antoine and Adams. (See fig. 1.) The Koppin was the single most important musical venue within the black community in the 1920s. One sign of the visibility of the Koppin is that an out-of-town African-American weekly, the *Chicago Defender,* had regular reviews of its shows.

"The biggest day in the history of the theater," Dudley told the *Michigan Chronicle* in 1959, was when Bessie Smith—the "Empress of the Blues"—packed the Koppin in 1921.[52] Bessie Smith was the best known of all classic blues singers and returned to the Koppin many times. A 1927 review in the *Chicago Defender* said that "Miss Smith, queen of them all, in several select blues, goes over with a bang, having

44. Peter Silvester, *A Left Hand Like God* (London: Omnibus Press, 1990), 112.

45. Paul Oliver, *The Meaning of the Blues* (New York: Collier Books, 1963), 53. Blind Blake's recording is found on *The Best of Blind Blake,* Wolf Records, WBJ-017-CD, an Austrian release.

46. "Hastings Street" is found on Various Artists, *The Paramount Piano Blues,* vol. 1, Black Swan Records, HCD-12011 (CD).

47. "Detroit Jump" is found on Big Maceo, *Chicago Breakdown,* RCA AXM2-5506 (LP). "Hastings Street Opera" is found on Various Artists, *Detroit Blues: The Early 1950s,* Blues Classics 12 (LP).

48. TOBA is an abbreviation of Theater Owners' Booking Association. Originally TOBA included 32 theaters nationwide; later it expanded to more than 80. "Theater Owners' Booking Association," *New Grove Dictionary of Jazz.*

49. *Chicago Defender* notices, December 13, 1919; September 27, 1919; July 31, 1920. Clarence Lee was a Chicago violinist who also later played at the Koppin. Willie Tyler had played the East Coast before coming to Detroit and later worked in orchestras backing black Broadway shows. He also spent time in Europe. Albert McCarthy, *Big Band Jazz* (New York: Berkley Publishing Corporation, 1974), 62, 310.

50. *Chicago Defender* notices February 19, 1921; June 4, 1921.

51. Elaine Moon, "Paradise Valley," *Detroit Discovery,* May/June 1974, 3, 16.

52. Cowens, "He's Seen All of Them."

Fig. 6. Advertisement for Ma Rainey's appearance at Detroit's Koppin Theatre on October 15, 1927. (From the *Detroit Independent*, October 14, 1927.)

53. H. D. Garnett, "Koppin Theater," *Chicago Defender*, February 5, 1927.

54. None of the Smith singers were related. "Koppin Theater" reviews from the *Chicago Defender*, May 26, 1923; June 13, 1925; April 25, 1924; September 5, 1925. Advertisement in *Detroit News*, September 26, 1926.

55. Derrick Stewart-Baxter, *Ma Rainey and the Classic Blues Singers* (New York: Stein and Day, 1970), 35–42.

56. H. D. Garnett, "Koppin Theater," *Chicago Defender*, July 3, 1926.

57. *Detroit Independent*, October 14, 1927.

58. H. D. Garnett, "City of Straits," *Chicago Defender*, October 3, 1925. See also Gang Jines, "Koppin Theater," *Chicago Defender*, July 4, 1925.

59. Chicago bandleader and columnist Dave Peyton considered the technical demands on the vaudeville orchestra musicians to be higher than for those who played in movie houses or cabarets. "The Musical Bunch," *Chicago Defender*, April 3, 1926.

60. Garvin Bushell, *Jazz from the Beginning* (Ann Arbor: University of Michigan Press, 1988), 13.

61. Ibid., 11–13.

62. Dave Peyton, "The Musical Bunch," *Chicago Defender*, August 21, 1926. Lee apparently cut an impressive figure in his Buick Country Club roadster according to a later column by Peyton in the *Chicago Defender*, February 12, 1927. This is also mentioned in Moore, interview by Bjorn.

63. Peyton, "Musical Bunch," August 21, 1926. Other musicians who played in the Koppin pit band during the decade include violinist John Long, celloist John Lain, drummer George Smith and his pianist wife Emma (both from Chicago), violinist Arnold Hooper, pianist Louis Hooper, cornetist Fred Hooper, and drummer Harry Bradley. "Koppin Theatre," *Chicago Defender*, December 15, 1923; October 3, 1925. The Hooper brothers were born in Canada and raised in Ypsilanti, Michigan. The family moved to Detroit in 1908 and had a Hooper Brothers orchestra. Louis played with the Koppin pit band in 1920 and 1927–28; between those two periods he lived in New York, where he recorded with Elmer Snowden and Bob Fuller. "Linwood's Letter," *Chicago Defender*, September 24, 1927; and Jim Kidd, "Louis Hooper," *Record Research* (June 1966): 2–8. Cornetist Thornton Brown came to the Koppin with Ethel Waters and her Original Vanities in 1926. Brown stayed on to become an important figure in Detroit jazz. "Koppin Theater," *Chicago Defender*, June 26, 1926.

to take encores on all numbers."[53] The *Defender* review from her March 3, 1924, visit gives us a picture of the vaudeville context in which she appeared.

> *Bessie Smith and company, the exclusive Columbia record artist, assisted by Irving Johns at the piano, with all new songs and costumes opened to a crowded house with hundreds still standing on the outside. . . . Miss Smith puts over her numbers with plenty of pep and vim. She is assisted by such well known acts as White and Moore, a male singing, talking and dancing team . . . ; Collins with his remarkable tenor voice puts over a number, "That old gang of mine"; . . . Dinah Scott Trio, a singing, talking and dancing [act], turn in a comedy farce . . . ; Duke (Quadrille) Johnson and Bebe Harding . . . go over big with their singing and dancing. . . . Miss Smith broke all records when she last played this house and it seems that she will repeat.*

Virtually all of the major classic blues singers appeared at the Koppin: Ida Cox, Ma Rainey, Clara Smith, Mamie Smith, and Sara Martin.[54] Ma Rainey was often called the "Mother of the Blues" since she is credited with training the

"Empress" Bessie Smith.[55] Rainey's stage show, according to many, was the most impressive of all. On her 1926 visit to the Koppin she brought an entourage of four comedians, two singers, nine dancers, and a five-piece jazz band.[56] In 1927 she returned with her Paramount Flappers in "A Show with Plenty of PEP—GINGER & JAZZ & A Chorus of Brown Skin Beauties" according to an advertisement.[57]

The Koppin also was a training ground for local musicians. While some touring acts brought their own accompanists, the four-piece Koppin pit band had to back most of them. The Koppin pit band was considered one of the very best on the TOBA circuit, or as one reviewer put it: "All performers playing that house state that they never have any trouble playing their song numbers."[58] The job of the pit band was no doubt a demanding one. Each show had a variety of musical acts; the shows changed every week; and rehearsal time was about an hour. This job required well-trained musicians who were familiar with the whole range of musical styles from light classics to popular and folk songs and, of course, the blues.[59]

Pianist Edward W. Bailey was the first leader of the band, which in 1921 included clarinetist Fred Kewley, one of the pioneering jazzmen in Detroit. Kewley's career illustrates another influence on early jazz—the circus. He had played with circus bands and was considered one of the best black clarinetists in the country.[60] Circus bands toured all over the country, and some of them came in contact with the Southern blues tradition.[61] Kewley later played with the Earl Walton band, one of Detroit's first jazz outfits. In 1926 Bailey left the Koppin for Chicago and toured with Mamie Smith. The new leader of the Koppin band was violinist Clarence Lee, who like Bailey spent much of his career in both Detroit and Chicago.[62] Lee's band included clarinetist Howard Bunts, who went on to lead one of Detroit's major big bands in the 1930s.[63]

The Koppin also featured other entertain-

Fig. 7. Fred Kewley saxophone class, unidentified setting, Detroit, 1923. (Courtesy E. Azalia Hackley Collection, Detroit Public Library.)

ment produced for a black audience, including movies and touring black musical comedy shows, which earlier could only be found at the large downtown theaters in Detroit. Sissle and Blake's pioneering musical *Shuffle Along* was a Broadway hit in 1921, and two years later it was shown downtown at the New Detroit.[64] The *Chicago Defender* reviewer commented: "Shuffle Along is doing a capacity business despite the fact that the Race folks, after being charged top prices, are being shunted to the rear of the main floor."[65] When the show returned in 1925 it came to the Koppin. Other shows followed, like James P. Johnson's *Runnin' Wild*.[66]

The audience at the Koppin was virtually all black and was "drawn from the simple working class of people within the neighborhood" according to *The Negro in Detroit*.[67] This probably also meant that most members of the audience were relatively recent migrants to the city. The classic blues tradition was a cultural innovation that well suited the changing black urban community of the early 1920s. It was an amalgam of the rural and the urban, vaudeville and concert performance, blues and jazz. Its demise came with the death of vaudeville, black and white, after the introduction of talking movies and the advent of the Great Depression. One of the casualties in Detroit was the Koppin Theatre, which closed in 1931.[68]

Society Band Music

Black Society Bands

An immediate precursor of the jazz orchestras that emerged in Detroit in the 1920s was the society band. Society dance bands and brass

64. *Detroit Saturday Night*, April 7, 1923.

65. "Koppin Theater," *Chicago Defender*, December 15, 1923.

66. "Koppin Theater," *Chicago Defender*, August 22, 1925; November 14, 1925.

67. Washington, "Recreation," 13. There were times when whites attended. When *Shuffle Along* was performed in 1925 "white performers who were playing the downtown houses were in attendance." *Chicago Defender*, August 22, 1925.

68. There is indirect evidence that the Koppin closed some time in 1931. The last advertisement for the Koppin in the *Chicago Defender* was on February 28, 1931. The Koppin was listed in the *Detroit City Directory* for 1931 but dropped for the 1932–33 edition.

Fig. 8. Advertisement for Arena Gardens. (From *Chicago Defender,* September 15, 1927.)

Fig. 9. Bob Cruzet business card, ca. early 1920s. (Courtesy Dorothy E. Jackson, Gallert Collection.)

bands flourished in most urban African-American communities by the end of the nineteenth century.[69] Society bands played a repertoire ranging from light classics to waltzes and the popular music of the day, such as ragtime. By the end of the century ragtime was all the rage in the country as well as in Detroit. Detroit was the home of ragtime composers like Fred S. Stone and Harry P. Guy.[70] When W. C. Handy visited Detroit in the 1890s, he is said to have been very impressed with two rags composed and performed by Fred Stone: "My Ragtime Baby" (written in 1898) and "Silks and Rags."[71] Stone was a member of the leading society band in the city, led by violinist Theodore Finney, but it is likely that Finney stayed away from ragtime.[72] After Finney died in 1899, Stone became the manager of "Finney's Orchestra," which is considered "one of the earliest professional bands to play ragtime in the country."[73] In the first decade of the new century the band performed in a variety of settings, including white elite cabarets in downtown Detroit.[74] One of the leading figures in the band was cornetist John W. "Jack" Johnson, who started out with the Detroit City Band in the early 1880s and toured as bandmaster with the Georgia Minstrels.[75] When Johnson came back to Detroit in 1890 he organized the Johnson Cornet Band, which was an important training ground for young musicians like Fred Stone and his brothers.[76] Both Johnson and the Stones would venture into occasional improvised passages with the Finney orchestra.[77] Another claimant to the Finney orchestra title was violinist Ben Shook, who ended up in court with the Stones over the right to use Finney's name.[78]

We know that young Ben Shook came to Detroit from Cleveland in the 1890s. He was trained as a violinist at Fisk University, and Stone hired him to take the place of Finney.[79] Saxophonist Johnny Trafton played with Shook in the 1920s and remembered him as

> *an outstanding leader in that he was pretty well educated and he spoke German very well. So he was able to book himself and his band for many of the elite affairs. Remember that the black population of Detroit at that time was very small and that most entertainment of any note was sponsored by whites. . . . Ben Shook's library would mostly consist of the music that was appreciated by whites. . . . I remember "Rain in Spain" (sings) . . . [and] waltzes, schottisches, rhumbas and tangos.*[80]

Bob Cruzet was another violinist/society bandleader, but he might have tilted more toward the African-American musical heritage than Shook if his business card is any indication. (See fig. 9.)

Cruzet was of Cuban and African-American heritage, and according to trumpeter Charles Victor Moore "he was such a loud violinist that a 10-piece band could not drown him out!"[81] Moore was a neighbor of Cruzet's on Erskine Street and played with his band around 1924. Like many contemporary bandleaders, Cruzet was also a booker, which in his case meant that at times he managed as many as 12 bands in

69. Eileen Southern, *The Music of Black Americans: A History* (New York: Norton, 1971), 340.

70. Ibid., 316. For Guy see also "Unsung Musical Genius," Fred Hart Williams Papers, Burton Historical Collection, Detroit Public Library; and Nan Bostick and Arthur LaBrew, "Harry P. Guy and the 'Ragtime Era' of Detroit, Michigan," *Rag-Time Ephemeralist* 1, no. 2 (1999): 116.

71. "Theodore Finney," Fred Hart Williams Papers, Burton Historical Collection, Detroit Public Library.

72. Theodore Finney was born in Columbus in 1837 and came to Detroit in 1857. Ibid.

73. Bostick and LaBrew, "Harry P. Guy," 116.

74. Ibid., 118.

75. Dave Peyton, "The Musical Bunch," *Chicago Defender,* May 1, 1926. Johnson was born in London, Ontario, in 1865 and came to Detroit at an early age. He toured with "Dr. Carver's Wild West Show" and the Georgia Minstrels between 1884 and 1890 as a cornetist and vocalist. "John W. (Jack) Johnson," Fred Hart Williams Papers, Burton Historical Collection, Detroit Public Library.

76. Fred was born in 1873, Charles in 1868, and William in 1876. Bostick and LaBrew, "Harry P. Guy," 113.

77. Ibid., 116.

78. Ibid., 120.

79. "Theodore Finney," Fred Hart Williams Papers.

80. Johnny Trafton, interview by Lars Bjorn, Detroit, Michigan, September 1, 1978.

81. Moore, interview by Bjorn.

southeast Michigan. These bands mostly played one-night "gigs" for black and white audiences, and their repertoire covered everything from light classics to jazz. One of his more jazz-oriented outfits was called Bob Cruzet's Alabamians and consisted of younger players. Moore remembers that the younger players in Cruzet's band were "more willing to improvise and also more advanced harmonically. They also played more 16ths and 32nds and bent notes more frequently."[82]

Two young improvisers were pianist Teddy Wilson and his brother Gus, a trombonist, who spent some summers in Detroit with a relative. In 1929 they worked with Cruzet before leaving town with Speed Webb's Orchestra.

> *We were both familiar with the city and our aunt was living there. However, we did not plan to live with her, and neither did we. We shared rented rooms with a bandleader called Bob [Cruzet]. He had no organized band on the road and did not make recordings. He just lived in Detroit and worked mostly on weekends. The result was that there were many small groups playing around the suburbs of Detroit on weekends under the name of the Bob [Cruzet] Orchestra, although it was difficult to tell which was supposed to be the Bob [Cruzet] Orchestra. Perhaps none of them!*
>
> *Bob himself did a kind of musical quick-change act, leaping in and out of his car, standing maybe fifteen minutes in front of one band, before rushing off again to the next band with which he was working. He was what we called a "club-date bandleader." The work we did for him was in the fall of 1929, around the time the school year would begin. That's how we started work, mostly on the weekends, with Bob [Cruzet] and other leaders in various bands around Detroit.*[83]

It seems that at least by the mid-1920s, if not earlier, both Shook and Cruzet were very successful bookers. Saxophonist Lawrence Mann remembered an incident.

> *Ben Shook and Bob Cruzet were the chief bookers at the time. . . . they had more engagements than they had musicians to supply. Shook would call people who had not even become too accomplished on their instruments. . . . so on this particular job Ben was there and the band sounded so terrible so the owner of the hall came up to find out what was happening. Shook came up off the bandstand and met him halfway and started patting him on the shoulder and said: "The boys are jazzy." . . . these were white dances.*[84]

All the musicians who played with Shook and Cruzet do agree that their audiences, whether found at dances, parties, or shows, were largely white.[85]

There were other society bands active in Detroit around the years of World War I that had a more discernible musical profile, maybe because they were able to land longer engagements as dance bands.[86] Detroit's best known black society band was led by Leroy Smith. Smith was born in Romeo, Michigan, in 1888, but his family moved to Detroit while he was still a baby.[87] His father was a cornetist with the Finney band, and Leroy's violin training "was

Fig. 10. Leroy Smith orchestra, Detroit, 1914. *Back row: Harold Henson, as/vcl/bs; Ed Beller, dms; Fred Peters, bbs; Stanley Peters, ts/bsn; Emerson Harper, as/cl/o. Front row: Smith; Harry Brooks, pno.* (Courtesy E. Azalia Hackley Collection, Detroit Public Library.)

82. Ibid.

83. Teddy Wilson with Arie Ligthart and Humphrey van Loo, *Teddy Wilson Talks Jazz* (London: Cassell, 1996), 10.

84. Lawrence Mann, interview by Jim Gallert, Detroit, Michigan, August 31, 1989.

85. In addition to Moore and Mann interviews, Wilson "Junior" Warren, interview by Lars Bjorn, Detroit, Michigan, July 14, 1978.

86. Charles "Doc" Cooke was a Kentucky-born pianist who worked as a composer and an arranger in Detroit starting in 1909. Little is known about his Detroit years. He eventually left for Chicago and by 1918 led a band that included both Detroit and Chicago players (Hennessey, *From Jazz to Swing*, 37). In the 1920s he employed many New Orleans jazz pioneers (McCarthy, *Big Band Jazz*, 22–23).

87. Harvey Taylor, "Content with His Memories," *Detroit Times*, October 2, 1958.

Fig. 11. Leroy Smith WPA band, 1941, St. Matthew's Church, Detroit. *Standing, L to R: Smith; Joe McCutcheon, vln; John "Shady" Lain, vln; Hank Warren, dms; unidentified; William McClure, bs; unidentified; Russell Green, tp; Rock Owens, tp; William Johnson, tb; unidentified; unidentified. Seated: Maurice King, as/arr; Lou Barnett, cl/ts; Norval "Flutes" Morton, flt/cl; George Lightfoot, bar/vcl; Ardine Illidge, cello.* (Courtesy Mrs. Russell Green, Gallert Collection.)

put in the hands of the best private teachers in Detroit," according to a 1939 *Detroit Tribune* interview with Leroy Smith.[88] Smith favorably contrasted the fundamental musical training that he and other young black musicians received in the second decade of the twentieth century to that of "the youngsters of today who only have swing on their mind." According to Emerson "Geechie" Harper, who worked with him prior to 1920, "Smith always insisted on musicians playing what was written, having been taught himself by European musicians. . . . he was rigid as to reading, improvisation, adlibbing and 'getting off.' . . . it was not until several years later that he gave in to the modern trend and even then only featured improvisation sparingly."[89]

Smith's longest engagement in Detroit was with his 16-piece band at the Pier Ballroom from 1914 to 1919.[90] The Pier was probably the most socially exclusive of Detroit ballrooms. It was designed by Albert Kahn and was "financed by men of prominence in Detroit. . . . so far this season . . . [it has been] chosen for Scarab Club Ball . . . [and] Shipmaster's Ball."[91] According to a 1919 weekly schedule only two nights of the week were devoted to "modern" dancing (the one-step), while the others were "old-style."[92] In the summer of 1921 Smith went to New York City, made recordings, and enjoyed an extended engagement at Connie's Inn (1923–26).[93] But by 1938 Smith was reestablished in Detroit and, according to his trumpeter Russell Green, "played for all the millionaires."[94] He was active well into the 1950s and died in 1962.

In his authoritative work *Big Band Jazz,* Albert McCarthy offers the following interpretation of Smith's music.

> *A lot has been heard about the white jazz musicians who spent years in commercial dance bands dreaming of escape. A band like Smith's must have seemed little better to the coloured jazz stylists who worked with it, however high its overall musical standards might be. On the other hand, the substantial number of coloured musicians who admired the Paul Whiteman band during the 'twenties might have viewed it in a very different light. That Leroy Smith's band should exist and succeed for so long is a salutary reminder that not all coloured big*

88. *Detroit Tribune,* February 11, 1939.

89. Emerson "Geechie" Harper in Bertrand Demeusy, "Leroy Smith and His Band," *Jazz Monthly,* April 1969, 5–7.

90. Taylor, "Content with His Memories."

91. *Detroit Saturday Night,* February 3, 1923.

92. Advertisement in *Detroit Saturday Night,* September 11, 1921.

93. "Connies Inn" entry under "Nightclubs" in *New Grove Dictionary of Jazz.*

94. Russell Green, interview by Lars Bjorn, Detroit, Michigan, October 28, 1977.

Fig. 12. Floyd Hickman orchestra, Palais de Danse, Detroit, ca. 1919. (Courtesy Bob Weller.)

bands were jazz units. The view we have of several of the leading black orchestras might be significantly different, but for the prejudices of recording directors of this period who considered black musicians incapable of playing anything other than jazz.[95]

Little is known about a band that violinist Floyd Hickman led at the Palais de Danse from 1919 to 1923.[96] The band was large, and the instrumentation indicates that it was a society band. A 1922 photo from a WWJ radio broadcast shows a 17-piece band with a string section.[97] The ads for the Palais also set the appropriate tone for society events.

Palais de Danse. Select Dancing nightly. Particular people prefer the Palais. Strictly censored. Highest Standard. Floyd Hickman's Superb Orchestra.[98]

Hickman left in 1923 and was followed by Earl Walton, a central figure in the Detroit African-American musical community.[99] Whereas Hickman played strictly for white audiences at the Palais, Walton's band would also play for black dancers. Walton's band straddled the boundary between society and early jazz music, and he was an early jazz pioneer, as we will see in the next chapter.

White Society Bands

THE WHITE SOCIETY BAND TRADITION proved more long lasting than its black counterpart. It was not until the Swing Era in the mid-1930s that white big bands completely adopted the features usually associated with big band jazz. There were a number of white bandleaders in Detroit who competed with the Stone, Shook, and Cruzet bands for dance jobs, and it is likely that there was an interchange of musical ideas across the racial divide. Some of these bandleaders were William Finzel, Stephan Pasternacki, Danny Russo, and Ted Fio Rito. However, there are few indications that these leaders allowed improvisation in their performances. They are therefore of less interest to jazz historians.[100]

From a jazz point of view the most interesting white society band in Detroit was that led by Paul Specht. His band achieved national prominence through its live radio broadcasts and recordings while headquartered in Detroit between 1919 and 1925.[101] Their best engagement in Detroit was at the Addison Hotel around 1923.[102] Located on Woodward Avenue and Charlotte, the Addison with its Florentine

95. McCarthy, *Big Band Jazz*, 53–54.

96. Advertisements in *Detroit Saturday Night* from 1919 to 1923.

97. "Orchestra Makes Big Hit over Radiophone," *Detroit News*, March 10, 1922.

98. *Detroit Saturday Night*, March 3, 1919.

99. After leaving Detroit Hickman played on Broadway with Will Vodrey and led the Orpheum Theater pit band in Newark, New Jersey. Barbara J. Kukla, *Swing City: Newark Nightlife, 1925–1950* (Philadelphia: Temple University Press, 1991), 200.

100. William Finzel's band often played at the Arcadia and recorded as Finzel's Arcadia Orchestra in 1923 and 1925 according to Brian Rust, *The American Dance Band Discography, 1917–1942* (New Rochelle, N.Y.: Arlington House, 1975), 521. Stephan Pasternacki formed a band around World War I, and he commented that "hot licks were an unknown phenomenon at the time except maybe by Satchmo" (*Keynote* 40 [1976]: 3). The Danny Russo–Ted Fio Rito orchestra from Chicago made its breakthrough at a longer engagement at the Oriole Terrace nightclub in Detroit (on East Grand Boulevard and Woodward). They recorded as the Oriole Terrace orchestra between 1922 and 1924, before returning to Chicago (Rust, *American Dance Band Discography*, 549–51; and Leo Walker, *The Big Band Almanac* [Pasadena, Calif.: Ward Ritchie Press, 1978], 368).

101. Leo Walker, *The Wonderful Era of the Great Dance Bands* (Berkeley: Howell-North Books, 1964), 29.

102. Walker, *Big Band Almanac*, 380.

Fig. 13. Paul Specht orchestra, Alamac Hotel, New York, 1924. *Unidentified, dms; possibly George Hamilton Green, x; Arthur Schutt, pno; Specht, dir/ldr; Russell Deppa, bjo; Joe Tarto, bs; unidentified, tp, tp, tb; saxophones, L to R: Johnny O'Donnell, Harold Sellers, unidentified.* (Courtesy Stan Kuwik, Gallert Collection.)

Room had "the largest dining room in Detroit, where 400 persons can be seated comfortably. . . . it is reached through a foyer with an Italian garden effect. . . . The Novelty of the Florentine Room is a crystal glass illuminated dance floor, 30 feet wide and 70 feet long."[103] Specht left for New York in 1925.

In his authoritative work on dance bands McCarthy says that Specht

> *was a prolific recorder, but little of his output was particularly striking, though jazz fans owe him a debt for featuring The Georgians, probably the first band within a band in the tradition of Bob Crosby's Bob Cats or Tommy Dorsey's Clambake Seven, and one that subsequently led an independent existence under its leader Frank Guarente.*[104]

It should be added that Specht influenced the Detroit jazz scene; some of his players remained in the city to join Jean Goldkette when Specht left for New York in 1925.[105] Goldkette led the premier white big band of the 1920s.

Early Jazz

JAZZ IN DETROIT was born from mixing its society band and blues traditions. A definition of jazz as music should be distinguished from the cultural use of the term *jazz*.[106] While today's jazz historian would say that society bands never crossed the line from dance bands to jazz bands, it is likely that the audiences in the second and third decades of the twentieth century were less discriminating in their use of the term *jazz*. The *Detroit Saturday Night* weekly's article entitled "Boys form Jazz Orchestra" from 1923 is a good illustration. The band was directed by Jules Stein (future founder of MCA) and consisted of students

103. Advertisement, *Detroit Saturday Night*, October 1, 1921.

104. Albert McCarthy, *The Dance Band Era: The Dancing Decades from Ragtime to Swing, 1910–1950* (Philadelphia: Chilton Book Co., 1971), 34.

105. Walker, *The Wonderful Era of the Great Dance Bands*, 29. These include drummer Chauncey Morehouse and trombonist Russ Morgan.

106. Kenney, *Chicago Jazz*, viii.

Fig. 14. Hank Duncan Kentucky Serenaders, Hotel Ellwood, Detroit, 1919. *Personnel includes George Robinson, dms; Jimmy Harrison, tb; Ernest "Sticky" Elliot, cl; Duncan, pno/ldr. The knife wielder is presumably a chef.* (Courtesy Burton Historical Collection, Detroit Public Library.)

from Northern High School who played "anything from the classical numbers to the syncopated tunes of the present day. . . . They have a novelty program which should prove interesting to all followers of syncopated music."[107] The association of the term *jazz* with novelty numbers was a common one. Neil Leonard has shown how "nut jazz"—the use of exaggerated growls and laughs—became popularized in the latter part of the second decade of the twentieth century by showmen like Ted Lewis.[108]

Jazz in Detroit before the emergence of big band jazz fell into two categories: small bands that played in black theaters, restaurants, or cabarets; and somewhat larger bands closer to the society band tradition. The latter played the larger ballrooms and were more likely to use written arrangements.

Theaters, restaurants, and cabarets in the black community provided some of the first jobs for jazz-oriented bands. As we have seen the Koppin was the main theater venue for Detroit jazz bands, where they had to play all the musical styles found in vaudeville. Several restaurants offered dancing according to *The Negro in Detroit*.[109] Black cabarets in New York around 1920 are vividly described by reedman Garvin Bushell.

> *New York jazz was nearer the ragtime style and had less blues. There wasn't an eastern performer who could really play the blues. We later absorbed it from the southern musicians we heard, but it wasn't original with us. . . . You could only hear the blues and real jazz in the gutbucket cabarets where the lower class went. . . . They improvised in the cabarets and what they played had different timbres from the big dance bands. . . . Most cabarets had a five-piece band and seven or eight singers. The singer would sing one chorus at each table and go*

107. *Detroit Saturday Night*, June 30, 1923.

108. Neil Leonard, *Jazz and the White Americans: The Acceptance of a New Art Form* (Chicago: University of Chicago Press, 1962), 13.

109. For example, the Crisis Cafe on Clinton Street, Turner's Hall on Sherman Street, the Cafe on Hastings, Melrose Tea Room on Brush, and Vaughan's Tea Room on St. Antoine. Washington, "Recreation," 16. See also advertisements for dance music at the Crisis Cafe in *Owl*, April 15, 1927; September 29, 1928.

Fig. 15. Advertisement for the Palms.
(From *Chicago Defender*, December 22, 1923.)

> *around to every table in the joint. . . . After each singer-entertainer was through, the band would play a dance number.*[110]

It is a good guess that the music of Detroit black cabarets was similar to that of New York. Bushell was born in Springfield, Ohio. He visited Detroit around 1920 and heard several Detroit jazzmen. His generalizations about how the jazz of northerners differed from that of southerners apply equally to Detroit. Only a small proportion of Detroit jazzmen came from the Deep South, so we would expect that the blues elements were not prominent in early Detroit jazz.[111] By contrast, Chicago jazz was closer to the blues since its cabarets received a very heavy inflow of New Orleans jazzmen toward the end of the second decade of the twentieth century.[112]

There were at least three cabarets around St. Antoine and Adams by the early 1920s, some of which were located in hotels.[113] One of Detroit's earliest jazzmen, trombonist Jimmy Harrison, played in the backroom of the Hotel Ellwood in late 1919. He was part of Hank Duncan's seven-piece Kentucky Jazz Band.[114] Duncan was a pianist born in Bowling Green, Kentucky, in 1896, who spent several years in Detroit before going to New York.[115] Another player headed for New York was reedman Ernest "Sticky" Elliott. Drummer George Robinson remained in Detroit and became a member of Earl Walton's band. But the most prominent jazzman in the group was Harrison. He went on to become "the father of swing trombone" and a member of the Fletcher Henderson orchestra before his early death in 1931.[116] Harrison was born in Louisville, Kentucky, in 1900, but moved with his parents to Detroit in 1906. He was a self-taught trombonist who started playing gigs at 16. His improvisational skills were well developed by his late teens. New York bandleader Charlie Johnson remembered hearing Harrison on tour in 1919: "Jimmy couldn't read a note of music at the time, but he could play in any key as if he were singing through his horn instead of blowing it."[117] Hank Duncan also recalled his entertaining skills: "Oh-h, man! He could really play. And he was a great showman. He was the first to play his instrument as he lay on his back manipulating the slide with his foot, and he would sometimes jump up on the piano to blow."[118]

Another cabaret with music was the Palms on St. Antoine, near Adams.[119] It advertised itself in the African-American press as "Detroit's Most Cosmopolitan Spot" in 1923 and seems to have been one of the first "black and tans" in Detroit. A black and tan provided black entertainment for black and white audiences. The Palms was described as follows for the mainly white readership of *Detroit Saturday Night*, March 28, 1925.

> *[T]here is more action in the Palms, when it is running, than in any spot in town. The girls dance, the boys dance, whites and blacks and all shades between, mingle in a welter of syncopation. They know how to have a good time, even the grind of cabaret performances, many times repeated, can not take the edge off the high spirits of the dusky youths and damsels who cavort professionally in these cafes. Some of the best buck-and-wing dancing anywhere to be seen will be sprung out at odd hours in the colored places.*

110. Bushell, *Jazz from the Beginning*, 19–20.

111. Lars Bjorn, "The Mass Society and Group Action Theories of Cultural Production: The Case of Stylistic Innovation in Jazz," *Social Forces* 60, no. 2 (1981): table 2.

112. Kenney, *Chicago Jazz*, chaps. 1 and 2.

113. Washington, "Recreation," 16.

114. George Hoefer, "Jimmy Harrison, Forgotten Giant!" *Jazz* 2, no. 5 (June 1963): 9.

115. Exactly when Duncan was in the city is not clear. The first time was at age 15 or 16 when he visited an uncle for the summer. This was also the time at which he had his first gig (Frank Owens, "Hank Duncan, 1896–1968," *Storyville* 25 [1969]: 4). In 1919–20 he led the band at the Hotel Ellwood according to Hoefer, "Jimmy Harrison, Forgotten Giant!"

116. Harrison moved to New York in 1922 and recorded with Henderson in 1927–30. "Jimmy Harrison," *New Grove Dictionary of Jazz*.

117. Hoefer, "Jimmy Harrison, Forgotten Giant!" 9.

118. Ibid.

119. The Palms' address was 1935 1/2 St. Antoine according to the 1924–25 *Detroit City Directory*.

The Palms seems to have been an ideal spot for "slumming" white audiences. It was open until 4 A.M. in the center of the developing black entertainment district of Detroit, and the music was jazz. The Bart Howard Syncopators played for dancing and the "Palm Revue."[120] While we do not know anything about his fellow Syncopators, Howard was one of Detroit's most prominent ragtime pianists. His style was very close to jazz, as it introduced "an element of rhythmic interruption or suspension to the regularity of ragtime oompah bass."[121] Tom Shea gave the following portrait of Howard.

> *Howard was a small man who always played with a cigar between his teeth. His hands were so small that he had trouble reaching octaves so he had a man named Dr. Alexander operate on them, cutting the skin between his thumb and index finger to increase his reach. . . . he was a strong piano player. He didn't play background music.*[122]

Like Detroit's blues pianists, Bart Howard also found employment in the blind pigs that inundated Detroit during the Prohibition years. Prohibition started as early as 1916 in Michigan, but law enforcement was lax and Canada lay just across the Detroit River.[123] One of the blind pigs was the Royal Garden Cabaret, run by society bandleader Benjamin Shook. Fred Hart Williams remembered the scene.

> *It was at the Royal Gardens while serving beer to Ben's patrons that Roy Lightfoot moved about the small tables, singing popular songs. Accompanying him at the piano would be Bart Howard, then one of Detroit's hottest pianists.*[124]

Roy Lightfoot was a musician who, like Shook, increasingly turned to business activities in the black community. He ran restaurants in the 1920s and in the 1930s opened his own after-hours club, the B & C, in the heart of Paradise Valley, as we will see in the third chapter. But first we will take a look at the birth of big band jazz in Detroit.

120. Ads in *Chicago Defender,* December 1 and 22, 1923.

121. Tom Shea, "Bart Howard," *Ragtimer* 6, no. 3 (1967). Charles V. Moore described Howard as a stride pianist in the style of James P. Johnson in an interview with Lars Bjorn.

122. Shea, "Bart Howard." On the basis of interviews with two of Howard's students Shea guesses that Howard was born around 1880 in Detroit or Toledo. He was playing in ragtime contests at the Turf Cafe on Mullett and Hastings by 1915 and played in Detroit and Windsor until his death in the mid-1930s.

123. Larry Engelmann, "Rum-running Gave Detroit Dim View of Prohibition Years," *Smithsonian,* June 1979.

124. Fred Hart Williams, "Paradise Valley Was a Paradise—and Here's Why," *Michigan Chronicle,* April 14, 1956. The Royal Garden Cabaret was on Gratiot at St. Antoine according to an advertisement in the *Chicago Defender,* December 15, 1923.

Detroit and the Creation of Big Band Jazz

Detroit played a major role in the development of big band jazz in the 1920s, largely on account of McKinney's Cotton Pickers. Through its recordings and national tours the band helped shape the new music more than any other band in the Midwest. This was partly due to the leadership of arranger Don Redman, but the Cotton Pickers was a band filled with talented players. The city was also home to the best of the white big bands in the 1920s, the Jean Goldkette Orchestra. Goldkette provided a home for star soloists like cornetist Bix Beiderbecke and saxophonist Frankie Trumbauer. The Cotton Pickers and the Goldkette bands are well known to jazz historians, but the history of a number of other remarkable Detroit outfits has never been told. Violinist Earl Walton led one of these lesser-known bands.

From Society to Jazz: Earl Walton

The story of big band jazz in Detroit begins with the Earl Walton band since it bridged the gap between black society bands and jazz bands. While several of the society bands mentioned in the first chapter occasionally ventured into jazz, Walton's band more consistently featured improvisation and jazz rhythms. Trumpeter Charles V. Moore joined the band about 1924 and compared it to Leroy Smith's society band.

> *Leroy was on a society kick, but Earl played society and other stuff for the younger ones. The Pier Ballroom was more society like, whereas Earl had the younger crowd at the Palais de Danse. . . . They had colored dances at the Palais on Monday nights before the Graystone. Earl rented the ballroom himself . . . and he'd have 10,000 people and pay his musicians $50 that night . . . for 3 hours work. . . . Earl was making more on one night than the [McKinney's] Cotton Pickers [at the Graystone in 1927] got all week. . . . he was a rich man. . . . He was offered the job at the Arcadia Ballroom before the Cotton Pickers came to town and he said: "Are you kidding?" . . . I quit 10th grade to join Earl Walton. I got $120 a week; my mother said "You can't pass this up!" . . . I was making more money than the principal of the*

Jean Goldkette Orchestra, Detroit, 1924.

Fig. 16. Earl Walton orchestra, unidentified setting, Detroit, early 1920s.
L to R: Unidentified; unidentified; possibly Eugene Calloway, as; Fred Kewley, reeds; Clyde Hayes, bbs; Earl Foley, bjo; Anthony Bush, pno; Earl Walton, vln/ldr; George Robinson, dms; Rock Owens, tp; John Tobias, tb; Al Goins, reeds.
(Courtesy E. Azalia Hackley Collection, Detroit Public Library.)

> *school. . . . I had studied cornet since I was 10 and I could sight-read. . . . Harry "Rock" Owens in the Walton band was one of my teachers on the trumpet.*[1]

Walton's 11-piece band was generally made up of younger players, which is not surprising since the leader was in his early twenties when he started the band. Walton was born in 1899 in Little Rock, Arkansas, and had a background in vaudeville. He played violin in the "Tennessee Ten" traveling show in 1917, which included other young jazzmen in the making.[2]

The hottest soloist in the Walton band in the early 1920s was trumpeter Charles Gaines. Gaines had spent several years in New York and was later featured on recordings organized by the legendary Clarence Williams. After an East Coast tour with the Walton band he returned to New York City to record with, among others, Leroy Smith.[3] Fred Kewley, who played clarinet at the Koppin, was also a saxophonist in the Walton band.[4] Charles V. Moore was replaced by cornetist Thornton "Nub" Brown. Brown came to Detroit when Ethel Waters and her Original Vanities played the Koppin Theatre in 1926 and was by many accounts an impressive player. He had earlier played with pianist Earl Hines and been the director of the Original Jazz Hounds as part of a touring vaudeville show.[5] Guitarist Wilson "Junior" Warren remembers that Brown "had a great sound" when he played with the Walton band.[6]

Walton's band stayed at the Palais for most of the 1920s and provided a training ground for many young Detroit jazzmen. Altoist Ted Buckner joined the band at age 15 in 1928, and his brother, Milton, wrote his first arrangement for the band at the same age (in 1930).[7] The Buckner brothers were orphaned at a young age and had been adopted by members of the band: trombonist John Tobias and drummer George Robinson (Milt) and Fred Kewley (Ted). Kewley no doubt trained his adopted son well, since he was a respected reed instrument teacher who taught in the back of his record shop in Paradise Valley.[8] Milt remembered that "my

1. Moore, interview by Bjorn. Charles V. Moore was born in Louisville, Kentucky, in 1908 and came to Detroit in 1922.

2. Earl Walton obituary, *Michigan Chronicle*, June 26, 1943. According to an article in the *Chicago Defender*, October 6, 1917, the Tennessee Ten included New Orleans bassist Ed Garland. The band also included trumpeter Gus Aiken and clarinetist Darnell Howard around this time according to Stanley Dance, *The World of Earl Hines* (New York: Scribner, 1977), 22.

3. "Charlie Gaines," *New Grove Dictionary of Jazz*.

4. Moore, interview by Bjorn.

5. *Chicago Defender*, January 13, 1923; September 19, 1925; Dance, *World of Earl Hines*, 21.

6. Warren, interview by Bjorn.

7. John Chilton, "Milt Buckner," "Ted Buckner," in *Who's Who of Jazz: Storyville to Swing Street*, rev. ed. (Philadelphia: Chilton, 1979). Ted Buckner replaced Joe Eldridge, the brother of trumpeter Roy Eldridge. The Buckners were born in St. Louis, Ted in 1913 and Milt in 1915.

8. Mann, interview by Gallert; and Jack Perkins, interview by Jim Gallert, Detroit, Michigan, April 26, 1995.

'uncle,' John Tobias, had started me on piano when I was ten and I took it for about three years."[9] The Buckner brothers in turn became central figures in the Detroit jazz world in the 1930s. Walton was an active bandleader until 1937, when he opened up his Studio Club restaurant, which was an after-hours stop for musicians. He died from appendicitis in 1943.[10]

McKinney's Cotton Pickers

BETWEEN 1923 AND 1929 the main features of big band jazz were worked out in New York City and the so-called territories.[11] To simplify, this involved infusing society bands with the rhythms and improvisational freedom found in smaller jazz bands. The two most important territories were the Southwest and the Midwest. In the latter, McKinney's Cotton Pickers was the most influential band.[12] Even though it is possible to delineate regional jazz styles, big band jazz grew out of a constant interchange between various regions.

The career of Don Redman illustrated this interchange in Detroit. Before he came to Detroit and the McKinney band in the summer of 1927, Redman spent three years as chief arranger for Fletcher Henderson's pioneering orchestra in New York City. After McKinney abandoned his role as musical leader of the Cotton Pickers about 1925, he served as its booker-manager even though it still carried his name. In the summer of 1931 Redman returned to New York to form his own band, and the McKinney band entered a different stage of its career, with less commercial and musical success.[13] "McKinney's Cotton Pickers," concluded Albert McCarthy, "can, with some justice, be described as an arranger's band—its good fortune was to have one of the greatest arrangers in jazz history."[14] This, of course, underscores Redman's importance, but what about the rest of the band? It turns out that it included a number of remarkable musicians from its start.

The Cotton Pickers were first known as

Fig. 17. Rhythm Stompers reed section, unidentified location, 1929.
L to R: Ted Buckner, Lawrence Mann, Billy Bowen.
(Courtesy Rilla Buckner.)

McKinney's Syncos, when they started playing in Springfield, Ohio, in the early 1920s. Springfield was the source of many early jazz pioneers, probably due to its sizable African-American population and the proximity to Wilberforce University, a historically black college. The black population of Springfield was as large as that of Detroit on the eve of the Great Migration.[15] Dave Wilborn was born in Springfield in 1904 and remembered how he joined McKinney's band in 1919.

> *My father was the leading undertaker in Springfield and he was grooming me to be an undertaker. . . . my father wouldn't purchase a banjo for me, so I got odd jobs, shined shoes and sold newspapers and bought my first banjo. I bought me a book and would walk across the street to a barn to practice, because I didn't want my father to know I was grooming myself to be a musician. . . . The McKinney Synco Septet were to perform at Memorial Hall . . . and their banjoist got ill. . . . McKinney went to the local barbershop and asked if there was anybody in town that was a banjo-player. The barber said there was a young kid up on Fair St., Dave Wilborn, that is a great banjo player*

9. Peter Vacher, "The Milt Buckner Story," *Jazz and Blues* 66, no. 9 (1972): 15.

10. Obituary in *Michigan Chronicle*, June 26, 1943.

11. Hennessey, *From Jazz to Swing*, chaps. 4–6.

12. Ibid., 111.

13. McCarthy, *Big Band Jazz*, 77; and John Chilton, *McKinney's Music* (London: Bloomsbury Book Shop, 1978), 49.

14. McCarthy, *Big Band Jazz*, 79.

15. In 1900 the black population of Springfield was 4,253, compared to 4,111 in Detroit. Bushell, *Jazz from the Beginning*, 14; and Holli, *Detroit*, 271.

Fig. 18. Synco Novelty Orchestra, Manitou Beach, Michigan, 1921.
L to R: Wesley Wilson, vln; Claude Jones, tb; Todd Rhodes, x/pno; probably Ralph Wilson, bjo; William McKinney, dms/ldr; Milt Senior, as/cl.
(Courtesy Mrs. Annie Mae Rhodes, Gallert Collection.)

16. Dave Wilborn, interview by Jim Gallert, *Jazz Yesterday,* WDET-FM, Detroit, Michigan, July 15, 1973; and August 10, 1979.

17. Dave Wilborn, interview by Lars Bjorn, Detroit, Michigan, October 21, 1977; and Chilton, *McKinney's Music,* 3.

18. Gunther Schuller, *The Swing Era: The Development of Jazz 1930–1945* (New York: Oxford University Press, 1989), 308.

19. Chilton, *McKinney's Music,* 4–6.

20. Wilborn, interview by Gallert, July 15, 1973.

who could fill the spot. . . . I guess I was an instant success, because the boys really liked me. I was a rhythm player at the time playing four beats to the measure and McKinney was playing two beats to the measure. . . . They were on their way to Manitou Beach, Michigan, so they asked if I could go along with them for a summer engagement. . . . My mother finally agreed but said I had to return to school for the fall session.[16]

One obstacle to a smoother four beat rhythm was actually William McKinney's own stiff drumbeat. The band lifted noticeably when Cuba Austin took over the drums and McKinney devoted his time to managing the band.[17] Austin was from Charleston, West Virginia, and his tap-dancing and comic skills added significantly to the show the band put on. The McKinney rhythm section developed into one of the hardest swinging in the late 1920s, and Austin is given major credit for this achievement.[18]

Other members were also added to the band, and it became more musically sophisticated. At first, there were few written arrangements, only "head arrangements." In 1925 booker-bandleader Jean Goldkette heard the band at the Green Mill in Toledo and hired them for the Arcadia Ballroom in Detroit in 1926.[19]

Before the band accepted the offer to go to the Arcadia, the Goldkette management suggested that the band change its name from McKinney's Syncos to McKinney's Cotton Pickers. Dave Wilborn recalled the conversation with Goldkette's manager, Charlie Stanton.

"You'll have to change the name. We should change it to a Southern name." But the boys stood there with their mouths open; they didn't want an Uncle Tom name. [Stanton replied that] "You can leave here with another name." . . . But after the McKinney's Cotton Pickers name went on the marquee that was it![20]

Consequently, this midwestern band was ad-

Fig. 19. McKinney's Cotton Pickers, Graystone Ballroom lobby, 1930.
Standing: Todd Rhodes, Dave Wilborn, Cuba Austin, Don Redman, Ralph Escudero, Ed Cuffee. Seated: George "Fathead" Thomas, Prince Robinson, Jimmy Dudley, Joe Smith, John Nesbitt, Langston Curl.
(Courtesy Frank Driggs, Gallert Collection.)

vertised for the Arcadia opening on September 1, 1926, as "the Cotton Pickers, colored, from Dixie."[21] This incident illustrates how black entertainment was packaged for white audiences as an exotic commodity in the 1920s. It also illustrates the commercial pressures on jazz artists.

The Cotton Pickers went over very well with the dancers at the Arcadia, and their contract was extended for five months.[22] Goldkette also hired the band for a week in April 1927 at his own Graystone Ballroom.[23] The house band at the Graystone was Goldkette's own band, but it was not a financial success, so he decided to try out a black band with obvious audience appeal. Dave Wilborn told the story this way.

> *We impressed Jean Goldkette because we stayed two weeks. . . . The beat was the basis of what made the McKinney's Cotton Pickers because the Jean Goldkette Orchestra was playing two beats to the measure, it was more of a sweet band, but we were playing four-four. . . . it gave the band a happy sound and the people could not resist dancing. . . . they would just go crazy.*[24]

Goldkette was so impressed with the band he decided to give it an indefinite contract starting in the fall season. In cooperation with McKinney the Goldkette management was also able to hire away Don Redman from the Fletcher Henderson orchestra in New York during the summer. Redman's arrangments and musical leadership added more substance and polish to the danceable music of the Cotton Pickers over the next four years. Redman ran a music school of sorts for the band in the Graystone locker room, and the reading skills of the band improved.[25] The band soon was broadcasting over WJR in Detroit, and the power of this station and national hookups gave it national as well as regional exposure. After the band landed a Victor recording contract in 1928 its popularity and influence spread rapidly, and national tours followed.

The recordings the Cotton Pickers made in 1928 in Chicago have been highly praised by jazz historians. In his seminal study *The Swing Era* Gunther Schuller says the following after commenting on Redman's music school at the Graystone.

21. The advertisement also mentioned that "during the summer the Arcadia management organized two great orchestras. The musicians have been chosen from all parts of the U.S." The other band was a white vocal group, the Bob-o-Links, which later recorded with Bob Crosby. No year is given for the advertisement, but September 1 was a Wednesday in 1926, and we do know that the band was at the Graystone by October that year according to Chilton, *McKinney's Music*, 8. The advertisement was found in the "Arcadia Auditorium. Misc. Material." file, Burton Historical Collection, Detroit Public Library. The Graystone house organ, *Graystone Topics* (1, no. 7), celebrated the supposed southern origins of the band as late as April 16, 1927: "the McKinney's Cotton Pickers . . . are the warmest lot of mirth and melody makers that ever wandered from the sunny South."

22. Chilton, *McKinney's Music*, 9.

23. *Graystone Topics* 1, no. 7, April 16, 1927.

24. Wilborn, interview by Gallert, August 10, 1979.

25. Chilton, *McKinney's Music*, 19.

Fig. 20. McKinney's Cotton Pickers handout, December 1930. (Courtesy Dorothy E. Jackson, Gallert Collection.)

> *The first recordings from July 11 and 12, 1928, are anything but tentative. It is clear that the band had already achieved a distinctive style and concept unlike any other and within that style a very high performance level, to my knowledge not matched by any other jazz orchestra of the time. It was a real orchestra: it had a highly developed sense of ensemble, and in its balanced precision sounded much bigger than its eleven-man personnel would lead one to expect.*[26]

Schuller credits Redman with some of these accomplishments, but he finds that as much credit should be given to John Nesbitt. Nesbitt was a trumpeter from Virginia who joined the band in 1924 and soon became its major arranger. Schuller calls Nesbitt's composition and arrangement "Crying and Sighing" "especially dazzling." His arrangement of pianist Todd Rhodes's "Put It There" "produces an amazing variety of compositional elements, worthy of the best of Morton and Ellington."[27] Nesbitt left the Cotton Pickers in 1930 to join another territory band, led by Zach Whyte.[28]

The Jean Goldkette Orchestra

JEAN GOLDKETTE'S MAIN CLAIM to fame among jazz enthusiasts is that he led a band that included cornetist Bix Beiderbecke, arguably the most important white jazz musician of the 1920s. Jazz historians would also point to the pioneering role the Goldkette orchestra had among white jazz bands. Among Detroiters Goldkette was also known as a concert pianist, the owner of the Graystone Ballroom, and the city's major booker of bands.

Goldkette was obviously a man of many talents. Born in France in 1899 and raised in Greece and Russia, he came to the United States in 1910. Because he had received piano training at the prestigious Moscow Music Conservatory, no doubt a career in classical music would have seemed to be in store for the young man. But by World War I he was playing in society bands for Chicago booker-bandleader Edgar Benson, with only occasional opportunities for classical concerts. In 1922 he was hired as musical director of the posh Detroit Athletic Club (DAC), where he first led a small concert band. He also organized a larger dance band for an engagement at the Graystone Ballroom with his Chicago friend and drummer Charles Horvath. In 1923 the two formed a corporation and took over the Graystone, with capital provided by friends from the DAC.[29]

An article about Goldkette in 1924 gives us an idea of Goldkette's musical goals and what they meant to the paper's music critic.

> *Jean, being a practical young man, believes in the taming, or the reformation, of American music from the bottom. Mr. Goldkette . . . sees some purpose in jazz. He believes that it is the creeping infant that one day will develop into a true school of American music. He points out that it has already shown vast signs of improvement. As proof of this he cited the fact that Paul Whiteman not so long ago invaded that inner temple of classical music, Aeolian Hall, New York. . . . Recently Mr. Goldkette conceived of the idea that the best way of improving the breed of jazz music was to organize a big public dance orchestra composed of real musicians. Hence the Graystone band. It seems that playing good dance music 100 percent right requires real talent, instead of mere physical durability as some of us used to think in the old days when the cow bell, the wash-boiler and the 38-caliber pistol seemed to feature the orchestration.*[30]

26. Gunther Schuller, *The Swing Era: The Development of Jazz 1930–1945* (New York: Oxford University Press, 1989), 302–3.

27. Ibid., 305–7.

28. Nesbitt died an untimely death in 1935. Chilton, *McKinney's Music,* 66.

29. Stan Kuwik, "From Prince to Pauper," *International Association of Jazz Record Collectors (IAJRC) Journal* 22, no. 1 (January 1989): 1–2.

30. "Personal and Confidential," *Detroit Saturday Night,* May 17, 1924.

Fig. 21. Jean Goldkette Orchestra, unidentified setting, Detroit, 1924. *Dewey Bergman, pno; Joe Venuti, vln; Charlie Horvath, dms; Paul Mertz, pno; "Irish" Henry, bbs; Don Murray, cl/C-m; Tommy Dorsey, tb; Jimmy Dorsey, as/cl/ss; Bill Rank, tb; Stanley "Doc" Ryker, as/bar; Fred "Fuzzy" Farrar, tp; Ray Lodwig, tp; Howdy Quicksell, bjo.* (Courtesy Frank Driggs, Gallert Collection.)

Paul Whiteman was known to the general public as "the King of Jazz," and Goldkette had aspirations to be the "Paul Whiteman of the West." One reason he never reached that goal could have been that he spread himself thin by organizing a number of bands and becoming more a manager than a bandleader. The musical leadership of the Graystone orchestra was eventually left in the hands of others, more comfortable with dance music. He did perform with orchestras under his name at the DAC and the Book-Cadillac Hotel, but others shared musical leadership.[31]

The heyday of the Graystone Ballroom orchestra was the years of 1926 and 1927, when Bix Beiderbecke rejoined the band. He had spent a few months with the band in 1924, including a recording date at the DAC, but Goldkette let him go with the remark that "The jazzing is well and good, but there are other skills you have to master."[32] These latter skills included facility in reading written music. When Bix's old friend saxophonist Frankie Trumbauer took over the leadership of the orchestra in May 1926, part of the bargain was the rehiring of Bix. After being split into smaller units for gigs at summer resorts in Michigan and Indiana, the band went on a successful eastern tour in the fall. This included recordings for RCA Victor, but unfortunately it seems that the band was prevented from recording some of its hottest numbers. Saxophonist Doc Ryker described the role of Victor's recording director this way in a 1967 interview.

> *He wanted it strictly stock, commercial. . . . I don't really know why he hired the band at all. The stuff he didn't want, why that was our style. We didn't get a chance to do anything we wanted until right at the end, when he let us put down "Clementine" and "My Pretty Girl." . . . But there were so many other gems.*[33]

The orchestra's "battle of the bands" with the Fletcher Henderson band at their home turf, the Roseland Ballroom in New York City, on

31. Ibid.; and Kuwik, "From Prince to Pauper," 4–6.

32. Richard Sudhalter and Philip Evans, *Bix: Man and Legend* (New Rochelle, N.Y.: Arlington House, 1974), 126.

33. Ryker, quoted in McCarthy, *Big Band Jazz*, 185.

Fig. 22. Jean Goldkette Orchestra, Detroit, 1927. *Front: Ray Lodwig, tp; Fred "Fuzzy" Farrar, tp; Bix Beiderbecke, cnt; Chauncey Morehouse, dms; Don Murray, as/clt; Frank Trumbauer, C-m; Stanley "Doc" Ryker, as/bar; Spiegle Wilcox, tb; Bill Rank, tb. Rear: Irving "Itzy" Riskin, pno; Steve Brown, bs; Howard "Howdy" Quicksell, bjo.* (Courtesy Gallert Collection.)

October 6, 1926, has become legendary since the Goldkette band "won." Henderson's trumpeter Rex Stewart put it this way.

> *We learned that Jean Goldkette's orchestra was, without any question, the greatest in the world and the first original white swing band in jazz history. . . . No other white orchestra boasted such an array of skilled jazzmen at one time. . . . Not even Paul Whiteman (who hired many of Goldkette's former stars after the group disbanded) was able to bring about such swinging or such esprit de corps. . . . Even Benny Goodman, swinger that he was, did not come close to the tremendous sound of Goldkette or the inventive arrangements. . . . Of this I am positive, because I was in Fletcher's band when that memorable confrontation took place at Roseland.*[34]

Stewart's testimony is one of many indications that in spite of racial segregation there was considerable borrowing of musical ideas between black and white musicians. The recordings made by Bix and Tram (Trumbauer) with a small group from the Goldkette band in 1927 influenced many musicians. The great tenorist Lester Young is reputed to have developed his unique style under the spell of Tram's solo on "Singin' the Blues." Bix's influence was even greater, and his solo on the same song is considered "one of the three most celebrated jazz solos in history."[35]

Bix's close musical kinship with John Nesbitt in McKinney's Cotton Pickers has also been commented on. The two bands did play together at the Graystone in 1926 and 1927, and according to Dave Wilborn: "Bix and Nesbitt were exchanging ideas and they both had a bottle. They had a place out in the Graystone Gardens, a loose brick, where they could hide their bottle."[36]

34. Rex Stewart, *Jazz Masters of the Thirties* (New York: Macmillan, 1972), 12, 16–17.

35. George Avakian, liner notes, Bix Beiderbecke, *The Bix Beiderbecke Story*, vol. 2, *Bix and Tram*, Columbia Records CL 845 (LP).

36. Wilborn, interview by Gallert, July 15, 1973. Since dancing in the Graystone Gardens did not start until the summer of 1928, the back of the Graystone was probably a better hiding place a year earlier.

The band was back at the Roseland in January 1927, and there were also more recordings. This was also the time when Bix and Trumbauer led a smaller group from the band in the classic recording of "Singin' the Blues."

While Bix and Trumbauer were the leading soloists in the Goldkette organization a number of pioneering jazzmen contributed to the Goldkette band: the Dorsey brothers (Tommy and Jimmy), trombonist and arranger Russ Morgan, saxophonist Don Murray, violinist Joe Venuti, bassist Steve Brown, and drummer Chauncey Morehouse. Such a collection of talent did come at a price however: the salaries were high, and the band was in the red. In contrast, the other bands under Goldkette's name were in the black. This eventually forced Goldkette to disband his Victor Recording Orchestra in September 1927. Several band members joined the Whiteman band, but few remained in Detroit. The new band at the Graystone was as mentioned McKinney's Cotton Pickers.

Other Goldkette Bands

SOME OF THE MOST EXCITING jazz outfits that played under Goldkette's name were the smaller bands that played at summer resorts in Michigan and northern Indiana. The summer of 1926 there were three such Goldkette units: at Island Lake, Sand Lake (south of Jackson, Michigan), and Hudson Lake (Indiana).[37] These bands adapted the arrangements of the Goldkette Graystone bands to fit a smaller band, but there was also a lot more improvisation. The Hudson Lake group included Bix Beiderbecke and has become legendary. Bix's biographers Sudhalter and Evans describe the weekends with visits from Chicago musicians as "an unending cycle of booze, 'mout' [marijuana] and music," but it was a summer when Bix's playing reached a peak.[38]

The unit at Sand Lake was called the Breeze Blowers and was led by pianist Fred Bergin, who later led his own band. Pianist Reuel Kenyon, who played with both the Breeze Blowers and the Graystone band, remembered the Breeze Blowers as one of the "hottest" of Goldkette's units.[39]

Mezz Mezzrow also gives an account of Goldkette's part in the music scene in Detroit in 1926 from the perspective of a Chicago white jazzman looking for work.

> *Stories from other musicians who'd been off to Detroit and New York kept drifting back to Chicago, making us know that King Jazz was romping up and down the land, and the wanderlust began to get to me. . . . Detroit in particular was one place I wanted to dig because the office for all the Jean Goldkette bands was there, Ray Miller's band was at the Addison Hotel, McKinney's Cotton Pickers were jumping at the Arcadia. . . . Next day I dropped around to the Goldkette office and . . . it looked like I was in. That same night they sent me on a club date with Tommy Dorsey in a pick-up band, where we played opposite McKinney's Cotton Pickers. . . . The corny stocks and jumbled-up special arrangements we had to read at sight must have sounded pretty cute to those colored boys, whose numbers were all fixed by solid arrangers like Don Redman. . . . the Cotton Pickers . . . came on with a steady rock that was really groovy.*[40]

The Orange Blossoms was a group formed by Hank Biagini that became one of the mainstays of the Goldkette office. Tubaist Oscar LaGassé was still in high school when he joined the band at the Orange Blossom Terrace in the early 1920s.

> *It was a dance hall with nickel dances. We were on the bandstand and all the US Steel workers used to come there and dance and make out with the ladies and drink. We used to lock ourselves in the stage part so nobody would chop us up. It was a pretty rough neighborhood! [Around 1926] the band was busy and Russ Morgan was our arranger and rehearser. We used to play opposite the Victor band at the Graystone. The Victor Recording orchestra had*

37. Kuwik," From Prince to Pauper," 7.

38. Sudhalter and Evans, *Bix*, 167–69.

39. Reuel Kenyon, interview by Lars Bjorn, Ann Arbor, Michigan, October 26, 1977.

40. Mezz Mezzrow and Bernard Wolfe, *Really the Blues* (Garden City, N.J.: Anchor Books, 1972), 76–77.

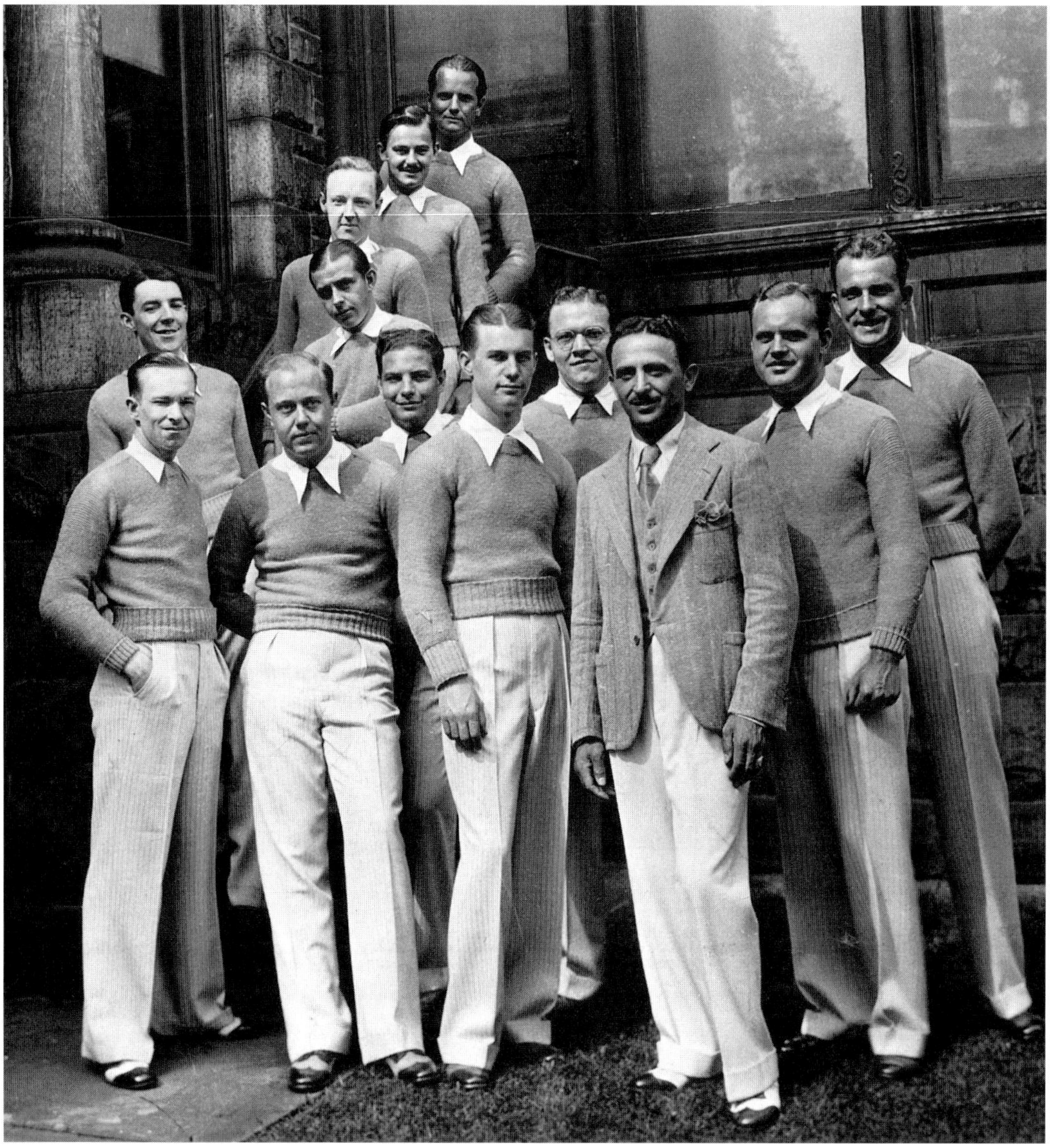

Fig. 23. Orange Blossoms, Visiting Nurse Association grounds, 4421 Woodward (one block north of the Graystone), 1929. *Standing on ground, L to R: "Chink" Dougherty, tp; Gene Gifford, bjo/arr; Howard Hall, pno; Pat Davis, as; Pee Wee Hunt, tb; Hank Biagini, vln/ldr; Les Arquette, ts; Glen Gray Knoblaugh, as/bar. Standing on first step, L to R: Dub Shoffner, tp; Harold George, bs. Standing above George, L to R: Wally Urban, dms; Billy Rauch, tb; Jack Richmond, vcl.* (Courtesy Frank Driggs, Gallert Collection.)

arrangers in the orchestra, but a lot of times someone would request a piece and they would just fake it and play it. We did that too.[41]

By 1929 the Orange Blossoms reorganized as a cooperative under the leadership of Glen Gray (born Glen "Spike" Knoblaugh) and added Gene Gifford as arranger.[42] Gifford had come to Detroit as a Goldkette staff arranger and eventually played a central role in developing the unique style of Glen Gray and the Casa Loma Orchestra, as the band eventually became known.[43] When work dried up in Detroit in 1929 the band moved to New York City and was soon recording.[44]

Goldkette's bands at the Detroit Athletic Club and the Book-Cadillac Hotel were more firmly within the society band tradition than the Orange Blossoms. As jazz styles developed rapidly in the 1920s bands like these became increasingly less attractive to both young musicians and dancers. Young white jazzmen voiced frequent complaints about having to suffer through "square" arrangements and leaders. Only by the mid-1930s did large white swing

41. Oscar LaGassé, interview by Lars Bjorn, Royal Oak, Michigan, August 28, 1996. The Orange Blossom Terrace was located on 8576 West Jefferson Avenue in southwest Detroit.

42. George T. Simon, *The Big Bands*, 4th ed. (New York: Schirmer, 1981), 117–18. Gray was an alto saxophonist who joined the Orange Blossoms about 1924. Other significant members of the band included trombonist Pee Wee Hunt, who came to Detroit in 1927.

43. Schuller, *Swing Era*, 632. Schuller characterizes the band as at best a semihot dance orchestra before Gifford joined. This did indeed seem to be the case in 1925 judging by the repertoire played in dinner broadcasts from Hotel Statler as reported in the *Detroit News*, April 12, 1925.

44. The first recordings for Okeh on October 29, 1929, still have Henry Biagini listed as director of the orchestra. Within a year Biagini returned to Detroit. One song has the band listed as the Palais de Danse orchestra, no doubt a reference to the Detroit ballroom. Rust, *American Dance Band Discography*, 310. Biagini (born 1899 in Italy) continued to work around Detroit. He died in a car accident on May 14, 1944, on his way back from a job with Mike Falk's orchestra.

bands emerge. Goldkette's Graystone orchestra and the Orange Blossoms/Casa Loma were important forerunners. When you add in the influence of the Cotton Pickers "a case could be made that the swing era started in Detroit," according to jazz writer Gene Lees.[45]

Other Black Bands

McKinney's Cotton Pickers was not the only Detroit band that benefited from the demand for black music in the ballrooms of the "Roaring Twenties." The Billy Minor Melodians and the Chocolate Dandies were more short lived than the Cotton Pickers but like their more famous cousins played ballrooms in Detroit and elsewhere.

The Billy Minor Melodians was an 11-piece big band organized around 1925. For the first three years the band seems to have spent a lot of time on the road touring dance halls in Ohio and Pennsylvania. By late 1928 the band was in residence at the Monticello Ballroom in Detroit.[46] Minor was the manager of the band and also played the piano, but the musical director was violinist and cellist John Lain. Charles V. Moore remembered that the band also played the Graystone.

Earl Walton turned down the Graystone job because he was offered better money at the Palais de Danse. Minor got the job. He hired me to play 1st trumpet. Minor was an OK pianist. He had lots of money. His parents owned a dress

Fig. 24. Minor's Melodians, Visiting Nurse Association grounds, 4421 Woodward (one block north of the Graystone), 1929.
L to R: Irving "Mouse" Randolph, tp; Ed Inge, cl; Cecil Lee, as; Jim Peters, bbs; Joe Johnson, dms; Walter Kennebrew, bjo/gtr; Eugene Calloway, as; Charles V. Moore, tp; John Anderson, tb; Billy Minor, pno/ldr.
(Courtesy Dorothy E. Jackson, Gallert Collection.)

45. Gene Lees, *Waiting for Dizzy* (New York: Oxford University Press, 1991), 98.

46. Peyton, "The Musical Bunch," *Chicago Defender*, March 5, 1927; July 2, 1927; November 24, 1928.

Fig. 25. Chocolate Dandies, Manitou Beach, Michigan, ca. 1927. *L to R: John Scott, bjo; Albert Holmes, pno; Joe Brown, tb; Charles V. Moore, tp; Joe Johnson, dms; Bill Canada, as; Rube Wardell, as/cl; Nick Veske, bbs; Charles "Lanky" Bowman, ts/cl.* (Courtesy Dorothy E. Jackson, Gallert Collection.)

> *shop behind the DAC, and they wanted him to become a dentist, not a musician. That was a good band, Will Hudson did arrangements.*[47]

Moore also remembered other members of the band.

> *Cecil Lee on clarinet and alto. . . . and our drummer Russell "Tacky" Madison was a Chick Webb look alike. . . . he could read like mad. . . . When you play floor shows you have the music written out. . . . if there was a fly speck he would read the speck. . . . We played 6 nights a week, Mondays off. . . for white audiences.*[48]

Several central figures in the Detroit jazz world got their first major big band experience with the Melodians: Cecil Lee became a major bandleader in the 1930s, and five Melodians turned Cotton Pickers in the 1930s.[49]

Before he joined the Billy Minor Melodians, Charles Victor Moore organized another big band dubbed the Chocolate Dandies in 1926. He remembered how the band got its first job.

> *When the McKinney's Cotton Pickers came to town, they left their summer job at Manitou Beach. . . . When they got a steady job at the Arcadia they could not go back to Manitou Beach; that's how we got the job at Manitou Beach. . . . We named the group the Chocolate Dandies. . . . We got paid real well: $100 a week and room and board. . . . after that we went to Toronto and the Silver Slipper. . . . I left the band when Lanky Bowman became the leader and they went to New York and to the Savoy Ballroom. . . . I rejoined the band when they came back to Detroit. . . . McKinney took over the booking of the band and called it McKinney's Chocolate Dandies. . . . we played the Graystone when the Cotton Pickers were out of town. . . . we worked at least 5 nights a week.*[50]

The Chocolate Dandies often used the same

47. Charles V. Moore, interview by Jim Gallert, Detroit, Michigan, March 3, 1989.

48. Moore, interview by Bjorn.

49. Future Cotton Pickers were John Lain, bassist Jim Peters, Cecil Lee, Charles V. Moore, and saxophonist Joe Moxley. Ibid.; and Chilton, *McKinney's Music*, 63–67.

50. Moore, interview by Bjorn.

arrangements as the Cotton Pickers, which is fitting since they worked as substitutes for the Cotton Pickers. When the Cotton Pickers headed for the Roseland Ballroom in New York City in the early fall of 1928, the Chocolate Dandies replaced them at the Graystone. This stint included a band battle with the Fletcher Henderson orchestra at the Graystone.[51]

Similarly to the Cotton Pickers the Chocolate Dandies were noted for putting on a show with plenty of song and humor.[52] Like the Melodians, the Chocolate Dandies band was made up of future bandleaders and Cotton Pickers. Charles "Lanky" Bowman eventually became the leader of the pit band at the Paradise Theatre in Detroit, and three members of the band became Cotton Pickers in the 1930s.[53]

Neither the Melodians nor the Chocolate Dandies had the chance to record, but in the case of the latter band it came curiously close. McKinney was booking the Dandies for the Goldkette office, and Goldkette came up with the idea of further promoting the band through recordings. However, Goldkette decided that his "first" band, the Cotton Pickers, should make the recordings under the name of the "second" band. As John Chilton points out in his history of the Cotton Pickers, "as with the best laid schemes, things did not turn out as anticipated, the impact of these recordings had no effect on the career of the 'real' Chocolate Dandies and at the end of 1928 their connection with Jean Goldkette ended."[54]

51. Advertisements in *Owl,* August 25, September 15, October 13, 1928.

52. Ibid.; and Warren, interview by Bjorn. The Chocolate Dandies was a nine-piece band, two less than the Cotton Pickers in 1928.

53. Future Cotton Pickers were Charles V. Moore, Lanky Bowman, and saxophonist William "Bill" Canada. Ibid.

54. Chilton, *McKinney's Music,* 21.

The 1930s: Paradise Valley Days

Those were the Valley days!
— Dave Wilborn

DURING THE 1930s Paradise Valley gradually became the new center for jazz in Detroit. The city's ballrooms were still where you would hear big bands, but they were increasingly rivaled by nightspots in the African-American community. Behind this shift were changes in the entertainment business amid the vagaries of the Great Depression.

During the 1930s big band jazz evolved into what is commonly called the "swing" style of jazz. Black bands around 1931 mostly worked out the elements of this style, but for a larger public the "official" beginning was Benny Goodman's performance at the Palomar Ballroom in Los Angeles in August 1935. The development of swing was associated with changes in the band business as well, where national bands came to dominate territorial bands. Thomas Hennessey has described the process this way: "The local variations of the territories were replaced by a uniform national structure and sound distributed by the mass media of records, radio, and motion pictures. Bands began to tour on a national level supported by complex publicity machines and highly organized schedules of bookings."[1]

What resulted was a "band business pyramid" with four to six national bands on top, territorial bands in the middle, and local bands on the bottom.[2] McKinney's Cotton Pickers was one of the national bands until about 1932, when it began a gradual decline.

"When the nation catches a cold, Detroit gets pneumonia" became a widespread saying in depression Detroit. Auto sales tumbled fourfold between 1929 and 1932. The result was that by 1933 almost half of all autoworkers in Detroit were unemployed.[3] Detroit recovered slowly and unevenly starting in 1933, and a sustained boom in the local economy did not occur until World War II.

The Great Depression dramatically slowed the influx of workers to Detroit, in comparison with the boom years of the preceding three decades. Still, the city added 55,000 inhabitants during the 1930s, and more than half of them were African Americans. The depression also reversed the growth of the black middle

Herb Thompson, Nub Brown, and Milton Buckner at the Cozy Corner Grill, ca. 1940.

1. Hennessey, *From Jazz to Swing*, 23.
2. Ibid., 135.
3. Holli, *Detroit*, 126.

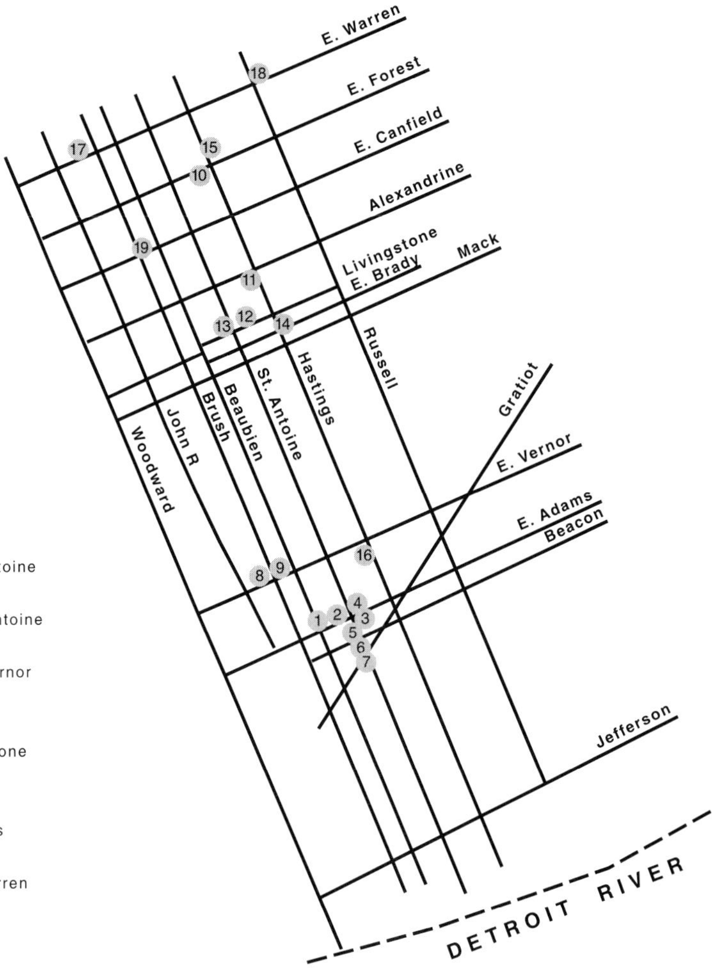

1 Club Plantation, 550 E Adams
2 Band Box, 602 E Adams
3 Buffalo's, 606 E Adams
4 Russell House, 615 E Adams
5 Melody Club/Club Paradise, 1933 St. Antoine
6 B&C, 1730 St. Antoine
7 Jess Faithful's Rhythm Club, 1701 St. Antoine
8 Club Harlem, 281 E Vernor
9 Brown Bomber Chicken Shack, 424 E Vernor
10 Forest Club, 700 E Forest
11 Cozy Corner, 4100 Hastings
12 Chocolate Bar/Cotton Club, 632 Livingstone
13 MDL Club, Livingstone/St. Antoine
14 Ace Bar, 3678 Hastings
15 Tuxedo Grill/Club Tuxedo, 4758 Hastings
16 Rose Bud Inn, 2337 Hastings
17 Garden Terrace/Rhythm Club, 301 E Warren
18 Palm Garden Café, Warren/Russell
19 Harlem Cave, Brush/Canfield

Fig. 26. Clubs in Paradise Valley and north to Warren Avenue, 1930s. (Map by Borkin and Kaplan.)

class that occurred in the previous decades. Business prospects remained uncertain, and the unionization of the auto industry in the middle of the 1930s did not immediately help the black working class.[4]

While economic conditions for black Detroiters stagnated during the 1930s, there were dramatic political changes. Blacks shifted their political allegiances from the Republican to the Democratic Party in 1936.[5] This helped reelect Roosevelt as president and also played a part in the election of Charles Diggs to the Michigan Senate. Diggs was a supporter of stronger civil rights laws and one of the main builders of the New Deal political coalition. In 1937 the State of Michigan passed a stronger civil rights law, but changes in discriminatory practices were slow to come.[6]

Racial discrimination in recreation and leisure activities was often reported in the African-American press, and it sometimes referred to places where jazz was heard. The first-page headline of the *Detroit Tribune* on June 29, 1935, was "Beer-Garden Discriminates."

> *At the Don Redman dance at Eastwood Park, Monday night, the dragon of racial discrimination raised its venomous head, when Ted Bedlipschitz, manager of the beer garden concession at the restaurant, refused to serve four prominent citizens of the race who had been in-*

4. Robert Conot, *American Odyssey* (New York: Morrow, 1974), 370.

5. Thomas, *Life for Us Is What We Make It*, 264.

6. Ibid., 129.

vited by Constable William Bradley and another white friend to partake of refreshments with them in the beer garden. . . . When Duke Ellington's orchestra was featured at Eastwood Park three weeks ago, no attempt was made to discriminate against colored patrons who attended in large numbers.

Eastwood Park was located at the city limits and was open during the summer season. It differed from several other seasonal ballrooms by featuring black big bands, sponsored by black promoters. The Graystone continued its Monday only dances for black dancers and also came in for criticism from the *Detroit Tribune*, without direct confrontation of its segregation policy. A 1933 editorial, "Economic Self-Defense," had the following to say about the Graystone.

We have spent thousands upon thousands of dollars there although it is neither owned nor managed by Negroes and what do we have to show for our money? Some of the colored individuals who have worked for the Graystone have complained to the Tribune that they are the last to be paid, and sometimes not paid at all. We know of cities much smaller than Detroit, in which the colored citizens own or manage up-to-date dance halls of their own.[7]

Thus one way of dealing with the humiliation of discrimination was black business development. This was already under way in Paradise Valley.

Paradise Valley

PARADISE VALLEY became a widely used term for the center of the African-American community in the 1930s. There is some dispute about who actually coined the term, but the most likely suspect is Rollo Vest, the theatrical editor of the *Detroit Tribune*.[8] Vest ran a contest to name the area, and Paradise Valley won. The business and entertainment center of the African-American community was the intersection of St. Antoine and Adams. The outer limits were roughly as follows: Gratiot on the south, Vernor on the north, Hastings on the east, and Brush on the west. (See fig. 26.)

Although Paradise Valley had legal as well as illegal business activities, it was considered safe. Fred Hart Williams explained it this way.

One of the reasons was that the men who operated, let us say, "legitimate" gambling games, and legitimate businessmen located in the Valley, ruled the roost with an iron hand and any outside dips, con men or tough hombres were promptly "discouraged" in remaining long within Valley limits.[9]

This strong sense of community also made possible an unusual degree of interracial mixing. While the Valley was predominantly black during the days, the nights and early mornings were evenly balanced along the color line. The major contributing factor was the development of the black and tan cabaret or nightclub.

As we saw in the first chapter there were a number of cabarets, theaters, and restaurants in Paradise Valley where jazz was heard by the 1920s. When the local economy started its slow road to recovery in 1933 Paradise Valley experienced its most rapid growth. Our research turned up 7 jazz spots for the 1920s, but 14 were added in the following decade.[10] A majority of these spots were owned by African Americans.[11] They were heavily concentrated in the "T" formed by East Adams across the top, from Beaubien on the west to Hastings on the east, and the vertical line consisting of St. Antoine south to Beacon and Gratiot at the bottom. (See fig. 26.) Let us explore the significant jazz landmarks along this T starting on Adams, or the top left of the T.

The Club Plantation was the "number one spot in the Valley" according to journalist Ulysses Boykin.[12] It was located in the Norwood Hotel at 550 East Adams, between Beaubien and St. Antoine. Like many other black and tan nightclubs its name evoked the Old South, as did the most famous of all black and tans:

7. "Economic Self-Defense," *Detroit Tribune*, August 19, 1933.

8. Moon, "Paradise Valley"; and Bill Lane column, *Michigan Chronicle*, September 29, 1959. For a different view see Hart Williams, "Paradise Valley Was a Paradise."

9. Hart Williams, "Paradise Valley Was a Paradise." A similar point is made by Sunnie Wilson in his memoirs: Sunnie Wilson with John Cohassey, *Toast of the Town: The Life and Times of Sunnie Wilson* (Detroit: Wayne State University Press, 1998), 50.

10. There were spurts of growth in 1933 and 1937. Using a wider definition of Paradise Valley, with Warren as the northern boundary, an additional 13 spots were added during the 1930s.

11. Some of these entrepreneurs probably got their capital from the underground (illegal) economy, specifically the numbers racket. Exactly who and how many were involved are difficult to establish, just as it is difficult to say with any assurance how many Jewish entrepreneurs were involved with organized crime. That several black and Jewish businessmen had reputations for being involved with illegal activities is clear from our interviews with musicians. Richard Thomas argues that there was a substantial overlap between legal and illegal business in the black community; for example, many businessmen were involved in both. Thomas, *Life for Us Is What We Make It*, 116–18. Sunnie Wilson argues that the numbers game was "the most important source of economic and political power" for black Detroiters in the 1930s. For example, "the numbers bought Walter Norwood's Norwood Hotel and Slim Jones' Chocolate Bar." Wilson, *Toast of the Town*, 66.

12. Ulysses Boykin and Wade Boykin, interview by Lars Bjorn, Detroit, Michigan, June 1, 1979.

Fig. 27. Club Plantation program (cover), 1935. (Courtesy Gallert Collection.)

CLUB PLANTATION

WE PRESENT

To our Detroit patrons and friends our show, comprising a very important part in the attractiveness and entertainment of the CLUB PLANTATION.

We have spared no efforts to secure real novelty and pep in the matter of harmoniously blending units from every section of the country into one grand entertainment.

Club Plantation this season is launching a drive to captivate our patrons by our attractions. We are hoping that our first attack will not fall short.

The floor show, the finest of this season, is directed and produced by "Dusty" Murray, well known producer and late of the Cotton Club. A hot number himself in comedy and equally as well in the straight roles he may be compelled to handle. He has lined up a production, at this time, we hope will please you.

A queen of mirth and song is Auzie Dial, abounding in pep, vitality and personality. She will bring to you her new offerings and interpretations in a manner and style, strictly original.

Quality
FRUITS and VEGETABLES
from the
QUALITY FRUIT SHOP
23 Broadway Market
DETROIT

OUR SHOW

EARL WALTON
presents THE SEASON'S FIRST EDITION OF THE FAMOUS
CLUB PLANTATION REVUE
SEPTEMBER « 20.h » 1935

PART I

1—OPENING: *Ensemble*
(a) An Introduction in Song
By the Plantation Sweathearts
(b) "TAKE IT EASY"
"Dusty" Murray and Girls

2—"GOT RHYTHM IN HIS FEET"
LITTLE NOODY BONMAN

3—"HOTCHA HOTCHA"
AUZIE DIAL

4—"RHYTHM OF THEIR OWN"
In Style and Grace
Plantation Sextette of Sepia Sweethearts

5—"A COMICAL CLASSIC
"DUSTY" MURRAY

6—"AINT MISBEHAVIN'"
On Her Toes
ERNESTINE FORD

7—"It Must Be a Devil in The Moon"
ERLINE AND GIRLS

8—"RHYTHM AND TAPS"
JAMES SIMMONS

9—"NONSENSE vs. SONG"
AUZIE DIAL AND "DUSTY" MURRAY

10—"Sophistication in Modern Dances"
TURNER AND BURELLE

11—"SMOOTH SAILING"
SEXTETTE ERLINE—ENTIRE COMPANY
PART II ON PAGE 10

ELECTRICAL WORK
and
FIXTURES
Installed by
Cochran Electric Company
Electrical Construction
Repairing
8873 Yates Ave. PLaza 2278

Meet me at "The Office"

Fig. 28. Club Plantation program (inside), 1935. (Courtesy Gallert Collection.)

Harlem's Cotton Club. We have already seen the same marketing strategy for white audiences when naming black bands.

Walter Norwood was the fifth African-American owner of the hotel since 1925, when it was purchased by bandleader-booker Ben Shook. Shook advertised the 105-room hotel as "Detroit's largest and finest hostelry devoted to the interest of colored people."[13] The Plantation was a swankier version of the cabarets that had been in the hotel in the 1920s. When it opened in 1933 its manager was Andrew "Jap" Sneed, also promoter for Joe Louis, Detroit's Brown Bomber.[14] Russell Green played the Plantation with Earl Walton and remembered its customers.

> *The Plantation drew a 95% white audience and it included the wealthy in town. Joe Louis also would hang out there, and guests at the finer hotels, like the Book-Cadillac, would come around too.*[15]

Club Plantation was replaced by Club Congo in 1941.

On the southeast corner of Adams and St. Antoine was the Musicians and Performers Club, better known as the Band Box.[16] Bandleader Johnny Trafton remembered that

> *The Band Box and the Rhythm Club were special rendezvous places where musicians congregated, met and hung out. They were less than two blocks from each other and this is where musicians congregated after hours in Paradise Valley.*[17]

Jam sessions at the Band Box could be competitive affairs, as tenorist Joe Norris remembered. He came to Detroit in 1934 and quickly established himself on the music scene after playing jam sessions.

> *Sometimes we would go through all of the keys . . . for instance: "Sweet Georgia Brown," in up tempo, starting in A flat, then B flat, then B, etc., and back up to A flat.*[18]

Piano player Wade Boykin remembered some notable visitors to the Band Box.

> *Say you had Fletcher Henderson at the Graystone. Everybody would congregate after 2*

13. 1925–26 *Detroit City Directory,* 1104. According to the *City Directories* the hotel was Hotel Dupont, 1921–25; Hotel Shook, 1925–26; Robinson Hotel, 1926–27; Hotel Williams, 1927–29; Dunbar Hotel, 1930–32; Hotel Norwood, 1932–48. See also "Old Hotel under New Management," *Owl,* August 19, 1927; "Finest Race Hotel in Middle West to Open Here in April," *Owl,* March 23, 1929; "Norwood Hotel Sold for $150,000," *Michigan Chronicle,* April 17, 1948.

14. Andrew "Jap" Sneed was born in Nashville, Tennessee, and ran away from home with a circus at age 14. He came to Detroit when the circus was stranded there in 1914. After working at many odd jobs Sneed opened up a haberdashery shop on Beacon and St. Antoine in 1926. Just before opening up the Plantation he opened up the Creole Kitchen at Beaubien and Madison with Alfred Pelham. He started as a dance promoter in 1928 and in 1941 opened up Club 666 on East Adams. Sneed file, Burton Historical Collection, Detroit Public Library.

15. Russell Green, interview by Lars Bjorn, Detroit, Michigan, October 28, 1977.

16. The Band Box was at 602 East Adams, where the Radio Inn cabaret was located in the mid-1920s according to Washington, "Recreation," 16. It was replaced by the Hollywood Cafe cabaret in 1927. Advertisement in *Owl,* December 17, 1927.

17. Johnny Trafton, interview by Lars Bjorn, Detroit, Michigan, September 11, 1978.

18. Joe Norris, interview by Jim Gallert, Detroit, Michigan, June 12, 1989. Norris, born in 1908 in Newark, New Jersey, switched from alto to tenor after hearing Coleman Hawkins. He worked with Earle Howard and Blanche Calloway and also led his own bands in Newark. His birth name was Joe St. John.

o'clock after the dance was over in the Valley. Go eat soul food and go to the Band Box.... Cab Calloway, Duke Ellington, were over there and... you'd see Earl Hines sitting over there.[19]

Ulysses Boykin added that

Jimmy Carlisle and Judge Nelson were the owners of the Band Box. The only thing illegal was that they served whiskey in coffee cups.... you could order all kinds of whiskey and it all came out of the same bottle.... Next door at 606 E. Adams was Buffalo's owned by John R. "Buffalo" James... later the 606 Horseshoe Lounge.... Buffalo's was frequented by the young Strohs and others and he would take clothes as temporary payment from the young affluent customers.[20]

Buffalo's in 1933 was known as Buffalo's 606 Club or Apex Club and featured a floor show, an orchestra, and Buffalo as emcee.[21] Buffalo was a "laughing little man who always carried a big cigar in his mouth" and also ran an after-hours spot called the Frogs Club. It was located in the southwest corner of the Valley and was frequented by "police inspectors, mayors, movie stars and other sundry nite crawlers, like Martha Raye . . . listening to George Bias sing and to Al Pearson play guitar with George Saunders on the Novochord."[22] What was of particular import was the presence of a certain high-ranking police officer. Buffalo "was raided regularly but always drove right down to the police station in his own car, fixed things up and went back to business as usual."[23] When his protector died in 1947 Buffalo's businesses were suddenly closed down.[24]

Across Adams from the Band Box was the Russell House Hotel. A side entrance in the basement led to the Night Club, which was a blind pig after hours "with a large white traffic" and jazz and blues piano players.[25] The same crowd also traveled south on St. Antoine to visit Earl Walton's Studio Club after 1938. It was upstairs and had "walls lined with framed autographs of famous visitors . . . Duke Ellington, Joe Louis, Cab Calloway, Teddy Wilson, Fats Waller."[26]

Fig. 29. Alberta Adams singing with pianist Wade Boykin and drummer Amos Woodward, Club B & C, June 1944.
(Courtesy Alberta Adams, Gallert Collection.)

Just south of the corner of Adams and St. Antoine at 1933 St. Antoine (and next door to the former Palms cabaret) was the Melody Club. It was another black and tan nightclub, owned by Judge Nelson and managed by William McKinney. Both were musicians, the latter of McKinney's Cotton Pickers fame. It opened in 1937 and closed two years later after the death of Nelson.[27] Club Paradise took over and in 1942 was replaced by the Turf Bar. The Turf Bar was one of the centers for "numbers" gambling according to Elaine Moon.

The Turf Bar was the gathering place for the fast crowd, a place where everyone waited for the winning number. When it was announced, if there were any winners present, that call was "Run 'em around." Everyone got a drink on the winner, and the bartender sweetened the bill.[28]

The next intersection traveling south on St. Antoine was Beacon. On the southeast corner were the Joe Louis Headquarters and the B & C Club.[29] The B & C was opened in 1937 by Roy Lightfoot, who started out in the basement of

19. Boykin and Boykin, interview by Bjorn.

20. Ibid.

21. *Detroit Times*, March 4, 1933; September 23, 1933.

22. Bill Lane column, *Michigan Chronicle*, June 24, 1950.

23. Moon, "Paradise Valley."

24. Larry Chism column, *Michigan Chronicle*, May 17, 1947. James became a full time executive with the Detroit Metropolitan Assurance Company, which he started with, among others, Charles Diggs Sr. "Buffalo James Dies; Community Saddened," *Michigan Chronicle*, February 18, 1956.

25. Advertisement for the Night Club in *Owl*, August 19, 1927. Boykin and Boykin, interview by Bjorn; and Trafton, interview by Bjorn.

26. "After Dark," *Detroit Times*, April 22, 1939.

27. *Detroit Times*, June 12, 1937; February 18, 1939.

28. Moon, "Paradise Valley."

29. The B & C was at 1730 St. Antoine.

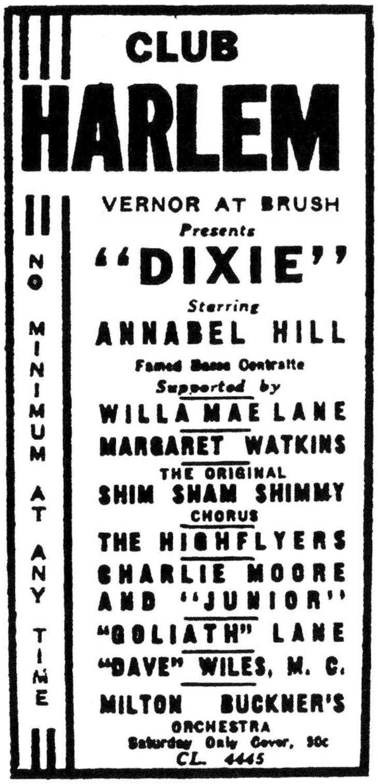
CLUB
HARLEM
VERNOR AT BRUSH
Presents
"DIXIE"
Starring
ANNABEL HILL
Supported by
WILLA MAE LANE
MARGARET WATKINS
THE ORIGINAL
SHIM SHAM SHIMMY
CHORUS
THE HIGHFLYERS
CHARLIE MOORE
AND "JUNIOR"
"GOLIATH" LANE
"DAVE" WILES, M. C.
MILTON BUCKNER'S
ORCHESTRA
Saturday Only Cover, 50c
CL. 4445
NO MINIMUM AT ANY TIME

Fig. 30. Advertisement for Club Harlem. "Charlie Moore" is trumpeter Charles V. Moore, and "Junior" is guitarist Wilson "Junior" Warren. (From *Friday Times*, May 11, 1934.)

the Hotel Biltmore (one block north) and in the 1920s was at the Royal Garden Cabaret (a block south from the B & C).[30] Lightfoot was a popular figure in Paradise Valley and was elected honorary mayor of the Valley in 1937. A *Detroit Tribune* article in 1940 said that "Roy Lightfoot has increased the size of the bar to 97 feet and he can seat 200."[31] The club was advertised as "Paradise Valley's Original Theatre Bar" and was replaced by Club Owens and the El Sino in the mid-1940s.[32]

Blues singer Alberta Adams was one of the headliners at the B & C in the early 1940s and remembered the stage shows.

> *The first show started at nine. The emcee, Bobby Keyes, would come out and the band would strike up a tune. Then the chorus girls—we had four or five of 'em—came out for a number. Behind them, there'd be a singer. Maybe a comedian next, the chorus girls again, and finally, me. I'd do about three numbers. Changed clothes every show. Red dress, red shoes. Yellow dress, yellow shoes.*[33]

Further south, just north of the northwest corner of St. Antoine and Gratiot, was the Musician's Booking and Service Bureau, better known as Jess Faithful's Rhythm Club. It was located on the second floor, as Johnny Trafton remembered.

> *Jess Faithful's wife, Biddy, owned a restaurant underneath, Biddy's Restaurant, one of the landmarks of Paradise Valley. . . . Jess Faithful was a musician, but he became more interested in his club.*[34]

Jess Faithful had traveled on the vaudeville circuit and in the early 1930s opened up the Rhythm Club.[35] This was the number one place for jam sessions in the Valley, and you needed a card to get in after hours.[36]

Saxophonist Lawrence Mann remembered what the scene was like on a typical day.

> *Musicians' Club . . . this was where most musicians would congregate and reminisce about jobs, sort of like family. . . . that's where the gigs came in. . . . We played cards.*[37]

Wilson "Stutz" Anderson had Faithful working occasionally in his big band and remembered the club well.

> *We'd sit around and play cards and bootleg liquor was served. The police didn't stop us. They'd walk the beat; you give them $2 and they'd walk out. We'd be open until 5 or 6 in the morning . . . jam all night long.*[38]

As the black population grew modestly in the 1930s it expanded north from the traditional center of Paradise Valley. Jazz spots were found along three major streets: Vernor, the northern boundary of Paradise Valley; Hastings, its eastern border; and Warren. (See fig. 26.)

Near the corner of Vernor and Brush were two spots: Club Harlem and the Brown Bomber Chicken Shack. Club Harlem was opened in 1933 by Morris Wasserman, a Jewish businessman who later opened the renowned Flame Show Bar. He was also the owner of a pawnshop, and some claim he had ties with the Pur-

30. Lightfoot also owned (with Isaac Petty) the short-lived Rose Palace Cabaret in 1927. It was located on the same block at 1708 St. Antoine. Advertisement, *Owl*, July 1, 1927.

31. *Detroit Times*, October 12, 1940.

32. Advertisement, *Michigan Chronicle*, January 31, 1942.

33. Adams, interview by Gallert.

34. Johnny Trafton, interview by Bjorn. Milt Buckner remembered Biddy's: "she started selling a bowl of beans for a nickel, and for a dime you could get a whole platter of beans, a pigfoot and a big piece of cornbread. Do you know, that woman got rich! . . . Paradise Valley was a jumpin' place." Vacher, "Milt Buckner Story."

35. Exactly when Faithful took over at this location is not clear. The 1930–31 *Detroit City Directory* lists the Musicians Club at 1701 St. Antoine. The following year the Musicians Booking and Service Bureau is found at this address, and the following year Jess Faithful is listed as part of this organization.

36. Green, interview by Bjorn.

37. Mann, interview by Gallert.

38. Anderson, interview by Bjorn.

ple Gang.[39] The Brown Bomber Chicken Shack was opened in 1937 by Leonard Reed, a black show producer, and later taken over by Sunnie Wilson. Wilson also had a show background but turned increasingly to business ventures. He became the first black owner of the Forest Club on Hastings in 1941 and was one of Paradise Valley's mayors. The mayors of Paradise Valley were not political officeholders but rather were symbolic leaders of the community.

Hastings Street had two major jazz spots in the 1930s. One, the Forest Club, was at the corner of Hastings and Forest and featured national bands since its opening around 1933. The other was the Cozy Corner, which was owned by Mack Ivey. Ivey was a Floridian who came to Detroit in 1916 and started out as a factory worker. In 1918 he opened up the Busy Bee Cafe and became one of the pioneering black businessmen on Hastings.[40] In the 1920s he ran two other businesses on the same block between Alfred and Brewster, one a barbershop and the other a poolroom.[41] This block also had the Dunbar Theatre, which was managed by E. B. Dudley. In 1935 Ivey opened the Cozy Corner further north on Hastings and Alexandrine. It was a popular black and tan, which lasted until 1950, but Ivey gave it up two years earlier. According to Sunnie Wilson, who managed the Cozy Corner, Ivey also ran a bar downstairs and a gambling joint upstairs.

> *Standing above six feet tall, Mac [sic] Ivey was a giant black man, with broad shoulders and massive forearms. He smoked El Producto cigars and carried a .44 revolver under his jacket. Always surrounded by his bouncers, Mac Ivey projected an imposing image. Everybody was afraid of Mac Ivey.*[42]

Not far from the Cozy Corner, on Livingstone and St. Antoine, the Chocolate Bar, another major black and tan, opened around 1935. It was in its four years of existence owned by (among others) Chester Rentie, another Paradise Valley mayor and booking agent. In 1938

Fig. 31. Advertisement for Cozy Corner.
(From *Detroit Free Press*, September 23, 1939.)

the Chocolate Bar was renamed the Cotton Club. Next to the Chocolate Bar was the Michigan Democratic League (MDL) Club, which opened after FDR's election in 1932. It was a black and tan as well as an after-hours spot. Slim Jones ran it before he started Club Congo in 1941.[43]

Other spots established on Hastings in the latter half of the 1930s were the Ace Bar, the Tuxedo, and the Rose Bud Inn.[44]

Warren Avenue—around 25 blocks north of Paradise Valley—was by the middle 1930s a new center for black business, as noted by a *Detroit Tribune* editorial on January 26, 1935.

> *There is a growing tendency of black business to leave "blighted areas" and locate in the new business center near E. Warren, Canfield, Hancock and other busy avenues between Beaubien and Russell.*

Among the new businesses established in this area were the Rhythm Club, managed by E. B. Dudley, the Palm Garden Café, and the

39. The Purple Gang was a Jewish criminal gang that got started in the illegal liquor trade in Detroit.

40. Larry Chism, "Legendary Nightspot Relinquished by Ivey," *Michigan Chronicle*, September 18, 1948. Also "Mack Ivey Dies at 71," *Michigan Chronicle*, August 19, 1950.

41. *Detroit City Directory*, 1923–24, 1924–25, 1928–29.

42. Wilson, *Toast of the Town*, 56.

43. MDL's first manager/owner was Frank Owens. The club relocated to Warren, between Hastings and St. Antoine, at some point. Warren, interview by Bjorn; and Ulysses Boykin, interview by Bjorn.

44. The Ace opened at 3678 Hastings in 1938; the Tuxedo Grill, later Club Tuxedo, at 4758 Hastings in 1937; and Rose Bud Inn at 2337 Hastings in 1935. Advertisements, *Detroit Times*, June 12, 1937; November 15, 1938.

Harlem Cave.[45] The Harlem Cave was opened in 1933 by "Little Sam" Brandt, a Jewish businessman, and Morris Wasserman, but soon they hired Sunnie Wilson as manager. By starting a small band booking business, Wilson got to know performers and businessmen in Paradise Valley, as he recalled in his memoirs.

> *Morris Wasserman and Sammy Brandt asked me to manage their club. The Harlem Cave got its name because it was downstairs. It had stucco walls, a good-sized stage, and a seating capacity of about two hundred people. . . . Working at the Harlem Cave, I met the boss of the Purple Gang and his lieutenant. Although the Purple Gang was a mean bunch, I got along fine with these two gentlemen. Since Sammy Brandt had married the lieutenant's sister, he often came to the Harlem Cave. One evening . . . the lieutenant got into an argument with Kate Francis, a black singer who was the featured act. . . . The lieutenant was a fist fighter. Angered, he turned and slapped Kate in the face. She let out a scream that drew the attention of the whole club. A black-and-tan, the Harlem Cave had a mixed crowd and the black fellas in the place looked as if they were going to tear him apart. Feeling the crowd grow uneasy, I called over the special police guard who worked for me and told him to hold the crowd while I ushered the lieutenant out into the lounge. . . . As the manager, it was my job to keep peace and I did it. . . . I'm sure that if I hadn't acted right away, several people would have lost their lives, including the lieutenant.*[46]

In 1936 Brandt opened Little Sam's on Hastings and in the 1940s moved it to Beaubien and East Warren.[47] The bar featured jazz and blues into the 1960s.

The very forefront of the expansion of the East Side black ghetto was the so-called North End, centered around Oakland Avenue. By 1937 two clubs opened there with frequent jazz shows: Heat Wave and Broad's Bar. Another black neighborhood was that on the West Side, around Tireman. Here we find the Blue Bird Inn and the Palm Garden Café by 1938. These areas will grow in importance as our story of Detroit jazz moves into the 1940s.

National Bands in Detroit

THE DEVELOPMENT of a band business pyramid was evident in Detroit, where we increasingly find national bands at local venues during the 1930s. Most of these venues were ballrooms. The Great Depression slowed down the entertainment industry, but its effects on ballroom dancing were not as severe as those on other types of musical entertainment. Most severely affected was vaudeville, which almost disappeared due to the economic downturn and the introduction of the talkies. The decline of the Koppin Theatre has already been chronicled in the first chapter.

Johnny Trafton played in a taxi-dance hall opposite the Graystone ballroom during the early years of the depression and saw the changes this way.

> *When the sound movies came . . . it was a turning point for the musical world, because any theater of note had live music. That's where a great many musicians worked. . . . The Depression was another problem. . . . During the whole of the Depression I worked as a musician; I was never out of work. But let me tell you what the salary was. The scale for taxi dance was $3 per night, per musician; that meant we worked seven nights for $21. In the heart of the Depression our money was half money and half scrip. Scrip was a promissory note with which you could buy groceries. The bank holiday happened at that time too. By the grace of God I was employed during that time. . . . Symphony musicians were out of work. . . . The Graystone suffered right along with other ballrooms. But I believe the theaters were hurt earlier and worse than the ballrooms, because people had gotten in the habit of dancing in the ballrooms. That was just one of the pleasures they did not give up so easily. The admission charge was very small. . . . They continued to*

45. The Rhythm Club opened in 1933 and was located at 301 East Warren. Its predecessor was the Garden Terrace, which in 1930 was the first black-owned nightery at this location. *Chicago Defender,* August 16, 1930. The Palm Garden Café opened in 1933 near Warren and Russell. *Detroit Times,* July 1, 1933. The Harlem Cave was on Brush and Canfield. Boykin and Boykin, interview by Bjorn.

46. Wilson, *Toast of the Town,* 50–51.

47. *Michigan Chronicle,* November 26, 1949.

patronize ballrooms. Although times were very hard, Stutz Anderson and Jap Sneed continued to bring in those name bands from New York. Although people did not have very much money, Duke Ellington and Cab Calloway would bring in a crowd. On that one night at the Graystone people would make that sacrifice to attend on Monday nights![48]

The Graystone was the main ballroom in Detroit for name black bands, and Monday nights black and white jazzmen came to listen amid black dancers.[49] Junior Warren, a young banjoist/guitarist, had just joined the Howard Bunts band when Bennie Moten's influential band came to town from Kansas City in the summer of 1932.

I learned a lot of guitar from Eddie Durham in the Bennie Moten band. They had played the Forest Club and Charlie Stanton [from the Goldkette office] heard them and got them a job at the Graystone for a week. . . . I had never heard anything like the Moten band in my life. Every chorus they set a different style of rhythm. You know, pushing rhythms where they pushed the soloists. They played riffs as background rhythm on every chorus. We didn't dance even though we had brought our girls to the Graystone; we forgot all about the girls! No band in Detroit played that well. The Moten band stayed at the Biltmore Hotel and we had jam sessions in the basement of the hotel on St. Antoine. I hung out every day with Eddie Durham, Ben Webster and Eddie Barefield and we became great friends. . . . every time Ben would come to Detroit with different bands my mom would always cook some greens for him.[50]

Drummer J. C. Heard got an early start in show business. At 10 he performed at the Koppin Theatre as the Child Wonder who tap danced, sang, and played the drums. He learned more about jazz drumming from live performances than from records when he entered his teens in the 1930s. Visits to the Graystone were central to his becoming one of the major jazz drummers in the country.

I used to hear every band that came to town.[51]

My mother used to take me to the Graystone Ballroom to see the bands. I listened to McKinney's Cotton Pickers when Don Redman led them, and Jimmie Lunceford too, when he had Jimmy Crawford on drums. It was a great show band, and a two-beat band, and although he wasn't a great soloist, Crawford just swung that band! Then Chick Webb came in 1937, and I had never heard anybody play drums like that in my life. In comparison, it seemed as though a lot of fellows had just been keeping time. . . . I'd sit up at the bandstand, right by Chick, listening to him on those accents all night long. . . . Basie came to Detroit with Jo Jones and his smooth four-four rhythm after I'd heard Chick. Jo was a master with the sock cymbal, but not so much with the ride cymbal, because they were not playing them so much in those days. . . . When Basie came to town again in 1938 . . . Jo came over to where I was playing [at the Cozy Corner] and said "You're going over and play with Basie tonight!" He could be very insistent, so I went, and Basie and all the boys liked me.[52]

The visits of name bands gave Detroit musicians a chance to keep up with the jazzmen of the Swing Era, almost all of whom worked in big bands. By also listening to records and radio broadcasts an aspiring young jazzman felt a part of a continually changing art form. In turn the visitors would listen to the local musicians and ferret out potential soloists or sidemen for their bands. For example, J. C. Heard was hired away by Teddy Wilson in 1939.

During the rest of the week the Graystone would feature local and national white bands of the sweet rather than hot variety. The major exceptions to this rule were McKinney's Cotton Pickers and the Howard Bunts band. McKinney's Cotton Pickers were in residence a few times at the Graystone up to early 1934 but spent most of their time touring the country. The Howard Bunts band from Detroit was in residence off and on for about two years.

48. Trafton, interview by Bjorn.

49. The Graystone's dominance can be seen from the visits to Detroit by the Fletcher Henderson band. According to Walter C. Allen's complete listing of Henderson engagements, the Graystone hosted the band 11 times during the 1930s. There were only two other known visits to Detroit: one at the Arcadia and the other at the Naval Armory. Walter C. Allen, *Hendersonia: The Music of Fletcher Henderson and His Musicians: A Biodiscography* (Highland Park, N.J., n.p., 1973), appendix.

50. Warren, interview by Bjorn.

51. Philip Hanson, "Catching up with J. C. Heard," *Jazz Monthly,* March 1968.

52. Stanley Dance, "J. C. Heard," *Jazz Journal International* 39 (November 1986). Heard was born in Dayton, Ohio, in 1917. He came to Detroit the following year and started out as a tap dancer at age 5. At 10 he performed at the Koppin Theatre as the Child Wonder with Butterbeans and Susie, and by 15 he toured on the TOBA circuit.

Fig. 32. McKinney's Cotton Pickers, Carlin's Park, Baltimore, Maryland, June 1934. *L to R: Prince Robinson, Roy Eldridge, Clyde Hart, Joe Eldridge, Ben Richardson, Bill McClure, Cuba Austin (kneeling), Eli Robinson, Billy Bowen, Andy Gibson, George "Buddy" Lee, Ed Cuffee.* (Courtesy Frank Driggs, Gallert Collection.)

It was more than two and a half years before the Benny Goodman band visited Detroit after its breakthrough in Los Angeles, and it was a long-awaited visit. The Fox Theater was packed for a week in February 1938. It is noteworthy that the band played a theater, rather than a ballroom like the Graystone. Due to its phenomenal popularity the band was simply too expensive for the Graystone, which was past its economic prime of the 1920s.

The popularity of the "King of Swing" can be seen by the attention his band received from the mainstream newspapers in Detroit. This was one of the very first times that a jazz concert got their undivided attention. The *Detroit Free Press* sent a general reporter, rather than an entertainment or music writer, to the event. He was none other than Edgar Guest, the paper's widely known columnist and poet. Guest focused on the youthful audience that came to see the band. He was particularly fascinated with the slang used by the young fans and adopted it in his article. He carefully defined each term, to the best of his abilities, in footnotes. Guest's disapproval of one of the first expressions of mass youth culture is also evident.

> *Although Benny and his boys didn't actually begin building a fire under the cats (people who are crazy about swing) until 12:45 P.M., the gates (same as cats) arrived at the scene of the festivities before dawn. At 10:15 Fox officials decided that the only way to save the front doors was to open them, and the cats pounded down the aisles to catch those front-row seats. As Benny and the band went through the first show, veteran stagehands looked on in amazement. Some of them had heard of jam sessions (concerts of swing music) but none had ever seen one. . . . "Take it right to town, Benny, and lay it down!" shouted a representative of the teen-aged group, a charming young miss who wouldn't have skipped school for anything less than a look and a listen of Benny Goodman. . . . The male swingeroos (same as cats and gates) took up the cheer at this point. "Send us-boys-send us!" ("to be sent": to be carried away from reality by the music) they exhorted. . . . What applause there was probably came from some citizens who had wandered in by mistake. Cats*

Fig. 33. McKinney's Cotton Pickers, Lowell Showboat, Lowell, Michigan, August 1935.
Jonah Jones, tp; Harold Wallace, ts/arr; Ted Buckner, as; Bill Canada, as; unidentified, gtr; Dorothy Derrick, vcl. A very rare photograph of one of McKinney's last working bands.
(Courtesy E. Azalia Hackley Collection, Detroit Public Library.)

don't applaud—they scream and cheer and shout and moan. They stamp their feet and waggle their fingers and punch the occupants of the adjoining seats. . . . Benny had to stay in his dressing room between shows; otherwise his admirers would mob him.[53]

Duke Ellington's band was one of the few black bands that could command salaries on the scale of the top white bands.[54] This put it out of reach of the Graystone after 1931, but it also played the Arcadia, Eastwood Park, and Detroit theaters, like the Michigan and the Fisher.[55] McKinney's Cotton Pickers was the only local band that toured much during the 1930s, even though at a lesser rate as the decade progressed.

Black Big Bands

McKinney's Cotton Pickers

A MAJOR CHANGE in the career of McKinney's Cotton Pickers was the nonrenewal of their recording contract with Victor in 1931. On the band's last recording session in September of 1931 Benny Carter had replaced Don Redman as musical director. Carter had, like Redman, been part of Fletcher Henderson's pioneering big band in the 1920s and was a noted altoist and arranger. In his year with the McKinney band Carter also developed as a trumpet player with the help of Doc Cheatham.[56] One of Carter's first engagements with the band was a battle of the bands against Duke Ellington at the Graystone. The *Chicago Defender* reported that a record breaking crowd of 7,000 fans forced a change from the Graystone Gardens to the main dance floor.[57]

Carter left the band because the management of the band was deteriorating. There were frequent conflicts between McKinney, Charlie Horvath, and Goldkette, adding to the already considerable strains of life on the road playing

53. Edgar Guest, "Alligators Line up at Dawn to Hear Benny Stretch Out," *Detroit Free Press,* February 19, 1938.

54. Hennessey, *From Jazz to Swing,* 132.

55. Ellington played the Arcadia in 1933 (*Detroit Tribune,* August 19, 1933), Eastwood Park in 1935 (*Detroit Tribune,* May 4, 1935) and 1936 (*Detroit Free Press,* June 4, 1936), the Fisher in 1931 (*Chicago Defender,* March 7, 1931), and the Michigan in 1931 (*Detroit Saturday Night,* March 21, 1931).

56. Morroe Berger, Edward Berger, and James Patrick, *Benny Carter: A Life in American Music,* vol. 1 (Metuchen, N.J.: Scarecrow Press and Institute of Jazz Studies, 1982), 107–8.

57. Fred Avendorph, "7,000 Present as Ellington Hits Detroit," *Chicago Defender,* September 12, 1931.

one-nighters. These management problems were one reason why the recording contract was not renewed. By 1931 the band no longer worked as a Goldkette unit, and in 1934 they stopped using the Graystone as their home base between tours.[58]

The Cotton Pickers had under the leadership of Redman and Carter attracted several top-notch players from the East Coast and the Midwest, but by 1933 the band was largely made up of locals.[59] In 1934 two original members from the 1920s left, pianist Todd Rhodes and altoist Jimmy Dudley, leaving Dave Wilborn as the sole survivor. Wilborn took part in sporadic re-creations of the band initiated by McKinney into the early 1940s.[60] He was also still around in 1972 when arranger David Hutson formed the New McKinney's Cotton Pickers.[61]

In spite of its checkered history in the 1930s, the Cotton Pickers band was an important training ground for a number of young Detroit musicians, who got a chance to go on the road and play next to more experienced jazzmen.[62] It is unfortunate that the band stopped recording so early in its career.

Howard Bunts

Howard Bunts led the only big band in Detroit that rivaled the Cotton Pickers in the 1930s. They were in residence at the Graystone off and on from about 1932 to 1934. Bunts had an academic background, with music studies at Atlanta University. He played seven instruments, even though in the big band he stuck to three: clarinet, alto saxophone, and soprano saxophone.[63] He also played clarinet in the pit band at the Koppin Theatre about the time he started his own band in 1926. His first bands went under various names: the Dixie Stompers, the Blue Blowers, the Dixie Ramblers, and simply the Howard Bunts Orchestra.[64] They increased gradually in size from 5 pieces to the big band size of 11.

In April 1928 Bunts reported in a letter to the *Chicago Defender* that "things are booming for Race musicians in the Motor City," an accurate depiction of conditions at the time. The letter probably also reflects Bunts's success in finding steady jobs for his band. Before they went into the Graystone they had a three-year stay at the Como Dancing Academy on Woodward Avenue. The Como was one of several taxi-dance ballrooms, where 10 cents was paid for each dance with a female teacher. These jobs were generally not as well paid as regular ballroom jobs, but Bunts had them during the worst years of the depression. The band was also able to broadcast nightly on WXYZ radio at another taxi-dance hall.[65]

By early 1933 the Howard Bunts Orchestra was at the Graystone for an indefinite engagement, which lasted into 1934. The band played four days a week, including a Sunday matinee. Twice a month they played Monday nights for black dancers, when a battle of the bands was organized. The battle was with out-of-town bands: Louis Armstrong, Duke Ellington, Fletcher Henderson, and Claude Hopkins.[66] Bunts's guitarist Junior Warren remembered that

> *During the Battle of the Bands we would trade sets of 45 minutes to an hour with the out-of-town band. On Monday nights we would play almost strictly jazz and blues, with only an occasional waltz. Other nights we would play everything including polkas. Polish people were crazy about Bunts; he got their names for future dance gigs. We started at $8 per night per man, but went down to $5 when times were bad. On Monday nights we would be paid from the door [receipts], and I could make $15 to $20. The Graystone was jammed on Monday nights. Jean Goldkette was the greatest man I ever worked for in my whole life. I am sorry he got broke. He always stood by us. He took us from nowhere and made us a great band, so we stuck with him even when he was late in paying us. . . . it was the Depression you know, he owed everybody and he could only give us so much.*[67]

58. Chilton, *McKinney's Music*, 49–52; *Chicago Defender*, April 18, 1931.

59. Some of the most prominent players with the band, not already mentioned, were trumpeters Roy Eldridge, Joe Smith, and Rex Stewart; trombonist Quentin Jackson; saxophonists Eddie Barefield and Hilton Jefferson; pianist Clyde Hart; bassist/tubaist Billy Taylor; and drummer Big Sid Catlett.

60. Chilton, *McKinney's Music*, 50–54.

61. Norman Gentieu, "McKinney's Cotton Pickers: Don Redman's Masterpiece," *IAJRC Journal* 14, no. 1 (January 1981): 15–16.

62. Some of these Detroiters were saxophonists Ted Buckner, Charles "Lanky" Bowman, Bill Canada, Wardell Gray, Cecil Lee, and Harold Wallace; trumpeters Frank Fryer, Karl George, Buddy Lee, and Charles V. Moore; trombonist Jake Wiley; pianist Milt Buckner; guitarist George Dawson; and drummer Kelly Martin.

63. Warren, interview by Bjorn. Notices in the *Chicago Defender* place the band at the Graystone in December 1932.

64. *Chicago Defender*, April 3, 1926; April 2, 1928; August 6, 1932.

65. This was the Woods Dancing Academy on Woodward. Ibid.

66. Warren, interview by Bjorn.

67. Warren was born in Atlanta in 1910 and came to Detroit in 1925. Before joining Bunts he toured with two territory big bands from Chicago and Cincinatti: J. Frank Terry and His Chicago Nightingales and Zack Whyte and His Chocolate Beau Brummels. Ibid.

One reason Goldkette was severely hit by the depression was a $400,000 renovation of the Graystone just before the 1929 crash.[68] A local black band like Bunts probably fit Goldkette's pocketbook well at the bottom of the depression.

Junior Warren remembered some of the major players in the Bunts band.

> *Clarence Ross, he was a great trumpet player, one of the best. . . . he would take that mute cup and swing that band; he would take a beat and just move. . . . that was a mainstay of Bunts' band. Clarence and I would do skits, like Cab Calloway. . . . Frank Fryer was also a star on trumpet. Harold Wallace was our arranger. . . . every Don Redman record Wallace'd sit down and put that record player on there man and in about 15 minutes he'd have that thing written almost note for note. . . . Once during intermission at the Graystone Don Redman told Harold "Jees, Crackers, do you know that you only left out about two notes on 'I Got Rhythm'!" He'd copy anybody's arrangement. He later went with Cootie Williams.*[69]

Howard Bunts continued to lead his big band until the mid-1940s, when he changed over to a smaller combo. The Graystone engagement was the most prominent ever held by the orchestra, and eventually his best players joined others. In the 1940s he opened a record shop on Hastings Street.

Stutz Anderson's Southbound Shufflers

Wilson "Stutz" Anderson played an important part in Detroit jazz as a promoter and bandleader. He was born in 1891 in Alabama and came to Detroit in 1920 on a Great Lake steamer, where he worked as a bellboy and waiter. As a child he had played French horn, and by the mid-1920s he was a dance promoter.

> *I started promoting dances at the Graystone ballroom with Fletcher Henderson and the Cotton Pickers, with Jean Goldkette. I had the Monday night lease; I leased it from him. I used to promote dances at the Pier and the Palais de Danse. I worked with [Professor J. F.] DeWitt and in the early 1930s Jap Sneed. . . . I started Monday night dances; it was my idea. . . . I was a theatrical booking agent . . . made connections with Louis Armstrong, Earl Hines, Chick Webb and Ella Fitzgerald, Cab Calloway. . . . My own band the Southbound Shufflers played school dances, the Urban League, Detroit Yacht Club, country clubs, Grosse Pointe . . . from the late twenties to the fifties. . . . I had about eleven pieces . . . Milt Buckner [piano and arranger] played with me when I first organized the Shufflers. Others I had over the years were Frank Fryer [trumpet], Alto Fryer [sax], Charlie Moore [trumpet].*[70]

Fig. 34. Stutz Anderson's Southbound Shufflers, Graystone Gardens, Detroit, ca. 1930.
Standing, L to R: "Duck" Collins, tb; Bill Canada, as; Joe Glover, dms; Charlie Carlyle, pno; Alfonso McKibbon, gtr; John Tobias, bs; Harvey Dial, tp; Lawrence Mann, ts; Charles V. Moore, tp; Jess Faithful, as/cl. Seated: John "Shady" Lain, vln/arr; Clarence Dorsey, tp; Anderson.
(Courtesy Dorothy E. Jackson, Gallert Collection.)

Milt Buckner remembered how the band was formed in 1930, when he was only 15.

> *I went with this young band called Stanley Miller's Harlem Syncopators. We were just a whole bunch of kids. . . . I was the youngest in the band but they were all young: sixteen or seventeen. . . . Stanley Miller left the band and Stutz Anderson took over and called it the Stutz Anderson Shufflers. We played Toledo, Ohio, and that's when I first met Art Tatum who was playing at a place of ill repute there. . . . In Toledo they had a big ballroom and Louis Armstrong and his band were there. . . . One time we*

68. Chilton, *McKinney's Music*, 50.

69. Warren, interview by Bjorn. Clarence Ross had earlier replaced the unreliable but brilliant trumpeter Joe Smith with the Cotton Pickers in 1930–31. Chilton, *McKinney's Music*, 33.

70. Anderson, interview by Bjorn. Anderson died in 1981. Professor J. F .DeWitt was not only an experienced dance promoter but also a proponent of "Preter-natural science" psychology. He ran an astrology/advice column in *Owl*. See *Owl*, April 15, 1927; May 4, 1928.

Fig. 35. Spirits of Swing, unidentified location, ca. 1939.
L to R: Priscilla Royster, vcl; brass: Leroy Willis, tb; Andrew Harkless, tp; Edgar Williams, tp; Mathew Rucker, tp/ldr; reeds: Bill Evans (Yusef Lateef), ts; Frank Porter, as; Johnnie Taylor, as; Alphonso Ford, ts; George Gleaton, gtr; Lawrence Hicks, dms; Willie Shorter, pno; Walter Bragg, bs.
(Courtesy Mathew Rucker, Gallert Collection.)

got through playing and looked over to the side and there's Pops listening. He liked it so well he invited us to his [30th] birthday party the next day at his apartment.

The band had two trumpets, trombone, four saxophones. Sonny Heard played trombone and I used to copy all the Lawrence Brown solos for him to play, like "The Sheik of Araby" and "Ducky-wucky." In fact, I used to play trombone myself. . . . In the saxophones . . . there was Tubby Bowen, great big fat cat, he played with Basie later on . . . but they [Basie] fired him because he couldn't read.[71]

Lawrence Mann, who played tenor saxophone and clarinet with the band, remembered that

We worked the Graystone one winter and Edgewater Park in the summer . . . Stutz's Southbound Shufflers. John Lain was the director and he rehearsed the band. We played a lot of arrangements by Will Hudson [who also arranged for Goldkette and the Cotton Pickers]. I don't recall Stutz playing anything; he was just a businessman. . . . While we were playing a formal affair in Grand Rapids John Lain got off the bandstand and Stutz got up on it and started directing. So the guys yelled: "Sit down Stutz!"[72]

The Shufflers was one of the Detroit bands that replaced the Cotton Pickers at the Graystone when they were on tour. Dave Wilborn remembered that the band borrowed some of the arrangements of the Cotton Pickers, which is analogous to the way the Chocolate Dandies were treated. In 1935 McKinney simply "borrowed" the Shufflers and changed their name to the Cotton Pickers.[73] At that point the band was also known as John Lain's Shufflers. Earlier Lain had been the musical director of the Billy Minor Melodians.

Joe Helm's Hot Dots/Earl Spencer's Rhythm Aces

Many big bands were started by high school students, and a few managed to survive beyond the school years. One of these was started by Joe Helm around 1930. Saxophonist Frank "Ditto" Perry remembered how it started.

Joe Helm started the band when everybody was still in school, 17 or 18 years of age. Five or six went to Cass, I was at Northeastern. Joe Helm left the band when the guys couldn't get along with him too well. We changed the name to Earl Spencer's Rhythm Aces. The band was a cooperative, there was no Earl Spencer. Ray Mimms [alto sax] and Neal "Ghandi" Robinson [piano] were the arrangers for the band. These

71. Vacher, "Milt Buckner Story."
72. Mann, interview by Gallert.
73. Chilton, *McKinney's Music*, 53.

boys took all the music off records with Don Redman, the Cotton Pickers, Ellington, and all them guys. Ernest Butler fronted the band and acted as road manager when we went on the road. We worked summertime, we went off on the lakes, and we worked a few jobs with Stutz Anderson who fronted the band for a while and Lanky Bowman fronted the band for a while as the Chocolate Dandies. . . . What happened to the band? When liquor came in every club would have five or six pieces in the band. And this band—all the guys could play so they got different jobs, working six or seven nights a week you could work anywhere.[74]

Fig. 36. Spirits of Swing reed section, Mirror Ballroom, ca. 1939–40.
L to R: Bill Evans (Yusef Lateef), Frank Porter, Johnnie Taylor, Alphonso Ford.
(Courtesy Mathew Rucker, Gallert Collection.)

Thus the Rhythm Aces dissolved when the economics of the entertainment industry changed. Other local bands, like Stutz Anderson's Shufflers, survived these conditions but at the cost of irregular employment. This was made possible by frequently changing personnel and members playing in several bands or having day jobs.

Mathew Rucker's Spirits of Swing

Another big band was started at Miller High School by trumpeter Mathew Rucker in 1938. Miller was in Black Bottom, and many of Detroit's most renowned jazzmen attended it. Tenorist Bill Evans, later Yusef Lateef, was one of them and he recalled that

> *The Spirits of Swing was Mathew Rucker's band. It was the first big band I played with while we're in high school [in 1938]. We left in 1939 and the band was fronted by Hartley Toots. And we toured all through the south, you know, to Florida. We played the Rockland Palace in Florida.*[75]
>
> *The band played mostly for dances in and around Detroit. Milt Buckner did most of the arranging for us, and, as a result, we had a lot of special arrangements. It was built around his compositional technique, and that's what put the band out in front at the time. Our music was unique, and we had this personal sound besides the stocks we played, like "Jumpin' at the Woodside." What got me into the 13 Spirits was that I could read music. I later found out that they were thinking of getting rid of me because I couldn't play a good solo, but fortunately they kept me. I learned to improvise as time went on.*[76]

Lateef left Detroit for New York in 1946. Like Lateef, Rucker remembered the contributions of Milt Buckner.

> *At first we used stock arrangements from Grinnell's [a local music store]. . . . Then Milt Buckner became interested in us. . . . It was incredible how he'd do it. He stood up and would write arrangements like he was writing a letter. He would write for every piece in the band. He only charged us $4 for those arrangements for a 12- or 14-piece band. He was working at a taxi-dance hall at the time. His arrangements for our band are partially responsible for him*

74. Frank "Ditto" Perry, interview by Lars Bjorn and Jim Gallert, Detroit, Michigan, September 2, 1992. Perry was born in Oklahoma in 1913 and came to Detroit in 1926 or 1927. He later toured with the big bands of Snookum Russell, Lloyd Hunter, and Ernie Fields. In 1948 he returned to Detroit and opened a music repair business in 1967.

75. Bob Rusch, "Interview with Yusef Lateef," *Cadence,* January 1989, 10.

76. Pete Welding, "Music as Color: Yusef Lateef," *Down Beat,* May 20, 1965.

joining Lionel Hampton. We played a Battle of Music against Hampton at the State Fairgrounds and we played just about all of Milt's arrangements. Lionel came up to me and said: "Who wrote all of those arrangements?" Two or three weeks later Milton was playing with Lionel.[77]

Buckner joined Hampton in 1941 and became a key arranger and pianist in the band for the next nine years. Rucker left his big band in the hands of trombonist Clarence "Pete" Peterson when he joined Fletcher Henderson's band in 1945. He returned to Detroit two years later and in the 1950s led a small band that included Lateef.[78]

Other Black Big Bands

Monk Culp, Billy Richardson, and Van Mosley were other bandleaders in the 1930s. These bands seem to have had relatively irregular employment as dance bands and used many musicians who played part-time. The Van Mosley band was known as the Chevrolet Syncopators, and all members, except the leader, worked at Chevrolet. Mosley was also a member of the Chocolate Fiends, a big band organized by very young players in Black Bottom in the early 1930s.[79]

White Bands

With the dissolution of the Goldkette band and the departure of the Orange Blossoms/Casa Loma band, there was a dearth of white jazz-oriented big bands in Detroit by the early 1930s. The remaining white big bands played "sweet" rather than "hot" dance music in the city's ballrooms and over the airwaves.[80]

One white big band leader who eventually led a national band in this period was Bob Chester. He started a band in Detroit in the mid-1930s, but it disbanded after an unsuccessful engagement at the Detroit Athletic Club. He moved to New York and with help from Tommy Dorsey started a more successful band with New York musicians. His band was at first closer to the "sweet" style of Glenn Miller than the "swing" style developed by Goodman.[81] Dance band historian Leo Walker gives us an idea of Chester's style with the following anecdote.

The band which Chester fronted in the late 1930s and early 1940s was so much like that of Glenn Miller's that on one of Miller's tours, in an area which he had not yet explored but in which Chester was already popular, Miller was asked why he copied the Chester sound.[82]

By 1941 Chester gave up the Miller sound and turned his band into a very professional all-round dance band that played both swing and sweet.[83]

Detroit's sweet dance bands did serve as an important training ground for aspiring young white jazzmen in the 1930s. The most unique soloist among them was no doubt pianist Bob Zurke. He seems to have played with most of the major Detroit dance bands of the day—those led by singer Seymour Simons, pianist Fred Bergin, and Hank Biagini of Casa Loma fame. Zurke was born in Detroit in 1912 and got his big break in January 1937 when he joined Bob Crosby. The Crosby band became known for its combination of swing and traditional (dixieland) jazz. By 1939 Zurke was voted "best pianist" by *Down Beat* magazine after making a mark with his boogie-woogie piano style. Gunther Schuller has this to say about Zurke's recordings with Crosby.

Zurke was Crosby's most interesting and original pianist. His sometimes wild, almost undisciplined playing lent the Crosby groups a dynamic hurricane-like force, that was light-years removed from the polite bubbling of most 1930s band pianists.[84]

Two other important soloists from Detroit who also tried their hand at leading bands should be mentioned: tenorist Sam Donahue and trombonist Bobby Byrne.[85] Donahue joined the Gene Krupa orchestra in 1938 and two years later played with Harry James and Benny

77. Mathew Rucker, interview by Lars Bjorn and Jim Gallert, Detroit, Michigan, July 7, 1991. Buckner's version is different—he first met Hampton at the Graystone around 1940. It was during a subsequent visit by Hampton that he joined the band. Buckner was working with Don Cox at Broad's Club Zombie. Vacher, "Milt Buckner's Story."

78. Ibid. Rucker left music in 1957 and bought a taxicab in Ecorse, Michigan. He later owned a cab company in Detroit.

79. Boykin and Boykin, interview by Bjorn.

80. Sweet vs. hot was not, however, an either-or choice, but rather it was a matter of degree. For example, white bands played mainly sweet music but also included some hot tunes and/or hot solos on a sweet tune. The reverse was true for black bands.

There are many factors that explain this state of affairs, but one of them is the greater opportunities afforded white musicians in theater and radio jobs. These jobs were relatively secure and high paying and therefore siphoned off some of the talent that otherwise would have been found in dance bands. As mentioned earlier, the center of the development of big band jazz was in the ballrooms of the United States.

The major white dance bands in Detroit in the 1930s were those led by Fred Bergin, Hank Biagini, Lowry Clark, Sammy Dibert, Tommy Marvin, and Seymour Simons.

81. Simon, *Big Bands*, 124–26.

82. Chester was related to the Fisher Body fortune on his mother's side, and this might have helped ensure the success of his big band venture, when coupled with help from Goldkette alumnus Tommy Dorsey (Walker, *Big Band Almanac*, 78; Simon, *Big Bands*, 124). Chester seems to have led a big band in Detroit at least as early as 1930, since his first recordings date from that year.

83. Schuller, *Swing Era*, 754. Schuller thinks the Chester band underrated in most histories of jazz.

84. Ibid., 656.

85. Another Detroiter who joined national big bands was trumpeter Charles "Chuck" Peterson (born 1915). After playing in Detroit with Henry Biagini's band he left Detroit in 1937 to join Artie Shaw's big band and in the 1940s played with Woody Herman. "Charles Peterson," *New Grove Dictionary of Jazz*.

Fig. 37. Bob Chester Orchestra, Detroit Athletic Club, 1936.
Chester is seated in right foreground lighting pipe.
(Courtesy Frank Driggs, Gallert Collection.)

Goodman. He was also a bandleader in Detroit (1933–38) and New York (1940–42).[86]

Bobby Byrne's father was part of the music department at Cass Technical High School, the most important training ground for Detroit musicians. This might explain why his son turned out to be a child prodigy. In 1935, at the ripe age of 16, Byrne joined the Jimmy Dorsey band to replace Tommy Dorsey. Tommy had left after an infamous fight that split the Dorsey brothers' band. According to many critics Byrne equaled Tommy Dorsey's playing in the sweet trombone style, and his jazz playing was even better.[87] Schuller goes as far as to say that

> *Byrne's jazz solos, cool, free flowing, structurally well-conceived, were in many ways well ahead of their time. He was in this sense—along with Jack Jenney—a transitional figure, looking ahead to the great white trombone virtuosos of a later day.*[88]

Byrne led his own big band in the early 1940s when he temporarily returned to Detroit. It seems a perfectionist bent prevented him from being a very successful bandleader.[89]

Radio became an important medium for popular music in the 1930s, and we have already mentioned black bands and their live broadcasts from dance halls. White bands were

86. Donahue was born in Detroit in 1918. "Sam Donahue," *New Grove Dictionary of Jazz.*

87. Schuller, *Swing Era,* 650–51; Simon, *Big Bands,* 148–49.

88. Schuller, *Swing Era,* 650–51.

89. Simon, *Big Bands,* 107–9.

Fig. 38. Sophistocats, unidentified setting, Detroit.
Paul Leash, cl/ldr; Clem Johnson, tp; Earl Striewski, ts; Roger Spiker, pno; Tappy Palmer, bs; Tom Cornell, dms.
(Courtesy Gallert Collection.)

even more likely to have opportunities for such broadcasts. When it came to radio studio work the picture was different: there were fewer jazz-oriented bands, and they were all white. One of the studio bands, the Sophistocats, played a fair amount of jazz. This sextet was featured on radio station WWJ in the late 1930s and 1940s and was led by clarinetist Paul Leash. It included several top-notch musicians, like tenorist Earl Striewski, but most prominent was Bill Stegmeyer, who worked as their arranger and saxophonist. Stegmeyer's remarkable talents as an arranger were obvious to Marvin Kahn, who under the name Tommy Marvin led a popular band in the late 1930s.

> *At a spot in Highland Park after work, Bill Stegmeyer was there and I said: I need an arrangement on "Running Wild" and I be damned; we sat there at the table, everybody talking, and Bill wrote the arrangement as we were all having coffee. That was the only arrangement he wrote for us. He was a marvel, music just poured out of him.*[90]

Stegmeyer left for New York in 1938 to work with Glenn Miller, Bob Crosby, and others. He returned to Detroit in the late 1940s for more radio work (for WXYZ).

Bands in Paradise Valley

The black and tan nightclubs in Paradise Valley increasingly provided jobs for Detroit jazzmen during the 1930s. Working in a black and tan was like working in a ballroom and a vaudeville theater all at once. The top black and tan, Club Plantation, is an illustration of what the job entailed, from the testimony of Russell Green.

> *I joined Earl Walton at Club Plantation in 1935. He had ten pieces and backed the show from the pit and played for dancing afterwards. You needed musicians who could read good because they changed shows every two to three weeks, and each with a new producer like Ted Blackman, Joe Johnson and Leonard Reed. The show had ten chorus girls and lasted an hour and fifteen minutes. The music was written down and we rehearsed a lot.*[91]

The Plantation had three shows every night,

90. Marvin Kahn, interview by Lars Bjorn, Southfield, Michigan, October 31, 1996.

91. Green, interview by Bjorn.

Fig. 39. Earl Walton Orchestra, Club Plantation, 1935.
Rear, L to R: Nub Brown, tp; Bill Canada, as; unidentified, bs; George Lightfoot, cl; Milton McNeil, ts. Front, L to R: Anthony Bush, pno; Walton, vln/ldr; George Robinson, dms.
(Courtesy Mrs. Russell Green, Gallert Collection.)

but most clubs had two floor shows, which usually featured a few singers, a comedian, and dancers. A former top-notch ballroom band like Earl Walton's was a logical choice for the job at the Plantation.

Earl Walton

The Walton band at the Plantation included several veterans from his days at the Palais de Danse, like drummer George Robinson and trumpeter Thornton "Nub" Brown. Some, like saxophonist Bill Canada, had other substantial big band experience. Russell Green was relatively inexperienced in this band and felt "it was my peak in Detroit." He remembered that other musicians in town would often be listeners. Sometimes out-of-town musicians like Fats Waller would sit in with the band.[92] The band also did radio broadcasts over WMBC each evening at 11 p.m.[93] By 1937 Walton decided to call it quits and turned his attention to his Studio Club a block away. His band was replaced by Cecil Lee's.

Cecil Lee Orchestra

One of the best Detroit bands of the 1930s was led by reedman Cecil Lee, a native Detroiter and a veteran of Billy Minor's Melodians and Lanky Bowman's orchestra. Cecil Lee worked with the Cotton Pickers in 1934 and with vocalist Clarence "Chic" Carter's Harlem Aces, a McKinney offshoot, in 1935. Lee organized his first band in 1936 for an engagement at the Chocolate Bar.[94] Harold Wallace played reeds and arranged for the band, no doubt building on what he learned with Howard Bunts in the early 1930s. Cecil Lee's bands were held in high regard. Dave Wilborn claimed that "if they had left the city, they could've become famous."[95]

Cecil Lee attracted good musicians because he worked for the best clubs, played high quality music, and paid regularly. He was regarded as a fine musician and a good organizer. Lee was a good soloist on both alto saxophone and clarinet when he applied himself, but he had a tendency to fall asleep on the bandstand—dur-

92. Ibid.

93. *Tribune Independent*, April 27, 1935. See also radio listings in the *Detroit Free Press*, October 5, 1935; September 3, 1937; September 10, 1937.

94. Jim Gallert, "Blue Sensation: The Todd Rhodes Story," *City Arts Quarterly* 4 (fall/winter 1989–90).

95. Wilborn, interview by Bjorn.

Fig. 40. Chic Carter's Harlem Aces, Graystone Ballroom, ca. 1935. *L to R: Clarence "Chic" Carter, ldr/vcl; Leonard Morrison, bs; Todd Rhodes, pno; Sam Simpson, dms; Jacob Wiley, tb; Joe Moxley, as/music director; unidentified; James "Buster" Baker, tp; Jimmy Strong, ts; Cecil Lee, as.* (Courtesy Mrs. Annie Mae Rhodes, Gallert Collection.)

ing sets! When Lee got too relaxed pianist Todd Rhodes, one of the original Cotton Pickers, would take over as musical leader of the band.[96]

In 1937 Lee took over the house band job at Club Plantation after Earl Walton disbanded, and the following year the band started an engagement at the Villa D Club. That the band was filled with talent became obvious in February 1939 when the *Detroit Tribune* reported, "Teddy Wilson Picks Three Detroiters for Band." One of the three was J. C. Heard, who was hired away from Bill Johnson's group at the Cozy Corner, and

> *a visit to the Villa D by Teddy Wilson listening to Cecil Lee's Cats brought contracts from: Karl George and Jake Wiley. Karl came to Detroit in 1933 with Monk Culp to open the defunct Club Harlem. He has been with Cecil Lee's orchestra for two years. Jake Wiley is a graduate of Cass Tech and was earlier with McKinney's Cotton Pickers.*[97]

George Dawson's Chocolateers

George Dawson was one of Detroit's top swing guitarists, who came to the city in the late 1920s with a vaudeville show at the Koppin. He was one of the first in the city to electrify his guitar.[98] In 1935 he formed his Chocolateers as the house band at the Chocolate Bar, where Dave Wilborn welcomed "Mr. and Mrs. Sepia Detroit" through an ad in the *Detroit Tribune*.[99] Wilborn served as a host and a singer at the club and "had a large white following" according to Russell Green. Wilborn later led his own band at the Melody Club. Green was one of the members of the eight-piece orchestra, which featured several veterans of the Cotton Pickers. The most prominent one was probably trumpeter George "Buddy" Lee. Russell Green might very well have been right in his judgment that "there wasn't a band in town that could touch us."[100]

Bill Johnson

Trumpeter Bill Johnson led a six-piece band at the Harlem Cave and the Tuxedo Grill before the group became the house band at the Cozy Corner from 1937 to 1940. Wade Boykin replaced Sam Price as pianist and remembered how he got hired.

> *Bill came to me at the Silver Lion. . . . Sam Price was his piano player then, but he went to New York. Sam was a good piano player, but he couldn't read and you had to do it in order to cut the shows. When those guys bring those reams in you better play what's on that paper! So, I was hired. We went on tour to Kentucky*

96. Gallert, "Blue Sensation."

97. "Teddy Wilson Picks Three Detroiters for Band," *Detroit Tribune*, February 11, 1939.

98. Warren, interview by Bjorn.

99. *Detroit Tribune*, September 7, 1935.

100. Green, interview by Bjorn. Dawson recorded five titles in 1948 for Paradise, a short-lived Detroit label owned by Mrs. Delmar Ray. The pickup session featured tenorist Joe Norris, who contributed charts and two originals, and altoist Joe Moxley. Paradise had only local distribution of its records. The label moved to Bakersfield, California, in early 1949.

Fig. 41. Cecil Lee orchestra, unidentified setting, Detroit, 1939.
L to R: Harold Wallace, ts/arr; Leonard Morrison, bs; Kelly Martin, dms; Jake Wiley, tb; Cecil Lee, as/ldr; Gerald Wilson, tp; Todd Rhodes, pno. (Howard Thompson, tp, and Karl George, tp, absent from photo.)
(Courtesy Mrs. C. Morrison, Gallert Collection.)

for a year [in 1938] and to Nashville as well. Then came word that Mack Ivey wanted us at the Cozy Corner in Detroit. We packed up and left Nashville.

Bill was very flashy, he was a showman but his reading was slow. We had to rehearse him like crazy! He was a handsome guy. Tubby Bowen [tenor sax] and J. C. Heard were the best. Tubby influenced Sammy Donahue. Donahue and the white cats would come down to the Cozy and dig the band. And we retaliated and went out to their place, somewhere out in Waterford. Sam Donahue went on to become a big thing, you know. . . . I also remember Gene Krupa, Roy Eldridge, and Benny Goodman jamming with us at the Cozy Corner. It was the place to go!

Teddy Wilson took J. C. Heard from our band. After he left Freddy Radcliffe joined. He went with Lionel Hampton, you know. He had to be great to play with Hampton. Hamp was a drummer extraordinaire himself.

We worked the Cozy Corner for three years. Bill couldn't get along with Charlie Nay, the doorman. He got in a fight with Charlie, knocked him down outside the door there. So Mack Ivey said "the hell with it!"[101]

Tubby Bowen led the remnants of the Bill Johnson band in 1941 under the name Tubby Bowen and His Tubs.

Black Bands on Woodward Avenue

During the 1930s black bands made further inroads in entertainment spots catering to whites. Many of these were found along Woodward Avenue, Detroit's main drag. Some of the major ballrooms already featured black bands in the 1920s, as we have seen, but lesser ballrooms (taxi-dance halls) and nightclubs did not follow until the 1930s.

Don Cox

Cassell "Don" Cox was a drummer and crooner with Howard Bunts and around 1932 formed a band to play the Woods Dancing Academy on Woodward Avenue. He kept his band there for almost 10 years until the dancing school closed in 1942.[102] Milt Buckner was the

101. Ibid. See also *Detroit Tribune* columns, February 12, 1938; November 15, 1938. Sam Price was a Texas pianist and singer who recorded with many jazz greats in New York. Freddy Radcliffe was a native Detroiter who played with Lionel Hampton, 1943–47. "Freddy Radcliffe," *Down Beat*, April 10, 1962.

102. "Union Plans Benefit for Cassell W. Cox," *Michigan Chronicle*, April 7, 1956.

Fig. 42. Nub Brown's Fingers, Cozy Corner Grill, Detroit, ca. 1940. *Unidentified, saxes; George Robinson, dms; Herb Thompson, bs; Brown, cnt/tp/ldr; Milton Buckner, tb/vbs/arr.* (Courtesy Gallert Collection.)

pianist with the band for about half that time, interrupted by his stints with Jimmy Raschel's territory band.[103] Buckner remembered how he developed his signature "locked hands style" on the piano when he played with Cox.

> *It was a long time before I could take a solo but I would copy after Earl Hines. Then in 1932 I heard Art Tatum. I said that's the style I want to play but I couldn't play it. I was playing with Don Cox's band in the dancing school. . . . We had five pieces and we were using stock music and I would take the little notes on top with the chords in the bass and I combined the whole bunch together to make it sound like a big band. It just came easy because my hands are small and that's how I started the locked hands style to give greater fullness to the orchestra. Whenever Art heard me he said "You keep on doing that." I said "I might as well, I can't play like you." Every time Art would come to Detroit, he would look up three piano players, an old*

103. *Down Beat*, June 15, 1955. The Raschel band was based in Danville, Illinois.

timer named "Buckles," Lannie Scott and myself.[104]

Another member of the five-piece band was trumpeter Clarence Ross. The Cox band was featured in a half-hour broadcast over WJLB. The band also played at the Melody Club in 1937–38 as the Creole Rhythm Boys.[105] When the dancing academy closed Cox took a day job as a streetcar driver.

Eric Bolen/Johnny Trafton

ERIC "NEMO" BOLEN led a six-piece band at the Tree Dance Studio, opposite the Graystone, around 1930. This band included one of Detroit's few New Orleans jazzmen, trumpeter Louis Prevost. He had earlier been a member of Billy Minor's Melodians. The band was Johnny Trafton's first regular job while he was still in high school, and the band moved into the Eldorado nightclub under his leadership. The Eldorado was also on Woodward and had a floor show and daily broadcasts over WJBK.

Johnny Trafton remembered feeling on the spot at the Eldorado and how he dealt with it.

> *Eric Bolen taught me a lot about musicianship and professionalism. You see, we were blacks in a white world. We played for whites and all the other acts at the Eldorado were white. If we were capable of cutting the mustard we kept employed. I kept up that same level of musicianship and the management at the Eldorado made me musical director of the nightclub. That meant that I was in charge of all the acts. We were always on the spot with people who were bigots. All the acts were white and some would patronize us. I realized that but I knew that we could cut the mustard if the music was right.*
>
> *I never did much arranging. Milt Buckner, Arnold Hooper, and Gloster Current wrote most of the arrangements. Milt Buckner was attending the Institute of Musical Arts at the time. He was studying counterpoint and arranging. Milt was unique in this way. Most arrangers have to write a score and then they copy the different instruments from this master score. Milt just wrote for instruments: alto sax, b-flat trumpet, whatever (laughs) . . . at a very young age. No score. That's the kind of mind he had. My arrangers were black musicians and their style was original. Those fellows made my band so much better and so much different. They were doing what black musicians always had done. They were writing what they heard in their mind. It had the rhythm, the beat and the sound of black music, which was entirely different from what the publishers were issuing in Tin Pan Alley. This made me sound different from the [white] bands that were playing at the Graystone.*[106]

Trafton's perception of being a black musician in a white world was shared by many Detroit musicians. The same sense of racial identity combined with a pride in craftsmanship was found among many who played in the big bands of the 1920s.[107]

The coming of World War II would bring changes in race relations in the United States and with it bebop, a new form of jazz where the sense of craftsmanship held by black musicians was modified by the rise of a more clearly articulated artistic consciousness.

104. Vacher, "Milt Buckner Story." Art Tatum was born in Toledo and lived there until 1932. He played after-hours joints in Detroit before that time and visited the city many times since. James Lester, *Too Marvelous for Words: The Life and Genius of Art Tatum* (New York: Oxford University Press, 1994), 59.

105. Advertisement, *Detroit Tribune*, August 14, 1937.

106. Trafton, interview by Bjorn.

107. Lars Bjorn, "The Mass Society and Group Action Theories," 377–94.

Detroit and the Birth of Bop

Phil Hill, Art Mardigan, and Eddie Jamison at the Blue Bird Inn, 1948.

Detroit played an important role in the birth of bop, a new form of jazz that emerged during World War II. Milt Jackson and Lucky Thompson grew up on the East Side of Detroit, where they played together as teenagers in the King's Aces big band. By 1945 they were back together again playing with the two major innovators of bop: Charlie Parker and Dizzy Gillespie. In later years Jackson explained his rapid immersion in bop as the result of the vitality of Detroit's jazz scene, which he likened to New York's Fifty-second Street.

What made the Detroit jazz scene so vital in the 1940s? Simply put, it was the combination of talent and opportunity. On the one hand, there were a number of well-trained musicians from the swing generation and a new crop of talent interested in the new sounds of bop. On the other hand, there was a thriving nightlife scene, which provided plenty of work at decent wages. Detroit's booming economy during and after the war was the source of the increased demand for entertainment.

Most bop pioneers were African American, which signaled a significant shift in the cultural identity of musicians who wanted to be taken seriously as artists. Bop was more complex than big band swing in melody, rhythm, and harmony. It celebrated the freedom of the improviser rather than the arrangements of the bandleader. In contrast to swing, which was easy to dance to, this music was more intellectual and more appealing to listeners. In the second half of the 1940s a modernist circle of musicians developed in Detroit as the bop revolution took a firm hold among the city's young jazzmen.

World War II, the Postwar Boom, and Race Relations

With the coming of World War II Detroit was transformed into "the Arsenal of Democracy."[1] The city that a decade earlier had been one of the most economically depressed in the country was now a boomtown. After the war fears of another depression proved unfounded, and economic expansion continued into the 1950s. This economic boom

1. Detroit's economy was improving before the bombing of Pearl Harbor in December 1941. President Roosevelt declared the United States the Arsenal of Democracy in January 1941, and the term was soon applied to Detroit. By the middle of 1941 several automakers had signed large defense contracts, and Ford had started construction of its Willow Run bomber plant. V. Dennis Wrynn, *Detroit Goes to War: The American Auto Industry in World War II* (Osceola, Wis.: Motorbooks International, 1993), 23.

presented Detroiters with new opportunities as well as new problems.

As the draft took more men into the service and manufacturing plants went into high gear producing war material, labor shortages developed. Employers responded with labor recruitment campaigns, and migrants from the South once again streamed into the city. About a half a million migrants came to Detroit in the first three years of the decade.[2] Over the decade the city added 225,000 inhabitants, 150,000 of whom were African Americans. While the overall city population grew by 14 percent during the 1940s the African-American population doubled.

The tight labor market in Detroit meant steady work and good wages, particularly in the eyes of southern migrants. On the other hand, there was a lack of leisure time, and consumption was limited by rationing and supply problems. Housing was in very short supply, even after government public housing programs began. For the African-American population housing was even harder to come by given patterns of racial discrimination in public and private housing. One of the major instances of racial conflict in 1942 was over the Sojourner Truth public housing project. A riot by whites in effect evicted black renters and kept public housing in Detroit racially segregated, at least temporarily. In the private market a prospective black home buyer faced the discriminatory practices of sellers, real-estate agents, and banks, which until 1948 were supported by law. Until 1948, it was legally permissible for a seller to include a "restricted covenant" that barred the selling of a house to a member of a minority group.[3]

In the workplace racial conflict also became more open during the war years. White workers in several plants started "hate strikes" to protest racial integration when black workers moved into new job classifications.[4] These strikes were not sanctioned by the UAW, which was part of the emerging liberal-labor coalition in the city.

Community racial conflict reached the boiling point in the Detroit riot in June 1943. It had its start on Belle Isle as 100,000 Detroiters were escaping the summer heat with a Sunday in the park. Sporadic fighting took place all day between blacks and whites, and by nighttime 5,000 people were participating. The fighting spread to Woodward Avenue and Hastings Street through the dissemination of false rumors. One of the rumors got started on the stage of the Forest Club at Hastings and Forest. By Monday fighting had spread to much of the city, and the turmoil did not stop until federal troops intervened. The riot left 25 blacks and 9 whites dead. The disparate death toll was largely due to the indiscriminate violence of the Detroit police against black citizens on Hastings Street. Most contemporary accounts of the riots blamed the rioting on young black "hoodlums" and white "hillbillies." A recent analysis by Capeci and Wilkerson shows that the rioters were from a broad spectrum of both communities. While white rioters often were motivated by "keeping blacks in their place," many black rioters had a new racial awareness that presaged the rioters of the 1960s. Capeci and Wilkerson argue that each generation of ghetto dwellers becomes "more physically segregated, racially aware, economically aggressive, politically mobilized, and—in lacking redress—collectively violent."[5]

One new element to race relations during the war was the increased political awareness of black Americans. In Detroit as in other cities, there were calls for Double Victory (Double V for short): against the fascists abroad and against racism at home. There were limits to how far the second victory could be pushed, as the demands for national unity were sometimes overpowering. Nevertheless, the NAACP organized a rally in Detroit in 1943 (only a few weeks before the riot) that stated the Double V message to an audience of 25,000 blacks and whites at Olympia Stadium.[6] Civil rights action

2. Walter White, "What Caused the Detroit Riot of 1943?" in *Detroit,* ed. Melvin Holli (New York: New Viewpoints, 1976), 187.

3. Thomas Sugrue, *The Origins of the Urban Crisis: Race and Inequality in Postwar Detroit* (Princeton: Princeton University Press, 1996), 44–47.

4. Steve Babson, *Working Detroit: The Making of a Union Town* (Detroit: Wayne State University Press, 1986), 117–18.

5. Dominic J. Capeci Jr. and Martha Wilkerson, *Layered Violence: The Detroit Rioters of 1943* (Jackson, Miss.: University of Mississippi Press, 1991), xiii.

6. Ibid., 190–91. Detroit even had a bar called the Double V bar that opened in late 1942 in Conant Gardens. It was black owned and featured jazz at times. Advertisements, *Michigan Chronicle,* December 12, 1942; November 15, 1947.

Fig. 43. Black neighborhoods in Detroit, 1940. One dot = 200 people. (Adapted from Sugrue, Map. 2.1.)

in the early war years had brought about a presidential executive order about nondiscrimination in war industries and the creation of the Fair Employment Practices Commission, and these in turn encouraged further civil rights action. In Detroit the local NAACP chapter became the largest in the nation, and after the riot the Mayor's Interracial Committee was created.[7]

One of the tasks of the Interracial Committee was to improve relations between the police and the African-American community. Complaints about police harassment of blacks were frequent, and the police, like the white rioters, also saw it as their task to draw the line on what were acceptable interactions between blacks and whites.[8] An illustration of how the police could draw the color line is provided by (white) singer Sheila Jordan, who started socializing with black musicians in her late teens. She had frequent run-ins with the police. She remembered that, around 1950,

> *I was constantly being harassed by the police . . . stopped in cars or walking down the street, it was horrendous, the treatment was not to be believed. . . . We were on our way to Belle Isle . . . I was going with Frank Foster who was my first boyfriend. We were in a car with Jenny King [also white] and the guy she was going with and the cops came and stopped us. I was smoking at the time and threw my cigarette out the window and the cop jumped under the car, picked up the cigarette and smelled it. Took us all down to the police station and gave us the third degree; it was heavy. He said: "I have a nine year old daughter at home and if I found her the way I found you tonight I would take this gun that I have and I would go home and I would blow her brains out!"*[9]

In spite of these problems the mood among Detroiters of all races was generally upbeat during the 1940s.[10] There was a sense that conditions were improving and that problems could be dealt with. During the war black workers got access to well-paid industrial jobs in auto

7. Sugrue, *Origins of the Urban Crisis*, 26–31.

8. On continued conflict with police 10 years after the riot, see "Police Relationship with Negroes Still Detroit's Sore Spot," *Michigan Chronicle*, March 21, 1953.

9. Sheila Jordan, interview by Lars Bjorn, Ann Arbor, Michigan, November 11, 1994.

10. Sugrue, *Origins of the Urban Crisis*, 30.

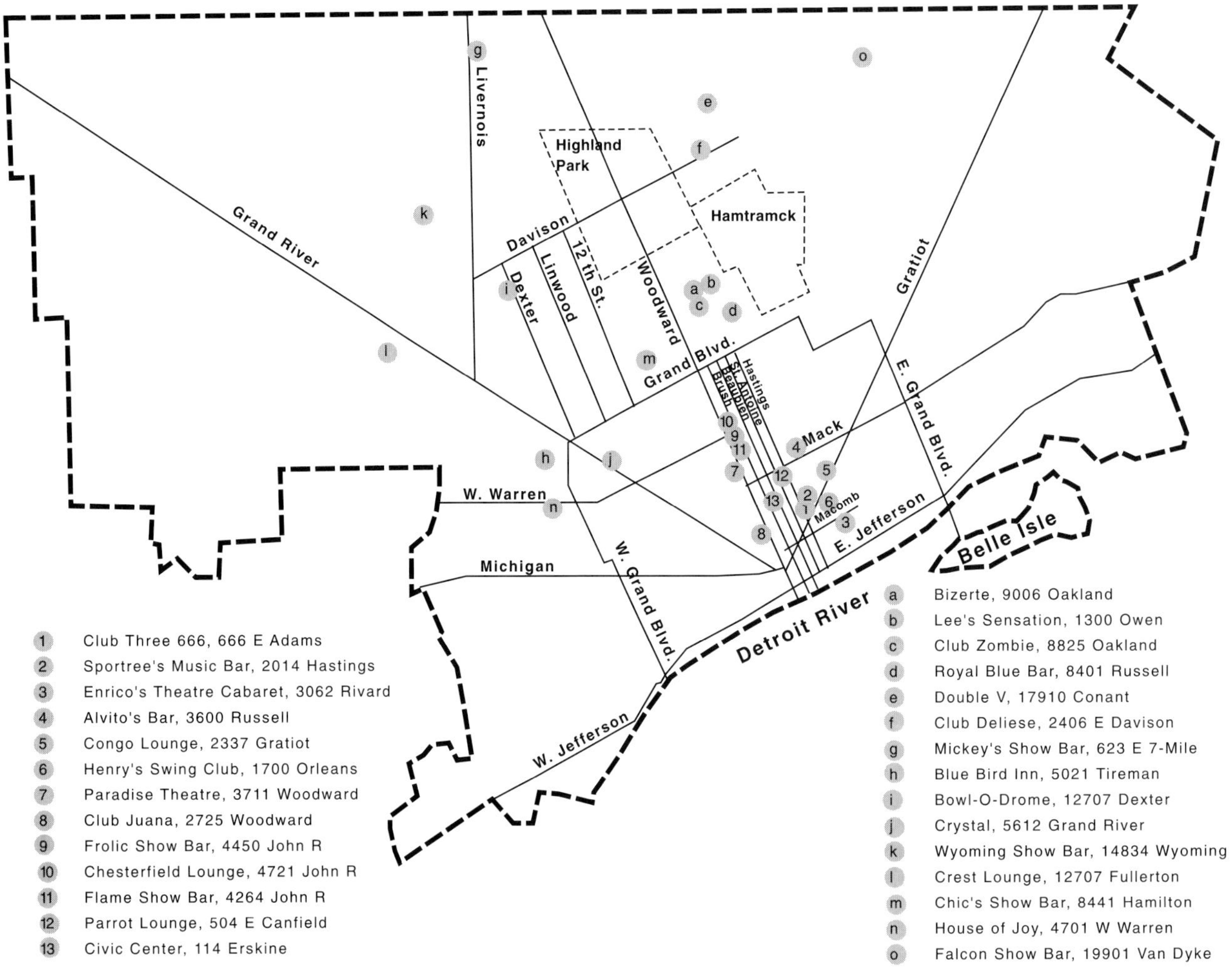

Fig. 44. New jazz spots in the 1940s, inside and outside Grand Boulevard. (Map by Borkin and Kaplan.)

plants that earlier had been closed to them. This advance was the combined result of the labor shortage, federal government prodding, and pressure from the UAW and civil rights leaders.[11]

Expansion of the Black Community and Jazz Venues

During the 1940s the black working class grew as more blacks moved into manufacturing jobs and the proportion in personal service jobs declined. While the skilled trades remained shut off to black industrial workers, the high wages of the auto industry made it possible for some to achieve middle-class status in terms of income. This typically involved leaving the Near East Side to become a homeowner further north and west.

With the expansion of the black population movement continued north from Paradise Valley on the east side of Woodward Avenue to the so-called North End, north of Grand Boulevard around Oakland Avenue. (See fig. 43.) The North End butted up against the cities of Highland Park and Hamtramck, which are cities within the city of Detroit (identified in fig. 44). The black population also spread continuously to the east.

Further to the north and to the west blacks had to "jump" to black enclaves, two of which

11. Ibid., 26–27.

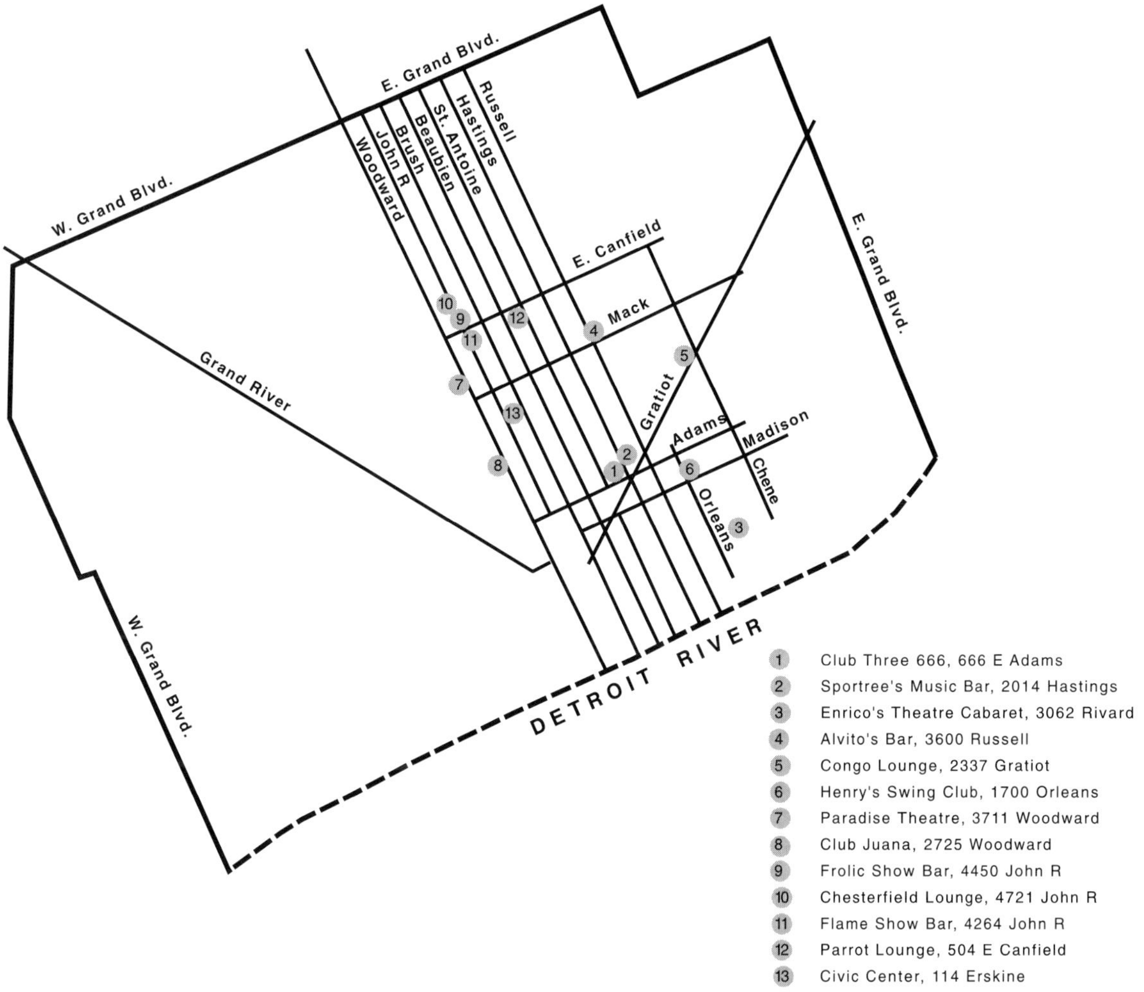

Fig. 45. New jazz spots in the 1940s, inside Grand Boulevard.
(Map by Borkin and Kaplan.)

were more middle class than the valley: Conant Gardens (north) and the West Side south of Tireman. About a quarter of Detroit blacks lived in such enclaves in the early 1940s.[12]

During the second half of the 1940s Paradise Valley lost some of its importance as an entertainment center for the black population. Expanded black enclaves produced rival centers, and there was also some opening up of entertainment along Woodward Avenue for African Americans. Figure 44 shows the location of all new jazz venues in the 1940s, whereas figure 45 gives a close-up of the new venues inside Grand Boulevard.

In the center of Paradise Valley, around St. Antoine and Adams, the Plantation and the B & C changed hands in the 1940s to become the Club Congo/Club Sudan and Club Owens/El Sino, respectively.[13] There was only a net increase of one new venue. The new venue was Club Three 666 (the Three Sixes), which was opened by Jap Sneed in 1941.[14] The Three Sixes was managed by Richard King, who told Elaine Moon:

> *The building was originally built for a dance hall, and adjacent to the Club Three 666 was the Paradise Bowl. . . . We served terrific food, and our customers were a wonderful group of people who worked in the downtown area. During this time, blacks couldn't eat just anyplace. People went to the YMCA, or some other business on St. Antoine, usually came to the Club*

12. Ibid., 37.

13. The B & C became Club Owens in 1945 and the El Sino in 1947. The Club Congo replaced Club Plantation in 1941 and became Club Sudan in 1946.

14. Sneed had opened Dance Paradise at 664 East Adams in February 1941, featuring John Kirby and Maxine Sullivan. But business was bad without a liquor license, and in October he opened the Club Three 666. Advertisement, *Detroit Tribune*, February 8, 1941. *Michigan Chronicle*, September 30, 1944.

Fig. 46. Advertisement for Sportree's Music Bar. (From *Michigan Chronicle*, September 21, 1946.)

Three 666 for lunch. Our club was first class all the way, and our clientele was well dressed at all times. . . . During the week we'd average two hundred people per night, and on Saturday we'd have a complete turnover. . . . When we lost the white business that we were getting, it was time to get out of the business. We sold the business in 1949.[15]

The Three Sixes was a show bar with a chorus line, and local and national acts were brought in by three of Detroit's main black bookers: Stutz Anderson, Rollo Vest, and Chester Rentie. In 1949 it became Club Valley.

In contrast, three new venues were added along Hastings Street, and four were added to the east and north, particularly along Russell Street. In the North End six new venues were added, mainly on Oakland Avenue and Russell.

By 1946 the *Michigan Chronicle*'s Larry Chism saw Paradise Valley in decline in the face of stiff competition.

> *During the past eight years as the theatrical editor of the Michigan Chronicle we have observed many changes in the habits of nite lifers. . . . The greatest change: the transformation of Paradise Valley. No longer is the Valley the gay, charming, and alluring young lady she once was, instead she is a withered, ugly old hag whom no one loves and whom everyone is beginning to forsake for a younger more beautiful companion. . . . only a small portion of the pre-war patrons now make the trip down to Paradise Valley.*[16]

One exception to this decline in the valley was the opening of Sportree's Music Bar on the corner of Hastings and Adams in 1946.[17] The owner was Raymond "Sportree" Jackson. It was a swankier bar than most along Hastings Street, and it presented local and national acts. According to the *Michigan Chronicle:*

> *The bar will seat 60 while the booths will seat several hundred more. . . . the establishment has a runway stretching in full length of the back bar. This runway leads to the half circular floor-space from which the entertainment is presented. The entire wall of the music box is lined with mirrors, which reflect the multi-colored ceiling. Booths are of red leather upholstery and are placed around one wall of the music box. . . .*

On October 28, 1946, the *Chronicle* noted:

> *Those blue Monday parties at Sportree Jackson's swank Music Bar are the talk of the town. Folks who like to mingle with celebrities and meet and greet old friends are wending their way to the fun spot where Sportree makes you welcome. Last week's celebrities included Dinah Washington, the Ink Spots, Eddie (Cleanhead) Vinson, and others.*[18]

Sportree's stayed in business until 1950 and was briefly replaced by the Rainbow Room.[19] By that time "financial paralysis was creeping across Paradise Valley," according to a front-page story in the *Michigan Chronicle*.[20]

Further to the east and north from the Valley several lesser spots were added during the 1940s. (See fig. 45.) Three of them were Italian owned: Enrico's Theatre Cabaret, Alvito's Bar, and the Congo Lounge.[21] Of the others at least one was black owned: Henry's Swing Club on Orleans and Madison.[22]

The North End

In contrast to the slow decline of the Valley, a front-page article in the *Chronicle* in 1948 pointed to the "amazing growth" of black business in the Oakland business area and likened it

15. Elaine Moon, *Untold Tales, Unsung Heroes: An Oral History of Detroit's African-American Community, 1918–1967* (Detroit: Wayne State University Press, 1994), 164–65.

16. Larry Chism, "Many Changes Seen in Night Life during Past 10 Years," *Michigan Chronicle*, April 13, 1946.

17. Another club that opened on Hastings and Columbia in 1940 was the Midway Club. It was owned by Marshall Harris, who earlier was one of the owners of the Rose Bud Inn two blocks north. The Midway seems to have lasted until Harris's death in 1946, but it was relatively insignificant as a spot for jazz. *Michigan Chronicle*, February 16, 1946. The Three Star Bar on Hastings and Brewster also featured occasional jazz in the 1940s. George Benson, interview by Lars Bjorn and Jim Gallert, Detroit, Michigan, March 17, 1991; and Alvin Jackson, interview by Lars Bjorn and Jim Gallert, Detroit, Michigan, October 10, 1991.

18. *Michigan Chronicle*, August 17, 1946.

19. Bill Lane, "Swinging down the Lane," *Michigan Chronicle*, March 11, 1950.

20. *Michigan Chronicle*, January 28, 1950.

21. Enrico's was located at Rivard and Wilkins (advertisement, *Michigan Chronicle*, December 26, 1942), Alvito's at Russell and Mack (advertisement, *Michigan Chronicle*, June 17, 1950), and the Congo Lounge on Gratiot at Chene (advertisement, *Michigan Chronicle*, February 12, 1949).

22. The owner was Henry Hare. His club went by different names: Henry's Café, Henry's Grill, and Henry's Swing Club. *Detroit Tribune*, May 11, 1940.

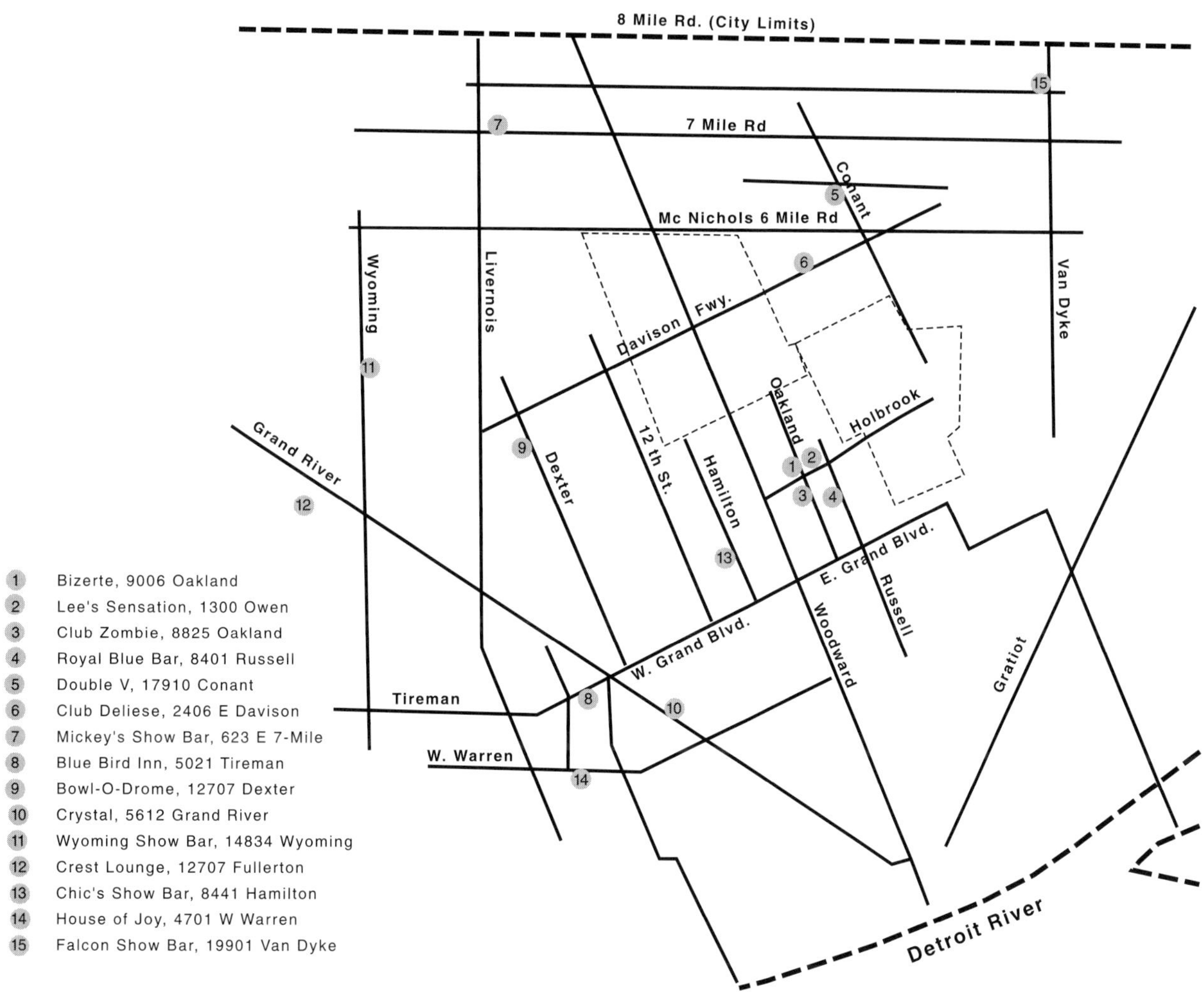

Fig. 47. New jazz spots, 1940s, outside Grand Boulevard. (Map by Borkin and Kaplan.)

to the "Miracle Mile" in Los Angeles. The Oakland area was predominantly Jewish by the late 1930s, but by the mid-1940s many Jews were moving on to the Twelfth Street area on the Near West Side.[23] By 1946 two major jazz venues in the North End had opened under black ownership: the Bizerte and Lee's Sensation.[24] (See fig. 47.)

Uzziel Lee was a businessman who saw economic opportunity in entertainment according to a *Michigan Chronicle* article, "Success of Club Sensation Due to Efforts of Owner Lee."

> *Uzziel Lee is 47. . . . [He was] born in Ensley, Alabama, and came to Detroit in 1923. . . . His first job [was] at the Pressed Steel Company. . . . [He] decided to go into business in 32. . . . [He] opened a shoe shine parlor at Owen and Cardoni, directly across the street from Sensation. . . . later he moved to the sunnier side of the corner and opened his confectionery. In 1943 he decided a nightclub was what his section of the North End needed. . . . first he opened a tavern at the rear of the confectionery. . . . [The] tavern became so popular he converted to a nightclub, but he lost money his first year. . . . Things got better when he started a talent show. . . . In 1945 he remodeled the Sensation, changed the lighting . . . [and] lowered ceilings . . . [creating] more intimacy. . . . [It was] the first really modern night club of black-and-tan class in Detroit. Places like the Frolic came later.*[25]

23. "Oakland's Business Area Shows Amazing Growth," *Michigan Chronicle*, May 8, 1948.

24. The Bizerte was known as a place for jam sessions at least by 1945 according to an article in a major national jazz publication. Don Hodges, "Detroit Remains Woefully Unhip," *Metronome*, October 1945.

25. *Michigan Chronicle*, July 15, 1950.

Fig. 48. Advertisement for Bizerte Bar. This is one of the few jazz clubs from the 1940s still standing. (From *Michigan Chronicle*, November 16, 1946.)

The Bizerte was a slightly different kind of venue. According to one frequent customer "it had pretensions of being a nightclub, but was really just a neighborhood bar."[26] Its audience was mainly black, but it also attracted aspiring white jazz musicians who would come there to listen or to take part in a jam session. One of them was singer Sheila Jordan.

> *To get to the Bizerte we all got on the Clairmount streetcar, and that was a wicked neighborhood, supposedly, and here's these little two white girls going into the Bizerte. I got in there and I don't think I was 21. . . . nobody ever bothered me. . . . I was always accepted with open arms.*[27]

The other jazz spots in the area were Jewish owned but catered to integrated or all-black audiences and often had black managers. The two major ones were the Club Zombie, earlier called Broad's Bar, and the Royal Blue Bar.[28] The Zombie was a black and tan nightclub with enough class to have valet parking. A *Michigan Chronicle* reporter visited the 1940 Christmas party and reported that

> *At last it has come to pass that Sepia Detroit has another first class nitery. . . . Broad's Club Zombie out Oakland way . . . has a seating capacity of 450, newly decorated and enlarged in the modern trend of such places . . . and a new six-piece band.*[29]

Conant Gardens

Conant Gardens, where a large number of black professionals and businesspeople lived, was the most exclusive of Detroit black neighborhoods in the 1940s.[30] It was located on the Northeast Side of Detroit, north of Hamtramck between Conant on the west and Highland Park on the east. Two spots with jazz opened up in this area in the 1940s: the Double V Bar in 1942[31] and Club Deliese in 1945. (See fig. 47.)

The Club Deliese was the more substantial jazz spot of the two. It opened in late December 1945 with a lineup of singers and dancers and a small group from the Paradise Theatre pit band. As "Detroit's Newest Black and Tan" it promised new shows every two weeks for a weekend cover of $1.[32] It was Jewish owned with a black manager.[33] Three years later it changed its name to Club El-Morocco, called itself a theater bar, and still offered a floor show. The club was active at least until 1953.[34]

The boundary line between the Conant Gardens area and a white Catholic working-class area was Seven Mile Road. By the late 1940s there was increasing white resistance to neighborhood integration, and violence often erupted. Mickey's Show Bar on Seven Mile and Irvington opened in 1944 and was increasingly on the fault line of racial division until about 1957, when it closed.[35] Mickey's featured various white dance bands and dixieland in its first year, but in 1945 it hired a black band, Clarence Dorsey's. The *Michigan Chronicle*'s Larry Chism commented:

> *Clarence Dorsey believes he is paving the way for other music note readers by being the first sepia band to open at Mickey's Show Bar, an ofay nitery with his six-piece combine.*[36]

26. Jack Duquette, interview by Lars Bjorn, Grosse Pointe Farms, Michigan, June 15, 1991. The same point is made by bassist Alvin Jackson. Jackson, interview by Bjorn and Gallert.

27. Jordan, interview by Bjorn.

28. The owner of the Royal Blue bar was Max Rott. He got started in the grocery store business and moved into taverns in 1941. The Royal Blue Bar was opened in 1946 on Russell and Euclid, and Rott advertised himself as "the Prince of Play." Bill Lane, "Profile of Max Rott," *Michigan Chronicle*, August 20, 1949.

29. *Michigan Chronicle*, January 4, 1941.

30. Sugrue, *Origins of the Urban Crisis*, 40–41.

31. The Double V was black owned, as the reference to the World War II slogan indicates, and lasted about five years. It was located at 17910 Conant, near Nevada, and was owned by Manco Jones. *Michigan Chronicle*, December 12, 1942. See also *Michigan Chronicle*, November 15, 1947.

32. Advertisement, *Michigan Chronicle*, December 29, 1945.

33. *Michigan Chronicle*, May 14, 1949.

34. Advertisements, *Michigan Chronicle*, November 20, 1948; April 25, 1953.

35. Advertisements, *Detroit Free Press*, January 14, 1944; February 8, 1957.

36. Larry Chism column, *Michigan Chronicle*, October 20, 1945.

Fig. 49. Cecil Lee orchestra, Broad's Club Zombie, 1941. *Band, L to R: George Favors, bar/vcl; Leonard Morrison, bs; Howard Thompson, tp; Charles "Chick" Williams, ts/vcl; Gene Shelton, dms; Cecil Lee, as/ldr; Todd Rhodes, pno. Others include Abe Broad, owner (left front), and Noah Brown, manager (right front). Sam Fouche (a.k.a. Peggy Joyce) is standing in front of Morrison; vocalist Al Tobin is standing in front of Rhodes. Fouche was a popular cross-dressing master of ceremonies.* (Courtesy Mrs. Annie Mae Rhodes, Gallert Collection.)

This turned out to be an exception: other local black bands did indeed play Mickey's in the 1950s, but they were not the rule.

West Side

THE BLUE BIRD INN became a major jazz spot in Detroit in the late 1940s. It was (and still is) located at 5021 Tireman near Beechwood. (See fig. 47.) Tireman was the northern boundary of the West Side black community until 1940. During the 1940s blacks started to move across Tireman. The history of the bar goes back to the late 1930s, when Robert DuBois Sr. opened up a bar/restaurant at 5021 Tireman.[37] He had come to Detroit from Valdosta, Georgia, and saved some money working at Ford Motor Company.[38] In 1938 Dubois was killed by his son Buddy, who was sent to prison.[39] Henry Black took over as manager of the bar until 1945.[40] By 1946 Buddy Dubois was back and running the bar.[41] The Blue Bird in the early 1940s had operated as a neighborhood bar with musical entertainment by a singer and a band.

> *Blue Bird Inn . . . Ella "Black Beauty" Lee, and Jimmy Caldwell and his orchestra . . . America's finest dishes, Chinese and American Foods, chop suey, chow mein, whiskey, wine and beer . . . H. H. Black, mgr.*[42]

By 1948 the Blue Bird became a center for modern jazz musicians.[43] This was a place where they could play what they wanted and also a place where they hung out. Almost all musicians and customers were African American. We will have ample reasons to come back to the history of the Blue Bird.

Jazz along Woodward in the 1940s

DURING THE 1943 RIOTS WHITES claimed Woodward Avenue as theirs by attacking black moviegoers at the all-night Roxy and Colonial Theaters, just a few blocks from the Near East Side ghetto. If this was a warning to African Americans to stay off Woodward it was only heeded for the duration of the riot. For much of the century blacks had slowly moved into entertainment venues on the city's main street, and by the 1940s civil rights activists increasingly focused on using protest and legal action to open up Woodward. A survey of downtown restaurants by the Mayor's Interracial Commit-

37. The DuBois family owned a restaurant at 5019–21 Tireman by 1938 according to the *Detroit City Directory*. The first advertisement for the Blue Bird appeared the same year in the *Detroit Tribune*, April 30, 1938. The restaurant advertised jam sessions on Thursdays and swing music by the Sonny Boy Williams quartet.

38. Carl Hill, interview by Lars Bjorn and Jim Gallert, Detroit, Michigan, December 12, 1991.

39. "Bluebird Inn Manager Ambushed," *Michigan Chronicle*, October 10, 1956.

40. Advertisements in the *Detroit Tribune*, April 30, 1938; *Michigan Chronicle*, January 4, 1940. Larry Chism column, *Michigan Chronicle*, August 4, 1945.

41. "The Chronicle Visits West Side Nightspot," *Michigan Chronicle*, June 1, 1946.

42. Advertisement, *Michigan Chronicle*, July 5, 1941.

43. *Michigan Chronicle*, October 2, 1948.

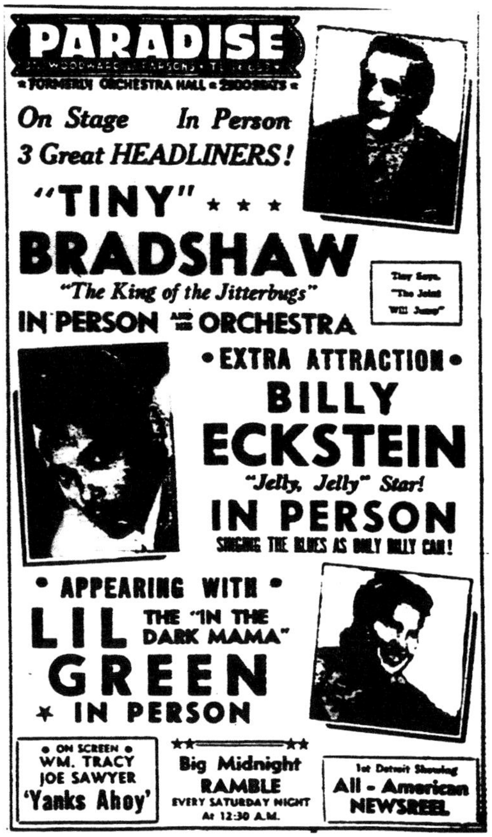

Fig. 50. Advertisement for Paradise Theatre.
(From *Michigan Chronicle*, December 11, 1943.)

tee in 1949 found two forms of discrimination: "whites only" policies and "partial discrimination," the latter including discourteous treatment of customers.[44] A few months later the NAACP launched a campaign against restaurant discrimination in Detroit and published a set of 10 points to follow when encountering discrimination. The first steps involved calling the police and the NAACP and then repeating the request to be served.[45]

These citizen actions seem to have had some effect because by March 1950 the NAACP could announce that it was possible for blacks to be served in the downtown area of Woodward.[46] However, this progress was by no means steady or irreversible, and the downtown area remained an area of civil rights contention into the 1950s.[47]

African-American music lovers had won a major foothold on Woodward Avenue with the establishment in late 1941 of the Paradise Theatre. For the next 10 years the Paradise was Detroit's most important venue for black musical entertainment, which meant jazz and rhythm and blues.

A few months after the Paradise had opened its doors the *Michigan Chronicle* informed its readers that

> *the Cohen Brothers, operators of the Roxy and Mayfair theaters on Woodward, took over the former Orchestra Hall last December and renamed it Paradise Theatre. . . . Their ambitious enterprise gave to the race one of the finest theaters in the country not excepting the Apollo in New York City and the Regal in Chicago. . . . [it] opened with Louis Armstrong.*[48]

The Paradise was a fine theater on many counts. Orchestra Hall had been built on Woodward at Parsons for the Detroit Symphony Orchestra (DSO) in 1919 and at first seated 2,250, later expanded to 3,000.[49] (See fig. 45.) The DSO's music director, Ossip Gabrilowitsch, had demanded a new hall as a condition for staying in Detroit, and he received what is generally considered a concert space with near perfect acoustics. The DSO left in 1939 for the Masonic Hall but returned in recent years.[50]

The Paradise was an instant success with its predominantly black audience.[51] By March 1942 the *Michigan Chronicle* reported that Cab Calloway held the attendance record for a week with 40,000, followed by Jimmy Lunceford's orchestra with 32,000 and Duke Ellington with 30,000. Audiences paid 60 cents for an evening or Sunday show, which started with a movie and continued with music and a floor show. Weekday matinees were 40 cents during the war years. In 1946 the Paradise started an amateur talent contest that provided a start for many aspiring Detroit musicians. Singer Betty Carter remembered that

> *When I was 16, I auditioned for the black amateur night they had every Wednesday at the*

44. *Michigan Chronicle*, August 6, 1949.

45. *Michigan Chronicle*, October 8, 1949. The NAACP had successfully fought the Bob-Lo Island Excursion company's "whites only" policy on their ferryboats between 1946 and 1949. The case was finally decided by the U.S. Supreme Court. Thomas, *Life for Us Is What We Make It*, 318–19.

46. *Michigan Chronicle*, March 4, 1950.

47. Charles J. Wartman, "Detroit 10 Years after the Riot," *Michigan Chronicle*, March 21, 1953.

48. *Michigan Chronicle*, April 25, 1942. Ben and Lou Cohen had operated a chain of theaters since around 1917 ("Paradise Owner Dies Suddenly," *Michigan Chronicle*, June 21, 1947).

49. The address of Orchestra Hall/Paradise Theatre is 3711 Woodward. Orchestra Hall was designed by C. Howard Crane, a prominent movie theater architect. Advertisement for the DSO, *Detroit Free Press*, October 5, 1994; and "Paradise Bows Out," *Detroit Times*, January 26, 1952.

50. The DSO returned in 1990 from another stopover, Ford Auditorium. Orchestra Hall/Paradise Theatre was saved from the wrecker's ball in 1970 by Paul Ganson, DSO bassoonist and preservationist.

51. Ann Campau, interview by Lars Bjorn, South Lyon, Michigan, July 29, 1993; and Duquette, interview by Bjorn.

Paradise Theater. I sang "The Man I Love," and accompanied myself, and I won second prize.[52]

I was the a capella choir student director in my school [Northwestern High School]. . . . After the amateur contest I thought I could strike out and become a singer.[53]

I did well enough for a couple of Detroit booking agents to pursue me for Sunday-afternoon cabarets and for appearances at the Elks Hall and at fashion shows.[54]

Just being in the audience was a learning experience for aspiring musicians, and often the big names on stage were actually quite approachable. Drummer Frank Gant remembered that

> *I must have been 13 or 14. . . . I [had] bought drumsticks, but I had no idea what drummers would do. So I went home and started beating around the chairs and tables and listening to the radio. But it was hard: you could hear the drummers, but to actually pick up on what they were doing was impossible. So by that time I became a fan of the Paradise Theatre, where the big bands were coming in, you know. So I'd go down there on Sunday. I might get there about 12 o'clock and stay all day, just to sit and watch and listen. And I caught all the big bands . . . Duke, Count, Billy Eckstine. . . . he [Eckstine] had all the stars in the band . . . Charlie Parker . . . Diz, and Miles . . . but I was watching the drummer . . . Art Blakey. So I went backstage and I said: "I'd like to talk to the drummer" and the stage manager said: "Art, somebody wanna see you!" He came over to the door said: "Hey kid, how're you doin'? Come on in!" He took me in, just like I was a regular, you know. . . . Buhaina [Blakey], I hung out with him the rest of the day, took me to his hotel, you know. . . . that's the way Art was, he was very positive about young guys getting into it. Made me feel very good you know, so I decided to study drums. . . . I just had a set of sticks, not even one drum.*[55]

Club Juana was another new spot on Woodward during the decade. (See fig. 45.) This nightclub opened in 1948 but did not become an important jazz spot until the early 1950s.[56] In May 1950 its management changed, and it openly advertised itself as a black and tan.[57] The use of the term *black and tan* was becoming increasingly irrelevant in the face of integration efforts, as this *Michigan Chronicle* article indicated.

Fig. 51. Advertisement for Club Juana.
(From *Michigan Chronicle*, February 23, 1947.)

> *It marks the first time in Detroit's history that an inter-racial night club has operated on Woodward Avenue . . . said Abe Rahaim, who with Cliff Gouton operates the beautiful new club. "We are going to have a strictly democratic policy in force at the Juana. It is not actually an interracial setup, it's just that we are a public establishment and we'll live up to the Constitutional law of admitting people as people as long as they are presentable and orderly."*[58]

John R.: The Street of Music

The latter half of the 1940s saw the development of "the Street of Music" in two blocks of John R., between Forest and Canfield. John R. is one block east of Woodward and marked the western border of the Near East Side ghetto. Looking west along Canfield you could see the Graystone on Woodward, while two blocks east were other clubs deeper inside the Near East Side ghetto. (See fig. 45.)

The Street of Music was dominated by three so-called show bars, sometimes called theater bars. In a show bar the music was not just incidental and background, as it would be if found in a neighborhood bar. The relative importance of the music can be seen in the elaborate stage constructed for the show. Often the stage floor was elevated to the eye level of a customer by the bar.

52. Whitney Balliet, "Betty Bebop," *New Yorker*, September 20, 1982.

53. Arthur Taylor, "Betty Carter," in *Notes and Tones* (New York: Da Capo Press, 1993), 272.

54. Balliet, "Betty Bebop."

55. Frank Gant, interview by Jim Gallert, Detroit, Michigan, July 7, 1992.

56. Advertisement, *Detroit Free Press*, May 28, 1948.

57. Advertisement, *Michigan Chronicle*, May 13, 1950.

58. *Michigan Chronicle*, May 20, 1950.

FROLIC SHOW BAR
"THERE'S NEVER A DULL MOMENT AT YOUR FAVORITE NITERY"
COMING JUNE 6
"LITTLE MISS CORNSHUCKS"
The Singing Voice of the Year
JIMMY MILLS
Emcee-Singer
TED BUCKNER
Hot and Sweet Music
TUESDAY NITES: "The World's Greatest Jazz Artists" in
BILL RANDLE'S JAM SESSION
MUSIC SWEET AND HOT
Wednesday Nites: Enjoy Our
AMATEUR TALENT CONTEST
Thursday Nites, Starting June 5
MARLYN CURRIE'S FASHION REVUE
Continuous Entertainment 9 - 2 A.M.
Call TE. 2-8553
FROLIC SHOW BAR 4450 John R
Have Fun at Our DECORATION DAY PARTY Friday, May 31

Fig. 52. Advertisement for the Frolic Show Bar. (From *Michigan Chronicle*, May 31, 1947.)

The Frolic Show Bar opened first, in December 1946. Owners Hymie and Bennie Gastman reportedly spent $60,000 to build what they called "the Showplace of Detroit," and the *Michigan Chronicle*'s Larry Chism told his readers that

> *There was standing room only as first-nighters made their way to the Frolic Show Bar which opened Friday. . . . from all walks of life they came to listen to Una Mae Carlisle and Savanna Churchill. . . . Gene Nero and his "3 Dukes and Duchess" band were groovey. . . . playboys, playgirls, hep-masters and hep-sisters, doctors, lawyers, and plain old funlovers were on hand.*[59]

The diverse audience described by Chism to his African-American readers probably included a minority of whites. The Frolic advertised as a black and tan, which tended to draw a small but select group of whites. One frequent customer to this and other black and tans in the area was Jack Duquette. He remembered the audience as "the sporting element and those who were interested in black music, and a few other folk, but not the general population."[60]

The Frolic continued to showcase top black musical talent, like the Louis Armstrong All Stars and Dinah Washington, as well as many significant local musicians, well into the 1960s.

The next addition to the street was the Chesterfield Lounge, which opened in November 1947. The Chesterfield was also a Jewish-owned black and tan but featured mainly local acts.[61]

The most prominent spot on the Street of Music was no doubt the Flame Show Bar, which was opened by Morris Wasserman on June 24, 1949.[62] Only the Paradise Theatre could offer a comparable quality floor show in Detroit in the late 1940s. The Flame was a more expensive alternative to the Paradise Theatre, since it offered more intimacy (only 250 patrons) and a 100-foot bar with a "three color flash motif and mirrors on three walls."[63] By the early 1950s the Paradise was gone, and the Flame ruled the roost until 1963. The Flame advertised as a black and tan but deviated from the standard model by offering some white entertainers as well as black ones. It is, for example, the place where singer Johnny Ray got his start in 1951. For the grand opening Wasserman brought in Nellie Lutcher and the Snookie Young band, featuring bassist Slam Stewart. Two weeks later Billie Holiday sang, accompanied by Horace Henderson on piano.[64] The Young band worked as a house band for only two months and was replaced by local groups led by Todd Rhodes and Maurice King.

Baritonist Thomas "Beans" Bowles was one of Maurice King's Wolverines and remembered the scene at the Flame.

> *The Flame was black and tan and more white than black. On the weekends the traffic would line up; you could not drive down Canfield or John R. That was hustle night, girls were on the street, pimps were out, everybody was makin' money. It was like Las Vegas. People would come from everywhere. It was the center of entertainment. There was no entertainment like that in the city at that time. We called it Sugar Hill really. Everything there was just poppin'. Lights and glitter, valet parking. . . . Nobody bother you or nothing. White people would come from all over to come to the Flame, because we had the top shows.*[65]

59. *Michigan Chronicle*, December 21, 1946.

60. Duquette, interview by Bjorn.

61. The Chesterfield was owned by Bill Goodman and was located at 4721 John R. *Michigan Chronicle*, December 6, 1947.

62. The Flame was located at 4264 John R on the corner of Canfield. Advertisement, *Detroit Tribune*, June 25, 1949. Wasserman was the owner of Club Harlem in the 1930s.

63. *Michigan Chronicle*, March 26, 1949. The Flame was clearly more than a neighborhood bar, since in 1949 it employed 26 people (*Michigan Chronicle*, July 9, 1949).

64. Advertisement, *Detroit Free Press*, July 9, 1949.

65. Beans Bowles, interview by Lars Bjorn, Detroit, Michigan, June 16, 1998.

There is Only One
Billie Holiday
. . . and she opens Friday,
July 8th at the . . .
SNOOKIE YOUNG and his Band
SLAM STEWART and his Bass
KITTY STEVENSON and her Songs
EMILE JONES Singing M. C.
FLAME SHOW BAR
4264 JOHN R ST.
AT CANFIELD
TE. 2-8714
Cocktail Hour On Sundays Starting at 5 p. m.
Four Shows Nightly
Morris Wasserman, Host
Always a Hot Time at The Flame!

Fig. 53. Advertisement for the Flame Show Bar. (From *Michigan Chronicle*, July 9, 1949.)

Fig. 54. Flame Show Bar interior showing stage and bar area. (Courtesy Lars Bjorn.)

Entry to the Flame was on a first come, first served basis—unless you offered the doorman a gratuity, according to Bowles: "That was one, and only one, of the little hustles going on. You could get anything at the Flame if you had enough money."[66]

Two blocks east of the Flame at the corner of Canfield and Beaubien was another show bar, the Parrot Lounge, which opened in 1947.[67] It was a simpler bar than the Flame or the Frolic, but it was an important spot for jazz until the 1960s. In the 1940s its musical manager was New York–born Al Green, who was becoming an important figure in Detroit's musical and social life according to the *Michigan Chronicle*'s Bill Lane.

He was the manager at Club Plantation in New York City where Cab Calloway got his start. . . . Later after arriving in Detroit he tried his hand at fight-management (Alfred "Big Boy" Brown) . . . promoted dances at the Mirror Ballroom and the Forest Club. . . . he is also promoting [singer] Kitty Stevenson and wants to take her to New York and TV. . . . a few months ago he opened Al's Bar-B-Que next to the Flame.[68]

Al Green became a partner in the Flame, where he also worked as a manager. He played an important part as a manager and promoter of many Detroit rhythm and blues figures until his death in 1957.[69]

In the latter half of the 1940s there was also a lot of musical activity at the Civic Center, several blocks south on John R., at the corner of Erskine. The Civic Center was run by a black men's association, the Twelve Horsemen's Club, and by 1944 they were having public dances in their own building. This became an important venue for big bands and jam sessions for the rest of the decade.[70]

Surveying the new clubs in Detroit in the 1940s observers in the local African-American press concluded that Detroit was a boomtown for black entertainers. "There is no longer any doubt that Detroit is becoming the sepia entertainment center of the nation," particularly "in light of the closing of large nighteries in Los Angeles and New York," according to the *Michi-*

66. Beans Bowles, interview by Jim Callert, Detroit, Michigan, February 18, 1997.

67. The Parrot was owned by Joe Jaffee. *Michigan Chronicle*, October 25, 1947.

68. Bill Lane, "Profile," *Michigan Chronicle*, September 10, 1949.

69. "Al Green Succumbs in New York Hotel Lobby," *Michigan Chronicle*, December 28, 1957.

70. Big band leader Jimmy Davenport was co-chair of the club and served as an emcee during the club's events. Larry Chism column, *Michigan Chronicle*, July 22, 1944. The club also arranged dances at ballrooms in the city.

gan Chronicle's Larry Chism in 1947.[71] Three years later columnist Bill Lane saw that Detroit had grown into a "Nite Club Mecca" starting with the opening of Sportree's Music Bar in 1946.[72] While the relative ranking of cities is beyond the scope of this book, we can say that these observers were on the mark in this regard: Detroit's black musical community was booming in the last part of the 1940s. From 1945 through 1949 venues for black music were opening up at a faster rate than ever, and the largest and most numerous venues were within the black community or within reach on Woodward Avenue.

New Jazz Venues outside the Black Community

The late 1940s saw the beginning of a boom in new jazz venues in white neighborhoods that was to last well into the 1950s. Most of these new venues were located on the West Side of Detroit, that is, west of Woodward Avenue.[73] The area where most of these venues were found is bounded on the south by Grand River, on the west by Wyoming, and on the north by Davison. (See fig. 47.) Detroit's Jewish community was a significant presence on the western side of this area, surrounding Twelfth Street, Linwood, and Dexter. On the other hand, there were few blacks in the area until 1947. In 1947 blacks started to move into the Twelfth Street Jewish community.[74] The major West Side black community was found further south, below Grand River along Tireman.

The first and most important jazz venue in this part of the West Side was the Bowl-O-Drome, which opened for music around 1945.[75] The Bowl-O-Drome was a bowling alley with a bar on Dexter Avenue at Leslie in the West Side Jewish neighborhood. There was a separate entrance to the bar from Dexter. The first advertisements for the Tropical Show Bar at the Bowl-O-Drome were in 1947, and it featured some of Detroit's top jazzmen.[76] By that time it was run by Lou Jacobs, who is remembered well by Ann Campau. Along with her husband, Jack, Ann was a regular customer at the Bowl-O-Drome.

> *Louie Jacobs owned the 'Drome. He didn't officially own it; it was in his father-in-law's name because he had a prison record. If you had a prison record you could not get a liquor license. We lost track of Louie after he went to jail . . . for gambling. . . . he had a gambling place close to the 'Drome too. . . . He had been a Purple Gangster, you know. . . . Louie was always in trouble. I thought he was a nice guy, because he was a nice guy as far as we were concerned. He would pay for our drinks, and he would put on a birthday party for me. . . . A lot of the same type of people frequented both the 'Drome and the Wyoming Show Bar. All white audiences. Black musicians were not allowed to sit down at the bar with you. . . . They had roughly sixty seats in there. People were there to listen to the music. You could see the music from everywhere. . . . It wasn't that people didn't talk, but they weren't excessive.*[77]

Jack Campau added that

> *If you didn't want to listen to the music you went somewhere where the drinks were cheaper. A shot of whiskey at the Bowl-O-Drome was 40¢ and you could go to a neighborhood bar and get it for 25¢.*[78]

The Bowl-O-Drome was to remain an important part of the Detroit jazz scene into the early 1970s.

In 1947 three additional jazz spots opened on the West Side: the Crystal Bar, the Wyoming Show Bar, and the Crest Lounge. The Crystal Bar was located on Grand River at Lawton and owned by Edmour Bertrand. The club changed its name and music policy over the years. It was a piano bar until 1951 and then became the Crystal Show Lounge with a black and tan policy.[79] The 1950s were the heyday for the Crystal as a jazz spot.

The Wyoming Show Bar started jazz on Monday nights in early 1947 and kept it up un-

71. Larry Chism, "Detroit May Become Entertainment Center of Nation," *Michigan Chronicle*, May 24, 1947; and "Local Clubs Offer Patrons Wealth of Theatrical Talent," *Michigan Chronicle*, July 26, 1947.

72. Bill Lane, "Detroit: Nite Club Mecca? City Blooms with New Spots, Top Talent," *Michigan Chronicle*, September 9, 1950.

73. The white Southeast Side of Detroit had relatively few jazz spots. Club Stevadora on Harper and Crane opened up in 1945 and lasted until about 1947. *Detroit Free Press*, June 15, 1945. The Stevadora featured Dixieland and white dance bands at first, but by 1947 it featured some black bands as well. *Detroit News*, April 13, 1947; April 20, 1947. It resurfaced as a jazz spot in the 1950s under the name "the Shangri-La." Duffy's Tavern on Harper and Gratiot featured black and white jazz between 1945 and 1946. Norris, interview by Gallert; *Michigan Chronicle*, August 4, 1945; advertisement, *Detroit Free Press*, October 4, 1946.

74. Sugrue, *Origins of the Urban Crisis*, 242.

75. Pianist Tommy Flanagan had his first gig with trombonist Frank Rosolino at the Bowl-O-Drome around 1945. Tommy Flanagan, interview by Lars Bjorn, Ann Arbor, Michigan, November 14, 1987.

76. *Detroit Free Press*, December 30, 1947. While advertisements always refer to the Tropical Show Bar, musicians and audiences called the spot the Bowl-O-Drome.

77. Jack and Ann Campau, interview by Lars Bjorn, South Lyon, Michigan, July 29, 1993. A newspaper article about Jacobs's 10-month sentence for gambling in 1957 indicated that he had a record of 32 arrests and five convictions. "Jailed in Gambling: Hoodlum Surprised by 10-Month Sentence," *Detroit Free Press*, February 22, 1957.

78. The Bowl-O-Drome did not have a cover charge in the late 1940s. Advertisement, *Detroit Free Press*, January 6, 1948.

79. *Detroit Free Press*, June 29, 1951; and *Detroit Tribune*, August 11, 1951.

til 1952. It was located on Wyoming, two blocks south of Fenkell, and drew an all-white audience. One frequent visitor was Jack Duquette, who gave this capsule description.

> *It had an all-white audience, but a few black players, like Rudy Rutherford. It was a then-yuppie crowd. A door charge. A bar in the middle and booths. A little lusher than a neighborhood bar like most show bars. A stage was an integral part of the design.*[80]

The youthful audience sometimes bothered more serious listeners like Bob Cornfoot.

> *I remember just before Easter of 1947 [someone] had written a piece in Metronome about jazz in Detroit and when Easter came all the college kids who were home on break jammed the place. Everybody was talking and nobody paid attention to the music. Just before midnight Sammy Carlisi, normally a very quiet player, started to bite down on his reed and started squealing and everybody went wild. Sammy cracked and could not play anymore, and one of the trumpet players had to take over.*[81]

The audience at the Wyoming probably varied depending on the music. Monday nights, for jam sessions with mainstream or modern musicians, *Down Beat*'s correspondent Lou Cramton sensed that "the intelligentsia" came around. On the other hand the "two-beat worshippers" who packed the Wyoming on Sundays were probably recruited more from the middle-class white population.[82]

The Crest Lounge was located just west of Wyoming, outside of the West Side area delimited earlier.[83] It drew a completely white audience with a mixture of nationally recognized Dixieland jazz and vocal groups. The vocal group the Four Freshmen was a mainstay in the 1950s, which were the heyday of the club.

The West Side had a few other minor spots for occasional jazz in the 1940s, but its prime period was really the 1950s.[84]

On the Northeast Side of the city a few clubs opened during the 1940s that featured some jazz. (See fig. 47.) We have already discussed Mickey's Show Bar, which opened in 1944 on Seven Mile Road, the boundary line between Conant Gardens and a white working-class area. In 1949 the Falcon Show Bar opened further east at the corner of Outer Drive and Van Dyke. It was a major spot for dixieland and swing jazz until the late 1950s and featured a few famous black entertainers. The Falcon started out with big names like Louis Armstrong in 1949 and kept that up until the mid-1950s, after which it mainly employed local groups.[85]

Bop Comes to Detroit

The History of Bop

During the years of World War II a new style of jazz was created in a few after-hours spots in Harlem. By 1946 it had become known as bebop, or bop for short.[86] The creators of bop were a circle of young musicians around altoist Charlie Parker, trumpeter Dizzy Gillespie, pianists Thelonious Monk and Bud Powell, and drummers Kenny Clarke and Max Roach. This circle intersected with a smaller circle consisting of established older musicians who shared a progressive or modernist outlook, like tenorists Coleman Hawkins and Lester Young.

What exactly defined the new music in strict musical terms is often discussed. In general the music was more complex in every way—melodically, harmonically, and rhythmically. For example, a steady four-four beat was complemented by off-beat and on-beat punctuations.[87] There was also more freedom for soloists than was typical in the swing era, where arranged big band music was the norm. Thus bop can be seen as just another stage in a slow evolutionary process that describes a progressive history of jazz.

Others see bop as a revolutionary break with the swing past. The revolutionary interpretation of the emergence of bop often brings in the social context of music making, most immedi-

80. Duquette, interview by Bjorn.

81. Bob Cornfoot, interview by Lars Bjorn, Westland, Michigan, March 18, 1991.

82. Lou Cramton, "Detroit," *Down Beat*, May 21, 1947.

83. The Crest was found on Fullerton, close to the intersection of Grand River and Myers.

84. These spots include Chic's Show Bar on Hamilton and Philadelphia, which became a serious jazz spot in 1953, and the House of Joy at 4701 West Warren, which operated intermittently between 1948 and 1952. Advertisements, *Michigan Chronicle*, June 26, 1948; July 19, 1952.

85. Advertisement, *Detroit Free Press*, March 22, 1949.

86. Bernard Gendron, "'Moldy Figs' and Modernists: Jazz at War," in *Jazz among the Discourses*, ed. Krin Gabbard (Durham, N.C.: Duke University Press, 1995), 48.

87. "Bop," *New Grove Dictionary of Jazz*.

ately the changing relationship between musicians and audiences. Whereas swing musicians played music for dancers, boppers played mainly for listeners. The ideal setting for listening would be a jam session or a concert, and both became more common in this period. Compared to swing musicians, the bop innovators were more likely to see themselves as artists, and they were often dissatisfied with the overly commercial nature of swing bands.[88] This interpretation is strengthened when race is factored into the equation. Almost all of the bop pioneers were African Americans, whereas the music business promoting swing was dominated by whites. Bop musicians were a new generation who came to musical maturity around the war years and had a more assertive outlook with regard to their civil rights when compared to previous generations.[89]

The emergence of bop did not kill earlier jazz styles. Rather jazz simply became a more varied musical form. The early 1940s saw a revival of New Orleans jazz, usually labeled Dixieland jazz. Early supporters of dixieland were often dissatisfied with the commercial nature of swing bands and favored a return to the true "folk roots" of jazz.[90] While some of the musicians who were active in this revival were black, almost all of the audiences were white. Big band swing also continued in full force during the first half of the 1940s, but by the second half of the decade a number of forces contributed to its decline.[91] One was simply the cyclical nature of popular taste, which by the latter half of the 1940s had shifted away from instrumental music to vocalists. Some of these vocalists, like Frank Sinatra, got their start with the big bands but could now go out on their own. Other vocalists were from rural musical traditions, country and western music and blues (rhythm and blues), which were now entering the music business.

The center of early bebop experimentation was New York City, specifically uptown (Harlem) and by late 1943 midtown (Fifty-second Street). The combo led by Dizzy Gillespie and bassist Oscar Pettiford at the Onyx Club on Fifty-second Street is generally considered the first bebop band. By February 1944 the first statement of the new music on record appeared, even though not explicitly under the bebop label. That year the first big band with a major bebop component in its repertoire, Billy Eckstine's, was formed. The band included both Parker and Gillespie. Dizzy Gillespie was inspired to create his own big band the following year, but it proved financially untenable, and he returned to a small group format. By late 1945 bebop had carved out a "niche on the periphery of the music business."[92] Its two major figures, Gillespie and Parker, had led a band together on Fifty-second Street, had made their first recordings together, and had also taken their band to Billy Berg's in Los Angeles. This first full exposure of the new music to general jazz audiences outside of New York was not exactly an instant success. Jazz historian Ira Gitler compares it to the negative reaction Gillespie's big band encountered earlier the same year.

> *The reception that Gillespie and Parker received from the public in California wasn't much better than Dizzy's big band got in the South. The difference here was the musicians, who had heard the New York recordings, came to hear their new idols in the flesh. These were the young musicians, but the older, established musicians such as Art Tatum and Benny Carter, came too, as did the Hollywood celebrity crowd. The music, however, was misunderstood in the main. . . . Opening night was big, but as the week went on the crowds diminished, and the hip minority did not order drinks enough to make the cash register ring with any consistency.*[93]

By 1946 the public at large became aware of bebop through a series of media reports about the new "craze." The media emphasized the deviant aspects of bebop: the strange musical

88. Ira Gitler, *From Swing to Bop: An Oral History of the Transition in Jazz in the 1940s* (New York: Oxford University Press, 1985), 4.

89. This is not to say that the beboppers tended to be political activists; rather it might be more accurate to describe their relationship to politics as "oblique at best," as does Scott DeVeaux in a recent study, *The Birth of Bop: A Social and Musical History* (Berkeley: University of California Press, 1997), 26. DeVeaux sees bebop as "an attempt to reconstitute jazz in such a way as to give its black creators the greatest professional autonomy within the marketplace," rather than as a direct rebellion against the music industry (DeVeaux, *Birth of Bop*, 27).

90. Gendron, " 'Moldy Figs' and Modernists," 39.

91. For a good discussion see McCarthy, *Big Band Jazz*, 348–55.

92. DeVeaux, *Birth of Bop*, 364.

93. Gitler, *From Swing to Bop*, 160.

sounds, the language, the drug use, and the personal appearance of some of its musicians and fans, like the beret and goatee worn by Dizzy Gillespie. The term *bebop* was coined, and this gave bebop some limited market potential, which lasted until roughly 1950. As was the case with swing a decade earlier, the music business again favored white over black musicians when this new market appeared.[94]

Bop Pioneers in Detroit

From the very beginning Detroit contributed to the development of bop. Some Detroit jazzmen played with the early bop pioneers in New York and on the road, while others helped form a viable modernist circle of musicians in Detroit after 1945.

The bop pioneers got their start in the national big bands in the late 1930s and early 1940s, and Detroit was part of the circuit for these bands. This meant that Detroit was in contact with what was going on musically in New York and that Detroit musicians were recruited by the name bands. Visiting bands met local musicians backstage, often at the Paradise Theatre, and at clubs and after-hours spots in Paradise Valley. The level of musicianship in Detroit was so high that young talent was continually snapped up. Some Detroit bands acted as virtual transmission belts for bebop talent and none more than the band at the Club Congo in the early 1940s.

The Club Congo Orchestra

This band was an important step in the careers of trumpeter Howard McGhee; tenor saxophonists George "Big Nick" Nicholas, Wardell Gray, and Teddy Edwards; and bassist Al McKibbon. Nicholas, McGhee, and Gray had earlier been members of the Jimmy Raschel territory band, so landing a job at the Club Congo represented a step up.[95]

Both McGhee and Gray were born in Oklahoma, in 1918 and 1921, respectively, but moved to Detroit at a young age. They both attended Cass Tech, as did Al McKibbon (born 1919), but only Gray graduated. McGhee traveled more widely than the others, who tended to stay in the Midwest and in Michigan in particular.[96]

Nicholas was born in Lansing, Michigan, in 1922 and joined Raschel some time between 1940 and 1941.

> *I went to Danville, Illinois [Raschel's home], and joined the band. Burnie Peacock was with us. Raschel sang a little song and we played dance music and arrangements and the main influence was Milt Buckner on piano. He was like an older brother to me and I learned a lot from him.*[97]

When Buckner left the band he was replaced by Detroiter Earl Van Riper who remembered that

> *Raschel had Sonny Stitt, Wardell Gray, and Howard McGhee. We were working in Grass Lake, Manistee, Ludington, Muncie [Indiana], Marion [Ohio] . . . Sonny Stitt was still in High School . . . I went to his graduation. . . . Wardell was the one who used to rave about him [Stitt] all the time. Wardell was about to leave and go with Bennie Carew and Wardell kept talking about Sonny. So we went to Saginaw and went to a football game. . . . Stitt was playing clarinet in this marching band during half-time and I said "I can't hear him!" so we went to this place called the Sunshine Gardens in Saginaw, and Hank Jones is playing and they would not let Sonny in because he was just a kid. They said: "If your mother finds out this place will be closed down . . . but you can come in and play one number. You can come in the back, then you got to get out of here!" When he played he sounded just like Benny Carter; that's what I was telling everybody. . . . He was always a great technician; he was all over that instrument.*[98]

The Raschel band was a band filled with talent, but the Congo orchestra was a further step up the band pyramid that was firmly in place by the late 1930s. The location of the Club Congo

94. DeVeaux, *Birth of Bop*, 440; Gitler, *From Swing to Bop*, 5.

95. This is not to say that the Raschel band was not full of talent as well, but work conditions were not as good in a regional traveling band. Among those who joined the Congo band, Edwards was a relative newcomer to Detroit. He was born in Jackson, Mississippi, in 1924, and in 1940 he came north with his uncle. After a visit to the musicians' hangout the Band Box, he got work on Hastings Street and with bassist Tweed Beard's band.

96. McKibbon played with a number of Detroit groups after leaving Cass Tech: Hans and Ocie Barnet, Monk Culp, and Dave Wilborn. Al McKibbon, interview by Jim Gallert, Hollywood, California, September 29, 1997.

97. Saxophonist Burnie Peacock was born in 1921 and later played with Lucky Millinder and Count Basie. Boyd and Sinclair, *Detroit Jazz Who's Who*, 53.

Earlier Nicholas had played a summer job with the Goofus Connel band in Saginaw, which included two of the Jones brothers from Pontiac: pianist Hank (born 1918) and trumpeter Thad (born 1923). George "Big Nick" Nicholas, *Jazz Oral History Project*, Institute of Jazz Studies, 1980.

98. Earl Van Riper, interview by Jim Gallert, *Jazz Yesterday*, WDET-FM, Detroit, Michigan, September 22, 1990. According to Mark Ladenson, Van Riper was born in Cleveland in 1922 and came to Detroit in 1926. He recorded with Eddie "Cleanhead" Vinson in 1945. Mark Ladenson, "Remembering Wardell," manuscript. Benny Carter's dominant influence on alto players in Detroit at the time is confirmed by Teddy Edwards in an interview in *Cadence*, April 1994. Sonny Stitt was born Edward Boatner in 1922 and grew up in Saginaw. After graduating from Saginaw High School in 1942 he played in Detroit clubs. Fred Reif, "Saginaw Musicians and Composers: The First Fifty Years of the Twentieth Century," manuscript. One of these gigs was with Phil Hill at the Silver Slipper. Teddy Edwards interview, *Cadence;* and Carl Hill, interview by Bjorn and Gallert. He left with Tiny Bradshaw in late 1942 or 1943. Gitler, *From Swing to Bop*, 73.

in Paradise Valley, still a vibrant center of nightlife in Detroit, was part of the equation.

The Club Congo replaced the Plantation Club in the basement of the Norwood Hotel. After its great success throughout the 1930s, the Plantation was closed in 1940, ostensibly for remodeling. In fact the owner, Walter Norwood, had numerous legal problems that cost him the right to "operate a tavern." The Plantation remained shuttered the first half of 1941 while Norwood searched for a partner. He made a deal with Benjamin Franklin "Slim" Jones to hold the liquor license and manage his club. The new club, Club Congo, opened July 5, 1941. Jones brought in Oliver "King" Perry's orchestra from Chicago for the opening, but he then recruited a local band.

The Club Congo was an upscale establishment that continued the "Jungle Nights" theme of the Plantation. For a nominal cover charge, patrons got a full floor show, which included a headline act, chorus girls, a comedian, one or two "not ready for headline status" acts, and music for dancing. The chefs knew their business, and the food was good. "The Congo was a very classy club," pianist Johnny Allen recalled. "There was a bar to the left as you entered from the street. The dance floor was in the middle and was lower [than the surrounding floor]. Tables and chairs were on either side of the dance floor. The bandstand was at the back end of the dance floor, between the kitchen and dressing rooms."[99] "That was a very small bandstand," bassist Al McKibbon recalled.[100] McKibbon, a burly man, had to stand near the front due to the low ceiling. The piano was on the dance floor, and Allen would cue the band during the show. A single microphone was available for singers and saxophone soloists. "The brass would just stand up and play," McKibbon said. "Unless he used a mute, then he'd walk out to the mike."

Veteran producers Leonard Reed or Larry Steele put on the shows, which lasted a little over an hour and usually changed biweekly. Jones brought in national acts that included vocalist Orlando Roberson (formerly with Claude Hopkins), the Mills Brothers, and vaudeville artists like "Sunshine Sammy" Morrison. "[The Club Congo] featured a full floor show, with dancers, comedians, and a headline act," McKibbon said. "Time for the show, we played a fanfare, the emcee came out. After the show, we played for dancing." The American Federation of Musicians (AFM) branch in Detroit, Local 5, was strong, and union membership was required. "We worked from 9 to 2, seven nights, matinee on Sunday," McKibbon recalled. "I think I got paid $17.50 per week."

Following the grand opening, Detroit drummer/vibraphonist Kelly Martin brought in a 12-piece band.[101] Martin was then leading a quartet at Buffalo James's popular Frogs Club. When Jones sounded him out about the job, Martin jumped at the chance. "We played at Buffalo James' place," Al McKibbon remembered. "Me, Kelly, Ted Smith [guitar], George Saunders [piano]. Kelly said, 'I got a chance to open the Club Congo with a big band. We'll be the nucleus of the band.'" He took his group, minus pianist George Saunders, and built the Club Congo orchestra around it.[102] Dave Spencer was slotted for the piano chair, but he failed to show for the critical "first rehearsal," and trumpeter Howard McGhee, already recruited, recommended Johnny Allen to Martin, who promptly hired him.

Allen (born 1917) grew up in East Chicago, Indiana, and caught Earl Hines's radio broadcasts from the Grand Terrace nightclub in Chicago. The sound of Hines's band, and the leader's unique keyboard style, deeply impressed young Allen. Allen tried to capture the fresh, crisp sound of the Hines orchestra in his orchestrations for the Congo band. He wrote four-beat arrangements of current pop tunes and jazz numbers such as "Second Balcony Jump" (composed by Earl Hines's arranger,

99. Johnny Allen, interview by Jim Gallert, Detroit, Michigan, February 8, 1984.

100. McKibbon, interview by Gallert.

101. Martin, born in Lake City, South Carolina, September 16, 1914, moved to Detroit with his family around 1927. He worked with McKinney's Cotton Pickers in 1932–34 and later spent several years with Cecil Lee's band. Martin took lessons during his stay at the Congo from vibraphonist Milt Jackson. Kelly Martin, interview by Jim Gallert, *Jazz Yesterday*, WDET-FM, Detroit, Michigan, October 27, 1989.

102. Saunders became the pianist in the Paradise Theatre pit band.

Fig. 55. Club Congo Orchestra, 1941.
Back row, L to R: Al Hayse, tb; "Red" Mitchell; Youngblood Davis; Lester Currant, tp; Kelly Martin, dms/ldr; Al McKibbon, bs. Front row: Alonzo "Stack" Walton, ts; Joe Moxley, as; Bill McCall, as; Lorenzo Lawson, ts; Johnny Allen, pno; Ted Smith, gtr; Orlando Roberson, vcl. Note the Count Basie–style seating of the reeds (ts/as/as/ts).
(Courtesy Al McKibbon, Gallert Collection.)

Jerry Valentine) and "C Jam Blues." Trumpeter Lester Current also arranged music for the band but "It wasn't as 'heavy' as what we'd been doing," McKibbon said. Howard McGhee contributed "McGhee Special," which he had written on an earlier job with Allen. Allen gave solo space to most of the musicians, except Al McKibbon, in his arrangements. "Bass players didn't solo back then," McKibbon remembered. "Only Blanton, and maybe Milt Hinton."[103]

Earl Hines influenced Allen's keyboard style, but he discerned a difference between the playing of Hines and Detroit-style piano.

> *As a soloist, Earl was one of the very first to "free up" the left hand from playing straight "stride." I don't think people in Detroit were too much into Teddy Wilson and Earl Hines. "Detroit style" piano came more from the East, stride piano.*[104]

The musicians' talents, the rigorous schedule, and Allen's arrangements helped the band jell into a cohesive unit, one that could execute tricky show arrangements and swing out. "We had a hell of a band," said McKibbon. "Once, Cab Calloway's band played the Paradise. The acts on the bill came over to the Congo with their music. Everybody but us was worrying about whether we could play the charts. We ate that music up." Howard McGhee, assessing the band 40 years later, agreed. "That band was swingin'. We had all the big names comin' in, all the cats that didn't have bands. . . . nobody knew none of us, but we were playin'."[105]

The Club Congo Orchestra developed a distinctive sound, as McKibbon recalled. "We played like Lunceford, we played like Basie, but we sounded like ourselves." In the opinion of Teddy Edwards, "We were a jazz band." The

103. Jimmy Blanton was with Duke Ellington's orchestra from late 1939 until his (premature) death in 1942. He was featured on many of Duke's recordings, for example, "Jack the Bear" and "In a Mellotone." Milt Hinton, featured with Cab Calloway's band from 1936 to 1951, solos on "Pluckin' the Bass."

104. Johnny Allen, interview by Gallert.

105. Gitler, *Swing to Bop*, 87.

Fig. 56. Club Congo Orchestra (partial), ca. 1941.
Howard McGhee, tp; Kelly Martin, dms; Joe Moxley; Bill McCall; Lorenzo Lawson, reeds; Ted Smith, gtr.
(Courtesy Al McKibbon, Gallert Collection.)

Congo band was seen as a harbinger of things to come by the younger musicians in the city. And, like Earl Hines's band, the Club Congo Orchestra served as Detroit's incubator for the incipient musical style later dubbed "Bebop" by the music press. "We weren't playing Bebop then," Edwards said. "But it was in the air."[106]

Many talented musicians worked in Martin's band. Some, like McGhee and trombonist Al Hayse, stayed only a few months. Allen, McKibbon, and Ted Smith were with the band until the club closed.[107] Teddy Edwards joined in the spring or summer of 1942 on alto sax and clarinet, replacing Burnie Peacock. Edwards, Alonzo "Stack" Walton, and Lorenzo Lawson comprised the reed section when Edwards joined.[108]

In 1943, Wardell Gray and George "Big Nick" Nicholas replaced Walton and Lawson.[109] Gray doubled on alto and tenor. He shared the tenor solos with Lawson and later with Nicholas. "Wardell was in transition at that time," Johnny Allen recalled. "He was sounding more like Chu Berry than Lester Young. Lorenzo sounded more like Prez."

Gray met Jeruth (Jeri) Walker, a dancer at Club 666, and the two became romantically involved and later married. Walker, a teenager at the time, remembered that Gray was

> *Very, very quiet and very articulate and very neat. He couldn't stand to see anything out of place. Before the band would set up, he would make sure that all the stands were right in a row. I just worshipped Wardell Gray. . . . we'd go out for food someplace, but most of the time we stayed at home in the bed. Sometimes he would sit in with Warren Hickey, Youngblood [Edwin Davis], Billy Frazier.*[110]

Howard McGhee, 23 years old, was heavily featured, and he impressed all who heard him, as Al McKibbon related.

> *Lionel Hampton came to town. Karl George was in the trumpet section, and he called Kelly up and said, "Hey man, you got a band; I'll*

106. Teddy Edwards, interview by Jim Gallert, Detroit, Michigan, April 26, 1997.

107. McKibbon went to New York, where he worked with Thelonious Monk's trio on Fifty-second Street. He also recorded with Lucky Millinder (1944), J. C. Heard, and Coleman Hawkins (1946), among others. In 1947 he joined Dizzy Gillespie's big band.

108. Edwards left Detroit in 1944 with the Ernie Fields orchestra. Mark Stryker, "A Jazz Legend Returns to Detroit after 51 Years," *Detroit Free Press,* June 28, 1996. Allen was drafted in 1943 and after returning to Detroit went on the road with the Lucky Millinder band in 1947. He replaced Sir Charles Thompson. Johnny Allen, interview by Gallert.

109. Lawson was a very impressive saxophonist in the eyes of many. He played briefly with Louis Armstrong and on returning to Detroit led his own groups for years, for example, at the Bizerte. One reason for his unfulfilled promise could have been the difficulty many had in working with him. Al Martin, interview by Lars Bjorn, Detroit, Michigan, August 2, 1993; Perkins, interview by Gallert; Jackson, interview by Bjorn and Gallert; Paul Foster, interview by Jim Gallert, Detroit, Michigan, February 10, 1991.

110. Jeri Gray, interview by Jim Gallert, Detroit, Michigan, October 26, 1994.

come down and play lead." "Fine," said Kelly. Karl came down, and after he heard Howard McGhee he never took his horn out (laughs). Howard had that strong lead. He was a high note player, played all kinds of stuff. Sounded like Roy Eldridge. He took practically all of the trumpet solos.[111]

Club Congo prospered; the shows were well produced, and the band made an impression on Detroit's hip nightlife crowd. The Congo became, in Teddy Edwards's opinion, "the hottest place in town." Also, the band regularly broadcast over radio station WWJ. There was a sense of community within the band; the guys liked playing together and enjoyed playing Allen's arrangements. There were funny moments, too, like when Teddy Edwards walked out front to solo on "C Jam Blues." "As I turned to play, the bell of my clarinet dropped off," he chuckled. "The whole band cracked up."

Shortly after the club's one-year anniversary (July 1942), Kelly Martin quit. According to Al McKibbon, Martin asked Slim Jones for a raise. "He said, '*NO!*'" McKibbon chuckles. "Kelly got mad and quit his own band!" Martin remembered it differently. "Slim Jones wanted to cut the band down to 9 pieces. I agreed only if the money would stay the same. He said 'no,' and I left."[112] Martin moved to New York and became best known as Erroll Garner's drummer (1958–64).

After Martin quit, newspaper ads list different musicians or the current headline singer as leader, but Johnny Allen remained music director and chief arranger. Amos Woodward first and, later, Vernon Brown filled the drum chair.[113] "He used to swing the shit out of the band," McKibbon said of Brown.

Club Congo's heyday lasted until November 25, 1942, when Slim Jones died at Harper Hospital after "a long illness." After Jones's passing, Norwood's problems escalated; he began a prison term for "conspiracy to violate gaming laws" three months later, which effectively closed the club until after the war.[114] The musicians kept a close eye on business at the club and stayed current on their wages. "We kinda knew something was up when they lost the liquor license," said Allen. "Without one, business fell off." Club Congo continued its downward spiral for several months. The end came suddenly but not unexpectedly. "We played a job at the Graystone from midnight to 2:00 A.M., and when we got back to the Congo, the place was locked up," Allen remembered. Club Congo is not listed in the Detroit telephone directories after October 1943. The site remained closed until Club Sudan opened on March 23, 1946.[115]

Of all the members of the Congo orchestra McGhee had the most direct impact on the course of bebop. He was an important sideman on classic recordings by both Coleman Hawkins (1945) and Charlie Parker (1946–47). Gray, who left Detroit in 1943 to join Earl Hines's orchestra, also recorded with Parker and McGhee.[116] Interestingly enough, McGhee, Gray, and Edwards played central roles on the modern jazz scene in Los Angeles after 1945.[117] Another key player on LA's Central Avenue was tenorist Lucky Thompson, who grew up on Detroit's East Side.

East Side Bop: Lucky and Bags

Two other important sidemen to Charlie Parker grew up together on Detroit's East Side: tenorist Lucky Thompson and vibraphonist Milt Jackson. Their musical talents were so plentiful that the pull of a musical career gave them trouble finishing high school. Their musical careers did differ in this regard: Thompson fit the already mentioned career pattern of going from national big bands into bebop, whereas Jackson's career illustrated another possible route into the new music.

Thompson described growing up near Hastings Street in an interview with *Cadence* in 1982.

111. George (born 1913, St. Louis, Missouri) spent most of the 1930s in Detroit with McKinney's Cotton Pickers and Cecil Lee's orchestra.

McGhee and Hayse left town with Hampton. McGhee's stay was short lived, as his salary was considerably lower than the $70 a week he had been drawing with Martin. He may have rejoined Martin's band following his stint with Hampton. He soon went with Andy Kirk's orchestra. DeVeaux, *Birth of Bop,* 197–98. McKibbon, interview by Gallert.

112. Kelly Martin, interview by Gallert.

113. Vernon Brown, was, according to McKibbon, "a big light-skinned fellow from Seattle." McKibbon actually preferred the drumming of his future brother-in-law J. C. Heard, with whom he attended Cass Tech, over that of Martin or Brown. "J. C. was a much 'hipper' drummer." McKibbon, interview by Gallert.

114. Norwood was sentenced to 1–5 years for conspiracy to violate gaming laws, a misdemeanor. He served 3 1/2 years at the Southern Michigan Prison at Jackson.

115. Club Sudan did not have a liquor license.

116. Jeri Gray claims she "got him his first big job. He had left the Club Congo and was working with Bennie Carew up in Lansing [Michigan]. He would play with the Jones brothers, Sonny Stitt on his nights off. . . . I started dancing at the Three Sixes with Teddy Buckner's band and Earl Hines came in one night and I told him, 'you should hear my boyfriend play saxophone' and he said 'what does he play?' and I said 'tenor saxophone.' He asked me if he could play alto. . . . I said, 'yeah.' So he gave me his number and I gave it to Wardell, and a week later Wardell was in Chicago with Earl Hines." Jeri and Wardell married while Wardell was with Hines. Jeri Gray was later hired by Hines to "travel with the girls, Sarah Vaughan and the Blue Bonnets, because they really didn't know how to dress too nice." Gray, interview with Gallert.

117. Ted Gioia, *West Coast Jazz: Modern Jazz in California 1945–1960* (New York: Oxford University Press, 1992), chaps. 1 and 3.

Fig. 57. Ted Buckner Orchestra, Club 666, 1943. *Ghandi Robinson, pno/arr; Al McKibbon, bs; Kelly Martin, dms; Buckner, as/ldr; Willie Wells, tp; Billy Frazier, as/bar; Henry Purifoy, tp; Tubby Bowen, ts; Youngblood Davis, tp.* (Courtesy Rilla Buckner.)

> *I lost my mother at a very early age—I was five. . . . In my home you could go to almost any block and you would hear people all day long playing. . . . It was a beautiful atmosphere. In elementary school [Bach School on Kirby near Hastings] they came up with a program with free music for everyone who could buy an instrument. . . . I had such a love for music that I was studying it myself. I ran errands and got myself enough money to buy a saxophone book. . . . I saw an old broom of my father's in the corner— so I chopped off the bristles and carved the main line of a saxophone into the hands. I carved keys into it and I couldn't do much with the side but imagine it. It's from that broom handle and that book that I got all my fingering on the saxophone. I read music all through the sixth grade. . . . My father could not afford an instrument and the first time he saw me playing he laughed out loud and if my love for music had been a fraction less, then it would have all been over.*[118]

Thompson finally got an instrument and was soon gigging around town with (among others) the King's Aces big band. This big band was made up of teenagers and played for teenage dances in ballrooms along Woodward Avenue, according to pianist Alma Smith. The band at one point included Milt Jackson, Willie Anderson, and Lucky Thompson.[119] Thompson also played with Smith and trumpeter Willie Wells in a band at Uncle Tom's Plantation, where they backed the floor show.[120]

He dropped out of the most prestigious high school in the city, Cass Tech, to support himself as a musician. He played with altoist Ted Buckner's band, "because he was so very much a professional." Buckner had spent six years with the Jimmie Lunceford orchestra and upon returning to Detroit in early 1943 became a bandleader at Club 666, one of the top jobs in Paradise Valley. The band backed the shows and also played for dancing.[121] It was from this job that Thompson left town with Lionel Hampton's orchestra in 1943.[122] By the following year Thompson was a member of the Billy Eckstine orchestra, where he also did small group num-

118. Christopher Kuhl, "Lucky Thompson: Interview, Part I," *Cadence,* January 1982.

119. Alma Smith, interview by Lars Bjorn, Detroit, Michigan, August 26, 1998. Smith visited the Thompson household along with other children, and part of the attraction was the meat brought home by Lucky's father, a meat packer. Mr. King was more of a businessman than a musician according to Smith. Smith replaced Anderson on piano with the King's Aces, and this version of the band also included bassist Al Martin and drummer Tim Kennedy. Al Martin, interview by Bjorn.

120. This band also included George Washington on bass and Al Harper on drums. An occasional member was trumpeter/French hornist Julius Watkins. The gig lasted a couple of months some time in 1941 or 1942. Smith left Detroit for California in 1945 with the Counts and Countess trio, which played in a Nat King Cole style. After some recordings Smith returned to Detroit in 1948 to play with Rudy Rutherford at the Parrot Lounge. Smith, interview by Bjorn.

121. *Michigan Chronicle,* November 27, 1943.

122. Kuhl, "Lucky Thompson: Interview."

Fig. 58. Lucky Thompson, publicity still, ca. 1951. The inscription is to Paul Foster and Alma Smith, who were recently wed.
(Courtesy Alma Smith, Gallert Collection.)

bers with Parker and Gillespie.[123] When Gillespie took Parker to California in 1945 he also hired Thompson.

Milt Jackson came from a family with more resources and especially strong ties to the church. His older brother Alvin, born in 1921, remembered what the Church of God in Christ on Adelaide was like.

> *They had a band in church . . . they called the Powerhouse. Five pieces; my father [Manley, a deacon in the church] played guitar. . . . They played every Sunday so that it was like the Power of Paradise. . . . It stopped everybody, because women of the evening was on the block; they were bootlegging next to the church. But when we had our services everybody came in.*

Manley Jackson played a number of instruments, and all of his six children played some instrument. They also sang.

> *How we started out: I sang and Milt played the piano or guitar; we were known as the Jackson brothers. . . . we were singing in all the churches all over the city. . . . we would sometimes sing with Sister Rosetta Tharpe. . . . I was 12, something like that. . . . My brother won a contest at 10 years old at the Plymouth Congregational Church for $10 . . . big bucks then. . . . he happened to win playing the organ which he had never played before.*

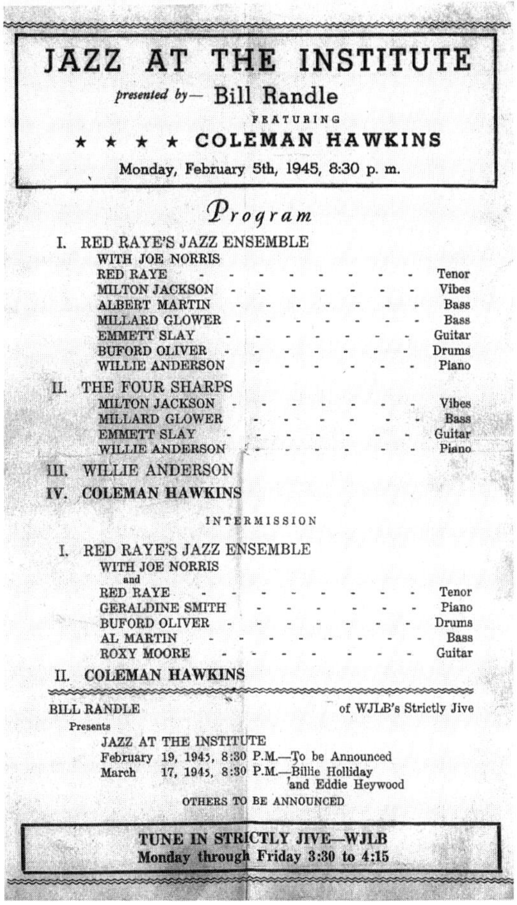

JAZZ AT THE INSTITUTE
presented by— Bill Randle
FEATURING
★ ★ ★ ★ COLEMAN HAWKINS
Monday, February 5th, 1945, 8:30 p. m.

Program

I. RED RAYE'S JAZZ ENSEMBLE
WITH JOE NORRIS
RED RAYE - Tenor
MILTON JACKSON - Vibes
ALBERT MARTIN - Bass
MILLARD GLOWER - Bass
EMMETT SLAY - Guitar
BUFORD OLIVER - Drums
WILLIE ANDERSON - Piano

II. THE FOUR SHARPS
MILTON JACKSON - Vibes
MILLARD GLOWER - Bass
EMMETT SLAY - Guitar
WILLIE ANDERSON - Piano

III. WILLIE ANDERSON
IV. COLEMAN HAWKINS

INTERMISSION

I. RED RAYE'S JAZZ ENSEMBLE
WITH JOE NORRIS
and
RED RAYE - Tenor
GERALDINE SMITH - Piano
BUFORD OLIVER - Drums
AL MARTIN - Bass
ROXY MOORE - Guitar

II. COLEMAN HAWKINS

BILL RANDLE of WJLB's Strictly Jive
Presents
JAZZ AT THE INSTITUTE
February 19, 1945, 8:30 P.M.—To be Announced
March 17, 1945, 8:30 P.M.—Billie Holliday and Eddie Heywood
OTHERS TO BE ANNOUNCED

TUNE IN STRICTLY JIVE—WJLB
Monday through Friday 3:30 to 4:15

Fig. 59. Program for "Jazz at the Institute" at the Detroit Institute of Arts, February 5, 1945.
Millard Glover's and Emitt Slay's names are misspelled.
(Courtesy Bob Setlik, Gallert Collection.)

Miller High School was another important musical training ground for the Jackson brothers.

> *At Miller we had a dance band. . . . the teacher's name was Louis Cabrera. . . . We would play for the other schools for dances, and we'd get paid $7. As a 14-piece band we would travel to the other schools, so actually we were professional all through school. . . . Milt played the xylophone in school; when my father bought him some vibes he could carry around, that's what he played with Art Mardigan all around in these clubs. . . . In those days they had "Swinging Clubs" for teenagers and just served ice cream, sodas, and we worked all kinds of spots for kids like that.*[124]

123. DeVeaux, *Birth of Bop*, 347.

124. Jackson, interview by Bjorn and Gallert.

Fig. 60. Bill Randle jam session, Club Sudan, 1946. *Alvin Jackson, bs; Joe Messina, gtr; Phil Hill, pno; Milt Jackson, vbs.* (Photo: Bob Douglas ©.)

The Miller dance band of the late 1930s was also a training ground for Yusef Lateef (Bill Evans), Lorenzo Lawson, and trombonist Frank Rosolino. Rosolino and drummer Mardigan were white, and both became important figures in modern jazz.[125] Rosolino remembered Miller and Jackson.

> *They had a stage band and a small group that we could play in. . . . It was great. The students at the school were 85–90% black. So I grew up in that environment, with jazz music around me all the time; this is where I developed a natural feel for it. . . . I guess the music that Milt and I were playing in school was considered Swing style . . . but there were a lot of jam sessions, a lot of small groups and places to play.*[126]

After about a year of playing in the Army Special Services, Jackson was back in Detroit in early 1944.[127] Local radio disc jockey Bill Randle heard him and hired him for the first of several jazz concerts on September 30, 1944.[128]

> *Bags [Milt] had just joined Ted Buckner . . . at the Club 666. Bags was playing the most tattered set of vibes I had ever seen, an octave and a half outfit held together, literally, by paper clips, rubber bands and string. The sound he got on the instrument was incredible and his playing was remarkably fresh and exciting. A few weeks [later] he was selected for the first jazz concert in Detroit held at the sacrosanct Detroit Institute of Arts. . . . Bags later formed a group with [pianist] Willie Anderson. This group, the Four Sharps, played an important role in the early Detroit modern jazz scene and was the rhythm section basis, with Art Mardigan added, for a number of important early jazz concerts . . . In March of 1945 Dizzy Gillespie was brought to Detroit for his first jazz*

125. Both were born in Detroit, Mardigan (Mardigian) in 1923 and Rosolino in 1926.

126. Les Tomkins, "Frank Rosolino Talking," *Crescendo International,* August 1973. Rosolino was drafted in 1944 and returned to Detroit in early 1946. Probably some time in 1945 he sat in with Charlie Parker at the Three Deuces on Fifty-second Street. Gitler, *Swing to Bop,* 140.

127. One of Jackson's first jobs was with Kansas City bandleader and entertainer George E. Lee. They played in Flint and at the Ace Bar on Hastings Street. Advertisement, *Michigan Chronicle,* July 5, 1941; Whitney Balliet, "Like a Family," in *American Musicians II* (New York: Oxford University Press, 1996), 314. Interview with Teddy Edwards, *Cadence.* He also led his own group, Milt Jackson and His Rhythm Boys, at Uncle Tom's Plantation in 1942. Advertisement, *Michigan Chronicle,* December 5, 1942.

128. See advertisement in *Michigan Chronicle,* September 30, 1944. Randle's *Strictly Jive* program on WJLB featured jazz in many forms and lasted from 1942 to 1948. He also ran a record store and promoted concerts. In 1949 Randle moved to Cleveland and became a very influential popular music disc jockey. Aunt Enna, "Bill Randle's Story: From Cool to Hot to Luke Warm . . . Turning the Tables!" *Down Beat,* May 7, 1952.

Fig. 61. Willie Anderson trio, Club 666, ca. 1947. *Anderson, Paul Foster, Billy Burrell.* (Photo: Bob Douglas ©.)

concert anywhere. . . . Dizzy was concerned first about the ability of local jazzmen to back him on the date. After 15 minutes of running down "Groovin High," "Dizzy Atmosphere," "Shaw Nuff" etc., Diz was ecstatic particularly about Willie and Bags. It was after this concert that Dizzy took Milt to New York.[129]

Randle's concerts were well attended; he had a large following and an arrangement with Al's Record Mart to sell tickets.[130] In addition to jazz, Randle presented left-wing authors and current political figures.

It was very political, very hip. All the shows were always sold out. I had nine or ten shows at the DIA [Detroit Institute of Arts] before they threw me out. They threw me out because they said the audience was a little "rowdy;" they left marijuana cigarettes in the john.[131]

The other members of the Four Sharps were Millard Glover on bass and guitarist Emitt Slay.[132] Glover gave Jackson the nickname Bags on account of the look of his eyes after too many nighttime club visits.[133] The Four Sharps were partly inspired by the then very influential (Nat) King Cole's trio. Jackson put it this way: "We did commercial vocals. I sang and the bass player sang." Willie Anderson's piano style has often been compared to that of Nat Cole's, and

129. Bill Randle, liner notes, Ray Charles and Milt Jackson, *Soul Brothers,* Atlantic Records 1279 (LP).

130. Al's (at 1450 Broadway) was "the place in town for jazz and classical records," according to Randle. "They supplied most of what I played on the air." Bill Randle, telephone interview by Jim Gallert, April 9, 2000.

131. Ibid.

132. Slay was born in Jackson, Mississippi, in 1917. When he applied for membership in Local 5 in 1943 he claimed to have worked with Louis Armstrong and the Cats and the Fiddle. American Federation of Musicians, Local 5, Membership Files. Slay led a Nat Cole–style trio with Willie Anderson off and on in the late 1940s. In the 1950s and 1960s he played blues and rhythm and blues with his Slayriders and had a hit with "My Kind of Woman" on Savoy in 1952. Frank Taylor, interview by Jim Gallert, Detroit, Michigan, January 6, 1991; and Roland Hanna, interview by Lars Bjorn, Ann Arbor, Michigan, February 8, 1992. Pianist Johnny Allen replaced Willie Anderson in the Slay trio at the Sudan in 1946 and remembers Slay as someone who could sing ballads or blues. Johnny Allen, interview by Gallert. Tenorist George Benson worked frequently with Slay in the 1950s and respected him as a leader and a musician: "Emitt was a good guitar player and had good ears. He wasn't a great singer, but he could sing well enough—blues, popular material. He was more of a jazz player than a blues player, but he would play whatever was popular at the time." George Benson, interview by Jim Gallert, Detroit, Michigan, December 29, 1998.

133. Milt Jackson, interview by Ed Love, *Ed Love Show,* WDET-FM, Detroit, Michigan, March 7, 1994.

Fig. 62. Emitt Slay trio, Club Sudan, summer 1946. *Slay, gtr; Willie Anderson, pno; Paul Foster, bs.* (Courtesy Alma Smith, Gallert Collection.)

like Cole he was stylistically a transitional figure between swing and bop. The group played the Civic Center, the Cotton Club and the B & C in late 1944 and the first half of 1945.

Willie Anderson (known as Willie A) was the premier modern pianist in Detroit in the 1940s according to many aspiring modernists like Tommy Flanagan.[134] Flanagan thinks Anderson combined Nat Cole's piano style with the fluidity of Art Tatum and managed to do so in spite of the fact that he did not read music. Others also liken him to Cole, no doubt because after the Four Sharps disbanded he used Cole's trio instrumentation: piano, guitar, and bass. Guitarist Kenny Burrell's brother Billy was a regular member of the trio, and Kenny used to sit in with them.

> *At the Club Sudan there was a very informal atmosphere in the late forties. Even though I think the trio was hired for the gig, it was really like an open jam session, so I really had a lot of chances to sit in. . . . I owe Willie Anderson a great debt, and I am very grateful for the opportunity he gave me. . . . Willie Anderson was phenomenal. . . . He had such a distinctive style of his own that [the trio] didn't sound like Nat Cole at all. Billy, even though he was strongly influenced by Charlie Christian,*

134. Flanagan, interview by Bjorn; Beans Richardson, interview by Lars Bjorn and Jim Gallert, Detroit, Michigan, May 31, 1990; Hindal Butts, interview by Lars Bjorn, Detroit, Michigan, July 29, 1993; Bess Bonnier, interview by Lars Bjorn, Detroit, Michigan, June 10, 1991. See also Sadik Hakim, "Reflections of an Era: My Experiences with Bird and Prez," *Jazz Journal* (August 1996).

Fig. 63. Bill Randle "Strictly Jive" concert, Detroit Institute of Arts, May 25, 1945. *Coleman Hawkins, ts; Willie Anderson, pno; James Glover, bs; Art Mardigan, dms. This was Hawkins's second appearance at the DIA.* (Photo: Bob Douglas ©.)

> *began to develop his own style as well. They had a very distinctive sound. I wish they would have gotten a record contract; I think they would have made it.*[135]

Bassist Paul Foster worked with Anderson in Emitt Slay's trio and later in Anderson's trio with Billy Burrell. He remembered Anderson as

> *Very much an introvert. He was intense inside. He was very aware of everything around him, but he didn't have much to say. Emitt sang; he was commercially oriented. Willie hardly talked, let alone sang. He was a nice person, big heart. He could play anything. . . . if you could hum it, he could play it. Had perfect pitch. When he played, he didn't need anybody else. Willie didn't want to leave Detroit—wouldn't go by himself. I used to tell him to go, and then send for us if it was appropriate.*[136]

Several major jazz artists, like Benny Goodman and Coleman Hawkins, tried to get Anderson to leave Detroit, but he remained in the city until his death at age 47 in 1971.[137] Barry Ulanov heard him in 1956 and was as impressed as he was on his visit to Detroit in the 1940s.

> *I had forgotten what a wit Willie is. . . . he's a Count Basie with 10 fingers, filling in with more notes and ideas than you or I ever thought could be sandwiched in-between the familiar measures of a "Billy Boy" or "Caravan" or anything else. . . . Not streams of meaningless notes, mind you, but delicate little phrases, counter-melodies in miniature, notes that are more like comments if you know what I mean. And Willie's right hand . . . has a looseness which only the great concert pianists usually possess or an Art Tatum may have. And with*

135. Kenny Burrell, interview by Jim Gallert, Detroit, Michigan, December 1, 1991. The trio did make two records for Jamboree and Fortune in 1947. Anderson also recorded two titles with drummer Charles Johnson's group for Prize records.

136. Paul Foster, interview by Gallert.

137. Others were Duke Ellington and John Hammond. Paul Foster, interview by Gallert. John Hammond nominated Anderson for Esquire's "All-American Jazz Band," but his was the only vote (Paul E. Miller, ed., *Esquire's 1945 Jazz Book* [New York: A. S. Barnes, 1945], 64). This is probably why Anderson often was touted locally as an "Esquire Award Winner."

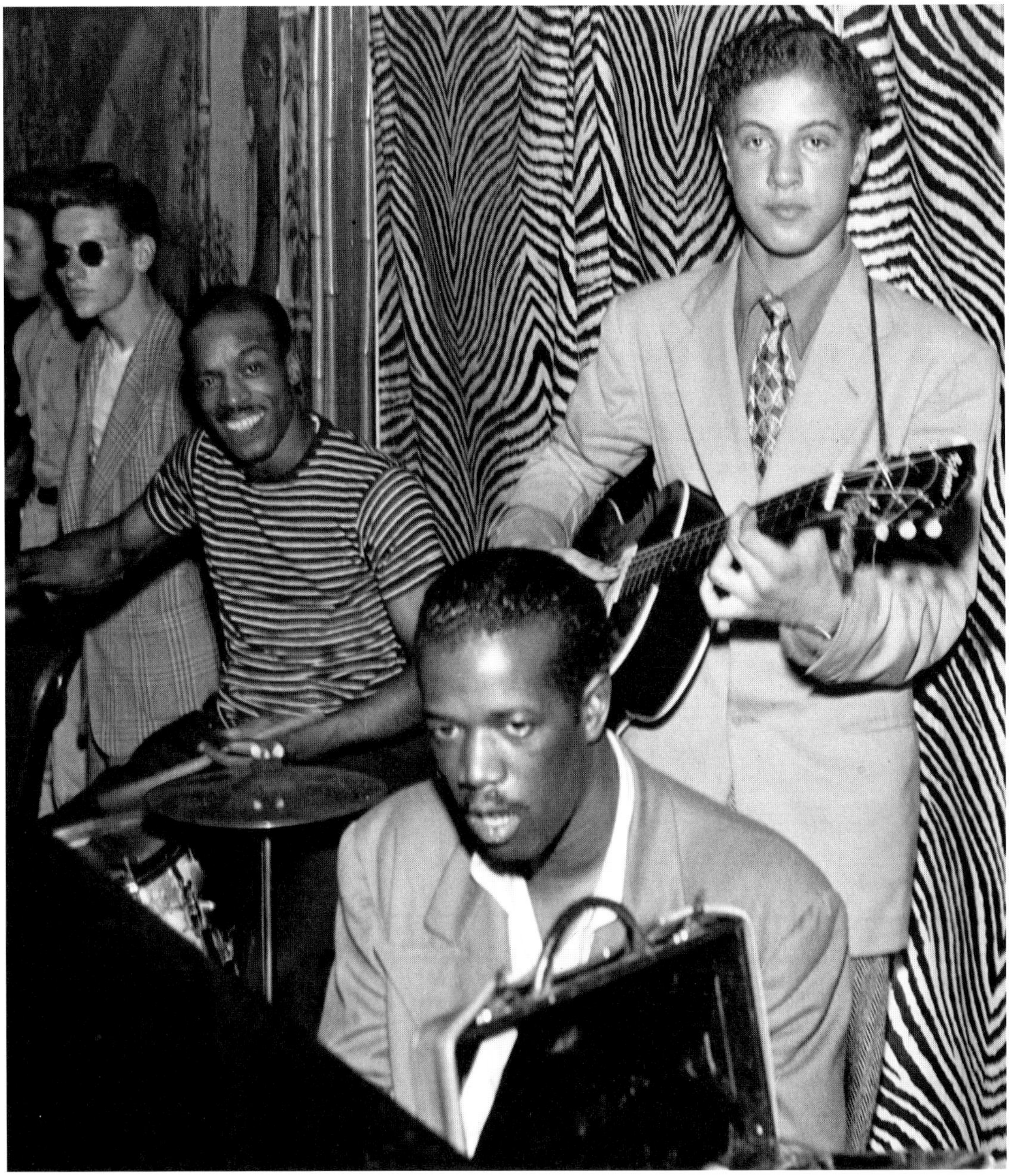

Fig. 64. Jam session, Club Sudan, 1946.
Jo Jones, dms; Willie Anderson, pno; Kenny Burrell, gtr.
(Photo: Bob Douglas ©.)

it, always, the steady beat, not pounded but insistently propelled by his left hand. Quite a musician.[138]

Anderson's playing also impressed a later generation of Detroit musicians. Kenn Cox (born 1940) was 15 years old when he first heard Willie Anderson and was "fascinated with his playing." Cox wanted to take lessons from Anderson, and other musicians told him to just go over to his house but to be sure to take a bottle of Anderson's favorite wine. This Cox did, and he spent the afternoon seated next to Anderson at the piano.

> *He didn't say anything. Being a holdover from the swing era, he thought of the left hand a lot differently from the latter-day pianists. He showed me some things about stride piano, a "cheat" guide. He wasn't quite Tatumish, more like Garner. I actually thought of him more like Nat "King" Cole.*[139]

138. Barry Ulanov column, *Down Beat,* April 18, 1956. Ulanov saw Anderson at Lavert's with the Paul Foster trio.

139. Kenn Cox, interview by Jim Gallert, Ferndale, Michigan, February 29, 2000. Cox came to prominence in the 1960s with the Contemporary Jazz Quintet.

The Four Sharps played local clubs and further DIA concerts and in jam sessions. Jackson was a frequent participant in jam sessions, hence the bags under his eyes. Willie Anderson often accompanied him to the Bizerte as pianist Earl Van Riper remembers

> *When I got out of the service [1945] I was working the Bizerte Bar and Willie would come by every night and I used to love to hear him play. I worked with whoever got there first! Milt Jackson, [tenorist] Tommy Burnette, Edwin Davis, [drummer] Dave Heard. . . . Whoever got there first was the bandleader!*[140]

Another favorite spot for informal sessions that year was the Civic Center, which was the location for jams following Bill Randle's concerts at the Art Institute. One such jam included many of the participants in the January 12 concert, which featured Art Tatum, the Four Sharps, and a "jam band" led by Art Mardigan.[141] The Civic Center had held regular jam sessions on Wednesday nights since 1944.[142]

By October 1945 the Four Sharps disbanded when Jackson left for New York to join the Dizzy Gillespie Sextet with Charlie Parker.[143] Jackson was a member of the group when it made its fabled trip to California. They recorded several classical sides in February 1946 in Los Angeles, and included on the date was Lucky Thompson. On returning to New York Jackson joined Dizzy Gillespie's newly formed big band as one of its major soloists.

Jackson's rapid adaptation of bebop without a lengthy apprenticeship in a touring national band was perhaps partly due to his exceptional musical gifts: perfect pitch and a photographic memory. But other factors were probably also at work. Jackson has himself remarked on the musical environment in Detroit of the early 1940s.

> *The Detroit environment in the early 1940s was very beautiful. I wish they could have kept that environment and enhanced it. The environment of the 1940s in Detroit was very similar to the environment of 52nd Street when I first came to New York.*[144]

Fig. 65. Bill Randle "Strictly Jive" concert, Schubert Lafayette Theater, March 11, 1945.
Bassist Paul Szglaggi played his fingers raw keeping the fast tempos Gillespie set.
(Photo: Bob Douglas ©.)

Detroit had a similar, but smaller, setup of nightclubs, after-hours spots, and concert venues compared to that on "the Street." Similarly, Detroit had experienced bandleaders, like Ted Buckner, who liked to take youngsters with new ideas, like Jackson and Thompson, under their wings.

A Modernist Circle Develops

As BEBOP BECAME more widely disseminated through recordings and visits by its flag bearers, a generation of musicians grew up who claimed the bebop language as their own. Many of Detroit's bop pioneers came back to the city for briefer periods, and this provided an immediate inspiration for the younger musicians.

Most musicians first heard the new music on record, and the experience was often earth shattering. A good illustration is provided by pianist Harold McKinney (born 1928), who first

140. Earl van Riper, interview, Graystone International Jazz Museum, *Community Jazz History Series: Earl van Riper,* 1989. Larry Gabriel, producer (video). See also *Metronome,* October 1945. Dave Heard was a drummer like his brother J. C. Heard.

141. "Tatum Thrills Thousands at Jazz Concert," *Michigan Chronicle,* January 20, 1945; and Barry Ulanov, *Metronome,* June 1946.

142. These sessions were led by Jimmy Davenport. *Michigan Chronicle,* July 7, 1944; August 5, 1944.

143. Before going to New York that band played in Washington, D.C. Balliet, "Like a Family," 314.

144. "Milt Jackson Interview," *Cadence,* May 1977.

Fig. 66. Bill Randle broadcasting over WJLB-AM, Club Sudan, 1946. *Doug Mettome, tp; unidentified, bs; Art Jordan, dms; Leo Osebold, ts.*
(Photo: Bob Douglas ©.)

heard bop around 1946 from a juke box in a confectionery in his West Side neighborhood.

> *These guys were sitting there with their knees crossed . . . and they said: "Hey baby, play A-25 and then hit B-30!" . . . That stuff hit me like an electrode to the base of my brain; I jumped around like a jack-in-the-box, the music tickled my innards; it was a magical form of music! . . . Parker, Diz, John Lewis . . . "One Bass Hit" . . . I was never the same since. Dropped almost all of my leanings to become a classical musician. . . . I became centered and focussed by the bebop tradition: it converted me into a young black boy.*[145]

Records were a major tool for learning the new music. Countless hours were spent trying to figure out how the new music was produced. Pianist Bess Bonnier remembered meeting fellow pianist Tommy Flanagan at Northern High School.

> *I was practicing on an upright piano in Room 323 during my 8th hour. Tommy would always appear, so we became friendly. . . . Downstairs there was a phonograph with variable speed so we would listen to Charlie Parker becoming a tenorist so we could pull the stuff off the record.*[146]

The overall impact of the early records by Parker and Gillespie on local musicians can be gauged from the observations of a visiting jazz writer. *Metronome* magazine's Barry Ulanov visited Detroit around May of 1946 and found that

> *[Detroit has] got enough Parker imitators on alto and Dizzy Gillespie copyists on trumpet to put those two esteemed gentlemen in business as a kind of hot Meyer Davis agency. Even the trombonists and tenor-men play Be-bop. It's astonishing: it is also progressive and refreshing.*[147]

The records also helped build an audience for modern jazz. The public success of Randle's DIA concerts, which included several modernists, indicated that there was the beginning of a modern jazz audience in Detroit as early as 1945. By early 1946 Ulanov concluded that

> *Detroit jumps. It jumps best after hours, at the Club Sudan, where Willie Anderson plays a lot of piano. . . . The Sudan is also the site of Bill Randle's jam sessions. One of these is an exhilarating experience, an amazing demonstration of the intense interest of Detroit's jazz fans in the music of their choice. . . . At the rate [the Sudan sessions] are going now, with broadcasts from them over Bill's station, WJLB, and audiences literally hanging over the lobby, the stairs and into the street, they should make jazz history. No other town that I know can boast such enthusiastic response to sessions.*[148]

The jam sessions at the Sudan were really just a continuation of Randle's *Strictly Jive* in-studio broadcasts at WJLB-AM.

> *They were parties, great parties. All the musicians used to come up. I'd bribe the elevator operator. We had two huge grand pianos. . . . musicians would come over and play those pianos. I had all the guys playing on the air. We had beer there. I was alone, just me and the board operator. . . . We'd start Friday night and never quit until Sunday morning. I mean, we'd sleep in the studio. At the Sudan, we had jam ses-*

145. Harold McKinney, interview by Lars Bjorn, Detroit, Michigan, April 2, 1991.

146. Bonnier, interview by Bjorn.

147. Barry Ulanov, "Jazz in Detroit," *Metronome*, June 1946.

148. Ibid.

sions. We used to broadcast them live for four hours. I used to have sessions there all the time. One time I had . . . Lionel Hampton's band and half the guys from Stan Kenton's orchestra. There was no liquor there; it came in the back door.[149]

When Parker and Gillespie finally came to the city with their own groups in 1947 the audience response was even more enthusiastic than at the Sudan.[150] Music promoters must have sensed this since Parker and Gillespie were booked for a total of two months in Detroit in 1947. This banner year for bebop started with the Gillespie big band at the Paradise Theatre in February. The *Michigan Chronicle* headline was "Hot Music Stirs Re-Bop Disciples into Near Riot."

Apparently angered when they clamored "Open the Door Richard" and the doors failed to open, a mob of re-bop disciples and music lovers bashed in the box office window and unhinged several doors at the Paradise Theatre Saturday. . . . The mob of adults and teenagers reached near riot proportions when patrons who entered the theater early Saturday morning failed to leave before time for the jam session at 5 P.M. The crowd began arriving at 10 A.M. and apparently intended to remain in their seats to hear the jam session. . . . Milt Herman, publicity director for the theater, said he sold 500 tickets in a half hour. . . . 600 people were in line at 1 P.M. . . . A short time later four police cars were called to assist the theater police. . . . when the audience who had seen the one show refused to leave the trouble started. . . . it took two hours to disperse the crowd.[151]

In April Howard McGhee came back to Detroit as a member of Norman Granz's Jazz at the Philharmonic concerts, and the *Michigan Chronicle*'s reviewer commented that the full house was

Proof that the be-bop school of music (or modern jazz) is becoming more clearly understood and appreciated by the layman was very evident by the capacity house. . . . the outstanding musician was Howard McGhee, local boy who is said by some music critics to be king of re-bop trumpeters. . . . the audience was the most receptive and responsive of any JATP session yet held in Detroit. . . . the yearly increase in attendance is evidence that Detroiters are becoming more musically conscious and appreciate the modern school of jazz, sometimes called re-bop.[152]

There were also indications that the attire of bebop audiences was different from that of other jazz audiences. When Milt Jackson and Sonny Stitt returned to Detroit for a concert in late 1947 the reviewer made note of the "cardigan jackets, hornrimmed glasses and goatees" in the audience and on stage.[153]

Thus Detroit had both modern musicians and an audience for the music. The two joined at jam sessions, as at the Sudan or the Bizerte,[154] and for concerts, as at the DIA or the Paradise, but what about more permanent jobs in nightspots? As we have seen, the late 1940s saw the rapid expansion of nightspots in many parts of the city. Employment opportunities were fewer for black than for white musicians, but they were expanding for all. Whether you saw yourself as a bebopper or not, if you were a young musician with the requisite skills you had plenty of work. And the work was rewarding even if you played with musicians more interested in playing swing music for dancers. Not until 1948 do we find the emergence of what is often thought of as the prototypical modern jazz club: a place with modern jazz only for listening. The Blue Bird Inn came closest to this prototype, and tenorist Billy Mitchell compared working there to work in other clubs in Detroit in the 1940s.

I was working with groups that were playing in clubs that were more show-oriented than actually jazz-oriented. Not all of them. In a lot of them, we were the show. . . . As far as show, man, we played music and the trumpet player sang, but that was it, that was the show. . . .

149. Randle, interview by Gallert.

150. Parker and Gillespie had both visited Detroit as sidemen before 1945. Parker came to the Paradise Theatre with Jay McShann in 1942 and with Earl Hines in 1943. His Paradise Theatre visit with Hines was noteworthy because he was fired after the engagement. According to Teddy Edwards, Parker "would be nodding but came out just in time to play. He came out to go to the microphone and knocked the music stand over, music all over the stage." Interview with Teddy Edwards, *Cadence*. Gillespie visited the Paradise as a member of the Billy Eckstine orchestra in November 1944. Gillespie, "the king of the trumpet," and Sarah Vaughan, "lovely ballad stylist," were advertised as the main figures in the band besides the leader, " 'Jelly Jelly' Star" Eckstine. Advertisement, *Michigan Chronicle*, November 11, 1944.

151. *Michigan Chronicle*, February 22, 1947.

152. The concert took place in the Music Hall. "Howard McGhee Scores in Jazz Concert Here," *Michigan Chronicle*, April 19, 1947.

153. *Michigan Chronicle*, December 6, 1947.

154. The Bizerte had Tuesday night jam sessions from about 1946 to 1948. An ad in 1946 encouraged listeners to come "hear big band stars blow with local boys" on those nights. On other days Lorenzo Lawson's group was featured with blues singer Alberta Adams for much of this period. Advertisements, *Michigan Chronicle*, November 30, 1946; December 25, 1948.

Fig. 67. Sudan sextet, Club Sudan, ca. 1946.
Phil Hill, pno; Earl Young, tb; Paul Szglaggi, bs; Doug Mettome, tp; Art Jordan, dms; "Box" Kroeger, ts.
(Courtesy L. Adrian.)

There was some jamming going on, but the time of the extended solo—Bird and them brought in different things. . . . For example, in those days it was almost an unwritten law that you played two choruses and then sat down. Whereas today, two choruses, ain't nobody took a deep breath yet. . . . That era came for us in Detroit . . . when the Blue Bird era started.[155]

The Blue Bird was the end result of the development of a modernist circle of players in the 1946–48 period. A detailed look at the activities of two modernist bandleaders from 1946 to 1948 will give us a sense of how this circle of bop players emerged.

Art Mardigan returned to Detroit in the middle of 1946 after spending about a year in New York with the Georgie Auld big band. In New York he had shared an apartment with pioneering bop drummers Stan Levey and Max Roach, and his drumming impressed those who heard him when he came back to his hometown.[156] Barry Ulanov had this to say about Mardigan's jam session group in River Rouge.

If you go out to the River Rouge Show Bar on a Sunday afternoon, you may find the city's and one of the country's best drummers, Art Mardigan. You'll certainly find Doug Mettome, a talented trumpeter who needs discipline and experience, and a less slavish attitude to Dizzy. You'll find Leo Osebald, a 15-yr old tenor man, with enough tone and technique and taste to indicate a very large future.[157]

Mettome was 21 when Ulanov heard him, and he lived in Detroit in the mid-1940s.[158] His bebop credentials were good enough to land him a job with Billy Eckstine, as Bill Randle has

155. Gitler, *From Swing to Bop*, 262.

156. "Art Mardigan," *New Grove Dictionary of Jazz*.

157. Ulanov, "Jazz in Detroit."

158. Mettome was born in Salt Lake City in 1925 and probably came to Detroit in 1945.

Fig. 68. Concert, unidentified setting, Detroit, ca. 1946–47. *Willie Anderson, pno; Warren Hickey, ts; James Glover, bs; Art Mardigan, dms; Youngblood Davis, tp; Kenneth "Cokie" Winfrey, ts.* (Photo: Bob Douglas ©.)

it: "Miles Davis heard Doug Mettome play with [pianist] Bobby Stevenson and persuaded Billy Eckstine to add him to the band. And Billy already had five trumpet players."[159]

The same group Ulanov heard at the River Rouge jammed at Club Sudan on Mondays in 1946, when it also included pianist Phil Hill.[160] The Sudan had opened up in March 1946 as the successor to the Club Congo. It was open until 5 A.M., and jamming took place on the nights the Willie Anderson trio played as well as on Monday nights.

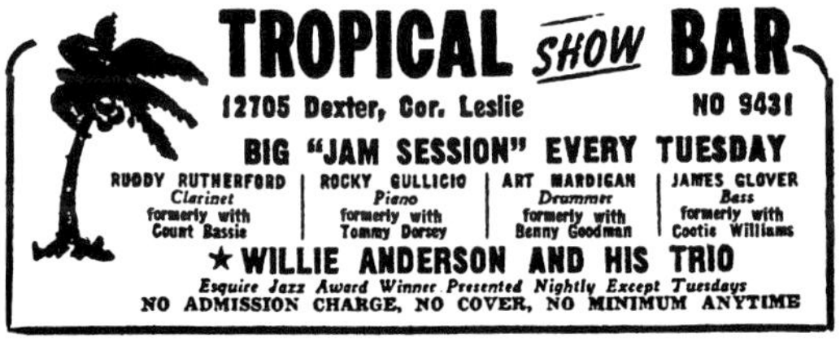

Fig. 69. Advertisement for the Tropical Show Bar. (From *Detroit Free Press*, February 17, 1948.)

By spring of 1948 Mardigan had moved his jamming over to the Bowl-O-Drome for Tuesday night sessions. The Bowl-O-Drome by then had become the home of Willie Anderson on other nights of the week.[161]

Mardigan was also a frequent participant in concerts: one in late 1946 at the DIA with Ted Buckner, Willie Anderson, and Edwin Davis and another in early 1947 with Sarah Vaughan at the Detroit Federation of Women's club.[162] A major event was his participation in a February 1948 concert at the Masonic Auditorium with several bebop stars: Charlie Parker, Milt Jackson, and trumpeter Fats Navarro. Detroit bassist Jimmy Glover also took part.[163] Mardigan had returned briefly to New York at the end of 1947 and recorded some classic bebop sides with Navarro and Dexter Gordon.[164]

Edwin Davis, like Art Mardigan, spent some time with a major big band and then returned to Detroit. In Davis's case it was the Benny Carter band that he recorded with in 1944.[165] By May 1945 he was back in Detroit and participated in a DIA concert as a member of Art Mardigan's sextet. This concert also featured the Coleman Hawkins group en route to California. *Metronome*'s Detroit correspondent had this to say about Davis.

> *Then there was Edwin Davis, trumpet, a graduate of Cass Tech . . . [who] has a very nice tone color on the more melodic tunes and shows that he is definitely influenced by Gillespie when he blows on jump numbers. This boy, as well as [Willie] Anderson, could stand watching, both may develop.*[166]

Davis's promise as a trumpeter was never completely fulfilled, but he became a central

159. Randle, liner notes, Charles and Jackson, *Soul Brothers.* Mettome left with Eckstine around New Year's Day 1947 (*Down Beat,* January 15, 1947). His most memorable recordings in the 1940s are those he did with Benny Goodman's orchestra ("Undercurrent Blues" from 1948) and small group ("Blue Lou" from 1948). Mettome and Wardell Gray were a major part of the King of Swing's much discussed effort to incorporate bebop into his repertoire. Jim Burns, "Doug Mettome," *Jazz Journal* (June 1975). He joined Woody Herman in 1950 and was sometimes referred to as "the White Dizzy." By the accounts of his fellow band members he was a brilliant trumpeter, when his substance abuse was under control. William D. Clancy and Andrea C. Kenton, *Woody Herman: Chronicles of the Herd* (New York: Schirmer Books, 1995), 169.

160. Lou Cramton, interview by Lars Bjorn, Ann Arbor, Michigan, June 2, 1991.

161. Advertisements, *Detroit Free Press,* April 27, 1948; July 23, 1948.

162. The Buckner group also included Jimmy Glover on bass. "Alto Star Slated for Jazz Matinee," *Detroit Free Press,* November 29, 1946. Other participants in the Vaughan concert were tenorist Sam Carlisi, pianist Bobby Stevenson, bassist Louis Popp, and Vaughan's husband and musical director, George Treadwell. *Michigan Chronicle,* March 15, 1947.

163. Other participants included Flip Phillips (tenor saxophone) and Jimmy Jones (piano). Roy Stephens, "Sarah Vaughan, Bird and Fats Spark Bash," *Michigan Chronicle,* February 14, 1948.

164. This recording by the Dexter Gordon quintet was done on December 22, 1947, for Savoy Records and can be found on Fats Navarro, *Nostalgia,* Savoy MG 12133 (LP).

165. Jorgen Grunnet Jepsen, *Jazz Records, 1942–1969* (Holte, Denmark: K. E. Knudsen, 1963).

166. Don Hodges, "'It Happens in the Best of . . . ,' Detroit Concert Jumbled," *Metronome,* July 1945.

Fig. 70. Leonard Morrison band, Club 666, 1948. *Johnny Allen, pno/arr; Frank Taylor, as; Morrison, bs/ldr; Frank Porter, as; Richard Moran, dms; Billy Horner, tp; Billy Mitchell, ts.* (Courtesy Mrs. C. Morrison, Gallert Collection.)

figure in Detroit's bop world. He was often the leader of groups of young musicians in concerts and at dances and sometimes at clubs. The latter was an achievement because there were few regular club dates led by modernists in 1946 and 1947. Davis led a group at Club Deliese in early 1946, and Ulanov was impressed with the

> *fine musicians in the band: Phil Hill, a brilliant block-chord pianist; Leon Rice, properly described in Michigan as "a very fly drummer," fast and light and even.*[167]

Davis was also able to get work for his group at dances, which shows that bebop was not strictly for listening. Some of these were Saturday night dances at the "Turntable" at the Civic Center, where the live bebop alternated with recorded hits.[168] Davis also had to work as a sideman much of his time in Detroit. Two of these gigs were major concerts: one appearance with Lester Young's quintet at the Masonic Auditorium (November 1946) and another with Ted Buckner and Willie Anderson at the DIA.[169] His major club date as a sideman was with tenorist Candy Johnson and his Peppermint Sticks in the winter of 1947–48.[170] Johnson had played with Andy Kirk's big band and decided to settle in Detroit by this time. He was a swing-style tenorist who knew how to entertain an audience with a combination of ballads, blues, and jump numbers, much in the style of Illinois Jacquet. *Michigan Chronicle* reviewer Roy Stephens described what he heard in an article

167. Others in the band were saxophonists Tommy Burnette and Warren Hickey. Ulanov, "Jazz in Detroit"; *Michigan Chronicle,* April 6, 1946.

168. " 'Turntable' Attractive to Bop Set," *Michigan Chronicle,* November 27, 1948.

169. The Young concert featured Young's sextet plus Ike Quebec and also the Willie Anderson trio. *Michigan Chronicle,* November 9, 1949. The Buckner group at the DIA featured Willie Anderson, James Glover, and Art Mardigan. "Alto Star Slated for Jazz Matinee," *Detroit Free Press.*

170. Other members of the group included Leonard White (bass) and William Benjamin (drums). *Michigan Chronicle,* October 11, 1947. Davis also worked as a sideman in altoist Gene Nero's Emperors of Swing at Arturo's on Woodward in 1945. *Michigan Chronicle,* May 26, 1945.

entitled "Candy Johnson Combo Gets in Modern Groove."

We offer one bit of advice to the fully competent tenor sax artist: for the cliches of Jacquet (those screeches and squeaks) substitute your own ideas. They're good enough. The combo at the Royal Blue Bar jumps. . . . Johnson's musical repertoire contains everything from the standard 12-bar blues themes, the customary novelties, to the excitingly modern scores from the pen of John Birks, the Dizzy one. Standout soloist, of course, is Edwin "Youngblood" Davis whose phrasing and trumpet technique are such that a lot of musicians ought to lend an ear to the "Blood." [171]

He also must have played with Ted Buckner's house band at the Frolic Show Bar. The regular trumpeter with the Buckner group was Willie Wells, another modernist with big band experience. Wells spent 1945–47 with the Fletcher Henderson orchestra.[172] In the fall of 1947 Davis recorded eight titles with the Ted Buckner orchestra for the local Staff label (later picked up by King Records).[173] Davis briefly went back to New York but was back in Detroit in September 1948 to lead a group at the Sudan. These performances were announced as a "Bop Opera," but the Sudan did not seem to provide anything like a concert setting. Most importantly this was a big break for two promising teenagers: Tommy Flanagan (18) and Kenny Burrell (17), who had the chance to perform with Detroiters with modern credentials. The *Chronicle*'s Roy Stephens commented on the music and the Sudan in an article called "Progressive Jazz Delightful."

Fig. 71. Advertisement for the John R–Erskine Center Ballroom.
(From *Michigan Chronicle*, November 6, 1948.)

Sessions presented Mondays at Club Sudan by Edwin "Youngblood" Davis and his invigorating group of young musicians are indicative of the direction toward which modern music is moving. For more than three years this thing called "bop" has puzzled thousands, irritated more and satisfied comparatively few. . . . the group on Mondays have "great" reputations among followers of modern jazz in Detroit. . . . They have agile forward-looking minds, a seriousness of purpose and an intent to master their instruments. . . . the combo included . . . Davis, Kenny Burrell (guitar), Tommy Flanagan (piano), Jimmy Richardson (bass), Leon Rice (drums). . . . guest star Lucky Thompson blew some magnificent tenor sax choruses on a beautifully woven "Sophisticated Lady." . . . The only possible distraction at Club Sudan . . . [is] the congestion which makes it a bit difficult to enjoy the subtle sounds coming from the bandstand. . . . the listener has to elbow his way near the bandstand . . . and lean against another listener.[174]

The Davis group at the Sudan changed personnel from one night to the other, but all the musicians were modernists no older than their

171. *Michigan Chronicle*, October 11, 1947.

172. Rucker, interview by Bjorn and Gallert. Allen, *Hendersonia*, 573.

173. The classical discography by Jepsen, *Jazz Records*, lists a trumpeter named Lewis Youngblood and a tenorist named Edwin Davis. More than likely this is simply one person: trumpeter Edwin "Youngblood" Davis. Others on the October 23, 1947, date are Neil "Ghandi" Robinson (piano), Jimmy Glover (bass), and "Big John" Johnson (drums). Vocalist Bobbie Caston is featured on four numbers. One of the instrumental songs is "Frolic Jump," probably named after the Buckner group's long engagement as a house band at the Frolic.

174. *Michigan Chronicle*, October 23, 1948.

late twenties. Alvin Jackson was one of the oldest at 27 yet part of something new.

The atmosphere at the Sudan was beautiful. We were the tops in the city at the time, Youngblood's beboppers; we were the young thing. . . . all the other bands were like Todd Rhodes . . . [and] Maurice King.[175]

French horn player Julius Watkins was the same age as Jackson and also a sometime member of the group. He had spent three years on the road playing trumpet with a nationally known band (Ernie Fields).[176] But it was probably Lucky Thompson's presence that dignified the group most. Thompson had become a major presence on the LA scene after his recordings with Parker. He returned to New York around the beginning of 1948 and also made his first of many trips to France.[177] Still he decided to come back to Detroit for a few months, as he was to do so several times in the next decade. Saxophonist Pepper Adams was another young member of the circle around Thompson, and in 1980 he remembered that

Lucky Thompson . . . came back to Detroit. I think it was in 48. He only spent a few months there. And we put together I think it was about a nine- or a ten-piece band. He had been obviously putting in a lot of time writing the book for it, he put in a lot of time rehearsing it, and only played a few gigs. It was all so difficult—well one, with that big a band; two, we can't play in a bar because there are about 4 people in it that are under age. Everything was stacked against it. When we worked in his band he was very kind to us, you know. I've always had a good feeling for him about that. He's had a lot of trouble in his lifetime, one thing and another.[178]

Tommy Flanagan played his first gig around 1945 with trombonist Frank Rosolino at the Bowl-O-Drome. He recalled that around that time

I started to meet well-known musicians around the city. This was the first time I really started hearing Charlie Parker. At this high school, in another part of town, the kids were a lot hipper than people from my part of town. [Flanagan attended Northern High School.] They were already into Bird. It was a little more affluent neighborhood, so they had the bread to buy the records. I used to hang out with them. It was the first time, other than a jukebox, that I got a chance to hear young kids trying to play this stuff. . . . Plus with four solid years of piano behind me I thought I could pick it up pretty quick, and I could. . . . At that time I was trying to play like Bud [Powell] and Hank [Jones] and Art Tatum; I was trying to fuse them all together. I practiced a lot at home or woodshedding at other people's houses. There were a lot of sessions going on in Detroit at that time too. I remember [pianist] Barry Harris [born 1929] coming over to my house or going over to somebody else's house. There was a real workshop feeling going on all over, with these all-day kinds of things.[179]

Barry Harris had very similar memories of those days.

The setting when we were growing up was unbelievable. Cats were playing all over the place. We didn't have segregation or integration. We weren't aware of it. Our families lived in houses, and we jammed a lot. In my home, there was always music going on.[180]

In another interview in 1977 Harris recalled that

My mother started me playing the piano. . . . I learned my first piece when I was 4 years old and she showed it to me. She plays well today, though she's half blind. . . . she's the one. My mother was a church pianist. That's how I grew up playing for the little choir, playing for Sunday School, stuff like that. . . . When we started High School [Northeastern], we got our little band together, went to an amateur show [at the Paradise Theatre], won first prize, started getting little jobs.[181]

Some of these jobs were at school dances and the Civic Center. Harris remembered that "be-

175. Jackson, interview by Bjorn and Gallert. Pianist Harold McKinney is also of the opinion that the Davis group was the first bebop group in Detroit. Harold McKinney, interview by Bjorn.

176. *Michigan Chronicle,* September 18, 1948.

177. Doug Norwood, liner notes, Lucky Thompson, *The Tenor Sax of Lucky Thompson: The Beginning Years,* IAJRC 1001 (CD).

178. Philip Hanson, "Pepper Adams: Detroit Roots," *Jazz Journal International* 33, no.1 (January 1980).

179. B. Primack and R. Dubin, "Detroit's Triple Gift to the Jazz Piano World," *Contemporary Keyboard* 12 (1979).

180. John S. Wilson, "Old Friends Bring Detroit Style to Series at Heavenly Restaurant," *New York Times,* January 23, 1981.

181. Allen Lowe, "Barry Harris," *Down Beat,* July 14, 1977.

bop was all we ever did. Tommy (Flanagan) was a little better than me. I didn't know I was older than Tommy until much later on. I always figured he was older because he and Kenny Burrell were the best of us, you know."[182] Like Flanagan, Harris played one of his first gigs with Frank Rosolino at the Bowl-O-Drome. Harris remembered that "it was a hip place. I remember the drummer Tiny Kahn came in."[183] Eventually he became one of the pianists for the Sudan affairs.[184]

Parker and Gillespie at the El Sino

Visits to town by the bebop pioneers were also inspiring events for younger musicians. Flanagan remembered that

> *I heard Charlie Parker with a small group—Miles, Duke Jordan, Tommy Potter and Max Roach—and it was great. I wasn't old enough to go in, but I could stand right by the side door, which was a better place to hear than being in the club.*[185]

The occasion was the Parker quintet's performance at the Club El Sino in Paradise Valley in the two last weeks of 1947.[186] The El Sino had just opened up that spring as the descendant of Club Owens.[187] During its first year of existence it featured Parker's group for two weeks and Gillespie's big band for two two-week stands.[188] The new music was presented along with what Club Owens, and before that the B & C, always had: a large dance floor and two floor shows per night (Larry Steele's dancers and singers). One of the chorus girls was Betty Carter.

> *At that time be-bop was the thing. You know how everybody in Detroit really latched into the new music. Sonny Stitt, Charles Greenlee, Tommy Flanagan, Barry Harris, and Yusef Lateef. . . . I came in contact with all these musicians. Dizzy Gillespie's first engagement in Detroit was at the El Sino club. Every time I came out to catch him at the club, he would ask me to sing with the band. . . . I ended up getting a job in the club, which really helped me. The next stint was when Charlie Parker came into the club. . . . We were supposed to rehearse on a Friday afternoon at about one o'clock and we waited until five o'clock for Charlie Parker to show up. It looked like he would never show. . . . The first person Bird saw when he showed up was me, and he grabbed me and said: "Do you know where I can find something to eat?" I was speechless! I said, "There's a restaurant across the street." He had never seen me before, and he never really looked at me. . . . Larry Steele had a chorus line at the club, which included . . . Charlie Parker's ex-wife. . . . Parker was rehearsing them with "Hot House," "Confirmation" and all these fast things. Those poor girls were kickin', and it was really something to see. How those girls managed the week I don't know! . . . Everybody came to hear Charlie Parker rather than to see Larry Steele's chorus, so the line had to suffer. It was one beautiful experience! After Bird discovered I could sing, it became a thing: "Come on up and sing!" I would go on up there and do my thing. . . . That's how I really got started. It's the chief reason I feel the way I do about jazz. . . . After that it was Lionel Hampton, and he got me with the band because I was modern. I had that bebop feeling he was trying to get at that particular time.*[189]

Another singer, Sheila Jordan, had the following reaction on first hearing Parker's music.

> *I thought I had a convulsion. . . . it was an unbelievable feeling. . . . it took my breath away. It was like someone hit me in the chest; I had tears in my eyes. This is what I want to be around. What a revelation!*[190]

The Parker quintet's stay at the El Sino was also memorable because some classical recordings took place. On December 21 the group recorded four sides for Savoy Records.[191]

The Gillespie band's El Sino engagements in

An Invitation to Paradise Valley Detroit's Newest, Finest Black & Tan
CLUB EL SINO
1730 ST. ANTOINE
PHONE: CL 1730
CONTINUOUS SHOWING
★ CHARLEY PARKER and his ORCHESTRA
Also LARRY STEELE REVUE ★ 6—DAZZLING DANCERS—6
DANCING EVERY NIGHT—No Cover Charge, Except Week-Ends—NO MINIMUM

Fig. 72. Advertisement for Club El Sino.
(From *Detroit Free Press*, December 26, 1947.)

182. Harris and Flanagan were close in many ways. One was that they shared a piano teacher, Mrs. Gladys Dillard. Barry Harris, interview by Lars Bjorn, Ann Arbor, Michigan, November 6, 1998.

183. Michael Bourne, "Barry Harris: Keeper of the Bebop Flame," *Down Beat*, September 1985.

184. Harold McKinney, interview by Bjorn.

185. Stanley Dance, "Tommy Flanagan: Out of the Background," *Down Beat*, January 13, 1966.

186. Advertisements, *Detroit Free Press*, December 19 and 31, 1947.

187. Advertisement, *Michigan Chronicle*, April 26, 1947.

188. The Gillespie big band was at the El Sino June 5–19 and November 21–December 4, 1947, according to advertisements in the *Michigan Chronicle*.

189. Taylor, "Betty Carter," 272–74.

190. Jordan, interview by Bjorn.

191. The tunes were "Bird Gets the Worm," "Klaunstance," "Another Hair-Do," and "Bluebird." Gitler, *From Swing to Bop*, 259.

Fig. 73. Jam session, Club Sudan, 1946.
Dave Heard, dms; Willie Anderson, pno; "Pancho" Hagood, vcl.
(Photo: Bob Douglas ©.)

June and November were also homecomings for two Detroiters in the band: Milt Jackson and vocalist Kenny "Pancho" Hagood. Hagood sang ballads in a way that later earned him the nickname the "Sepia Sinatra." He also sang scat with Gillespie on popular numbers like "Oop-Pop-A-Da."[192]

Two other significant modernists also appeared at the El Sino during its first year: tenorists Gene Ammons and Illinois Jacquet. Both were pioneers in the school of hard-hitting saxophone honkers who combined the modern sounds of bebop with danceable backbeats. On October 4, 1947, Ammons was part of a Detroit recording date with baritone saxophonist Leo Parker in which they recorded "El Sino," a slow blues penned by Detroit trombonist Charles Greenlee.[193] This tribute to the club is reminiscent of the well-known "Walkin,'" made famous by Miles Davis.[194] While Greenlee was not part of this recording, Howard McGhee was as he was in town for a Jazz at the Philhar-

192. Hagood was born in Detroit in 1927 and left in 1944 with the Benny Carter band. After returning to Detroit he joined the Gillespie band in 1946. Obituary, *Detroit Free Press*, November 11, 1989. Barry Ulanov, "Pancho!" *Metronome*, August 1948.

193. Greenlee was not part of the session but was in Detroit around this time. He had been a member of Dizzy Gillespie's big band in 1946 and returned to New York and the Gillespie band in 1949. He later changed his name to Harneefan Majeed.

194. Bob Porter, liner notes, Gene Ammons, *Red Top: The Savoy Sessions*, Savoy SJL 1103 (LP).

monic concert the same day.[195] Leo Parker was also part of a recording with other members of the Jacquet band for the local Sensation label in 1948. This recording also featured Sonny Stitt, as Joe Newman recalled.

> *We did a record in Detroit early one morning with Sonny Stitt and [Illinois's brother and trumpeter] Russell Jacquet. It was his record. Russell stayed up with Sonny Stitt all night to make sure he made the record date 'cause Stitt was strung out. We used to go to Detroit all the time with that band. They really loved us there.*[196]

Fig. 74. El Sino photo card. (Courtesy Lars Bjorn.)

Stitt seems to have spent about half a year in Detroit from late 1947. He was the headliner for a "Special Bebop Session" at the Mirror Ballroom on Thanksgiving night. Milt Jackson and Rudy Rutherford also participated along with some younger Detroiters, including bassist Jimmy Glover and drummer Dave Heard.[197] In June 1948 Stitt led a modified lineup of this group in another Sensation recording session under the name Lord Nelson and His Boppers.[198] The major soloist on these four sides was Stitt, while Willie Wells and Will Davis were held to brief appearances. Stitt generally displayed the Parker influenced alto style that he had developed at least three years earlier, by the time of his classic recordings with Dizzy Gillespie.[199] There were also reminders of his major early influence on the alto, Benny Carter, particularly on "Stardust."[200] Stitt was developing his own version of these masters, and his accomplishments were recognized by critics a year earlier when he was voted New Star on the alto by *Esquire*.[201]

Even though the El Sino survived until 1962 it never again reached the musical heights of its first year of existence, when it was a true bebop haven.

The Blue Bird Turns to Bop

The Blue Bird Inn on the Near West Side had music intermittently in the late 1930s, but in the fall of 1948 it presented modern jazz for the first time and was to do so into the early 1970s.

In contrast to the Sudan, which had dancing for those over 18, the Blue Bird was a bar and had to enforce the drinking age limit of 21. The Blue Bird was a neighborhood tavern, similar to the Bizerte, except that it featured strictly modern jazz several days a week. It eventually outlasted the Bizerte. In the process the Blue Bird turned into a musicians' hangout.

A notice in a *Michigan Chronicle* column in October 1948 announced that "The Blue Bird Inn is making a bid for the younger 'over 21' set with a group of modernists, including pianist Phil Hill and Abe Woodley, brilliant vibe and piano star." The group also included altoist Eddie Jamison, bassist Jimmy "Beans" Richardson, and drummer Art Mardigan. This group was the house band at the Blue Bird for about two years and in 1948 played regularly Thursday through Sunday and Blue Monday jam sessions.

Phil Hill was born in 1921, grew up near the

195. The Ammons group played the El Sino for a week starting October 2. The other participants in the recording were pianist Junior Mance and bassist Gene Wright, both from the Ammons group, and drummer Chuck Williams. The four sides recorded on the date can be found on Ammons, *Red Top*. See also *Michigan Chronicle*, October 4 and 11, 1947.

196. This recording also included trombonist J. J. Johnson and baritonist Leo Parker, probably the most prominent modernists on either instrument. Gitler, *From Swing to Bop*, 259. Sensation Records was one of the few local record companies and is discussed in the seventh chapter.

197. The group also included Charles Greenlee (trombone), Warren Hickey (tenor saxophone), Alvin Jackson (bass), and George Jenkins (drums). *Michigan Chronicle*, December 6, 1947.

198. The group included Milt Jackson (vibraphone), Willie Wells (trumpet), Will Davis (piano), Jimmy Glover (bass), and Dave Heard (drums). These recordings are available on an English CD release called *The Roots of Modern Jazz: The 1948 Sensation Recordings*, Boplicity, CDBOPD 017.

199. Stitt always maintained that he developed his alto style independently of that of Charlie Parker and that when he first met Parker in 1942–43 they sounded alike. Miles Davis is one of the people who supported this view. Gitler, *From Swing to Bop*, 74. If so, his style must have changed rapidly since a year or two earlier, when Teddy Edwards and Earl Van Riper heard him. Both describe his style as being very close to that of Benny Carter. See note 98.

200. Jim Burns, "Early Stitt," *Jazz Journal* 22, no. 10 (1969).

201. Roger House, "Sonny Stitt: A Fond Remembrance," *Coda*, Issue 221 (1988).

Fig. 75. Eddie Jamison's last name is mistaken and Art Mardigan's and Abe Woodley's names are misspelled in this advertisement for the Blue Bird Inn. (From *Michigan Chronicle*, February 26, 1949.)

Blue Bird, and attended Cass Tech for a few years. Before starting at the Blue Bird he had become part of the modernist circle playing at the Sudan, the Bizerte, and the Zombie.[202] He had also worked with tenorist Billy Mitchell, himself a future leader of the house band, and in drummer George Jenkins's band at the Old Time Café in 1947.[203] Beans Richardson was two years older than Hill and had come to Detroit upon release from the army in January 1946. Richardson remembered that

> *I had a cousin in Detroit, Al Cavett, a bass and guitar player with Jimmy and Sue Caldwell. They had previously played the Blue Bird. Played almost like R & B stuff, hits. . . . To me that was old-fashioned stuff; I wanted to be where the action was. . . . I met Phil Hill and went to the Bizerte where I heard Tommy Burnette, Youngblood Davis, Warren Hickey.*[204]

Woodley was the youngest member of the group at 22 years of age and was generally considered a very promising vibraphonist.[205] Eddie Jamison was, like many young altoists, close to Parker in style. Judging from a live tape recording done by Porter Crutcher at the Blue Bird he had a great sense of swing.[206] Mardigan was the only member of the group with a national reputation, yet he was not the leader. While at the Blue Bird, Mardigan also headed jam sessions at the Bowl-O-Drome on Tuesday nights.[207] He also led his "Be Boppers" in the first of a new series of concerts at the Broadway Capitol Theater downtown.[208]

The *Michigan Chronicle*'s Roy Stephens was very enthusiastic about the group.

> *The unit provides more kicks in 15 minutes than could be culled from spending 4 hours in a lot of other joints. . . . Woodley's . . . ideas, sense of restraint, technique, bop inflections and all-round musicianship are attributes which most horn-blowers would give 4 sharps to match. . . . Woodley interjects that extra "something" which is the difference between a musician and a guy who carries an instrument around. . . . Both Hill and Jamison are followers of the modern idiom and this trend toward the progressive is reflected in things like "Just You, Just Me," "Donna Lee," and "Good Bait."*[209]

Younger musicians like Barry Harris had a special affection for the band.

> *Then there was the Blue Bird, the joint I would run to when I was too young to get in. The bandstand was in the window. I'd knock on the window and the pianist, a cat named Phil Hill, would turn and look at me. When he finished a song I'd run and play a couple of tunes and run back out.*[210]

> *My twenty-first birthday was celebrated in the Blue Bird to make sure they knew I was twenty one.*[211]

The house band added a guest artist when Detroit greats visited their hometown for an extended period of time. Beans Richardson remembered that

> *Wardell Gray was working with us at the Blue Bird whenever he was in town, sometimes as*

202. Hill was part of drummer David Heard's sextet at the Club Zombie, which included trumpeter Doug Mettome. Advertisement, *Michigan Chronicle*, February 1, 1947.

203. Jenkins was born in 1917 and had plenty of big band experience before coming to Detroit in 1947: Lionel Hampton, Buddy Johnson, and Charlie Barnet. In Detroit he played with Ted Buckner at the Frolic and led his own band. Dick Jennings, "Drummer Man Jenkins," *Swingsation*, April 1948. "Old Time Bar Jumps Nightly with Jenkins," *Michigan Chronicle*, August 16, 1947.

204. Richardson was born in New Orleans but grew up in Chattanooga, Tennessee. His older brother Rodney was also a bassist and played with Count Basie in 1943–47. Beans learned a lot of music in the army from pianist Billy Kyle. He also played with Detroit pianist Willie Hawkins in the service. Beans Richardson, interview. Jimmy Caldwell and his Blue Bird Trio played the Blue Bird in 1942 and 1943 according to advertisements in the *Michigan Chronicle*.

205. "Three Js Rollick at Sixes," *Michigan Chronicle*, February 7, 1948. Hill, interview by Bjorn and Gallert. Eddie Jamison was probably also a West Sider since he attended Northwestern High School. Little else is known about him. Harold McKinney, interview by Bjorn.

206. Crutcher caught Jamison with the Hill trio playing "Lover Man," "Body and Soul," and "Idaho." The exact date of the recording is not known.

207. Advertisement, *Detroit Free Press*, September 3, 1948; *Down Beat*, March 11, 1949; *Detroit Free Press*, May 31, 1949.

208. The "Jazz at Broadway Capitol" Saturday night concert also featured the city's major traditional jazz group: Frank Gillis and the Dixie Five. Advertisement, *Detroit Free Press*, October 7, 1949. The series typically also featured a national band visiting a local club.

209. "Abe Woodley Sparks Phil Hill Combo at Blue Bird Inn," *Michigan Chronicle*, October 23, 1948.

210. M. Bourne, "Barry Harris: Keeper of the Bebop Flame," *Down Beat*, September 1985.

211. Barry Harris, interview by Bjorn.

Fig. 76. George Jenkins group, unidentified location (possibly Old Time Café), 1947.
Billy Holiday, tp; possibly Leonard "Heavy" Swain, bs; Jenkins, dms/ldr; Phil Hill, pno; Billy Mitchell, ts.
(Photo: Bob Douglas ©.)

> *long as two months. . . . He lived with his sister and his brother Harry was also in town.*[212]

The first of these visits was in July–August of 1949 before Gray rejoined the Benny Goodman orchestra.[213] The *Michigan Chronicle*'s Bill Lane drew a portrait of Gray in an article called "Wardell Gray Says Feeling Rates in Bop."

> *Wardell Gray is the unusual young tenor sax man who has been knocking out overflow audiences at Blue Bird Inn over the past week. . . . He says that "Bop is something that is highly spontaneous. Something in music that flows right out as the mood strikes the player. So, if he doesn't feel anything he can't play anything." . . . An expert showman, he cuts a well-groomed, fluid appearance while in action. Looking more like a young college frosh than a bop musician, Gray blows with great expression, moving his arms and shoulders in short rhythmical accompaniment. Backing him . . . sitting in usually are several young white bop musicians, one on bongo drums and another on trombone. The Blue Bird audiences are always greatly inter-racial on the nights Gray plays. Gray got his start in Detroit in the band of Isaac Goodwin. He lists his favorite musicians as: Charlie Parker, Diz and Fats Navarro. . . . all have the feeling of their music . . . similarly when Wardell plays "I Don't Stand a Ghost of a Chance with You."*[214]

Musicians also remember Gray's stint at the Blue Bird.[215] Drummer Elvin Jones was 22 at the time and remembered the occasion in a conversation with Art Taylor.

> *In 1949 I got out of the Army. There was a place in Detroit called the Blue Bird Inn and I was working there with Billy Mitchell [in the 1950s]. . . . Before I met Billy Mitchell, and he hired me, I used to go to the club and listen to*

212. Richardson, interview by Bjorn and Gallert.

213. Gray recorded with both the Goodman orchestra and Goodman septet in 1949. His last recording was on October 15, and on October 27 he was replaced by Zoot Sims. D. Russell Connor, *Benny Goodman: Listen to His Legacy* (Methuen, N.J.: Scarecrow Press and Institute for Jazz Studies, 1988).

214. *Michigan Chronicle*, August 6, 1949.

215. Many sat in with Gray. A column in the *Michigan Chronicle*, July 30, 1949, mentions Kenny Burrell and Rudy Rutherford.

Fig. 77. Phil Hill combo, Blue Bird Inn, 1948. *Beans Richardson, bs; Hill, pno/ldr; Eddie Jamison, as; Art Mardigan, dms; Abe Woodley, vbs.* (Photo: Bob Douglas ©.)

Wardell Gray and all these cats. Art Mardigan was the drummer, and he was always very friendly and helpful to me. He used to ask me to sit in, but I would never do it. I thought it was presumptuous to sit in with these musicians, because to me, they were the greatest people I knew. I found it an honor even to speak to these cats and to know them socially. I never had the faintest idea that I would actually become a member of the group and be a regular.[216]

Jones was soon playing gigs around Detroit with a new drum set bought with his army savings and a $35 loan from his sister Melinda.[217] By 1952 he had joined the house band at the Blue Bird.

Pepper Adams was a student at Wayne University (later Wayne State University) at the time and had recently switched from the clarinet to the baritone. He heard Gray at the Blue Bird and got to know him.

I worked many gigs with Wardell Gray. Spent a lot of time together when we weren't working because we traded authors. . . . I was going to the university at the time majoring in English. Wardell was very interested in what I was doing at college. We compared notes on novelists, movies, staged performances, went out of our way to watch Omnibus every Sunday. . . . Wardell was one of the finest baritone players I have ever heard. If I had to think of any influence on baritone sax it was Wardell Gray.[218]

After returning to the Goodman band, Gray was back at the Blue Bird in December.[219] He remained in Detroit for about a half a year playing with several groups. In April 1950 Gray recorded four classic sides for Prestige Records with the Blue Bird house band.

In October 1949 Charlie Parker also sat in at the Blue Bird for the first time. What made this visit unusual was that it was recorded, thanks to the efforts of Porter Crutcher. Crutcher was a

216. Arthur Taylor, "Elvin Jones," in *Notes and Tones* (New York: Da Capo Press, 1993), 219–20.

217. "Elvin Jones Jazz Machine," *Down Beat,* November 1992. Jones's first gigs ended abruptly. The first one, in a club on Grand River, ended when the leader ran away with the money on Christmas Eve, and the second one, back home in Pontiac, ended when an incompetent singer fired him. His next job was at the Blue Bird with Billy Mitchell. Whitney Balliet, "A Walk in the Park," in *American Musicians II,* 464.

218. P. Danson, "Pepper Adams," *Coda,* no. 191, 1983.

219. *Michigan Chronicle,* December 24, 1949.

regular at the Blue Bird and had the foresight to buy a Presto portable disc recorder and cut records there on several occasions. He remembered that

> *We were sittin' at the Blue Bird, back in the back [at the time the bandstand was up front]. Someone said: "Yard just came in!" I looked up, and sure enough, he was sittin' up in the front booth. I said "Wow!" and jumped in my car. I lived on Woodrow, the next street over, three blocks down. Went home and got my machine and came back. When I got back, I couldn't get in the place! I wasn't gone for more than fifteen minutes! I was outside, so I took my microphone and passed it inside to somebody. . . . I caught the last part of "Now's the Time."*[220]

Crutcher caught Parker with the Hill trio and baritonist Tate Houston, who was featured regularly at the Blue Bird at that time. Houston was a West Sider with modernist credentials: he recorded with the Billy Eckstine band in 1946 and J. C. Heard and Wardell Gray in 1948. He came back to Detroit in between stints with various big bands and had played with Sonny Stitt and Milt Jackson at the Mirror in late 1947.

The presence of the single most important figure in bebop at the Blue Bird was a further sign that it had arrived in the late 1940s. The club had established itself as a major center for Detroit modernists, and its centrality was further solidified in the next decade.

220. "Yard" is short for "Yardbird/Bird," Parker's nickname. The recording was done on October 11, 1949. It also includes Jack Tiant on congas. Porter Crutcher, interview by Lars Bjorn and Jim Gallert, Detroit, Michigan, March 19, 1994. Crutcher also caught Wardell Gray on two tracks with the house band in the summer of 1949.

West Side Modern: Detroit Jazz Clubs in the 1950s

A REMARKABLE GROUP OF MODERNISTS emerged in the 1950s in Detroit. Modern jazz in the 1950s was found mainly on the West Side of the city at the Blue Bird Inn and other jazz clubs. The movement of jazz spots from the East Side to the more middle-class West Side can better be understood within the context of the economic and social changes during the decade.

Economic Progress and Social Conflict

"WHAT'S GOOD FOR GENERAL MOTORS is good for the country," GM president Charles E. Wilson told a congressional committee in 1953.[1] In many ways this statement reflected the political mood of the United States at the time: capitalism and the social good were seen as naturally linked to each other. The economic boom of the postwar years showed no signs of slowing down, and Americans enjoyed unprecedented levels of affluence. The turmoil of the Great Depression was rapidly receding from public memory, and the middle class was expanding. But underneath this political consensus there were signs of social conflict along class and race lines.

Ironically, what was good for General Motors was not necessarily good for the city of Detroit, the home of its headquarters. New auto plants in the postwar era were built in the suburbs, while older plants in the central city were phased out.[2] The boom and bust cycle of the auto industry had already created havoc in the city during the depression years, and by the late 1950s another severe downturn appeared. While the car companies sold about 6.5 million cars in 1950, in 1958 this slowed drastically to 4.25 million.[3] The consequences for the city were substantial. Unemployment skyrocketed, and many plants closed for good. Between 1950 and the early 1960s the East Side alone lost 71,000 jobs.[4] While blacks had moved rapidly into the auto industry in the 1940s this movement slowed down and reversed itself during the latter half of the 1950s. While overall unem-

Philly Joe Jones and Billy Mitchell at the Blue Bird Inn, 1958.

1. Conot, *American Odyssey*, 428.

2. One estimate is that the Big Three auto companies constructed some 20 new plants in suburban Detroit between 1947 and 1955. No plants were built in the central city during this period. In fact the General Motors Poletown plant, which opened in 1983, was the first auto plant built in Detroit since 1928. Joe T. Darden et al., *Detroit: Race and Uneven Development* (Philadelphia: Temple University Press, 1987), 16, 180.

3. Holli, *Detroit*, appendix, 281.

4. Conot, *American Odyssey*, 430.

Fig. 78. Black population in Detroit, 1950. One dot = 200 people. (Adapted from Sugrue, Map 7.1(b).)

ployment in the city remained virtually unchanged at around 7.5 percent between 1950 and 1960, black unemployment rose from 12 to 18 percent.[5]

The movement of jobs to the suburbs was part of a process of suburbanization that began in the 1940s and picked up its pace during the 1950s.[6] The city of Detroit stopped growing in 1952 at 1.85 million people. During the rest of the decade it lost 10 percent of its population. This population decline hides an even more dramatic change when race is taken into account. The black population continued to expand during the 1950s at the rate of 60 percent, whereas the white population declined by 23 percent. The net result was that Detroit was 29 percent black in 1960 compared to 16 percent in 1950.[7] With white flight on this scale it was very difficult to achieve anything like a stable integrated neighborhood. Saul Alinsky put it this way: "Integration is the period of time that elapses between the appearance of the first Negro and the exit of the last white."[8]

During the 1940s a tight housing market combined with housing discrimination led to overcrowding and poor living conditions in the Near East Side ghetto. Housing discrimination persisted in the 1950s and took organized form as white homeowners formed neighborhood associations to resist racial integration. This resistance was sometimes violent and was most common in neighborhoods made up of blue-collar workers, Catholics, and homeowners.[9] While housing discrimination persisted, the housing market eased, and with continued growth of the black population the geography of race changed.[10] A look at figure 78 in comparison with figure 79 gives an immediate sense of how things changed. In 1950 the majority of the black population was found on the Near East Side and in outlying enclaves. By the end of the 1950s a large number of blacks had crossed

5. Sugrue, *Origins of the Urban Crisis*, table 5.5, 151.

6. The rate of suburbanization doubled during the 1950s as compared to the 1940s. Compared to other metropolitan areas, Detroit had one of the highest rates in the 1950s. Karl E. Taeuber and Alma F. Taeuber, *Negroes in Cities* (Chicago: Aldine, 1965), table 49, 153.

7. Author's calculations based on Holli, *Detroit*, appendix, 271.

8. Quoted in Detroit Urban League, *A Profile of the Detroit Negro, 1959–1964* (Detroit: Detroit Urban League, 1965), 5.

9. Sugrue explains these correlations as follows. Working-class whites had fewer opportunities to move to the suburbs than those from the middle class. Catholic congregations are more territorially defined than Protestants and thus more likely to resist black newcomers. Sugrue, *Origins of the Urban Crisis*, chap. 9.

10. The increased white resistance to housing integration in the 1950s is well described by Sugrue, *Origins of the Urban Crisis*, chaps. 8 and 9.

Fig. 79. Black population in Detroit, 1960. One dot = 200 people. (Adapted from Sugrue, Map 7.1(c).)

Woodward Avenue into the near Northwest Side and dissolved the West Side black enclave that existed before. However, this change in physical location did not create a united African-American community, since class differences became more pronounced at the same time. This was an unintended consequence of the gradual opening up of the housing market as many whites fled the city.[11] A black elite settled in the Boston-Edison district and Arden Park, and a middle class of some professionals and many well-paid factory workers were the black pioneers on the Near Northwest Side in the neighborhoods of Twelfth Street, Russell Woods, and Bagley.[12] At the bottom were the poor people left behind on the Near East Side. The development of these neighborhoods was not so much a reflection of increased income differentials among blacks in the 1950s as an expression of the new possibility of living in the neighborhood of your choice.[13]

The Near East Side ghetto faced new enemies in this period: urban renewal and freeway building. After some initial attempts in the 1940s, the city in cooperation with the federal government started to clear land in an area that was designated as the Gratiot Redevelopment Site in 1950, bounded by Gratiot on the north, Lafayette on the south, Hastings on the west, and Dequindre on the east.[14] The displaced population, 98 percent black, was given insufficient assistance in finding new housing and contributed to an already severe housing shortage for the poor.[15] Matters were made worse with the building in 1959 of what became the Chrysler Freeway, which wiped out the lower end of Hastings Street, thus destroying Paradise Valley.[16]

Location of Jazz Spots in the 1950s

DURING THE 1950s jazz spots consolidated their hold on Woodward Avenue and

11. Sugrue, *Origins of the Urban Crisis,* 188.

12. These pioneers moved into the Twelfth Street area starting in 1947. Sugrue, *Origins of the Urban Crisis,* 242.

13. In fact the black industrial working class that had expanded during the 1940s, retained its relative size during the 1950s. Sugrue, *Origins of the Urban Crisis,* table B1, 276.

14. Robert J. Mowitz and Deil S. Wright, *Profile of a Metropolis* (Detroit: Wayne State University Press, 1962), 16.

15. Sugrue, *Origins of the Urban Crisis,* 50–55.

16. Ibid., 47; and "Chrysler Kin, Officials Say Start X-Way on East Side," *Detroit News,* January 30, 1959.

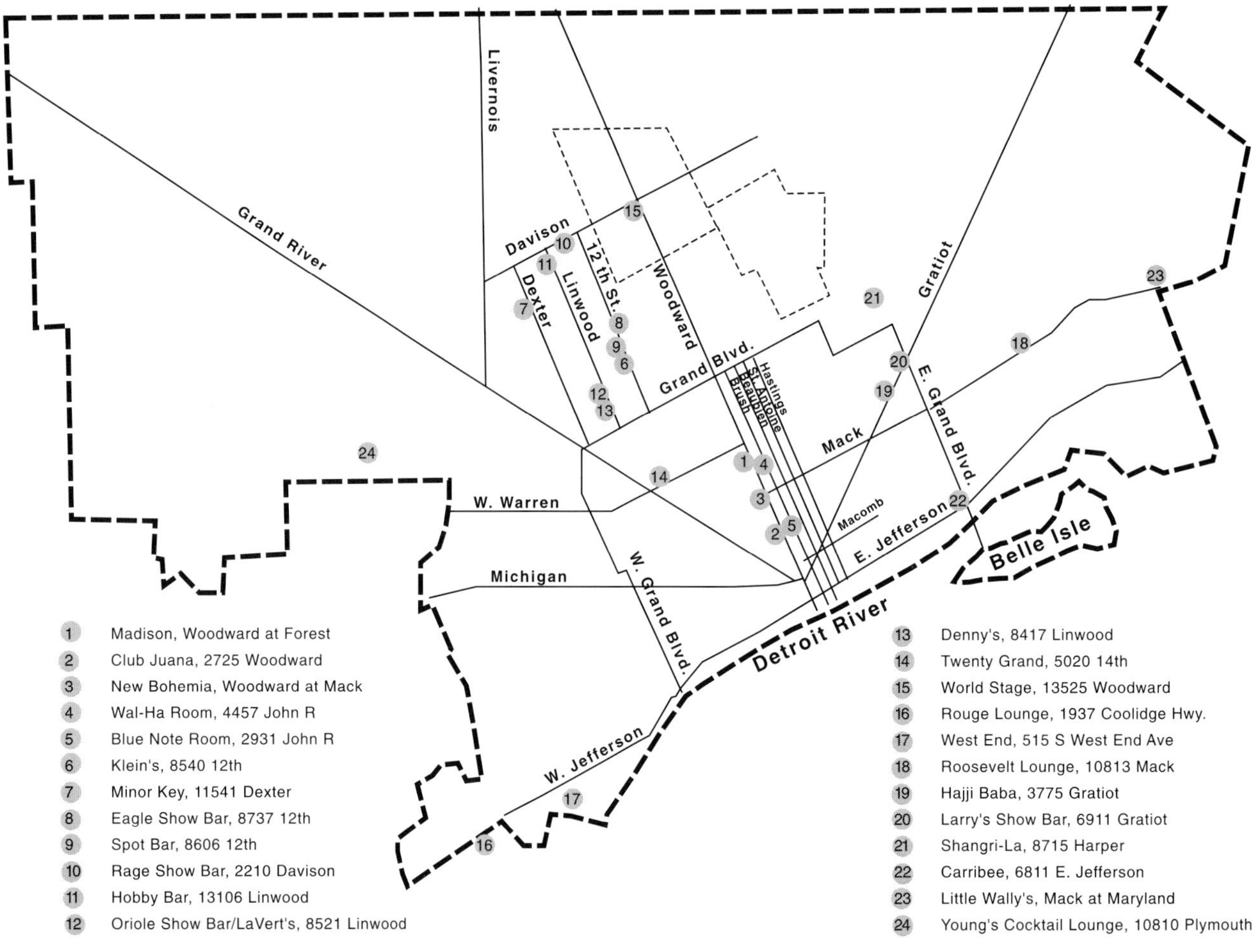

Fig. 80. New jazz spots in the 1950s.
(Map by Borkin and Kaplan.)

John R., while expanding on the West Side. Most of the new jazz venues in the late 1940s and 1950s were on the Near West Side of Detroit, a middle-class area in rapid racial transition. (See fig. 80.) This was a repetition of an earlier pattern of ethnic relations in the city: the particular areas of the West Side where blacks moved were predominantly Jewish, and most owners of jazz venues were Jewish or black. As seen in previous chapters this had happened earlier on the North End and on Hastings Street. In fact, if we consider all jazz venues in the postwar era, 70 percent were either Jewish or black owned.[17]

The Last Dance in Paradise Valley

The increased concentration of poor blacks in Paradise Valley and the determination of the city to engage in "Negro removal," as urban renewal policies became known in the black community, spelled the end of Paradise Valley. Sportree's was the last major jazz spot to open in the Valley, in 1946, but by 1950 it was gone. The El Sino was the lone surviving nightclub by 1958 and managed to stay in business until 1962.[18]

The late 1940s and early 1950s witnessed an effort by two clubs to transform themselves from nightclubs to teenage dance halls. This strategy worked for a few years. The Club Su-

17. For the 93 jazz venues identified after the war (up to 1960) it was possible to determine the ethnicity of 50 of the owners. Of the 50, 20 were Jewish American, 18 African American, 6 Italian American, and 6 other whites.

18. "Paradise Valley Gets Shot in Arm from Association," *Michigan Chronicle,* May 31, 1958.

Fig. 81. Advertisement for Club Valley. (From *Michigan Chronicle*, November 12, 1949.)

dan and Club Valley were at one time both owned by Howard Pyle, who was Jewish. Both clubs had an age limit of 17. Pyle complained to the *Michigan Chronicle*'s Roy Stephens that the interracial nature of his audience was the source of police harassment.

> *The police and fire department brands the teen age club a fire trap. . . . Owner Howard Pyle said their efforts are based solely on racial issues. . . . police ejected only a handful of white girls from the club. . . . no questions were asked of the white boys or black boys or girls. . . . he also reports that police had asked him to move his business out of the Negro neighborhood, but he refused. . . . The Rev. Horace White, pastor of Plymouth Congregational Church, said it has been widely known that certain members of the police department have resented the mixed recreational activities of the Club Sudan. . . . the officers also lectured the white girls "on going to recreate with young people of color."*[19]

The *Michigan Chronicle*'s Bill Lane agreed.

> *Young people at Club Valley are more orderly than their adult counterparts. . . . then too, where else can Negro youth find a place to dance in the city that compares in beauty and accessibility to Club Valley? If they go to dance on Woodward at the Graystone they can't even get meals at adjoining cafes. Not even the greasy, nasty ones.*[20]

Pyle brought in many national jazz and rhythm and blues acts to Club Valley in 1949 and 1950, such as Ella Fitzgerald, Miles Davis, Wardell Gray, Lester Young, and Earl Bostic. The club changed managers twice before closing around 1951.[21] Club Sudan lasted a few years more.[22]

Woodward and John R.

Howard Pyle moved his formula of jazz and rhythm and blues for dancing to Woodward Avenue in 1951. Throughout the 1950s he presented major jazz figures at the Madison Ballroom: Charlie Parker, Clifford Brown–Max Roach, Stan Getz, James Moody, Gene Ammons–Sonny Stitt, Stan Kenton, Duke Ellington, and Lester Young.[23]

Other promoters also saw the possibilities of teens dancing to modern jazz. Frank Brown organized a number of dances at the Graystone and Mirror Ballrooms throughout the 1950s. A particularly memorable one took place in 1953 at the Graystone when Charlie Parker was pitted in a "Battle Royal" against Illinois Jacquet and Arnett Cobb.[24] The event got some media attention as Parker was arrested after the performance for nonsupport of his ex-wife, who lived in Inkster, a Detroit suburb. Frank Brown was also quoted as "berating the musician when he arrived at the dance at 11 P.M. without his band. . . . he was slated to start playing at 10 P.M."[25] This is very likely the same event that Barry Harris remembered as follows.

> *We saw Bird at ballrooms way before we saw him at nightclubs. We sat in with him at the Graystone because his band didn't show up on*

19. "Club Sudan Owner Charges Race Issue Involved: Rap Police 'Gestapo Tactics,'" *Michigan Chronicle*, January 29, 1949.

20. *Michigan Chronicle*, November 12, 1949.

21. *Michigan Chronicle*, July 28, 1951.

22. The last advertisement for the Sudan in the *Michigan Chronicle* was on March 21, 1953. At this time the Sudan was under black ownership. Louis Hayes, interview by Lars Bjorn, Detroit, Michigan, September 7, 1998.

23. Parker probably played the Madison more than once. The last time was on February 4–6 in 1955 with the Candy Johnson quartet. Drummer Rudy Tucich and altoist Charles McPherson were in the audience. Rudy Tucich, telephone interview with Lars Bjorn, May 29, 2000.

24. Advertisement, *Michigan Chronicle*, August 29, 1953.

25. "'Cool Blues' Hits Sour Note as Cops Nab 'Yardbird,'" *Michigan Chronicle*, September 5, 1953.

> *time. So I sat in, I think Beans [Richardson] sat in, and Freddie Metcalf played drums. It was nice, man, because he [Bird] was really nice too. I sat in with Bird a few times. I never played a gig with Bird. There's a great deal of difference.*[26]

Fifteen-year-old drummer Roy Brooks was also in the audience.

> *When I heard Charlie Parker that was it. . . . I was shy of dancing until I heard his music. I grabbed the lady and got out on the floor. . . . the music was social and it was done to be-bop music. . . . Bird played up-tempo. . . . you cut time in half, dance slower and it fits. . . . you can dance to it. . . . People need to know they can dance to jazz. . . . We called it progressive jazz at that time. . . . [Like] Stan Kenton, we were listening to it all, but Charlie Parker was the master of that time; he was the prophet of modern jazz. . . . When he played at the Graystone the floor was packed.*[27]

Parker also played for a dance at the Forest Club in 1950, and Bob Cornfoot was one of the few whites in attendance.

> *The number of dancers always outnumbered the listeners around the bandstand. Not really all that different from [when] the big bands [played]. The dancers almost used to knock me out as much as the music. The ones I always thought were the best were not dancing in the jitterbug style; they would dance separately from each other, the way the rock dancers do, and they knew the music. They would follow along even when there were solos. . . . It wasn't parallel; everybody had their own thing going on, and it was the most creative dancing I have ever seen. . . . people came just to dance to, say, Lester or Bird.*[28]

By 1953 Brown organized dances at the Graystone, which featured jazz and rhythm and blues artists opposite each other. This lead to some interesting combinations like one in July 1956 that combined jazz groups led by Clifford Brown–Max Roach, Miles Davis, and Lester Young with several rhythm and blues quartets: the Orioles, El Dorados, Moonglows, Drifters, and Turbans.[29] Such dances continued through the 1950s at the Graystone.

Club Juana opened on Woodward in 1948, and in 1950 the *Michigan Chronicle* reported that it "only recently swung open its doors to Negro patronage, [and] is doing rush-order trade, with crowds packing it for all shows."[30] During 1951 and 1952 the Juana presented many national jazz acts within a floor-show context: Count Basie's sextet, Dizzy Gillespie's sextet, Billie Holiday (both years), and Johnny Hodges.[31] On July 14, 1951, a *Michigan Chronicle* column reported that "Billie Holiday, at Club Juana for a nine day stint, has drawn a full house every night and has a waiting line of at least a block."[32] In 1953 the Juana closed for remodeling. It seems not to have reopened until 1956 and then only for a few months.[33]

The New Bohemia (also called Club Bohemia), a modern jazz club, opened up on Woodward in 1958. It was the kind of place that reminded some of clubs in Greenwich Village. Arnold Hirsch's survey of jazz clubs in 1959 noted that

> *By far the city's most offbeat (no pun intended) jazz temple is the New Bohemia, a double-store grotto on Woodward just above Mack. Its dark-toned walls are hung with modern paintings and sketches, its drinks served by waitresses in wildly assorted street clothes, its tables furnished with chess or checker boards. The music is supplied alternately by a fine hi-fi record system and by a live and earnest fivesome known as the Informal Jazz Quintet.*[34]

Columns in the *Michigan Chronicle* commented on the audience, which, the *Chronicle* noted on May 24, 1958, included "[a]rtists, sculptors, writers, college teachers. . . ." According to the *Chronicle*,

> *Artists, plain music lovers and plain ordinary folks congregate to listen to symphony music, occasional juke box selections, live jazz shows*

26. Barry Harris, interview with Bjorn. In another interview Harris guesses that Doug Watkins or Paul Chambers could have been on bass. Michael Bourne, "Barry Harris: Keeper of the Bebop Flame," *Down Beat,* September 1985. It could also have taken place on March 18, 1953, when Parker appeared with Duke Ellington at the Graystone. Advertisement, *Michigan Chronicle,* March 16, 1953.

27. Roy Brooks, interview, Graystone International Jazz Museum, *Community Jazz History Series: Roy Brooks,* 1989. Larry Gabriel, producer (video). Brooks also remembered that dancing audiences were thoroughly familiar with modern recordings like Miles Davis's "Blue Haze." Roy Brooks, interview by Lars Bjorn and Jim Gallert, Detroit, Michigan, November 23, 1999.

28. Cornfoot, interview by Bjorn.

29. Advertisement, *Michigan Chronicle,* June 30, 1956.

30. *Michigan Chronicle,* September 9, 1950.

31. Advertisements in the *Detroit Free Press* (January 19, 1951; February 23, 1951); *Michigan Chronicle* (June 6, 1951); *Detroit Free Press* (July 13, 1951; January 21, 1952).

32. Even though there were full houses for Holiday this proved not to be much of a moneymaker for owner Abe Rahaim. He paid Holiday $17,500 a week and netted far more money on dancer Baby Scruggs, whom he paid less than a tenth of that amount. *Michigan Chronicle,* August 15, 1959.

33. *Detroit Tribune,* March 14, 1953; and advertisement, *Michigan Chronicle,* October 13, 1956.

34. Arnold Hirsch, "Jazz Goes Uptown: Neighborhood Spots Popular," *Detroit Sunday Times,* May 10, 1959.

and to play chess while drinking beer during weekday nights.[35]

The Bohemia featured national and local modern jazz. Unfortunately it lasted only a year or so.

On John R. several of the spots started in the 1940s—the Flame, the Frolic, and the Chesterfield—did good business throughout the 1950s. The Flame was the number one show bar in the city and offered the best in black entertainment throughout the decade. This meant a heavy emphasis on vocalists singing blues, rhythm and blues, popular songs, and sometimes strictly jazz-oriented material. The jazz singers included Billie Holiday, Anita O'Day, Chris Connor, Betty Carter, and Dinah Washington. Dizzy Gillespie led the only modern jazz group at the Flame for a week in 1958.[36] Two new spots also opened up in the 1950s, both hotel cocktail lounges: the Garfield Lounge and the Blue Note.

The Garfield Lounge opened in the Garfield Hotel in 1945, but it became an important jazz spot in 1950 when the Wal-Ha Room opened. In 1950 its owner, Randolph Wallace, received what he claimed was "the first Negro-operated hotel-lounge license in Michigan." Mississippi-born, he came to Detroit in 1936 and started a grocery, even though he was trained as a pharmacist. The *Michigan Chronicle,* in a September 20, 1952, article entitled, "Garfield Lounge Glitters behind Modern Exteriors," described the bar and the adjoining "jewel-like" Wal-Ha Room in glowing terms.

> *The circular bar is flanked by 35 chairs. . . . plush booths line the walls. . . . The Wal-Ha Room is entered through accordion-like doors from the main lounge. . . . recitals by local singers and dramatic readers are staged often in the Wal-Ha on Sunday evenings. . . . It has thick carpeting. . . . the name is a contraction of Wallace and Harris (after Charles Harris, former manager).*

According to the *Chronicle,* "The predominant color scheme is burgundy, chartreuse and white (lounge); blue and white (Wal-Ha); and sea green and white (hotel lobby)."[37]

During the 1950s the Wal-Ha room featured some of Detroit's best modern jazz players in no larger format than a trio. In 1958 the same players got work in the newly opened Blue Note Room of the Hotel Capri Plaza at John R. and Edmund Place.[38]

New Jazz Spots in the 1950s

The boom in new jazz venues from the late 1940s continued into the 1950s but at a somewhat slower pace. The peak was in 1949, and many of these clubs lasted through the 1950s. In 1953 there were also many new venues, and this prompted the *Michigan Chronicle* to look for an explanation of the growth in nightspots.

> *In 1949 John R was emblazoned anew when a chummy little fellow named Morris Wasserman opened a big blase spot. . . . the Flame . . . reeked with talent and patrons. . . . it is still busy. . . . now the city is loaded with places for entertainment . . . all around town . . . all sizes of places. . . . most of the new spots were formerly "all-white." But the dollar changes many hearts—and viewpoints. It opens many doors. Every club that has opened to Negroes since 1951 has been enjoying phenomenal success monetarily. What they lost in white patronage they have made up triplefold in colored patrons. In many spots there was no noticeable loss of white patronage.*
>
> *Take Klein's Show Bar on Twelfth. Or the Crystal Lounge on Grand River . . . or the Oriole on Linwood. Today they serve all comers. They never suffer a lack of audience. . . . .The Club Basin Street opened the Delray district to Negro patronage. . . . patronage . . . picked up enormously at the Garfield Lounge, the only big Negro-owned bar-club on John R. Its Wal-ha Room is a favorite place for people who love organ music and intimate surroundings. . . . On 12th and Warren Mike Murphy opened his*

35. *Michigan Chronicle,* July 5, 1958.

36. *Down Beat,* June 26, 1958.

37. Larry Chism, "New Garfield Lounge Is 'Dream Come True,' " *Michigan Chronicle,* October 21, 1950.

38. Art Cartwright was the owner of the Blue Note Room. Advertisement, *Michigan Chronicle,* June 7, 1958; June 14, 1958.

club to all patrons and the Glen Lodge Show Bar came into being on Eight-Mile Road. . . . And now comes news that the Rouge Lounge out Schaeffer Highway is admitting Negro patrons by reservation. Max Speigelman is serving Negro patrons by phone call arrangements in his smart Club Alamo on Livernois. From an overall scanning, it appears that Detroit is progressing strongly in racial amity along nightclub row. And the truth of the matter is nobody is losing any money or sleep over the change.[39]

What was not so obvious in 1953, but can be well observed today, is that most of the spots welcoming black customers were located on the Near Northwest Side. Figure 80 shows that this is where much of the growth in new jazz spots occurred in the 1950s, and, as already noted, this was an area in rapid transition during the decade. Blacks moved into the Jewish neighborhood around Twelfth Street starting in 1947, and by 1950 the area was over one-third black. By 1960 less than 4 percent of Twelfth Street was white. The Twelfth Street, Linwood, and Dexter areas saw several new jazz clubs in the 1950s in addition to the ones already in existence. The major new clubs were Klein's and the Minor Key.

Klein's

Klein's Show Bar opened to jazz fans in the early 1950s and abandoned an earlier policy of excluding black customers.[40] Drummer Hindal Butts played there with Kenny Burrell's group in 1953–55 and remembered the club and its owner.

The bandstand used to be up behind the bar. George Klein enlarged it. . . . he was going to put the bandstand around the bar in a circle. . . . Fortunately enough he talked with the musicians. "Oh, George, come on: that won't look good!" and when we got through begging and crying he wouldn't do it. Instead it was put along a wall. . . . That was the darndest guy I ever worked with when it came to money. He paid good. . . . like if you asked him for a raise he'd grumble but it'd be in your pay envelope the next week. Owning the club was a hobby with him. He was making money with it and his pride and joy was his son and he went to med school with it. . . . He made money off that place. Very classy audience; you had a lot of players on 12th of course, but jazz audiences inside. . . . Black and Jewish people . . . people from Grosse Pointe . . . they came to listen and if you were out there making a noise someone in the audience would tell you to shut up. . . . The musicians performed to these people and played your instrument, because people appreciated what you did. Same thing at the Blue Bird, though the Blue Bird was a little more of a neighborhood place and ran like one. The audience was about 60/40 black/white, all jazz lovers. . . . the area was slowly changing . . . as blacks moved northward.[41]

Bassist Will Austin played at Klein's in 1958–59 with the Yusef Lateef quintet. He also had positive things to say about the club and its owner.

Klein's was a very good place to work. George Klein was nice. It was a jazz club, a mixed club. There was no food, no dancing, only drink. The bar . . . was constantly full, lot of good drinkers. Monday night, jam session, was really a sold out night, no cover charge, he'd give all of us an extra $10. Klein was cool. He had a few troubles with the police sometimes. They didn't like whites coming into Klein's, and I think Klein . . . wouldn't give them drinks like some of the other clubs.[42]

Klein's featured local bands for extended periods and also brought in many nationally known modern jazz artists, including Milt Jackson and Frank Rosolino in 1954. Monday night jam sessions were a regular feature and attracted many visiting musicians. In 1959 Klein sold the club to Al Mendelson, who renamed it the Club 12 Show Bar. Mendelson brought in a galaxy of modern jazz stars in

39. "New Spots Blaze Trails in Racial Amity and Dollar," *Michigan Chronicle*, October 3, 1953.

40. Kenn Cox, "Reflections on Klein's Show Bar," program booklet, *Blue Bird Reunion 6* (Detroit: Societie of the Culturally Concerned, 1996). Klein's was located at 8540 Twelfth Street, between Philadelphia and Pingree.

41. Butts, interview by Bjorn.

42. Will Austin, interview by Jim Gallert, Detroit, Michigan, December 6, 1999.

1959: Thelonius Monk's quartet, Miles Davis's quintet (with John Coltrane), and Sonny Stitt.

The Minor Key

THE MINOR KEY OPENED in the winter of 1958–59 on Dexter and featured top local modernists for the first year and then nationally known groups until it closed in 1963.[43] The Minor Key was Detroit's first jazz coffeehouse and a major presence in the early 1960s. Dexter was already the home of the Bowl-O-Drome, discussed in the previous chapter. It continued as a major jazz spot through the 1960s.

Other Near West Side Spots

THERE WERE SEVERAL SPOTS on the Near West Side that featured local acts. Part of the Twelfth Street neighborhood was Chic's Show Bar on Hamilton. It opened in 1945 and for many years featured its owner, Chic Cohen, who advertised himself as Detroit's Al Jolson. Around 1953 Chic's started to book jazz combos and singers and continued with black music until 1966.[44] Other Twelfth Street bars with jazz were the Eagle Show Bar, which opened in 1954 in what earlier was Zeman's Bakery, and the Spot Bar, which opened in 1953.[45] At the northern end of the neighborhood was the Rage Show Bar, which opened in 1955.[46]

On Linwood the Hobby Bar opened in 1952 and was primarily a piano bar. It started with jazz combos in 1960.[47] Further south on Linwood the Oriole Show Bar opened as a black and tan in 1953, and two years later it was replaced by LaVert's Lounge.[48] The Oriole and LaVert's were bar–bowling alley combinations. Both showcased several important Detroit modernists. Close by was Denny's Show Bar, which opened in 1953 and also featured Detroit modernists in the late 1950s.[49]

Twenty Grand

SOUTH OF THE JEWISH NEIGHBORHOOD, along Warren Avenue and on the western edge of the expanding West Side black neighborhood, new clubs opened up in the 1950s. One of them was the Twenty Grand, a major site for African-American music until the early 1970s.[50] It was opened as the Twenty Grand Recreation by Leo and Bill Kabbush in 1953 and featured two floors of activities. On the first floor were 22 bowling lanes, and on the second floor the Driftwood Lounge and the Terrace Garden both featured music.[51] After a fire and renovations in 1958 the *Michigan Chronicle*'s Bill Lane described the Twenty Grand in glowing terms.

> *Bill Kabbush and Marty Eisner have a truly beautiful spot in their new 20 Grand . . . with [the] majestically decorated, carpeted, smartly lighted and sound-perfect main play room with the Levi Mann band and special dance nights, its modern bowling facilities, . . . its cozy and unique Fireside Room with Mary De Loach and midget bar stools and its soon to open Cabaret room, the Gold Room, which will feature top-name attractions. . . . About the most welcome feature is the extensive carpeting, something seldom found in a place patronized extensively by Negroes. Owners, white or Negro, seemingly have been reluctant to place carpeting on floors in their establishments . . . [except in] smaller clubs like the Blue Note Room and the Wal-Ha Room.*[52]

The Twenty Grand did indeed bring in the best in black entertainment, and it also employed many Detroit jazz and rhythm and blues artists from 1953 until the early 1970s.

Crystal Show Bar

JUST WEST OF THE TWENTY GRAND on Grand River and Lawton was the Crystal Show Bar, which had opened in 1947. In 1951 Creflo "Buffalo" Mims was brought in as manager, and the Crystal was advertised as a black and tan. The *Detroit Tribune* commented that

> *The Crystal Bar, one of Detroit's two new interracial nightclubs, this week appeared ready to switch from the sweet song, piano-playing en-*

43. The exact date for the opening of the Minor Key is unclear. Kenn Cox remembers being the pianist in a group during the winter of 1958–59, but the first newspaper notice is not until late 1959. Kenn Cox, Jazz Symposium, Detroit Historical Museum, February 10, 1991; and *Down Beat,* December 10, 1959.

44. Chic's was located at 8441 Hamilton. Advertisement, *Detroit Free Press,* April 16, 1948. Advertisement, *Michigan Chronicle,* November 21, 1953. Singers during the 1950s included Arthur Prysock and Jimmy Witherspoon.

45. The Eagle Show Bar was located on Twelfth Street at Gladstone. It was owned by Sol Bloom. *Michigan Chronicle,* June 26, 1954; March 24, 1956. The Spot Bar was located at 8606 Twelfth Street. Advertisement, *Michigan Chronicle,* October 3, 1953.

46. The Rage was located on Davison at Fourteenth Street. It was owned by Joe Greenberg and opened in 1955 with Candy Johnson. Advertisement, *Michigan Chronicle,* May 14, 1955.

47. The Hobby Bar was located at 13106 Linwood, near Buena Vista. When it featured jazz in the early 1960s it was owned by Nat and Betty Gold. *Michigan Chronicle,* January 23, 1960.

48. The Oriole and LaVert's were located at 8521 Linwood, near Philadelphia. LaVert's was named after the owner, LaVert Beaman, who also owned a hotel on Pingree. *Michigan Chronicle,* April 21, 1955.

49. Denny's was located at 8417 Linwood at Euclid and was owned by Denny Protopappas. *Michigan Chronicle,* April 11, 1953; and 1953 *Detroit City Directory.*

50. Close to the Twenty Grand on Grand River and Fourteenth, the Strand Bar and Grill opened in 1956. It was owned by Basil and Mike Simon and featured local jazz for at least two years. Advertisement, *Michigan Chronicle,* March 24, 1956.

51. Advertisement, *Michigan Chronicle,* October 31, 1953.

52. *Michigan Chronicle,* October 3, 1959.

tertainment, to rousing, jumping combo music. Edmour Bertrand [is the] affable owner of the smart and decorous Crystal. . . . The Crystal is the city's most beautiful interracial nightclub in the spoken opinion of many club-goers. It has been in operation for only about a month. It has two rooms, one of which is its famed Sports Room, which since its inception has attracted many high sports figures.[53]

For three years it featured top local jazz groups. In early 1954 it dropped the black and tan label and advertised itself as a modern jazz club.[54] National acts were brought in weekly, and there was music five nights a week, including a Sunday matinee. Over the next two years the performers included the following: Gene Ammons, Charlie Parker, Coleman Hawkins, Terry Gibbs, Dinah Washington, the Modern Jazz Quartet (with Milt Jackson), James Moody, Clifford Brown–Max Roach, and Dizzy Gillespie.[55]

All of Charlie Parker's visits to Detroit have become legendary, and his two stints at the club in 1954 are no exception. At this stage of his career Parker worked as a solo act with local rhythm sections. During his first visit in April he was backed by a trio led by bassist Major "Mule" Holley, back temporarily after a few years in New York.[56] Parker's drug use was well known, so everyone watched for signs of it. Carl Hill was in the audience at the Crystal.

At the Crystal he had Will Davis on piano. . . . You'd never know Charlie Parker was a drug addict. . . . He told each of them you play what you play, because I am going to play what I play. He played his ass off. All night long he would drink Champale, had it on top of the piano . . . He was very articulate.[57]

When Parker returned for two weeks in October he played with altoist Gene Nero's group. Nero remembered that

I first met Charlie when he was with Jay McShann's band. I brought him to Detroit for the engagement at the Crystal. He stayed at my home even though he had a room at the Statler; the same hotel where my wife worked as a hostess. At the end of the night we went home to go to sleep; there was no hanging out. Bird was clean; he drank some.[58]

While at the Crystal, Parker also appeared on comedian Soupy Sales's evening TV show, *Soupy's On,* on WXYZ-TV.[59] Sales was a jazz fan, and the theme song of the show was Parker's "Yardbird Suite."[60] Charlie Parker very rarely appeared on television, and it is unfortunate that no tapes of his Detroit appearances exist. The Crystal was an important modern jazz club, but even more important was the Blue Bird further west on Tireman. In chapter 4 the history of the Blue Bird in the 1940s was discussed, but the club reached its zenith in the 1950s.

Blue Bird

Whereas the Blue Bird was on the northern end of the black West Side in 1940, black population movements across Tireman put the club in the center of the neighborhood by the early 1950s. In 1950 the area just north of the Blue Bird was about a quarter black, and only 10 years later it was 90 percent black.[61] The black population around the Blue Bird can be described as middle class, by virtue of income rather than occupation. Throughout this period they were in the upper third of black income earners, and a majority were in blue-collar occupations.[62] In addition by 1960 more than half of the residents of the neighborhood were homeowners, a traditional symbol of middle-class status.

Who was in the audience at the Blue Bird? It was a composite made up largely of three segments: people from the neighborhood, jazz fans from all over the city, and modernist musicians. The relative sizes of these audience segments are in some dispute among observers, but many say that most people in the Blue Bird were not from the neighborhood. All observers agree on

53. "Crystal Bar to Bring in Earl Belcher," *Detroit Tribune,* August 11, 1951.

54. The Crystal advertised in both the *Detroit Free Press* and the *Michigan Chronicle. Detroit Free Press,* March 12, 1954.

55. Advertisements in the *Michigan Chronicle* and the *Detroit Free Press.*

56. His trio also backed Coleman Hawkins at the Crystal. "Interview with Major Holley," *Cadence,* July 1989.

57. Hill, interview by Bjorn and Gallert. The exact makeup of the Holley trio is in some dispute among those who were present. Most agree that Will Davis played piano and Major Holley bass. The drummers were Phil Demino, at least some of the time, and Hindal Butts. Holley was born in Detroit in 1924 and had played with Parker in New York in the late 1940s. "Interview with Major Holley," *Cadence*; Butts, interview by Bjorn.

58. Gene Nero, interview by Lars Bjorn and Jim Gallert, Detroit, Michigan, May 27, 1990.

59. Parker appeared on the *Soupy's On* program on April 7, July 16, and July 21, 1954, according to TV schedules in the *Detroit Free Press.* Other Crystal performers on the same television show during 1954 included Lester Young, Earl Bostic, Clifford Brown–Max Roach, and Arnett Cobb. Sales also had a children's show in the daytime.

60. Jack Brokensha, interview by Lars Bjorn, Bloomfield Hills, Michigan, July 20, 1998.

61. The area south of the Blue Bird was 90 percent black in 1940 and 94 percent black in 1950 (census tract no. 120). The area just north of the Blue Bird consists of census tracts numbered 157 and 158.

62. The median family income in tract no. 120 was $3,098 in 1950 and $4,993 in 1960 according to census data. The lower limit for the upper third of black incomes in these years was $2,710 in 1950 and $4,160 in 1960 according to Sugrue, *Origins of the Urban Crisis,* map 7.2 (a) and (b). In 1960 craft workers made up 16 percent and operatives 44 percent of the nonwhite males in tract no. 120 according to census data.

Fig. 82. Clarence Eddins in front of the Blue Bird Inn, late 1950s.
(Photo: James Richardson ©.)

two issues: it was a knowledgeable audience, and it included only a handful of whites.

Baritonist Pepper Adams worked at the Blue Bird after returning from the army in 1953.

> *The Blue Bird [was] . . . a marvelous club. Very unique in its way. And I think the way a jazz club should be when it was at its peak. Great place. Great atmosphere. Nothing phony about it in any way. No pretensions and great swinging music. Klein's was similar but a little more high class. . . . The clientele at the Blue Bird was 99 1/2 percent black.*[63] *It was strictly a black scene—in which I felt no uneasiness at all.*[64]

Tommy Flanagan remembered the club from the same time.

> *It was a beautiful club with all the atmosphere that is not in Detroit anymore. It's gone for that matter practically everywhere in the country. I never saw a place like that even in New York. It had a neighborhood atmosphere and all the support a jazz club needed. Everyone who loved jazz in Detroit came, and it was a very inspired group that played there. . . . We*

63. Danson, "Pepper Adams."

64. P. Hanson, "Pepper Adams: Detroit Roots," *Jazz Journal International* (January 1980).

Fig. 83. Bar scene at the Blue Bird Inn, 1958. *L to R: Philly Joe Jones, Billy Mitchell, Cannonball Adderley.* (Photo: James Richardson ©.)

were always able to play what we wanted to play, and the people liked what they heard.[65]

Beans Richardson played the Blue Bird longer than any other Detroit musician.

I found out the majority of the people who was in there played some kind of an instrument, so music-wise they were very up, you know. . . . the talking that went on never bothered nobody. There was a jukebox at the Blue Bird and when they had a bad thing on there, even the bartenders would get on them, get that record off.[66]

The owner of the Blue Bird for most of the 1950s was Clarence Eddins. He became one of several owners in 1953, and in 1956 he took over the club after the violent death of Buddy Dubois.[67] On September 29, 1956, the front-page headline of the *Michigan Chronicle* read "Blue Bird Inn Manager Ambushed. Link Woman to Dubois Slaying," and the article detailed what happened.

Buddy Dubois . . . shot to death mysteriously only a few blocks from the club . . . in front of [the] home of his alleged sweetheart. . . . police believe motive is old grudge. . . . police say Dubois is said to have hit the numbers for several thousand dollars in the last year.

The murder was never solved, but it left

65. Stanley Dance, "Tommy Flanagan: Out of the Background," *Down Beat,* January 13, 1966.

66. Richardson, interview by Bjorn and Gallert.

67. The other owners were Cliff Cheeks, who died after a heart attack, and Creflo Mims, former manager of the Crystal. Hill, interview by Bjorn and Gallert.

Clarence Eddins in charge of the club. He was a resident of the West Side black community and had opened a cleaner's shop on Milford, a few blocks southwest of the Blue Bird, at the end of World War II. Eddins was a well-known numbers man in the neighborhood.

Eddins carried out a major renovation of the Blue Bird in 1957. The stage was moved from its window location at the front to back of the room, where the kitchen was once located. The new stage was a semicircle in the middle of the back wall and could narrowly accommodate a combo with an upright piano. Along the left wall was the bar and to the right a row of booths. The middle of the room was filled with tables, bringing the capacity of the club to 125.

Eddins was soon bringing in more national jazz acts for five- to six-day engagements. This included a teenage matinee on Sundays, which cost $1.25 compared to $2.50 for an evening performance. The groups in the last two years of the decade included hard bop favorites like the Miles Davis sextet, Art Blakey's Jazz Messengers, Jimmy Smith's trio, Horace Silver's quintet, and J. J. Johnson. The Blue Bird was also able to bring back Milt Jackson and Sonny Stitt to play with the house band throughout the decade. It was the combination of a high quality house band and a steady flow of jazz stars that made the Blue Bird the premier jazz club in the city.

On the Far Northwest Side of the city was another spot that turned toward modern jazz in the late 1950s: Baker's Keyboard Lounge.

Baker's

Baker's Keyboard Lounge, just south of the Detroit city limits on Livernois, had already been in operation for 20 years by the mid-1950s. In later years it advertised itself as "the World's Oldest Jazz Club," and there was some truth to the slogan. Its major competitor for the title would be the Village Vanguard in New York City, which opened in February 1934, three months before Baker's. What is debatable for both clubs is exactly when they started as jazz clubs. Baker's featured pianists in late 1934 but was known mainly as a restaurant. The Vanguard began to feature music in 1935, as a complement to its poetry readings.[68] Neither was a major jazz club until the 1950s.

Clarence Baker took over Baker's Bar from his father, Chris, in 1939, when out-of-town pianists were brought in for the first time.[69] A renovation in 1952 expanded the club and gave it its elegant Moderne look, which is still in existence today.[70] The audience at Baker's was predominantly white through the 1950s.[71]

The main attraction from 1940 until about 1954 was Detroit pianist Pat Flowers, who played in the style of Fats Waller, Teddy Wilson, and Art Tatum.[72] Tatum played Baker's during the last two years of his life. Baker remembered that during his last performance, in April 1956, "Tatum was very sick. He lived at the Cadillac [Hotel], but had a hard time making all three shows."

Tatum was one of the major jazz acts that Baker started to bring in around 1955. Others included mainstream piano trios, small groups, and vocalists. Modern jazz was less common at Baker's during the 1950s. The major acts were Dave Brubeck in 1957 and Gerry Mulligan in 1958. In the 1960s Baker's turned more toward the hard bop varieties of modern jazz.

Next door to Baker's on Livernois was the Club Alamo, which opened in 1948 and lasted through the 1950s. It featured singers, comedians (including Lenny Bruce), and pianists. Art Tatum was there frequently from 1949 to 1953. When Tatum first appeared in October 1949 he stopped playing when a black friend was refused service. The owner of the Alamo, Max Spiegelman, wrote the *Michigan Chronicle* two months later to inform its readers that blacks were welcome at the Alamo and that Tatum was back for another engagement.[73]

Whereas Baker's in the 1950s turned into a

68. Clarence Baker, interview by Lars Bjorn, Detroit, Michigan, September 28, 1977. "Nightclubs and Other Venues: USA, New York. Village Vanguard." *New Grove Dictionary of Jazz.*

69. Baker, interview by Bjorn.

70. The renovation moved the door and the bar from the Livernois side to the north side of the building. Baker's features booths, tilted mirrors, a bar with a painted keyboard, and wall paintings by Harry Julian Carew. Baker's had seating for 99 people. Baker, interview by Bjorn.

71. Baker, interview by Bjorn.

72. Flowers recorded for Hit/Guild in 1944 and RCA Victor in 1946–47. The latter recordings were done with Fats Waller's old band. Jepsen, *Jazz Records.* Detroit pianist Harold McKinney was very impressed with Flowers as a pianist and compared his style to that of Wilson and Tatum. Harold McKinney, interview by Bjorn.

73. *Michigan Chronicle,* October 15, 1949; December 17, 1949. South of Grand River on Plymouth Road (near Meyers) in northwest Detroit was also Young's Cocktail Lounge, which in the mid-1950s featured some jazz mixed with white dance bands. *Detroit Free Press,* June 19, 1954; June 25, 1957.

classic modern jazz club, a new kind of jazz spot was also found on the North Side of town: the World Stage.

World Stage

While studying at Wayne University, Kenny Burrell got the idea of forming an association of musicians that would put on performances and facilitate the passing on of musical knowledge from one generation to the other. Around 1953 some Wayne students organized the World Stage, a theater in the round, under the direction of Fred Barnett. The World Stage was located in Highland Park, a couple of miles north of campus on Woodward Avenue.[74] Pepper Adams remembered the World Stage.

> *Through the manager of the place at the time, who Kenny Burrell and I had known for many years, somehow it was suggested that we put on concerts there on a weekly basis. So the New Music Society was formed with Kenny as President and a whole slate of officers; pretty good size membership as I recall. It was quite a nice feeling, good musically and very nice socially; a lot of good friends getting together on a regular basis, which happened all the time in Detroit, but that sort of formalized it somewhat.*[75]

In June 1955 the *Michigan Chronicle* reported that

> *The World Stage Inc. may well be the beginning of mass legitimate theatre and a vehicle for the furtherance of jazz in Detroit. Located at 13525 Woodward in a dinky hard-to-find one-room-building, it may surprise play lovers to find a full production of Shaw, Tennessee Williams, or Shakespeare in well-acted performances. A group of local musicians known jointly as the New Music Society stage concerts every Tuesday night, usually playing to a full house. The New Music Society headed by Oliver Shearer, Acting President, is trying to give free expression to jazz in Detroit where mostly young people gather at the concerts. . . . the true purpose of the society . . . is offering young, inexperienced musicians a chance to play with seasoned veterans and before an audience appreciative of modern musical endeavors. . . . . Big names sit in after work. . . . The New Music Society was headed by Kenny Burrell before he was signed to the JATP group and went to Europe. . . . Oliver Shearer is assisted by Yusef Lateef, Vice President. . . . Low admission ($1.50 to the public and 50¢ for members). . . . [There are] 300 odd members of the organization.*[76]

The Tuesday concerts referred to by the *Chronicle* were in fact more like jam sessions, while concerts were started every other Sunday afternoon in early 1955.[77] Elvin Jones remembered the World Stage as a very special performance space.

> *The World Stage . . . was supported heavily by the community. . . . This was near the Wayne University campus so a lot of the audience would be college students. The respect that the audience would show, even in that little place. One hundred and fifty people would have been a really large crowd, because the place wasn't big. It was just as if you were in Carnegie Hall. It was the same kind of reverence, the same sort of atmosphere.*[78]

One unusual feature of the World Stage was the fact that some performances were recorded. On August 23, 1955, seven tracks were recorded by Transition Records, a company formed that year in Cambridge, Massachusetts.[79] This was Donald Byrd's first record as a leader, and the group included Yusef Lateef, Bernard McKinney, Barry Harris, Alvin Jackson, and Frank Gant.

The New Music Society also sponsored jams at the Blue Bird Inn and concerts at the Detroit Institute of Arts, but its sessions at the World Stage remained the main focus.[80] This society was the first effort of Detroit jazz musicians to collectively organize and control the conditions of music production, outside of their participation in the American Federation of Musicians. This was at once a more far reaching and a more focused effort than union action. It was

74. The World Stage was located at the corner of Woodward and the Davison freeway. Its address was 13525 Woodward. The World Stage is listed under social clubs as a theater club in the 1953 *Detroit City Directory*.

75. Danson, "Pepper Adams."

76. Shearer was a vibraphone player and a Wayne student. The Board of Directors of the society included Alvin Jackson. "Hard to Find but World Stage Boasts Top-Flight Artists," *Michigan Chronicle*, June 4, 1955. Rudy Tucich remembers that concerts at the World Stage allowed younger players like him to perform with those more experienced during the first set of the evening. Tucich, interview by Bjorn.

77. *Down Beat*, February 3, 1955.

78. Taylor, "Elvin Jones," 221.

79. Transition lasted for two years and recorded 20 albums with many important modernists. Byrd's album was later released by Delmark as *First Flight*, Delmark DL-407 (LP). "Transition," *New Grove Dictionary of Jazz*.

80. *Down Beat*, October 19, 1955. At least two concerts were held at the DIA: March 28, 1955, and June 26, 1956. Performers included Sonny Stitt, Kenny Burrell, Yusef Lateef, Pepper Adams, Tommy Flanagan, Barry Harris, Elvin Jones, Bernard and Harold McKinney, and Pancho Hagood. Tucich, interview by Bjorn.

more far reaching because musicians organized the performance function, rather than just the labor contract. It was more focused since it only involved a group of modern jazz musicians at the local level. The New Music Society lasted at least through 1956 and became an important forerunner of organizing efforts in the late 1960s.[81]

On Detroit's Southwest Side two major jazz spots emerged in the 1950s: the Rouge Lounge and the West End.

Rouge Lounge

The Rouge Lounge was located in River Rouge, a suburb between the Detroit River and the southwest tip of the city. River Rouge was one of the first Detroit suburbs with a sizable black population. During the 1950s it was one-third black, and by 1960 it was predominantly black.[82] The Rouge Lounge was just a block south of the Detroit city limits on Coolidge Highway.[83] In 1953 owners Tom and Ed Sarkesian started a jazz policy that lasted for five years. This policy coincided with the opening of the lounge to black patrons, and since then audiences were well balanced along racial lines. The Rouge had a bowling alley, as Pepper Adams remembered.

> *Rouge Lounge was a combination bowling alley and bar. I heard tales of people who would circumvent the door charge to hear the band by bringing a bowling ball and going through the alley, and then coming out the other way as if they were just on their way home after bowling a few frames.*[84]

Many of the top names in modern and mainstream jazz visited the Rouge for six-day stays, including Sunday matinees.[85] Some groups were frequent visitors: Terry Gibbs's quartet with Detroiter Terry Pollard on piano; Dave Brubeck's quartet; the Modern Jazz Quartet (with Milt Jackson); the Chet Baker Quartet; the Gerry Mulligan Quartet; Dizzy Gillespie's quintet; the Stan Getz Quartet and Sextet; the Bud Powell Trio; Carmen McRae; the Clifford Brown–Max Roach Quintet; the J. J. Johnson Quintet; the Sonny Stitt Quartet; and the Australian Jazz Quintet.[86]

The Rouge was able to get some media exposure, at least for a while. On Friday nights in 1954 radio station WXYZ had a half-hour *Jazz at the Rouge* program. Several of the artists at the Rouge were also able to get on Soupy Sales's show.[87]

The Rouge also gave two prominent local modernists a place to play. Kenny Burrell and his Four Sharps played for jam sessions on Monday nights in 1954–55, and by September 1955 they shared the bill with out-of-town names. Barry Harris was called on to back up visiting solo acts with a local rhythm section and eventually led his own quartet at the Rouge in 1956 and 1957.[88]

By 1957 Ed Sarkesian left the management of the Rouge to Peter and Augie Evangelista, who ran it for another year before it closed. In a 1959 interview Sarkesian explained the economics of jazz clubs this way.

> *It's a two-way problem. First for the club owner, then for the patron. Say an act does real well. Fine. Then he wants $500 more the next time, and $500 more the third time. The club owner has a limited capacity and all he can do is raise the admission and the price of drinks. The average guy out on a date can spend $10 without batting an eye. He may do it once or twice, but he's not going to come back to hear a performer a third or fourth time no matter how much he likes him.*[89]

Sarkesian went on to explain that "the rising cost of top-name jazz talent [was] causing major jazz cabarets all over the country to retrench or close shop altogether."[90] In addition to running his club Sarkesian had been involved as a producer of national jazz concert tours in the last half of the 1950s. In 1959 Sarkesian put on the first "American Jazz Festival" at the State Fair grounds in Detroit. The *Michigan*

81. Charles Gunter became president of the society in 1956. *Michigan Chronicle,* September 22, 1956. Boyd, "Black Bottom and Beyond," 86.

82. River Rouge lost 12 percent of its population in the 1950s and was one of the first suburbs to do so. U.S. Department of Commerce, Bureau of the Census, *Census of Population: 1950,* vol. 2, *Characteristics of the Population,* pt. 22, table 10; and *Census of Population: 1960,* pt. 24, table 13.

83. The Rouge Lounge was located at 1937 Coolidge Highway. Coolidge becomes Schaefer once in Detroit.

84. Danson, "Pepper Adams."

85. Matinees gave teenagers a chance to attend but were discontinued in late 1955 due to poor attendance. *Down Beat,* October 30, 1955.

86. Other notable appearances were from the Miles Davis quintet, the Roy Eldridge–Ben Webster–Bill Harris Sextet, Billie Holiday, the Art Tatum Trio, Lester Young, the Cannonball Adderley Quintet, the Charles Mingus Quintet, and Charlie Parker. Parker played at the Rouge February 15–20 in 1955, a month before his death. Advertisements, *Detroit Free Press,* February 14, 1955; and *Michigan Chronicle,* February 19, 1955. See also Ken Vail, *Bird's Diary* (Chessington, England: Castle Communications, 1996), 171.

87. In 1954 these included Earl Hines, Stan Getz, Chet Baker, and Chris Conner. In 1955 it included Charlie Parker from February 15 to 20 and a February 4 TV appearance on *Soupy's On.* Parker died on March 12 in New York City. Vail, *Bird's Diary,* 169–71.

88. Harris backed Eldridge-Webster-Harris (1955), Flip Phillips (1956), Lee Konitz (1957), and Lester Young (1957). He also played in the Clifford Brown–Max Roach Quintet. Advertisements in the *Detroit Free Press;* and Michael Bourne, "Barry Harris: Keeper of the Bebop Flame," *Down Beat,* July 1985.

89. Arnold Hirsch, "Jazz Goes Uptown: Neighborhood Spots Popular," *Detroit Sunday Times,* May 10, 1959.

90. Ibid.

Chronicle hoped that "Detroit was ready to occupy a position in the picture, equal in stature to the nationally recognized Newport Jazz Festival," which had started in 1954.[91] The Detroit festival did not fulfill those high hopes and lasted only for another year. It did however present a number of prominent jazz performers, including Duke Ellington, Dave Brubeck, Ahmad Jamal, Thelonious Monk, Max Roach, Jack Teagarden, and Maynard Ferguson, as well as a number of local groups. *Down Beat*'s Ira Gitler visited the second year and was impressed with the quality of the local musicians.[92] Sarkesian eventually abandoned jazz for folk music.[93]

West End

The West End Hotel was the major place for after-hours sessions on weekends in the late 1950s. It was located in Delray, a formerly Hungarian working-class neighborhood in southwest Detroit surrounded by industrial plants. Just north of the hotel was the large Cadillac Fleetwood plant, and to the south was a Hungarian church.[94] The West End was owned by Joseph Blair, who "was an older man who was an inventor with cars, having worked at Ford. He was building a car in the shed behind his hotel" according to Pepper Adams. Hindal Butts was the drummer in Kenny Burrell's band and remembered playing there around 1954–55.

> *We worked six nights at Klein's and three nights at the West End . . . in Delray, owned by Mr. and Mrs. Blair. . . . How that happened . . . Mrs. Blair had a permanently bad heart and she couldn't get out. So she's got this dining room out there and she'd say: "Let's put some music in here after 2 o'clock"—food and coffee, no booze, nothing illegal. . . . The primary thing was for her to listen to some music, to enhance her business. She was doing nothing illegal but she was constantly getting harassed by the police. They'd harass her and she'd harass them. If you had some whiskey, they [the Blairs] would run you outside; they ran a clean joint. The only thing she wanted was to hear some jazz and then she got enthused because the reputation of the club became so wide. . . . everybody that was in town would come out there. The Blairs were black. He was an old inventor from Ford's and she had a heart attack when Ray Robinson won his title bout. . . . Kenny's wife was her daughter, Laura.*[95]

Elvin Jones also remembered the West End fondly.

> *There was a club near there called the Rouge Lounge that would bring in topflight musicians from all over the country, and when they were off, they would come out to the place if only to have breakfast, because they had some good food there. A lady cooked homemade bread and biscuits, grits and eggs, chops and steaks and things. It was very nice.*[96]

The sessions at the West End lasted for at least six years until 1961.[97] An effort to revive them in 1965 lasted only for two weekends.[98]

East Side Spots

The East Side of Detroit had few jazz spots in comparison with the West Side. The Roosevelt Lounge on Mack was the only one to feature national talent and only for a couple of years at most. It opened in 1955 with Phineas Newborn and his band. In 1956 it featured James Moody, Lester Young, and Paul Bley. That year the Roosevelt presumptuously advertised itself as the New Birdland of Detroit (after New York's major modern jazz spot), but it was not to be.[99]

Other spots were Hajji Baba (1957–60)[100] and Larry's Show Bar (opened in 1955) on Gratiot,[101] Shangri-La (formerly Club Stevadora) on Harper,[102] and Dick and Ernie's Carribee on East Jefferson (opened 1953).[103]

Further east at the border to Grosse Pointe Park on Mack was Little Wally's, which was an important spot for white modernists. Accord-

91. "American Jazz to Debut in Detroit," *Michigan Chronicle*, June 27, 1959.

92. Ira Gitler, *Down Beat*, September 29, 1960.

93. Brokensha, interview by Bjorn.

94. The West End Hotel was located at 515–21 South West End Avenue.

95. Butts, interview by Bjorn.

96. Taylor, "Elvin Jones," 222.

97. The West End probably started its sessions some time in 1953. Harold McKinney remembers playing there in January 1954 just before getting drafted. McKinney, interview by Bjorn. See also Azalea Thorpe, "'Exciting' Detroit Bash," *Down Beat*, September 21, 1955.

98. *Down Beat*, January 28, 1965; February 25, 1965.

99. The Roosevelt Lounge was located at 10813 Mack, near Montclair. Advertisements, *Michigan Chronicle*, August 8, 1955; April 13, 1956; October 27, 1956.

100. Hajji Baba was at 3775 Gratiot near Mount Elliot. Advertisement, *Michigan Chronicle*, April 18, 1957.

101. Larry's was at 6911 Gratiot at Canton. Advertisement, *Michigan Chronicle*, January 13, 1955.

102. Shangri-La was at 8715 Harper between Van Dyke and Gratiot. In 1953 it featured Kenny Burrell. Advertisement, *Detroit Free Press*, March 12, 1953.

103. *Michigan Chronicle*, May 2, 1953.

ing to a survey of jazz clubs in the *Detroit Sunday Times* in 1959, Little Wally's featured Bess Bonnier's "very hep, moving jazz which transcends the bar's complete lack of suitable atmosphere . . . attracts the same sort of young crowd the other jazz places do, only dressed a little less elegantly."[104] Bonnier does not have much praise for the way Little Wally's worked.

> *I was there in 1959, lasted maybe a year and a half. The owner was a gambler (horse races). It is a terrible thing to have the musician be given the responsibility of bringing people in. I don't want it. . . . I had the place jammed. All by word of mouth, forget advertising.*[105]

Let us now take a closer look at the music produced in Detroit during the 1950s.

104. Little Wally's was located on Mack and Maryland. Hirsch, "Jazz Goes Uptown."

105. Bonnier, interview by Bjorn.

The 1950s: The Golden Age of Jazz in Detroit

Jazz in the 1950s

If the 1940s were a time of stylistic revolution in jazz, the 1950s were a time of evolution. The bop style in the 1950s evolved into two varieties: cool and hard bop. The cool school was generally the music of white modernists and was the dominant style on the West Coast. Hard bop on the other hand was the work of mainly black modernists on the East Coast and began in the mid-1950s. Hard bop expanded the emotional range of bop and under the influence of rhythm and blues developed a heavier beat. The expanded emotional range allowed for more lyricism but also for starker and more somber moods.[1]

Detroit was one of the main feeders of talent to New York hard bop groups in the latter half of the decade and thus a vital part of its development. However, Detroit remained handicapped by the lack of major record labels, and this eventually forced young aspiring players to leave for New York or the West Coast. The Detroiters who arrived in New York were already highly accomplished modernists and had little trouble taking part in the highly competitive New York scene. Tommy Flanagan's first year in New York is a case in point. During 1956 he played with bassist Oscar Pettiford, subbed for Bud Powell at Birdland, toured with Miles Davis and J. J. Johnson, and recorded now classic LPs with Miles Davis (*Collector's Items*) and Sonny Rollins (*Saxophone Colossus*). The experiences of baritone saxophonist Pepper Adams, who joined the army in 1951 after having been part of the Detroit modern jazz scene for about three years, followed a similar path. Adams had not planned on becoming a professional musician, but his army experiences changed his mind.

> *Most of the fellows in the Army band were considerable older, some had been on the road with name bands. I didn't even consider myself to be a professional musician, and here I find myself in a milieu of professional musicians and they*

Sonny Stitt, Lonnie Hillyer, and Charles McPherson at the Blue Bird Inn, ca. 1957.

1. David Rosenthal compares hard bop as a stylistic category to Stanley Dance's "mainstream" label for jazz in the 1930s. David Rosenthal, *Hard Bop: Jazz and Black Music 1955–1965* (New York: Oxford University Press, 1992), 43–45.

don't know a damn thing close to what I know. You see in Detroit the standards were so high that to compete for local gigs you had to really play awful goddamn good! If you were good enough to be competitive in Detroit, you were far ahead of what the rest of the world's standards were.[2]

Detroit had contributed to the development of jazz since the 1920s, but the 1950s were clearly the golden age of jazz in Detroit.

1950s Modern at the Blue Bird

THE HOUSE BANDS AT THE BLUE BIRD in the 1950s were at the center of modern jazz in Detroit and by extension at the center of modern jazz in the country. A number of talented modernists in their twenties fine-tuned their art in Detroit and eventually moved on to New York. There were other modern bands in other places, but the center was at 5021 Tireman.

The story of the Blue Bird can be told through the succession of house bands that played there. The house bands usually ruled the roost, but they also accompanied touring jazz artists and locals who sat in. As we saw in the fourth chapter, Phil Hill started the modern jazz period at the Blue Bird with his house band in 1948. He was followed by Billy Mitchell in 1951, Beans Richardson in 1954, Alvin Jackson in 1955, and Ernie Farrow in 1958.

Phil Hill with Frank Foster and Wardell Gray

TATE HOUSTON WAS the featured saxophonist with the Phil Hill group at the Blue Bird in the fall of 1949. Some time that fall he was replaced by tenorist Frank Foster.[3] Foster had come to Detroit from Wilberforce University in Ohio to join Snooky Young's band at the Flame in the summer, but things did not turn out as planned.

I never played the Flame with Snooky Young. They were there seven weeks, but I played with them for another seven weeks at the Club Valley.... I only had three years of college at Wilberforce when I left for Detroit. I was a music major. I was supposed to come back to school after the job in Detroit. While I'm there at the Club Valley my three instruments, clarinet, alto sax and tenor sax, bought by my parents, were stolen by a flunkie who worked there. He also stole Ziggy Johnson's suits.... I left my horns in the dressing room. I came there the day before my birthday [September 23] and they were stolen.... The night before a black cat crossed my path, but I paid it no mind! But I didn't forget it. The next night I had to borrow a baritone sax from someone.... I used the investigation by the Detroit Police Department as an excuse not to go back to Wilberforce. I was failing most of my courses, except music.... Also I knew as much about music as most of my teachers.

When I first came to Detroit I heard great musicians at the Club Sudan, Tommy Flanagan, Kenny Burrell. I met Barry Harris and Billy Mitchell.... I was hanging out at the Blue Bird. I happened to be there when Tate Houston got into a quarrel with Phil Hill and Phil hired me.... I started out four nights a week Thursday through Sunday, but after a while things got hard and we were cut to three nights a week. ... We got $50 for four nights and $36 for three nights.... I met so many beautiful Detroit musicians there: Ted Sheely, Lefty Edwards, Warren Hickey, Joe Alexander, Moon Mullins.... I was at the Blue Bird over a year.... When Wardell Gray and Milt Jackson came to town they played there. I learned from Detroit tenorists like Joe Alexander and Lefty Edwards. They knew how to swing and they knew their chord changes.[4]

Fortunately an acetate recording by Porter Crutcher made in late April 1950 has preserved the sound of the Foster quartet at the Blue Bird. The pianist was Tommy Flanagan, who was one of the frequent subs at the club, and this tape represents the earliest recordings by both Foster and Flanagan. Both Foster and Flanagan play fluently in the bebop style, even though their individual approaches were still in the

2. Adams returned to Detroit in 1953 and went to New York in 1956. Gary Carner, "Pepper Adams' 'Rue Serpente,'" *Jazz Research* 22 (1990): 121.

3. This probably occurred some time after October 11 when Houston was recorded with Charlie Parker at the Blue Bird.

4. Frank Foster, interview by Lars Bjorn, Detroit, Michigan, March 29, 1997. Joe "Ziggy" Johnson was a show producer and a former dancer. In the 1940s he toured with Count Basie, and he was also a columnist in the *Michigan Chronicle*. "The Production Number on Upgrade: Ziggy," *Michigan Chronicle*, October 18, 1947. Joe Alexander was active in Detroit in the late 1940s and then moved to Cleveland. Lefty Edwards was born in 1927 and was a Cass graduate. His playing was in the school of Lester Young. He played with King Porter around the time Foster was in Detroit. Boyd and Sinclair, *Detroit Jazz Who's Who*, 27.

process of formation. The quartet swings nicely on some bebop and Tin Pan Alley standards.[5]

In December 1949 Foster was temporarily replaced by Wardell Gray, who stayed in Detroit until the middle of 1950. Beans Richardson remembered: "Wardell was working with us at the Blue Bird whenever he was in town, sometimes as long as two months. . . . He lived with his sister and his brother Harry, a bassist who left music."[6] In April Gray and Phil Hill, Beans Richardson, and Art Mardigan recorded at United Sounds studios for Prestige. Four sides were logged: "A Sinner Kissed an Angel," "Blue Gray," "Grayhound," and "Treadin' with Treadwell." They were included on the *Wardell Gray Memorial Album* released by Prestige in 1955 and are an important part of Gray's jazz legacy.[7] Gray was a unique saxophone stylist who developed his own mix of the tradition of Lester Young and the new sounds of Parker. Critics have argued that Gray's strengths were a "power of unfaltering linear invention," which produced "flowing melodic shapes," together with a "constant emotional pulse"[8] and "a sense of swing almost unrivalled in jazz."[9] All these qualities are nicely illustrated on his four Detroit sides, most particularly on "Treadin' with Treadwell," an up-tempo blues of particular emotional and rhythmic intensity. This tune also showcases the power of the rhythm section, particularly Hill's vibrant chords and Mardigan's propulsive drumming.

Gray played several places outside the Blue Bird during his half year in Detroit. In late January he was part of what must have been a remarkable dance at Club Valley where the popular rhythm and blues singer Lil Green was featured along with Miles Davis and his Capitol Recordings Stars, as well as Gray's orchestra.[10] The *Michigan Chronicle* reported that "Gray jammed the luxurious dance precinct, playing a double date with Miles Davis, the boy trumpet ace."[11] Gray returned to Club Valley over several weekends in what was billed as a "Bop Battle" against Little John and His Merry Men and Candy Johnson and his Peppermint Sticks. In May Gray participated with Richardson in the Monday night jams organized by Art Mardigan at the Bowl-O-Drome.[12] He was also a member of Todd Rhodes's jump band at several spots during the spring.[13] Gray returned to Detroit and the Blue Bird in 1954.

In August 1950 Foster was briefly spelled at the Blue Bird by Milt Jackson, who was back in town after a tour with the Woody Herman big band. Jackson had joined Herman a year earlier with another Detroiter, tenorist Billy Mitchell.[14] Mitchell only lasted for a couple of months, returned to Detroit, and was soon leading his "Be-Boppers" at concerts. His group was part of the "Jazz at the Broadway Capitol" series of concerts on Saturday nights until early 1950.[15] When Jackson returned to Detroit and the Blue Bird he worked with some of the players who played with Mitchell: Tommy Flanagan on piano, Tate Houston on baritone, and his brother Alvin Jackson on bass.[16]

Foster also played with Little John and His Merry Men, a seven-piece band that used unusually sophisticated arrangements for its size.[17] With this band Foster could further develop his arranging skills, for which he was increasingly becoming known. The gigs with Little John included a trip to Cleveland.

> *I played the Globe Theater in Cleveland with [trumpeter] Little John Wilson. Pepper Adams was also in the band. . . . "Cleveland" Willie Smith was a wonderful writer for the band. I only wrote a few arrangements for the band, 1 or maybe 2. . . . I did write a lot for the Charles Johnson big band. He was a drummer. There was not many big bands around Detroit then. . . . I started writing in high school.*[18]

Pepper Adams also remembered the Little John band.

> *The Club Valley was a dance hall for teenagers. Mostly jazz was played there and I worked there with a band called Little John and his*

5. Crutcher caught the quartet playing "Bouncing with Bud," "Yesterdays," "The Way You Look Tonight," "Move," "Dance of the Infidels," and "There's a Small Hotel."

6. Richardson, interview by Bjorn and Gallert.

7. James "Beans" Richardson is incorrectly identified as Johnny Richardson on this and other releases.

8. Max Harrison, "Backlog Ten-Wardell Gray," *Jazz Monthly,* May 1962, 19.

9. Alun Morgan, "Wardell Gray," *Jazz Monthly,* February 1956, 7.

10. "Bop Greats Join Lil Green at the Valley," *Michigan Chronicle,* January 21, 1950.

11. "Wardell Gray Held over at Valley," *Michigan Chronicle,* January 28, 1950.

12. *Down Beat,* May 5, 1950.

13. "Todd Rhodes to Play Last Local Dance at Valley," *Michigan Chronicle,* April 29, 1950. Advertisement for Club Juana, *Michigan Chronicle,* May 13, 1950.

14. Clancy and Kenton, *Woody Herman,* 152–53.

15. Mitchell's group was advertised at the Broadway Capitol in the *Michigan Chronicle* from October 1949 to February 1950. In October the group also was featured at the Radio City Theater on Woodward and 9-Mile. This concert also featured Milt Jackson. Advertisement, *Detroit Free Press,* October 28, 1949. Mitchell, Flanagan, and Kenny Burrell also played dances at the Mirror Ballroom in December 1949. "Boppers to Bop at Mirror Christmas," *Michigan Chronicle,* December 24, 1949.

16. *Michigan Chronicle,* August 5, 12, and 19, 1950. The drummer could possibly have been Elvin Jones since Flanagan remembered a quartet gig at the Latin Quarter in Toronto with the two Jacksons and Jones. Flanagan, interview with Bjorn.

17. Tenorist Lamonte Hamilton played alto with the band and remembered the high quality arrangements compared to those of other bands that typically relied on head arrangements. Graystone International Jazz Museum, *Community Jazz History Series: Lamonte Hamilton,* 1989. Larry Gabriel, producer (video).

18. The moniker "Cleveland" was used to separate this Willie Smith from the more well-known one who played with Jimmie Lunceford. Frank Foster, interview with Bjorn.

Merrymen, if you believe that. . . . leader John Wilson had worked with Buddy Johnson and briefly with Lunceford (though I am not positive). . . . for a long time Cleveland Willie Smith, an alto player and a student of Tadd Dameron, played in the band and wrote a good deal of the book. . . . The quality of the writing was fine. . . . He could make three-piece voicings that were extraordinary. . . . Barry Harris played piano for a long time. Another long tenure was Otis "Bu Bu" Turner on piano and Ali Mohammed Jackson on bass and several good drummers. Frank Foster played in the band . . . [and] Yusef Lateef played in the band for a while. . . . The quality of writing was fine. Frank Foster . . . contributed arrangements and I wrote some. . . . Basically we played Club Valley; we got other gigs now and then.[19]

Foster spent two years in the service and was back briefly at the Blue Bird in 1953, before moving to New York.

I was drafted in March 1951. Someone told me that because I had flat feet I would get out of it. I got out in May of 53. Billy Mitchell hired me at the Blue Bird; then he fired me. I don't know why. I auditioned for [Count] Basie in May and he sent for me in July. Ernie and Jimmy Wilkins told Basie about me. . . . Basie was playing at the Graystone, I think. . . . Jimmy Wilkins says I met him in the Gotham Hotel coffee shop and he told me to come by and audition. I did two numbers: "Perdido" and "Body and Soul." . . . I replaced Lockjaw [Davis].[20]

Billy Mitchell

Some time in the last half of 1951 Phil Hill was fired from his job as leader of the Blue Bird house band. His brother Carl, who was the doorman at the club in the 1950s, remembered that

Phil was doubling between the Crystal and the Blue Bird, and that's how he lost his job at the Blue Bird, because Buddy DuBois told him he could not play both places. That's how Billy Mitchell ended up with the band, because Phil and Buddy had a big blow-up over it. Edmour [Bertrand] was paying Phil more than Buddy was, plus Edmour had a black and tan. . . . Phil had told Buddy he was out of town Friday–Sunday, in fact he was at the Crystal. The Blue Bird had a little spinet piano and Edmour had a baby grand. . . . They had to wear a navy blue suit at the Crystal whereas you wore what you had at the Blue Bird.[21]

One indication that Phil Hill knew he was doing something questionable was that his group at the Crystal was called Baron Emanuel and His Progressive Jazz Group. Emanuel was Phil's middle name, and he was sometimes referred to as Baron Hill.[22] The inadvertent beneficiary of Hill's firing was Billy Mitchell who remembered that

Phil had the band and . . . something happened and the lady asked me to form another band. That was when I formed the band at the Blue Bird. In the original band was—it could have been anybody working with me at various times: the Jackson brothers [drummer] Oliver and [bassist] Ali. But when the band finally did get settled down I had a quartet . . . [pianist] Terry Pollard and Beans [Richardson and] . . . Elvin [Jones].[23]

When the *Michigan Chronicle*'s Roy Stephens heard the Mitchell group in April 1952 he was very impressed.

Occasionally the music is good, more often it's better, but the musicians who take chorus after chorus on the Blue Bird Inn bandstand are just about the most uninhibited, relaxed and frenetic bunch of men in the city. Years ago, back in the late forties perhaps, the Inn was a Mecca for the goatee and beret, a sort of cave for the "musically misunderstood" and a gallery for the set who talked rapidly (and often vaguely) in terms of "atonal qualities, polyphonic melodies and counterpoint." . . . Currently, something of a renaissance is taking place at the West side night spot where tenorman Billy Mitchell has surrounded himself with Jimmy Richardson, Terry Pollard, and Elvin Jones.

19. Danson, "Pepper Adams." In another interview Adams claimed the band played teenage clubs like Club Valley frequently because the band included underage players. Hanson, "Pepper Adams: Detroit Roots." Little John's band at one time included many other Detroit modernists, among them Tommy Flanagan and drummers Lawrence "Jacktown" Jackson and Frank Gant. *Michigan Chronicle,* January 29, 1949; June 18, 1949. Gant was with the band in 1954 when it backed Billie Holiday for four days at the Madison Ballroom. Gant, interview with Gallert; and advertisement, *Michigan Chronicle,* December 11, 1954.

20. Frank Foster, interview with Bjorn. Foster stayed with Basie for 11 years and became one of the principal arrangers and soloists in the band. In 1986, after Basie's death, he took over leadership of the band. St. Louis born Jimmy Wilkins was a trombonist and his brother Ernie an arranger with the Basie band. Jimmy settled in Detroit in 1955 and started a big band in December of that year that lasted into the 1990s, when he moved to Las Vegas. "Fifteeen 'Swinging' Sidemen," *Michigan Chronicle,* August 3, 1957.

21. Hill, interview with Bjorn and Gallert.

22. Richardson, interview with Bjorn and Gallert. Baron Emanuel and His Progressive Jazz Group at the Crystal included Lamonte Hamilton (tenor saxophone), Kenny Burrell (guitar), Beans Richardson (bass), and Art Mardigan (drums). At times tenorist Leo Osebold also played with the group. Advertisements, *Michigan Chronicle,* September 29, 1951; December 1 and 22, 1951.

23. Gitler, *From Swing to Bop,* 262. The Jackson brothers are likely to have played with Mitchell during the fall of 1951 since at this time Beans Richardson played with Phil Hill at the Crystal.

Then there's always the chance that "anybody" may drop in for a series of choruses. Anybody, of course, refers to somebody who is somebody, musically. Mitchell's group is a progressive one that emphasizes solo lines more than harmonic construction. . . . Anchored by Terry Pollard's piano and Richardson's bass, Mitchell carried most of the load on such niceties as "Robbin's Nest," "I Had the Craziest Dream" and "Stardust," the latter in which he used the not-too-familiar but strikingly beautiful verse. The pianist, a 23-year-old Pershing High School graduate who disavows any formal training, also denies any musical kinship to George Shearing, but it's there from her swift runs to her block chords. On her it wears well, however, and Terry's interludes on "Someone to Watch over Me," "Breathless" or any of the other modernisms are a good indication that the attractive young woman will, with experience and study, develop into a skilled jazz pianist. With the augmentation of the combo by musicians from all over the city, the unit romped, and only on occasion did noise replace music.[24]

Fig. 84. Advertisement for the Broadway Capitol Theater.
(From *Detroit Free Press*, January 6, 1950.)

Billy Mitchell was 25 years old when he took over the Blue Bird house band, but he had been a musician for 10 years, as he told Ira Gitler.

I was involved with music all my life in one way or another. . . . I knew exactly what I wanted to do and never wavered from it really. I began studying music in the public schools. Actually I started in McMichael Intermediate School. I was lucky. . . . They had a very good music program there. . . .There were a lot of people on the Detroit scene still, in my classes, people like Tate Houston. . . . Julius Watkins was sort of one of our teachers. . . . A little later . . . Major Holley. Quite a few came out of that school and went on to the high school, Northwestern, or if they wanted to take music, specifically, they went down to Cass Tech, which was a pretty good school at the time. I went to Cass. I had a cousin . . . George Favors, and he played in a band in one of the finest clubs in the city . . . Club Zombie. . . . They had a fine, nine-piece band . . . [led by] . . . Harold Wallace. I'd go with him to rehearsals. . . . We were playing for acts, people like Billy Eckstine, Lena Horne. . . . I went on the road with my first gig at fifteen. . . . After I left Nat Towles' band I went back to Detroit in 1946. It was at that time that I met people like Kenny Burrell. . . . For about two years I spent [my time] mostly with King Porter. . . . Then I came back to New York in '48 with Lucky Millinder's band . . . and with Milton Buckner—we had a small group at that time; myself and Julius Watkins were the front line.[25]

Mitchell also recorded with Buckner's short-lived big band in March 1949.[26] He can be heard in tenor sax duels with Paul Quinichette, and on "M. B. Blues" he takes a convincing solo.[27] After a brief stay with the Woody Herman band Mitchell was back in Detroit in the fall of 1949 ready to lead his own band of modernists at the Broadway Capitol. By then Mitchell had a solid grounding in the classic tenor saxophone tradi-

24. Roy Stephens, "Blue Bird May Still Sing as in Those '47–'49 Years—and That's Not Bad," *Michigan Chronicle*, April 12, 1952.

25. Gitler, *From Swing to Bop*, 260–62. Wallace had taken over leadership of Cecil Lee's band at the Zombie after Lee was drafted.

26. Mitchell recorded four sides with Milt Jackson and His New Sound Group, which included Julius Watkins on French horn. Mitchell solos on three of the sides and is his best on the blues "Bubu," while his other solos sound tentative. These sides can be found on Milt Jackson, *Meet Milt Jackson*, Savoy SV-0172, in a Japanese CD release.

27. Other Detroiters can be heard on these big band sides, in addition to the leader. Julius Watkins solos on French horn on the medium tempo "Oo-Be-Doop" and plays the lead and a nice coda on "Yesterdays." The drummer is Ed "Chips" Grant. Buckner's big band was started at the time that most big bands were disbanding, and it lasted only a few months. The recordings were on MGM and have been rereleased on Official. Milt Buckner, *The Early Years*, Official 3033 (LP).

tion of Coleman Hawkins from his work in big bands. He was also actively participating in the jump blues honking tradition in his work with King Porter and others. With these two strands of playing he merged the modernistic approaches of the late 1940s and came up with his own brand of gutsy modern saxophone playing, which eventually fed right into the hard bop movement of the 1950s. It was at the Blue Bird that he perfected this approach with his colleagues in the house band.

TERRY POLLARD was the youngest member of the band and had become a professional musician while in her teens. She had perfect pitch and never learned to read or notate music. Her father played piano and exposed Terry and her younger brother to the instrument at an early age.

> *My dad used to sit me between his legs at the piano and show me how to play. I learned "Stardust" with one finger. He used to take me to local talent shows and show me off.*[28]

Pollard began formal lessons with a neighborhood woman who was impressed with her ear but insisted that the youngster use conventional fingering.

> *She would play something for me and I could hear it, but when I played it I used different fingering than she did. She smacked me on the knuckles, hard. After that I didn't go back.*[29]

By the time Pollard was in Pershing High School, she was hooked on music. With a phony ID and dressed to look older, she went to clubs and bars and asked to sit in.[30] This led to her first professional job at age 17 with baritonist Johnny Hill in 1948. Hill led a horn-driven jump band at the Cozy Corner. "That was a rough, blood and bucket type place," she recalled. "When they started fightin', we'd still play."[31]

Pollard's talent attracted the attention of established Detroit musicians, and she joined Emitt Slay's combo and remained for nearly two years.

> *We traveled all over . . . used to play parties and cocktail rooms. He would play guitar and I'd be playin' the cocktail drums and Bill Ware would play bass and sing. We did risque songs. . . . I was singing then.*[32]

Inspired by Milt Jackson while she worked for Slay, Pollard began to play the vibraphone.

> *Dizzy Gillespie was working at the Paradise, and he had Milt Jackson and Kenny Hagood with him. . . . Milt just gassed me so much until I just had to get some vibes. And I got the vibes . . . and just started playin' them. It went over real well.*[33]

Through her friendship with Beans Richardson she joined the Billy Mitchell group at the Blue Bird in 1952. Pollard decided early in her career that she would play "like a man" and would not be pushed aside because of her gender. She acted and talked tough and gained respect as a pianist. At the Blue Bird, Pollard would put a copy of *Jet* magazine on the piano and read it while she played. "I DARED Billy to say a word! (*laughs*) . . . I'd laugh and turn the pages and read and have a ball." She also remembered that the Blue Bird gig gave her a lot of exposure: "Every musician came to hear us . . . and sit in with us, 'cause we had the best rhythm section."[34]

One musician who was especially impressed with Pollard in August 1953 was vibist Terry Gibbs, who praised her vibraphone playing and her "fabulous ear" for music.[35] A week later she went to New York to join the Gibbs quartet as a pianist/vibraphonist and remained until 1957, when she returned to Detroit "to be a mother to my son."[36]

Her stay with Gibbs brought her national recognition, and in 1956 she was chosen as the "New Star" on vibraphone in the *Down Beat* critics' poll.[37] She recorded one album under her own name in 1955, and it was very favorably reviewed in *Down Beat*.

> *Terry, as in person, is an exuberant gas. She swings hard, and while her range of dynamics*

28. Terry Pollard, interview by Jim Gallert, Detroit, Michigan, February 13, 1999.

29. Ibid.

30. She also seems to have fooled Roy Stephens from the *Michigan Chronicle* about her age. Pollard was born in August 1931, which means she was 21 and not 23 at the time she was heard at the Blue Bird by Stephens.

31. Pollard, interview by Gallert. The Hill combo played the Cozy Corner in 1948 according to advertisements in the *Michigan Chronicle*, October 2 and November 20, 1948.

32. Ibid.

33. Ibid.

34. Ibid.

35. "Terry's Other Terry Gives Gibbs a Weight Problem," *Down Beat*, November 18, 1953.

36. *Down Beat* reported that Pollard at this time was pregnant, which she denies. Pollard, interview by Gallert.

37. *Down Beat*, August 8, 1956.

could be wider, she has [a] generally interesting conception on both jumpers and ballads. Terry is a forceful talent, and it's good to see her with an album of her own.[38]

Pollard eventually returned to Detroit and became an important member of the Yusef Lateef Quintet at Klein's, as we will discuss subsequently.

Elvin Jones was one of the younger children in a large and very musical family from Pontiac, Michigan, a small city on the northwest fringe of Detroit's suburbs.[39] His brother Hank (nine years older) was a piano player and had left for New York during World War II. His brother Thad (four years older) played the trumpet and had also gone on the road during the war but eventually returned to the Detroit area. Hank and Thad's main contact with Detroit players during the prewar years was through playing together in various territory bands stationed in Flint and Saginaw, as briefly mentioned in the fourth chapter. To Elvin joining the Blue Bird house band was a major step in his career because he considered the group his musical heroes.[40]

Elvin Jones in turn became a hero to younger drummers like Frank Gant.

> *Out of all the gigs that was the one gig I really wanted to get, because I thought that was the proof you know. Once you could play at the Blue Bird with the different people that were playing there, man, you were in. But Elvin had the gig over there. . . . Elvin Jones wiped me out. Talking about burnin'! And then with his own style. He was an innovator, because at that time I always thought that a drummer's right hand had to be super-strong, but Elvin's hand didn't seem to be that strong. The way he played it was like tick-tah, tick-tah. Billy Mitchell taught him: "Look man, your right hand is not strong enough. Why don't you fill it up with your left hand!" So that's when he would start to fill it in with triplets from the left hand, you know, and making those tremendous rolls and kicking people all out in the street and stuff. (laughs) Elvin Jones: bad dude man! . . . Any band he got in, he'd take over. No surprise what he did with Coltrane.*[41]

Fig. 85. Elvin Jones and Barry Harris shaking hands, Rouge Lounge, late 1950s. (Photo: James Richardson ©.)

Jones's approach to drumming was more polyrhythmic than that of other drummers at the time, and Beans Richardson remembered comments from his brother Rodney, who was a well-known bass player.

> *I never understood what people were talking about when they said Elvin was seen as difficult to play with. My brother would come in and say it is difficult to play with him. I never had problems, even at first. I don't know why the triplet would throw them; it was in meter you know.*[42]

Others had problems with the volume of Jones's playing. For example, pianist Wynton Kelly complained about this at a gig Richardson and Jones had with Dinah Washington at the Frolic.[43]

38. *Down Beat* review of Terry Pollard, Bethlehem LP BCP-15, September 21, 1955.

39. The Joneses' father played guitar, and their mother played piano. Their father was a deacon in the Baptist church in Pontiac, and two sisters sang in the senior choir. An uncle was a trumpet player and a very important influence on Thad. *Different Drummer: Elvin Jones*, video directed by Ed Gray. Rhapsody Films, 1986. Nat Hentoff, "They're All Talking about the Jones Boy," *Down Beat*, November 16, 1955. Primack and Dubin, "Detroit's Triple Gift." *Contemporary Keyboard*, December 1979.

40. Taylor, "Elvin Jones," 220.

41. Gant, interview by Gallert. Elvin Jones is best known for being John Coltrane's drummer from 1960 to 1966.

42. Richardson, interview by Bjorn and Gallert.

43. Ibid.

THAD JONES joined the Billy Mitchell house band some time in the fall of 1952, and even though he was Mitchell's senior by three years he had less experience with name bands. Jones had spent most of the 1940s on the road with bands in the Midwest and Southwest. When his father got ill he returned to Detroit and played for a while with Candy Johnson's band. This was followed by two-and-a-half years on the road with the Larry Steele "Smart Affairs" show.[44] Joining the Mitchell band gave Jones a chance to explore more freely his modern jazz inclinations. Soon he was the dominant member of the group in choice of material, and he contributed a number of his own tunes. His trumpet (cornet) solos were an even more significant contribution.

In an interview three years later Jones told Nat Hentoff: "That was one of the high points of my playing career. . . . That group was about the finest five-piece combo I've ever heard."[45] Musicians who heard the band clearly saw Thad's contribution to the band. One of them was pianist Roland Hanna.

Thad Jones was a genius as an arranger, not yet at the Blue Bird Inn, but his soloing on the cornet. There was only one other person who was his equal and that was Dizzy. Miles [Davis] would stand under the air conditioner with tears running out of his eyes when he heard Thad play.[46]

Pianist Bess Bonnier also visited in those years and was impressed.

The Thad Jones–Billy Mitchell quintet was the best group at the Blue Bird. It was world class, and Thaddeus was not to be believed; I consider him a genius. He had so much in that head of his, you were just mesmerized when he played, no question about it. . . . He was brilliant. Thad was also a very encouraging person, would tell me when I played something good. I got to know him well.[47]

Bassist Charles Mingus heard Thad Jones at the Blue Bird and wrote an enthusiastic and idiosyncratic letter to critic Bill Coss.

I have just heard the greatest trumpet player that I've ever heard in this life. He uses all the classical techniques and is the first man to make them swing. . . . his brother Elvin is just about as good on drums. The cats call Thad Jones the Messiah of the trumpet. . . . Thad was too much for me to believe. He does things that Diz[zy Gillespie] and Fats [Navarro] made difficult for the trumpet. The things Miles [Davis] never made. The things Diz heard Bird do, and Fats made us think were possible. . . . Here is Bartok with valves for a pencil that's directed by God.[48]

Mingus's enthusiasm for Jones was translated into some now classic modernist recordings on Mingus's Debut label once Jones moved to New York in 1954.[49]

The Jones brothers brought an additional dimension to the Blue Bird sessions: jam sessions at their Pontiac home. Elvin recalled that

There was a great interest and an undercurrent of support for the music all over Detroit and that area. Everybody loved the music. They loved to see a young cat develop, to follow his development and to encourage and support him. Consequently, where I lived in Pontiac . . . on our off nights at the club, I started asking the cats if they wouldn't like to come out to my house just to jam. My mother made everything comfortable for everybody. Every Monday the house would be mine and all the musicians from Detroit would flock out there. We would jam and have a ball. That went on for a couple of years. It was that kind of community support.[50]

The Pontiac sessions were at an advanced level of playing as Roland Hanna remembered them.

Every Thursday night there was a jam session in Pontiac at Jones' house. I didn't play often. They'd play "How Long Has This Been Going On" and I did not hear the right chords, espe-

44. The band for the Steele show was led by Jimmy Tyler, a veteran from Sabby Lewis's band in Boston. McCarthy, *Big Band Jazz,* 158. Hentoff, "They're All Talking about the Jones Boy." Raymond Horricks, *Count Basie and His Orchestra* (New York: Citadel Press, 1957), 201.

45. Hentoff, "They're All Talking about the Jones Boy."

46. Roland Hanna, interview by Jim Gallert, "Meet the Artist," Montreux-Detroit Jazz Festival, September 1, 1997.

47. Bonnier, interview by Bjorn. Bonnier played a lot of gigs in the 1950s and formed her own trio around the middle of the decade. This trio for a while included drummer Frank Isola. She felt at the top of her game when she recorded for Argo with her trio in 1958. In the 1960s she was part of a quartet with vibraphonist Jack Brokensha.

48. Bill Coss, "Thad Jones: Horn of Plenty," *Down Beat,* May 9, 1963.

49. On August 11, 1954, six sides were recorded for Debut under the name of the Thad Jones Quintet. This group was a recording unit as Jones worked regularly with Count Basie at the time. The quintet included Thad's brother Hank on piano and Mingus on bass. Others were saxophonist Frank Wess (also with Basie) and drummer Kenny Clarke. On March 10, 1955, the Thad Jones Quartet with Mingus, Max Roach on drums, and pianist John Dennis recorded four additional sides. The quartet sides received five stars in *Down Beat,* and the reviewer thought that Jones "blows with the emotional power and individual conception that announce the arrival of another major jazz figure." *Down Beat,* September 7, 1955.

50. Taylor, "Elvin Jones," 219.

cially the way Thad played all around the chords.[51]

Hanna's perception of the level of playing takes on added significance in light of his own substantial accomplishments by the early 1950s. He started on the piano at age 5 and from 11 received formal classical lessons. His interest in jazz was piqued around 1945 when he met Tommy Flanagan at Northern High School. In the late 1940s Hanna was part of a cooperative modern group, the AHJOs, from the first initials of the players: Ali Jackson (bass), "Hac" Hanna, Joe Alexander (tenor sax), Oliver Jackson (drums). He also played with Lucky Thompson, Emitt Slay, and Candy Johnson before the Pontiac sessions.[52]

Bess Bonnier went to several sessions about the time Barry Harris and Tommy Flanagan were pianists in the house band.

> *Before Thad left town I remember going to perhaps a dozen sessions at the Jones' house in Pontiac. Barry and Tommy would come and many other top musicians. I remember playing there with Paul Chambers. There was a grand piano in the house.*[53]

Billy Mitchell Presents Thad Jones. Before Terry Pollard left the house band in August 1953, the Billy Mitchell Quintet recorded four sides for an EP record on the local Dee Gee label.[54] The EP format keeps each song brief and only provides a glimpse of what the band must have accomplished on extended solos. The first cut is a blues, "Compulsory," played in a raucous style with Mitchell's jumping tenor and Elvin Jones's backbeat. When Terry Pollard takes a swinging vibraphone solo, the horns provide background riffs and Jones adopts a shuffle beat. Another fast song, "Zec," is a tricky Thad Jones composition that is the highlight of the EP.[55] After stating the elegant and witty theme, Mitchell launches into a muscular tenor solo, and Thad Jones follows with a beautifully constructed cornet solo. His brother's comments on the snare greatly increase the rhythmic intensity in a tune that starts out as a cool technical tour de force.

Thad is the sole feature on "Alone Together," where the slower tempo allows him to showcase his deep and full-toned trumpet and to create a somber mood. The old swing standard, "Blue Room," is given a decidedly hip treatment, with witty ensembles that bear the trademark of Thad Jones and a gently walking tempo. Terry Pollard's piano leads off the soloing in a romping bebop style, with no hints of the Shearing influence detected by others. Mitchell's solo on this tune is contemplative and laid back and shows his beautiful tone. Thad Jones's solo on this one is brief, but he comes away as the main discovery of this recording date.

Tommy Flanagan took over Terry Pollard's piano chair when she left in the fall of 1953. The 23-year-old had just returned to Detroit in the summer after two years in the army. In the late 1940s Flanagan had been considered the most promising young pianist in town and started to gig at the Blue Bird. His last year before the service (1951) was spent with clarinetist Rudy Rutherford's band. Rutherford was a veteran of the Basie band who surrounded himself with younger and more modern musicians like Flanagan and drummer Oliver Jackson. After Rutherford returned to Basie in early 1951, Flanagan played with tenorist George Benson's band in Toledo. Benson remembered: "We would play jazz the first set or two, until the people would come, and then we'd break out and play R & B. [Guitarist] Calvin Frazier would have a long cord, walk all over the club and we would have that place packed EVERY night!"[56]

Flanagan remembered the other members of the Blue Bird band when he joined.

> *It seemed to me that Thad and Billy were already fully developed, and Elvin was playing not far from the way he does now. He was al-*

51. Hanna, interview by Bjorn.

52. Ibid. Hanna, interview by Gallert. Hanna remembered playing the Chesterfield Lounge and the Frolic with the AHJOs. Hanna joined the military service in 1950 and in 1953 spent some time at the Eastman School in New York. He returned to Detroit in early 1954 and led a trio (with Ray McKinney on bass and Benny Benjamin on drums) at Chic's Show Bar for a year and a half. In 1955 Hanna moved to New York for more than four years of study at Juilliard but played jazz with, among others, Benny Goodman to survive. In the 1960s his modernist jazz career took off when he played with Charles Mingus and the Thad Jones–Mel Lewis big band.

53. Bonnier, interview by Bjorn.

54. An article in the *Michigan Chronicle* in October announced that the EP *Billy Mitchell Presents Thad Jones* would be out in a few weeks. "Thad Jones Makes EP Record Album," *Michigan Chronicle,* October 3, 1953. The standard discographies have dated this record to 1948, which must be in error. Savoy picked up these four sides and released them on Various Artists, *Swing Not Spring* (SV-0188), now available in a Japanese CD release.

55. The album gives Mitchell credit for this song, but it is generally considered to be the work of Thad Jones.

56. The Benson band played Tate's in Toledo and included Alvin Jackson on bass and George Buckner on drums. Benson, interview by Bjorn and Gallert.

Fig. 86. Rudy Rutherford Quartet, Parrot Lounge, 1948.
Dagwood Langford, dms; Alma Smith, vbs/pno; Harry Gray, bs; Rutherford, cl/bar/ldr.
(Courtesy Alma Smith, Gallert Collection.)

ways an interesting part of the band because no one else in Detroit was playing like that, and the more you play with him the more you CAN *play with him.*[57]

Flanagan's own development as a pianist is difficult to study given the lack of recordings between the 1950 Blue Bird acetates and his first recordings in New York in 1956. The Blue Bird band was definitely a challenge to Flanagan as he remembered it.

We got into some of the things that Bird played, "Billie's Bounce," "Now's the Time," "Night in Tunisia" and Thad started to introduce his music. That stuff was advanced at the time, you know, and it still holds up, I'm still trying to play it, like "Elusive." I think it was the most advanced group in the city at that time. And it was pretty much acknowledged all over the country; people used to come through. The place had a reputation: There's this trumpet player, Thad Jones, who writes these tunes. When Max and Clifford used to come to town later on you'd hear the influence of some of those things that Thad was writing. That one arrangement he had on "I Get a Kick Out of You," which had that waltz time that Max [Roach] was crazy about and those tempo changes. A lot of people came through and were always encouraged to play. Sonny Stitt used to come, Miles was there in residence for a long time, getting his act together. Rehabilitation, cleaning up his habit. Before he went back to

57. Dance, "Tommy Flanagan."

New York and formed that quintet that became quite a quintet.[58]

Flanagan was in the house band when Miles Davis came to Detroit for his first extended stay in 1953. Miles dropped by the Blue Bird as an occasional guest with the house band.

Miles at the Blue Bird

Miles Davis's stay in Detroit and appearances at the Blue Bird have become the stuff of local legend. In his autobiography Davis details how he decided to go to Detroit to kick his heroin habit for good. He had started out going cold turkey by locking himself up in his parents' home in St. Louis for a week in early fall 1953.

As soon as I kicked my habit I went to Detroit. I didn't trust myself being in New York where everything was available. I figured that even if I did backslide a little, then the heroin that I would get in Detroit wasn't going to be as pure as what I could get in New York. . . . When I got to Detroit I began playing in some local clubs with Elvin Jones on drums and Tommy Flanagan on piano. I did use some heroin up there, but it wasn't so strong and there wasn't a lot of it around. . . . I stayed in Detroit for about six months. . . . Anyway, I was staying in a hotel, and I would never eat or anything. . . . There were some good musicians in Detroit and I was starting to play with some of them. That helped me and a lot of them were clean. A lot of musicians in Detroit looked up to me because of all

Fig. 87. George Benson Quintet, unidentified setting, Toledo, Ohio, ca. 1951.
Tommy Flanagan, pno; Benson, as; Ali Jackson, bs; George Buckner, dms; Calvin Frazier, gtr.
(Courtesy George Benson, Gallert Collection.)

58. Flanagan, interview with Bjorn.

the things I had done. . . . There was this great trumpet player named Claire Roquemore, I think that was his name. Man, that motherfucker was bad. He was one of the best I ever heard. And then me and Elvin Jones was getting it on. People were packing in to see us when we played this little club called the Blue Bird. . . . I had been playing at the Blue Bird several months as a guest soloist in Billy Mitchell's house-band. . . . Betty Carter used to come and sit in with Yusef Lateef, Barry Harris, Curtis Fuller and Donald Byrd. It was a real hip city for music. Now when Max [Roach] came to town with Clifford [Brown] and their new group—Richie Powell, Harold Land, George Morrow . . . Max asked me to sit in with them at Baker's. . . . [It is not true that] Clifford let me play because he felt sorry for me . . . . I came back to New York in February 1954, after spending about five months in Detroit, I really felt good for the first time in a long time. My chops were together because I had been playing every night and I had finally kicked heroin.[59]

Davis's appearances at the Blue Bird in 1953 were irregular and not advertised in the press, and it is impossible to verify exactly when he was at the club. It is certain that he returned in mid-August the following year and stayed for at least six weeks. Davis, like other participants and observers, easily conflates these separate stays when trying to recall these long past events. The time he sat in with the Roach-Brown quintet, for example, could not have taken place in 1953 but possibly might have occurred the following year.[60] The Roach-Brown group was definitely in Detroit at the end of November 1954 but at the Crystal rather than Baker's.[61] Frank Gant was present at the Crystal, which was located not far from the Blue Bird.

At the Blue Bird they LOVED *Miles! Clarence Eddins loved Miles! That was Miles' second home outside of New York. He could always come to Detroit and just hang. He didn't have to worry about a horn or anything because some local cats like Lonnie Hillyer would lend him the horn. So this particular night Max was at the Crystal Show Bar and he had Brownie [Clifford Brown] with him and he might have had Harold Land. I know he had Richie Powell and George Morrow. They were burnin'. Brownie was flawless, in the stratosphere, clear as a bell! And in come the Blue Bird people. The barmaid who used to be over there, Grace Silvertop, said: "Come on Miles! Get him Miles, go ahead! You know you can outplay Brownie go ahead Miles!" (laughs) Everybody said: "Oh-Oh! Miles and Brownie right here!" The word went out; people came from everywhere man! The place just became packed in seconds it seemed like. So Miles walked up to Brownie: "Brownie you think I can play some?" And Brownie said: "Well, ask Max. It's alright with me, but ask Max." Max said: "Yeah come on Miles!" And the Blue Bird said: "Miles get him! Get him!" And Miles walked up on the bandstand took Brownie's horn, he had his own mouthpiece, and he started fingering the keys, blowing the air in that horn, turned his back, faced Max and the cats, and then he turned around and put that bell of the horn right in the mike [and played] "My Funny Valentine." You could have heard a rat pissing on cotton when he finished. That was the most soulful thing I'd ever heard in my* LIFE*! I mean the way Miles played that ballad. And then he just put the horn down and walked out of the place.*[62]

Carl Hill was a doorman at the Blue Bird and shed more light on Davis's situation in Detroit in the fall and winter of 1953–54.

When Miles first came to the Blue Bird . . . he was strung out and was living in Sunnie Wilson's hotel on Grand River and the Boulevard [Grand Boulevard]. . . . It was in the winter and Miles walked from the hotel to the Blue Bird, and the joint was packed; everybody was waiting for Miles Davis. So when he came in he had on this old grimy white shirt and a navy blue sweater and Clarence [Eddins] told him to go home and put on a tie. At the Blue Bird

59. Claire Roquemore was by many accounts a very promising trumpeter who never fulfilled his promise. Frank Gant's assessment is that "Claire had technical fluidity; I saw him wipe Miles out many a time. He seemed like he had that breath control where he can play forever." On the other hand Gant says he did not have the tone of another trumpeter who did not fulfill his promise: Teeter Ford. Gant, interview with Gallert. Bassist Ray McKinney (born 1931) knew Roquemore from the time they were in grade school. McKinney remembered when "the teacher got Claire up in front of the class to play 'Ciribiribin.' I said, 'What the?' but he played it right." Ray McKinney, interview by Jim Gallert, Detroit, Michigan, January 7, 1999. Roquemore was a boy wonder at 13 when he participated in a concert with, among others, Rudy Rutherford, Art Mardigan, and Kenny Burrell. "Newman Club at Michigan State College Sponsor Jazz Concert," *Michigan Chronicle,* May 8, 1948. A couple of years later he participated in the "Moods and Idioms" concerts at the DIA organized by Harold McKinney. Harold McKinney, interview by Bjorn. Roquemore was one of the musicians in the circle around Barry Harris. McKinney remembered how impressive Roquemore was at jam sessions in Maurice Wash's basement in the late 1940s: "Me, Barry Harris, Sonny Red, and Donald Byrd would be there, but when Claire Roquemore was there, [Donald] didn't want to pick up his horn." Ray McKinney, interview by Gallert. Tenorist Charlie Gabriel (born 1932) went to high school with Roquemore and remembers an occasion when both youngsters sat in with Lionel Hampton's band at the Paradise Theatre in 1948: "After the show, they had 'Lionel Hampton's Junior BeBoppers' come out on stage and play. It was his rhythm section and local kids. Claire and me played, and Fats Navarro was so impressed with Claire that he came over and started trading solos with him. Claire was the most advanced trumpet player around." Charlie Gabriel, interview by Jim Gallert, Detroit, Michigan, May 28, 2000. Gabriel is a fourth generation New Orleans musician.

Miles Davis with Quincy Troupe, *Miles: The Autobiography* (New York: Touchstone, 1990), 171–75.

60. Davis's autobiography and biographies are silent on his activities during the fall of 1954, but advertisements from the *Michigan Chronicle* indicate that Davis was at the Blue Bird between August 14 and October 2, 1954. The incident at Baker's could not have happened in 1953, given the composition of the Roach-Brown quintet. Harold Land joined the group in Los Angeles in August 1954, and it is possible that the group stopped in Detroit on their way to New York. Gioia, *West Coast Jazz,* 310–17.

61. Advertisement, *Michigan Chronicle,* November 30, 1954; *Detroit Free Press,* December 3, 1954.

62. Gant, interview by Gallert.

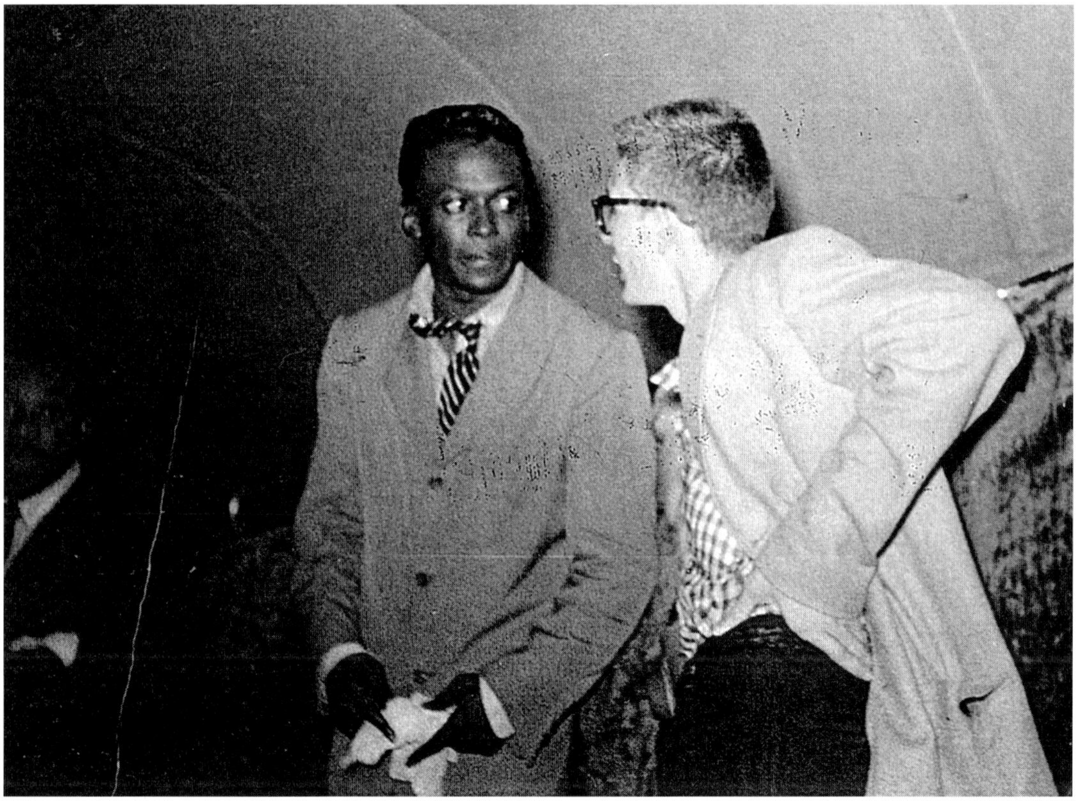

Fig. 88. Kenny Clarke, Miles Davis, and Rudy Tucich, Madison Ballroom, June 2, 1952.
Clarke and Davis were performing with a "Symphony Sid" Torin jazz tour.
(Photo: Rudy Tucich ©. Courtesy Rudy Tucich.)

there is an inside and an outside door. So Miles went outside and took a shoelace out of his shoe and tied it up under his shirt and said: "How do you like this, boss? and went on the bandstand and played. So Miles was stranded here in Detroit maybe for the next two or three years, and Clarence befriended him to a certain degree, because he was a little small guy and Miles was a little small guy and he gave Miles a lot of his clothes to wear. . . . When Miles first came to the Blue Bird, Willie Wells played circles around his ass because Miles was all messed up . . . debilitated. . . . he was buying things on credit.[63]

Willie Wells was the trumpeter in John "Moon" Mullins's band, which temporarily replaced the Mitchell-Jones unit at the club at the end of November 1953. Mullins was a promising tenorist. His quintet included Otis "Bu Bu" Turner on piano, Major Holley on bass, and Freddie Metcalf on drums.[64] While Turner was one of the better modern Detroit players, Holley was temporarily back in his hometown after several years in New York, where he had played with Dexter Gordon, Oscar Peterson, and Charlie Parker.[65]

Davis's desperate straits did indeed lead him to borrow Lonnie Hillyer's trumpet. Hillyer lived in the neighborhood and was only 14 at the time. Billy Mitchell recalled how Mrs. Hillyer walked up to the stage and took her son's trumpet right out of Davis's mouth. "If he's such a great trumpet player, how come he does not have his own trumpet?" she announced to the baffled audience.[66]

At the end of January 1954 a modified house band returned without Billy Mitchell and instead under the leadership of Beans Richardson.[67] In March Sonny Stitt came in as a guest, and in May Thad Jones left after almost two years with the house band. Jones joined Count Basie and was one of its major soloists and arrangers until 1963.[68] He was replaced in the front line of the house band by Pepper Adams on baritone saxophone, and Barry Harris was

63. Carl Hill worked as a doorman at the Blue Bird while in college and returned in the 1990s to book music at the club. Carl is a brother of pianist Phil Hill. Hill, interview by Bjorn and Gallert.

64. "Flying at the Blue Bird," *Michigan Chronicle,* November 28, 1953. According to a December 5 *Chronicle* article the band played bebop standards.

65. Holley led the house band at the Crystal that accompanied Coleman Hawkins and Charlie Parker in April 1954. Advertisements, *Michigan Chronicle,* March 27 and April 10, 1954. Holley returned to New York in the late 1950s after three years in England and played with Kenny Burrell, Coleman Hawkins, and Duke Ellington. "Major Holley," *New Grove Dictionary of Jazz.*

66. Billy Mitchell, interview by Rudy Tucich, *52nd Street,* WDET-FM, Detroit, Michigan, April 28, 1990. Charles McPherson has a different version of events, as we will see subsequently.

67. Mitchell led a quintet at the Crystal Lounge from mid-November 1953 until early February. This group included Tommy Flanagan on piano and backed vocalist Austin Cromer, who also sang at the Blue Bird. Advertisements, *Michigan Chronicle,* November 14–December 19, 1953; and column, *Michigan Chronicle,* January 2, 1954.

68. Thad Jones joined Basie on May 12, 1954 after encouragement by tenorist Frank Wess. Hentoff, "They're All Talking about the Jones Boy."

the new pianist. This refurbished band backed Wardell Gray by the end of July, and Miles Davis was added to the bill two weeks later.[69]

Beans Richardson remembered that Gray was a different man from his previous stay at the Blue Bird in 1949–50.

> *He was different then; we didn't even hang out. . . . any other time we would hang out all night, go over to his sister's place, and I would cook food. . . . I guess he had got his habit going. . . . Wardell did get a big tone out of his instrument, but he wasn't bigger than a flea. . . . He was a great musician; every chorus was different.*[70]

Gray appeared on the Soupy Sales TV show during the stay at the Blue Bird and played for the last time in Detroit before Christmas with the Will Davis trio.[71] Gray died under mysterious circumstances in Las Vegas on May 25, 1955.[72] His death made the front page of the *Michigan Chronicle*.[73]

Richardson also remembered Davis's impact on the band's repertoire at this time.

> *I remember playing "Bitty Ditty," one of Thad's numbers, where the band had played the melody with the chords, but then when soloing we got into a blues thing. Miles suggested changing it around, to play the chords during the solo as well, and this became the standard way of playing the song.*[74]

Davis in turn must have become fond of "Bitty Ditty," because he recorded it in New York the following year.[75] The next time Davis came to the Blue Bird he did not come alone but as the leader of his newly formed quintet, which included John Coltrane on tenor saxophone and Paul Chambers, a 20-year-old Detroiter, on bass. Davis recalled the six days in Detroit in early October 1955.

> *On our first tour after Coltrane joined the group in late September 1955, we were having a lot of fun together, hanging out, eating together, walking around Detroit. Paul Chambers was from Detroit and I had lived there and so for us it was like a homecoming. My man Clarence, the numbers man, brought all his boys down every night to see the shows. Detroit was a gas.*[76]

BARRY HARRIS'S chance to play with Davis was an important part in his development, as was the chance to join the Blue Bird house band. Harris was 24 years old and already established on the Detroit scene as a top pianist and bandleader. After Tommy Flanagan he was considered the main modern pianist in Detroit, but what really distinguished him was his role as a teacher, mentor, and bandleader.

As early as 1949 he led his own orchestra in a concert at the Detroit Institute of Arts organized by fellow pianist Harold McKinney.[77] His band also played dances at places like the Madison Ballroom.[78] Frank Gant remembered joining the circle of musicians around Harris by knowing bassist Doug Watkins.

> *I practiced real hard and I became friends with Doug Watkins. Now there was a place over on Fleming Street, called Joe Brazil's or Joe B's, and he was having a lot of sessions and all the guys would go over there. But I didn't know about it. So I had become proficient enough, in Doug's eyes, to go by the session one day. He didn't tell me where he was taking me. . . . He came by my house and got me . . . and we go over there and here is Donald Byrd, Doug, Barry [Harris], Sonny Red and Joe Brazil [played alto] and they were jamming. They said: "We got everything except a drummer" I said: "Oh no, not me!" and naturally they said: "Man, come on!" So I sat down and they played a fast tempo the first tune. Somehow or another, I don't know, I kept the tempo, and didn't drop anything. I just stayed where I was supposed to be and from that time on I started getting gigs with these people. I really wanted to work with Barry, because he had some bebop arrangements, and he was really into Tadd Dameron. But the thing about Barry: one week he would use Doug Watkins and the next week he'd use*

69. For at least three weeks Billy Mitchell returned to the house band to play with Davis. Advertisements, *Michigan Chronicle*, September 11–October 2, 1954.

70. Richardson, interview by Bjorn and Gallert.

71. *Michigan Chronicle*, December 11, 1954.

72. Gray had developed a heroin habit, but it is unclear exactly how this figured into his death. Gioia, *West Coast Jazz*, 56–59.

73. "Dancer Teddy Hale Held for Murder of Wardell Gray," *Michigan Chronicle*, June 4, 1955.

74. Richardson, interview by Bjorn and Gallert.

75. *Miles Davis and Milt Jackson All Stars*, Prestige 7034 (LP). Recorded August 5, 1955.

76. The Davis quintet spent October 5–10 in Detroit. Davis, *Miles*, 198. Jack Chambers, *Milestones*, vol. 1 (Toronto: University of Toronto Press, 1983), 217–18.

77. Advertisement, *Michigan Chronicle*, September 17, 1949. McKinney's "Moods and Idioms" concert also featured music by his own "Bopateers" and classical numbers by pianist Roland Hanna and dancers. This series spanned about three years. Participants included Thad Jones, who contributed arrangements. Harold McKinney, interview by Bjorn.

78. *Detroit Tribune*, March 22, 1952. Harris was also a member of Little John and His Merry Men around this time. The Merry Men often played their bebop for dancers. Danson, "Pepper Adams."

Paul Chambers and I don't know who was the hippest at that time you know, both of them were great, you know, feeling-wise. But as far as I was concerned, my ear was so limited, that's the way I began.[79]

Harris often gathered musicians at his house.

My mother was beautiful to all of us, Donald Byrd, Paul [Chambers] and Doug [Watkins]. My house was a classroom. We could practice all we wanted.[80]

Pepper Adams remembered that the two bassists, who were cousins, learned a lot from Harris.

Paul and Doug spent a lot of time with Barry Harris. . . . He showed them what specific patterns to walk and everything. . . . this gave them a tremendous educational advantage. Aside from [Oscar] Pettiford, I don't think there was anyone to compare with Paul and Doug.[81]

Adams's own learning from Harris was most intense when they were together in the Blue Bird house band: "I couldn't begin to tell you how much I've learned from him, I call him Uncle Barry."[82]

In the early 1950s Harris also led a trio that sometimes backed the Brown-Walls Trio, a vocal group that included his wife, Christine Brown. Bassist Ray McKinney remembered those days.

We'd go by the Brown family house every day. . . . Barry was writing original music. He had a very analytical mind. Whatever game he played—bridge, scrabble, chess—he played with a ferocity that was almost unhealthy. Too serious about it. He'd suddenly jump up from a game and go to the piano. . . . he wrote some slick music. A lot of the stuff was complicated, that's why Paul and Doug liked it. Barry's writing arrangements for [the Brown-Walls Trio], and John Evans [guitar] and Barry and I had this group, really delightful. It wasn't quite like a Nat King Cole trio thing. . . . He [Barry] had quite a few originals. They [Brown-Walls] sang more ballad stuff. We auditioned [for a radio talent show] and the guy . . . said the music was obscene. . . . The music wasn't obscene. . . . I think we didn't sound amateurish enough or somethin'; we sounded really professional.[83]

Harris cut his first recording around 1950 with tenorist Wild Bill Moore, who played in a jump band style. More memorable was a 1952 quartet recording with Frank Rosolino, who had just joined the Stan Kenton orchestra.[84] Rosolino's trombone is the main feature on the four sides, and they showcase his great facility, swing, and melodic inventiveness on a difficult instrument. "Take Me out to the Ballgame" is taken at breakneck speed and challenges all players. Harris's piano technique is definitely up to the task, but he has not yet clearly arrived at a personal approach.

In late 1953 Harris took over the piano chair Tommy Flanagan once had with the Rudy Rutherford band. Harris brought along Doug Watkins on bass and the drummer Oliver Jackson, who had played with Rutherford off and on since Flanagan's days. Rutherford played Klein's Show Bar for much of 1952 and 1953, and Harris joined for gigs at two other West Side spots: Chic's and the Crystal.[85] By May 1954 he was in the Blue Bird house band, thus once again following in Flanagan's footsteps.

Charles McPherson and Lonnie Hillyer grew up a few blocks from the Blue Bird, and McPherson remembered seeing Harris and Miles at the club.

Miles . . . lived in a hotel that was right down the street. . . . I would see him all the time during the daytime, going to the store. . . . we knew who he was, by that time we were playing music so we knew who he was. In fact, Miles used to use Lonnie's horn. Everybody knew Miles' reputation for drugs and this was the period when he was actually stopping, he was cooling out. . . . Anyway, Lonnie's mother or somebody said: "You can use Lonnie's horn but you can

79. Gant, interview by Gallert. Another member of the group of musicians around Harris was saxophonist Robert Pierson. Pierson led a big band in Detroit in the 1960s and also joined Woody Herman's band. He eventually settled in Las Vegas. Barry Harris, interview by Bjorn.

80. Bourne, "Barry Harris," September 1985.

81. Danson, "Pepper Adams."

82. John Tynan, "Doctor Pepper: Valuable Detroit Internship Helped Adams Find Himself," *Down Beat,* November 14, 1957.

83. Ray McKinney, interview by Gallert. This group with the addition of Frank Foster recorded two titles for the Toledo, Ohio, based New Song record company around 1950.

84. The Rosolino sides were recorded on Dee Gee Records in September and were later rereleased by Savoy. They are available on Various Artists, *Swing Not Spring,* Savoy SV-0188 (Japanese CD). The other participants were Detroit bassist Billy Christ and Kenton drummer Stan Levey. Rosolino and Levey were at the time touring the Midwest with the Kenton band. Rosolino had been back in Detroit in 1951 when he was still with tenorist Georgie Auld's quintet. He spent some time in May and October of that year at the Bowl-O-Drome with Willie Anderson's All Stars. Advertisements, *Detroit Free Press,* May 11 and October 12, 1951. By 1952 he had left Auld and was back in Detroit. He participated in a jazz concert at the DIA in March with Kenny Burrell, Leo Osebold, Barry Harris, and Art Mardigan. "Jazz Concert Slated for Art Institute," *Michigan Chronicle,* March 15, 1952. In June he was hired by Kenton. John Tynan, "Funny Frank," *Down Beat,* February 6, 1957; and William F. Lee, *Stan Kenton: Artistry in Rhythm* (Los Angeles: Creative Press, 1980), 160.

85. For much of 1952 and 1953 Silas Walker was the pianist and Alvin Jackson the bassist with Rutherford. In 1953 trumpeter Billy Adams, who had played with Stan Kenton, was an added attraction with the band at Klein's. Advertisements, *Michigan Chronicle,* April 12, 1952; February 7, 1953; November 21, 1953; February 27, 1954; *Detroit Free Press,* April 20 and November 2, 1953.

Fig. 89. Jammin' at the Blue Bird Inn, ca. 1957.
L to R: Roy Brooks, dms; Sonny Stitt, as; unidentified, bs; Lonnie Hillyer, tp; Charles McPherson, as; Ira Jackson, as.
(Photo: James Richardson ©.)

not take it home over night. Every night you have to come by here and drop that horn off. You can't keep it!" Because people would worry about him pawning it. . . . So every night after the gig at the Blue Bird, Miles would come to Mrs. Hillyer with his horn . . . so that worked. . . . On Sunday afternoon a couple of times we sat in with Miles. We were only about 14–15 years old. . . . We couldn't play a damn thing. . . . We could play the melodies of certain tunes, but we couldn't solo, a little bit, half-assed maybe . . . not really playing right. I didn't know a damn thing about chords. . . . I started playing with Barry about 15 and he started showing me what all that stuff was about. . . . I knew about scales, but I didn't know anything about Minors or Majors and augmenteds. I didn't know any theory, chords, dominant sevenths and so on. . . . There weren't many guys that I knew that I had access to during that period . . . that would have been nice, but I was very fortunate to have Barry live around the corner from me. . . . he lived on Stanford . . . two minutes away. I met Barry when he was working at the Blue Bird which was just down the street. . . . When he heard Lonnie and [me], when we sat in that time, I guess he figured these guys have some talent. He knew we couldn't play a damn thing, but he said: "You guys need to learn some kind of theory and harmony. Maybe some time you can come by and I'll show you some things." We took him up on it. "You really have to learn all your scales, your minor scales before you start learning about chords, then I'll see you and I'll take you to the next step and show you what a chord is." So I knew the major scales, but I didn't know the harmonic minor, the melodic minor, and so on. And I wasn't fluent with the major scales, because I came back on time and he said: "Naw Naw that's not really it. . . . you got to be able to rattle these things off." Then we finally got that he said: "Here's what a C major chord is" and so on.[86]

Thus Harris served as a mentor to a new generation of players only about 10 years younger. His skills as a teacher were exceptional, and today he is regarded as one of the great jazz teachers. Reflecting back on his own teaching in 1977, Harris had the following to say.

I've taught quite a few musicians that are well known. It really started out when I was a youngster, 'cause maybe I was just a little ahead of the next cat. So it was just like we really grew together. I have a few that I teach now, but I wouldn't want to make it regular. I feel sort of funny about charging for teaching jazz, teaching music. . . . We had a music society with membership of about five thousand way back in the fifties, so that young musicians could come up and play there, like Charles McPherson and Lonnie Hillyer. They really had the opportunity through our little jazz organization. We had a close kind of thing.[87]

86. Charles McPherson, telephone interview by Lars Bjorn, September 6, 1997.

87. Allen Lowe, "Barry Harris," *Down Beat*, July 14, 1977. The membership numbers for the New Music Society are likely to be inflated by a factor of 10. See the discussion in chapter 5.

Fig. 90. New Music Society concert rehearsal, Detroit Institute of Arts, ca. 1955–56.
Sonny Red, as; Bernard McKinney, euphonium; Barry Harris; Bess Bonnier at piano; Bert Myrick, dms.
(Courtesy Rudy Tucich ©.)

Harris eventually softened his resistance to regularizing his teaching and started his own Jazz Cultural Center in New York City in 1982. But his fees were very modest.[88]

Harris played occasionally at the Blue Bird for the remainder of the 1950s, but his steadiest job was as an intermittent house pianist at the Rouge Lounge. There he accompanied a series of jazz greats, including Roy Eldridge, Ben Webster, Bill Harris (1955), Lee Konitz (1955 and 1957), Kenny Burrell (1957), and Lester Young (1957). Harris also led his own trio, quartet, and quintet at the Rouge. In the summer of 1956 he joined the Max Roach quintet soon after the deaths of Clifford Brown and Richie Powell, and he stayed for three months, including one week at the Rouge Lounge. Detroiter Donald Byrd also joined this quintet with the unenviable job of replacing Clifford Brown, widely considered the most promising young trumpet player of his age.

In July 1958 Harris traveled with his trio to Chicago to make his first record under his own name for Argo Records, under the direction of Dave Usher. With bassist Will Austin and drummer Frank Gant he produced the *Breakin' It Up* LP.[89] The trio also backed Sonny Stitt on his *Burnin'* LP date.[90] Both sessions were done without rehearsal to satisfy Stitt's agreement with Chess Records, as Usher recalled.

> *Sonny owed Chess a record, and because I liked Barry's playing I took his trio to Chicago to back Sonny. The next day I did a session with just the trio.*[91]

Both records are among the best either Stitt or Harris ever made and give a good idea of the high level of playing in Detroit at the time. *Breakin' It Up* includes a number of bebop standards, on which Harris puts his own trademark. His playing is perfectly calibrated between the rapid fire of bebop piano lines and the laid-back elegance of earlier pianists. The

88. Bourne, "Barry Harris," September 1985. Gunnar Holmberg, "Barry Harris: Fascinerande Pianolärare" (Barry Harris: Fascinating piano teacher), *Orkesterjournalen* (June 1981).

89. Barry Harris Trio, *Breakin' It Up*, Argo/Cadet LP(S)644, recorded July 31, 1958.

90. Sonny Stitt Quartet, *Burnin'*, Argo LP(S)661, recorded August 1, 1958.

91. Dave Usher, interview by Jim Gallert, Detroit, Michigan, March 10, 2000. Usher was artists and repertoire (A&R) man for Chess, of which Argo was a division.

opener "All the Things You Are" is a perfect illustration of Harris's individual and carefully crafted approach. He takes it at an unusually slow tempo, and Austin and Gant provide the elastic bounce that allows Harris's piano lines to come alive.

Harris and Byrd were both active in the New Music Society and were part of sessions at the Blue Bird Inn and the World Stage in mid-1955. The group was under the leadership of bassist Alvin Jackson and became the Blue Bird's new house band.

Alvin Jackson

Alvin Jackson was the first East Sider to lead the house band at the Blue Bird. When interviewed in 1991, after a celebration of the Blue Bird Inn and Clarence Eddins, he was asked if the Blue Bird was different than other clubs.

> *Naw, the Blue Bird was just the West Side. See they didn't say nothing about the other clubs [at the Blue Bird celebration]. . . . On the East Side it was the Bizerte, and it was just like the Blue Bird; before the Blue Bird . . . Lee's Sensation . . . and . . . the Cotton Club were also on the East Side.*[92]

It is often said that there are two kinds of Detroiters—East and West Siders—and that the two never meet. While this generalization should be taken with a grain of salt, it is interesting that after more than 30 years in New York Jackson still saw the symbolic wall along Woodward Avenue.

Jackson became a leader of the band at the Blue Bird in 1955, but he had been a member of the modernist circle in Detroit since its birth. In the 1950s he had played with Rudy Rutherford for some time because "he had a name . . . [and] . . . we all worked with Rudy because he would get all the young guys." He was also one of the musicians who gigged at the Blue Bird and took part in sessions at the Joneses' home in Pontiac.

The personnel of Jackson's group varied, and the size alternated between five or six pieces. The larger group had Yusef Lateef on tenor sax and flute, Donald Byrd on trumpet, Bernard McKinney on euphonium or trombone, Barry Harris on piano, Alvin Jackson on bass, and Art Mardigan or Frank Gant on drums.

Down Beat's columnist Barry Ulanov heard the quintet at the Blue Bird in April 1955 on a brief visit to the city.

> *What an amazing thing it is, really—what a mysterious one—the way Detroiters accept jazz. They take it for granted, but don't avoid it as a result. They keep a warmth alive for the best of the old, but don't reject any of the new in consequence. Symptomatic of the Detroit approach to jazz is the atmosphere, the look and the feel and the sound, of the Blue Bird. Over the door hangs what seems to be an oil painting. No masterpiece, but a recognizable quartet of jazzmen: Illinois Jacquet, Oscar Peterson, Nat Cole, Charlie Parker. That's about the shape and size of Detroit tastes—nearly everything that's around or has been. And on the stage—if that's what we should call the platform to the left of the door—a quintet of blowing musicians as up-to-date in their thinking and their playing as wise and sensitive youngsters should be. Maybe "youngsters" isn't the word. At least not the word to describe the elder statesman of Alvin's group, the veteran tenorman Yusef Lateef, who boasts a big tone and a melodic gift that is best described as tender and mature. . . . They're a pert, perky group of musicians who deserve every sort of support, at home in Detroit, and abroad in the rest of the country, for the simple, swinging modernity of their music. Barry Harris is a notably articulate fingerer, articulate in the precise sense of the word: his fingers are superlatively well-jointed, and every note in his fleet solos comes out clean and clear and incisively defined. It's been a long time since I've heard a modern pianist with such old-fashioned elegance of style and new-fashioned length of line. How he holds the interest! Apart from Yusef and Barry, the choruses are Bernard McKinney's on euphonium, and he*

92. Jackson, interview with Bjorn and Gallert.

makes the most of them, or as much as anybody could make of them on his billowy horn. I shouldn't like to finish this notice of a notable band without putting in a word for and about Curtis Fuller, a remarkably facile trombonist, who sat in the night I was at the Blue Bird, and made the evening considerably richer for his presence.[93]

In August the larger group was recorded in performance at the World Stage for Transition Records. An LP was released under Donald Byrd's name and received a favorable review by Nat Hentoff in *Down Beat*.[94] Hentoff was most impressed with Byrd and Harris and saw the recording as "further proof that there's a lot of worthwhile jazz being created in other localities besides New York, Chicago and the West Coast."[95] The quality of the recording was mediocre, and this makes it particularly hard to get a good sense of the rhythm section, especially with a poorly tuned piano! Lateef stands out on most tracks. His playing is mature and individual, and he sounds much like on recordings under his own name. Lateef also gets a very enthusiastic response from the audience, which cheers him on as he turns up the temperature, for example, on "Blues" and "Parisian Thoroughfare."

By October the Jackson group was also offering music six nights a week at the Blue Bird, one of them under the auspices of the New Music Society. Even though Alvin Jackson was the same age as Lateef and the formal leader of the group, the musical leadership was split between Lateef and Harris. Harris remembered that "we used to rehearse every week and I came up with a way for us to practice. I was in charge of the rehearsals. I came up with ways to run scales and stuff that I still use."[96] Lateef was the major soloist in the group and brought years of experience with modern jazz to it.

Yusef Lateef, under the name Bill Evans, had spent the last half of the 1940s on the road with a number of big bands, including the Bama State Collegians (with Sonny Stitt), Lucky Millinder, Ernie Fields (with Julius Watkins and Tate Houston), and Dizzy Gillespie. The Gillespie job lasted for close to a year and included recordings in the spring of 1949. Lateef was the tenor saxophone soloist with the band and recorded a particularly effective solo on "Jump Did-Le Ba."[97] He came back to Detroit in early 1950 at the age of 30 because of his wife's illness. Around 1951 he became a follower of the Ahmadiyya Islamic movement and changed his name to Yusef Lateef. He was a sideman for a few years in a band led by pianist Floyd Taylor. Frank Gant remembered a job at the Old Time Café on Russell Street.

It was the strangest gig I had ever been on. . . . We were backing some female impersonators. Everybody in the band had a day-time job, so everybody in the band was asleep except me and the piano-player (laughs). But the impersonators didn't care as long as they heard that drum pounding behind them. But the bass player was standing up there sleeping, Yusef was asleep, the trumpet player [Elliot Escoe] was asleep.[98]

What made it difficult for Lateef to stay awake was a job at the Chrysler Jefferson plant. Lateef rejoined Mathew Rucker as a sideman for a couple of years. This time Rucker had downsized from a big band to a quintet and was very busy playing places like Uncle Tom's Plantation and the Congo Lounge. Rucker remembered the difference in Yusef's playing from the early 1940s.

The difference was as much as night and day. The man could play and he was awesome on that tenor saxophone. The owner of Uncle Tom's Plantation [Doc Washington] commented on Yusef when playing his feature "Flyin' Home": "Man, Illinois Jacquet's got nothing on you; he should come in here and hear Yusef play 'Flyin' Home.'"[99]

Jump tunes like "Flyin' Home" were a staple

93. Barry Ulanov column, *Down Beat*, April 18, 1956. Fuller became a regular member of Lateef's quintet at Klein's a year later, as we will see subsequently.

94. The Transition LP was *Byrd Jazz*, later reissued by Delmark as *First Flight*, Delmark DL-407.

95. *Down Beat*, February 22, 1956. *Byrd Jazz* received a four (of five) star rating.

96. Barry Harris, interview by Bjorn.

97. Lateef recorded with the Gillespie band between April 14 and July 6, 1949. Charles Greenlee and Al McKibbon were other Detroiters present on these recordings. Dizzy Gillespie, *The Complete RCA Victor Recordings*, Bluebird 07863-66528-2 (CD). He is also featured on two titles with the Johnson Orchestra on the local Prize label in 1949.

98. Gant, interview by Gallert. In 1950 Lateef was a member of the Everett "Mack" McCrary's All Stars at Sunnie Wilson's Show Bar. Lateef alternated with Candy Johnson as a tenorist in the band. McCrary was a bassist born in Alabama in 1908. Bowles, interview by Bjorn.

99. Rucker, interview by Bjorn and Gallert.

of Rucker's band, and Lateef became the widely known star of the band, as he was with the Floyd Taylor band. For a while in 1953 Lateef formed his own band to play Dick and Ernie's Lounge on the East Side of Detroit. He was advertised as "the Sax Man with the Turban," and an issue of the *Michigan Chronicle* featured a drawing of the exotic musician.[100] His band included Will Davis on piano, Ray McKinney on bass, and Reethan Mallet on drums.

By early 1955 Lateef was a Wayne student and heavily involved with the New Music Society, of which he was vice president. According to a *Michigan Chronicle* article he was regarded as "the grand master of the local saxophonists," and some considered him "the only true genius around here."[101] Lateef's own group played in Music Society concerts at the Detroit Institute of Arts, and he was a member of the Alvin Jackson group at the World Stage and the Blue Bird Inn.

Donald Byrd was the youngest member of the group at 22 and a rapidly developing trumpeter. He grew up on the East Side, where his father was a Methodist minister, and he graduated from Cass. At Cass he hung around with Paul Chambers, who remembered that "I used to get together with Doug Watkins, Donald Byrd and piano player Hugh Lawson in rest periods and we'd play." Barry Harris was another pianist he played with before going into the army. Byrd received a bachelor's degree in music from Wayne University in 1954, interrupted by over two years of service in the air force. Luckily he was stationed near New York City, as he told Bill Quinn of *Down Beat* in October 1971.

> *That was one of the most formative times in my life. I went to Manhattan where I met Max Roach, John Lewis, Julius Watkins, Joe Wilder and many others.*

Back in Detroit he finished his degree and gigged around, including stints at the Blue Bird with the Alvin Jackson group. After his first recording at the World Stage in August 1955 he spent two months in New York with pianist George Wallington at the Café Bohemia. In late September he recorded an LP for Savoy under his own name released before his World Stage date. The album featured his buddy from Cass, Paul Chambers, on bass, as well as two other ex-Detroiters: Frank Foster and Hank Jones.[102] Nat Hentoff's review in *Down Beat* called Byrd "one of the most important jazz trumpet talents in the past few years. Byrd has a swinging tone, generally inventive ideas, and a feeling for wholeness in his choruses."[103] In between numerous recordings in New York, Byrd was briefly back in Detroit for another Transition recording in November, this one led by Doug Watkins. In December Byrd got his big break: he replaced Kenny Dorham as one of Art Blakey's Jazz Messengers, a group that defined the hard bop style.[104]

Frank Gant was just a year older than Byrd and like him spent two years in the service. Upon his return he played drums behind Billy Mitchell, Pepper Adams, and Little John and His Merry Men.

> *Then I started working with Little John Wilson and his Merry Men. We used to work at the Madison ballroom all the time. People would dance and that was a great book. And during that time, one of the weekends, Billie Holiday came and we backed Billie up for four days. That was so beautiful, man, that was really a beautiful gig. She was so wonderful, so gracious, so soulful, it was like it was seventh heaven.*

He finally got the coveted gig at the Blue Bird.

> *I worked with Alvin's group at the Blue Bird.... Berry Gordy used to come and we used to rehearse at Alvin's house and Berry would come there every rehearsal and just sit behind Barry Harris and listen and watch, and pick up some changes and stuff. I don't know why, I didn't*

100. *Michigan Chronicle,* March 28, 1953.

101. "Hard to Find but World Stage Boasts Top-Flight Artists," *Michigan Chronicle.*

102. Long Green, Savoy MG-12032, was recorded on September 29, 1955, and rereleased in 1976 as Savoy 1101. Both are LPs. The drummer was Kenny Clarke. Byrd's first recording in Detroit was with the Bobby Barnes Sextette in 1949 for Fortune records.

103. *Down Beat,* January 25, 1956.

104. Ira Steingroot, liner notes, Donald Byrd, *House of Byrd,* Prestige P-24066 (LP).

hear what he did later on with Motown and everything, but he would do that, he'd be there. . . . Donald Byrd went to New York soon after that. . . . he could play.[105]

Bernard McKinney (later Kiane Zawadi) came from a large Detroit family filled with musicians. His mother, Bessie, was a church organist and managed to get all the 10 children interested in the arts. Three became jazz musicians: Harold was a pianist, Ray was a bassist, and Bernard played the euphonium, a four-valved instrument with a similar range to that of a trombone. The family first lived on the East Side but eventually moved into a large industrial building on the West Side as Harold remembered.

> *We moved to 23rd Street during the war. . . . we had been evicted onto the street when my mother just had a new baby. . . . The constables were kind of on the redneck side and stole $54 from my brother . . . rummaging through things. . . . At the time living quarters were at a premium in Detroit, so my father found this abandoned creamery building, Horger Creamery, an industrial building, and we had to spend the whole winter cleaning the place out to live. . . . the girls had to stay with my aunts, while we slept in the building. There were no windows at all . . . no heat . . . no toilet facilities. . . . my feet would stick to the floor it was so cold, it was really a hard time. . . . we put in 350 industrial type windows. . . . my father was able to turn it into a living dwelling . . . and he eventually owned the building. Upstairs we used to rehearse the bands that I had. . . . I remember the guys who would come up: the Jones boys, Elvin and Thad, Thad was probably the Charlie Parker of the arranging/composition world . . . and Barry Harris, Don Slaughter, Claire Roquemore, Sonny Red. . . . I remember one day we were rehearsing the small group and guys used to stop in off the street, and one of them was . . . Roland Hanna, about 14 years old.*[106]

Bernard, three years younger, remembered having sessions in the same space with Pepper Adams, Donald Byrd, Doug Watkins, and Hugh Lawson. There were also sessions at Club Valley, and eventually he landed at the Blue Bird in the Jackson group.[107]

International Jazz Quartet

The Blue Bird was closed for remodeling in the summer of 1957, and the following year the club embarked on a new policy. Clarence Eddins decided to bring in national jazz talent on a regular basis and did so for much of the year. This policy continued for about two years but eventually ran into the same problems that prompted Ed Sarkesian at the Rouge Lounge to give it up in 1957. The cost of national talent was going up and became out of reach for small clubs. Eddins claimed he was able to get a good price for the talents of Miles Davis, who was a frequent visitor to the Blue Bird, and the same might have been true for other former locals, like Milt Jackson and Sonny Stitt. The Blue Bird was helped briefly by the lack of competition, since in 1958 and early 1959 it was the only jazz club in Detroit presenting modern jazz in the city. Competition stiffened in the latter half of 1959 when Club 12 (formerly Klein's) opened. By the first two years of the 1960s Club 12 faded, but the Minor Key arose, and Baker's brought in more modern jazz. The result was fewer big names at Tireman and Beechwood.

1958 was a banner year for the Blue Bird as a big name jazz club. Miles Davis brought in his sextet twice. April found John Coltrane, Cannonball Adderley, Red Garland, Paul Chambers, and Philly Joe Jones cramped on the small stage in the back of the club. When September came around Bill Evans had replaced Garland at the piano, and Jimmy Cobb had replaced Jones. The Davis sextets were at the forefront of hard bop, as were the Horace Silver, Art Blakey, and Jimmy Smith groups, who also came for weeklong engagements.[108]

105. Gant, interview by Gallert.

106. Harold McKinney, interview by Bjorn.

107. McKinney moved to New York in 1960 and joined Slide Hampton. He later changed his name to Kiane Zawadi. Fred Bouchard, liner notes, Pepper Adams, *Pure Pepper,* Savoy SV-1098 (LP).

108. Others were Terry Gibbs, Chico Hamilton, Johnny Smith, J. J. Johnson, and Melba Liston.

Fig. 91. International Jazz Quartet, Blue Bird Inn, late 1950s.
Ernie Farrow, bs; Sonny Red, as; Oliver Jackson (Bops Jr.), dms; Hugh Lawson (not shown) was probably on piano.
(Photo: James Richardson ©.)

There were also visits from the now established former Blue Bird regulars. Billy Mitchell and Thad Jones returned for a week with the Count Basie All Stars, and Sonny Stitt began a string of return engagements that lasted for several years. Milt Jackson came in early in the year and was backed by a new house band, which played only when big name groups were not in residence.

The house band was a unit called the International Jazz Quartet, led by Ernie Farrow. It included altoist Sonny Red, pianist Hugh Lawson, bassist Farrow, and drummer Oliver Jackson. With the new music policy in effect the house band was not as tied to the Blue Bird as its predecessors, and in 1958 it seems to have worked an equal amount of time at the newly opened Bohemian Club. Sonny Red was the only member of the band who had not been a regular member of Yusef Lateef's group at Klein's.

SONNY RED was born Sylvester Kyner in 1932 and had grown up in the North End. After starting out on C melody he switched to alto sax in 1949.[109] He was friends with Frank Gant, who remembered well how they discovered a common interest in music making.

> *I used to hang out on the streets of the North End and I was into some little things like picking up numbers. It's legal now so you can talk about it, you know. I was friends with a guy*

109. Ira Gitler, liner notes, Curtis Fuller, *New Trombone*, OJC-077 (LP).

named Sonny Red and he had his little hustle going. You know, we were all North End people, and we had to make it one way or another. So me and my friends, we go down to the Craftsmen's Club one night and here is Sonny Red playing alto and it floored me because I didn't know he had that talent. I said "Wow!" because he sounded like Charlie Parker to me. And I went up to him and I said: "Red, I didn't know you could do this!" He said "Yeah man." I said "How long have you been playing? Tell me!" He said "You just do it!" So he became a motivator to me. I said if he can do it, I can do it. You know he was with Barry Harris, Doug Watkins on bass, Sid Roman on drums and Claire Roquemore on trumpet. Man, you can hardly believe what these guys were blowing. And the thing about it, no matter how much they played we could still dance. We were dancing to the music.[110]

Red was plagued by lung trouble for much of his life, and his material situation was not helped by a steadfast resistance to playing anything but bebop. After his tutelage in the group around Barry Harris he landed some name gigs in 1954. He played at Klein's with Frank Rosolino and made his first of many trips to New York that year to briefly join Art Blakey's Jazz Messengers.[111] In 1957 he moved to New York with Curtis Fuller and made his first recordings. After a recording date with Paul Quinichette he was part of Fuller's first album, *New Trombone*, in 1957. His father's death brought him back to Detroit and the Blue Bird in 1958, but the following year he settled in New York and recorded his first album under his own name.[112]

JOE HENDERSON was an occasional member of Farrow's group at the Blue Bird and at the Bohemian Club. Eventually he led his own group at the Blue Bird at the very end of the decade.

Tenorist Joe Henderson came to Detroit to attend Wayne University in 1956 at the "tail end of the flourishing Detroit jazz scene," as he put it in a 1975 interview.[113] He grew up in Lima, Ohio, and his brother got him interested in jazz.

He'd play these Lester Young and Ben Webster records. . . . When I picked up the saxophone I had an idea of how it could be played as far as bebop style was concerned. After that, I started playing in high school bands, which didn't play bebop, and thus got a full appreciation of other kinds of music—classical and marches. I liked Bartok and Stravinsky and Schoenberg instantly; nobody had to prepare me for that. . . . My intellectual pilgrimage began at Kentucky State College in the mid-fifties. I was there for about a year, then I moved to Detroit and was there for about five years, until 1960. I studied composition, strings, brass, woodwinds, percussion and began to develop an intellectual appreciation of orchestral forms. At that time, jazz wasn't in the schools—you had to learn it in the clubs.[114]

As a newcomer Henderson made the rounds to sit in with a number of local bands. Drummer Roy Brooks remembered when the young tenorist dropped by the Blue Bird some time in 1956 to sit in with Sonny Stitt.

Beans [Richardson] got me my first gig at the Blue Bird with Lamonte Hamilton and Abe Woodley. Sonny Stitt came in for a week or so. I was still in High School, I was 18. I graduated in June of 1956. Joe [Henderson] came in with his horn. Sonny asked him his name and where he was from. "You want to play?" Joe took his horn out and Sonny asked: "What do you wanna play?" He said "Bye Bye Blackbird." Joe went into some Pres shit with his horn held here [sideways], right? And Sonny said, "Oh-oh, next tune!" Sonny started changing the keys, but that shit didn't work on Joe. So Sonny got off the stand and let Joe blow. Sonny went to the bar and said: "give me five singles!" Vodka, I guess. He went on back up and Joe just kicked ass.[115]

One of Henderson's first regular jobs was with Hindal Butts's quartet at Denny's Show Bar in 1957 as the leader remembered.

110. Gant, interview by Gallert. Tenorist Malvin McCray first met Red in a pool hall and later at Joe Brazil's. He was impressed with Red's fluent solos and also his skills as a composer. Malvin McCray, phone interview by Jim Gallert, October 6, 2000.

111. Advertisements, *Michigan Chronicle*, April 24 and May 1, 1954. Gitler, liner notes, Fuller, *New Trombone*.

112. Red did record earlier under his own name but not enough for an album. In November 1957 his group (Pepper Adams, Elvin Jones, Doug Watkins, Wynton Kelly) recorded for Savoy and the session was issued on Savoy SV-0161, *Two Altos: Sonny Red and Art Pepper*. For more on Red, see Anders Svanoe, *The Music and Life of Sonny Red* (New York: Second Floor Music, forthcoming).

113. Ray Townley, "The Herculean Tenor of Joe Henderson," *Down Beat*, January 16, 1975.

114. Mark Gilbert, "Joe's Mode," *Jazz Journal International* 38, no. 8 (August 1985).

115. Brooks, interview by Bjorn and Gallert.

That was Joe Henderson's first job. I had Teddy Harris playing tenor first. Johnny Cleaver, this drummer friend of mine, told me about Joe and I went to listen to him and we rehearsed. . . . Denny's was a bar. We started playing jazz in it and they started serving chicken-in-the-basket, stuff like that, but basically just a bar. No floor shows—they had that before I went in there. . . . Whatever I wanted to play is what we played in there and he [the owner] listened. . . . Sonny Stitt taught Joe a lot; he taught him how to breathe. . . . Sonny Stitt, he could play forever and forever, but I got a knot on my wrist and I just quit.[116]

By 1958 Henderson was playing with Beans Bowles's group at Lavert's together with two other young modernists: pianist Kirk Lightsey and drummer Roy Brooks.[117] Bowles recalled his band.

Kirk Lightsey was playing Horace Silver like nobody else in the city was playing it. . . . Horace was his man. That's what I built my thing around. . . . We played straight rhythm and blues and jazz, hard bop. . . . Benny Golson gave me "Stablemates." . . . LaVert Beaman was a businessman, he brought in jazz because he made money. . . . We also would be called borderline jazz people because we played everything. Some places were just hard jazz, like the Crystal, and the Blue Bird. They would not play "Flying Home," but we walked the bar [walked on top of the bar]. I signed for Joe Henderson's first Selmer saxophone. We were at the Blue Bird and he was fumbling with that saxophone. I said: "why don't you buy yourself a Selmer, you play too much not to have a Selmer." He took that horn, he practiced hours, days, weeks and he never turned around. . . . He knew all the bebop tunes. . . . He started experimenting with the lower parts of the instrument because that's a hard part to play. . . . He learned to master the saxophone. . . . His sound was fat and warm when he was here. He was different. Henderson was not a dancer, but he was a swinger; he was fiery, with great technique. . . . He was in development and on the top edge of the tradition. He could play like Coleman Hawkins, he could play like Lester Young, he could play like Jacquet; but he was not a squealer.[118]

Henderson also played with the International Jazz Quartet at the Bohemian Club that year and the Blue Bird in 1959.[119] On these occasions Barry Harris was the pianist, and he became an important part of Henderson's musical development. Henderson told an interviewer that he "hadn't been into bebop very heavily" before coming to Detroit. By the end of 1959 Henderson was leading his own quartet at the Blue Bird with Terry Pollard on piano and was getting interested in postbop styles.[120]

Henderson's tenor style has often been thought of as in the John Coltrane school, but Henderson argues vehemently that his own development was largely independent of Coltrane's. As early as 1956 he says that he sounded akin to Coltrane because of similar influences on their playing. Henderson had the chance to meet Coltrane for the first time at a private recording session in Detroit in 1957.

He sat right next to me as we played, and I thought "Wow, this guy sounds like he's got his scales together." As a result of his hearing me there, maybe a year later, he used to talk about me and he appreciated whatever it was that I had at that time.[121]

By the late 1950s Henderson was also becoming increasingly impressed with new sounds in jazz that eventually led to the "free jazz" of the 1960s. This was not always appreciated in Detroit's bebop-oriented scene according to Henderson.

Ornette [Coleman] came on. There wasn't always strict 4/4. . . . At that time, I was probably a man alone listening to Ornette. . . . nobody around Detroit could use him. It was a constant putdown, the first time I had heard musicians grouped together. . . . Here's somebody whom I knew was into something but whom everybody else was down on, so I broke away from the bebop scene.[122]

116. Butts, interview by Bjorn. Butts's Four Tones also included Johnny Griffith on piano and Al Martin on bass. Advertisement, *Michigan Chronicle,* March 16, 1957; *Down Beat,* April 4, 1957.

117. *Down Beat,* June 26, 1958. Lightsey was 21 and Brooks 19 years old at the time. Lightsey had played with the group for more than a year and refers to this as his first professional job. He joined the army in 1960 and in the 1960s became a major figure in Detroit jazz. He recorded with Sonny Stitt and Chet Baker in 1965, and in 1979 he joined Dexter Gordon. (Kenn Cox, "Kirk Lightsey," program booklet, *Blue Bird Reunion 5* [Detroit: Societie of the Culturally Concerned, 1995]).

118. Bowles was born in South Bend, Indiana, in 1926 and came to Detroit in 1943. From 1950 to 1956 he was the baritonist in Maurice King's house band at the Flame Show Bar and then went on the road with Illinois Jacquet and Bill Doggett. Trumpeter Al Aarons was also a member of the band while he spent 2–3 years in Detroit. Aarons spent the 1960s with the Basie band. Bowles, interview by Bjorn.

119. *Michigan Chronicle,* May 31, 1958; *Down Beat,* December 25, 1958; February 19, 1959.

120. *Down Beat,* December 10, 1959.

121. Gilbert, "Joe's Mode."

122. Townley, "Herculean Tenor."

Fig. 92. Joe Henderson quartet, Blue Bird Inn, 1958. *Henderson, ts; Kirk Lightsey, pno; Ernie Farrow, bs; Roy Brooks, dms.* (Courtesy Gallert Collection.)

In 1960 Henderson joined the army for a two-year stint, after which he settled in New York. By 1963 he was recording for Blue Note Records and became one of the label's leading modernists.

Beyond the Blue Bird

While the Blue Bird was the focal point for Detroit modernists there were several other clubs in the city that encouraged modern jazz. In the early 1950s the Crystal and Klein's increasingly featured the jazz of the day, and by the middle of the decade the Rouge Lounge and the West End came on board. When club jobs fell short musicians organized their own gigs at the World Stage. Kenny Burrell and Yusef Lateef were the two leading figures at these spots.

Kenny Burrell

Kenny Burrell grew up in a musical family on the East Side of Detroit. His brother Billy, 11 years older, played guitar and was an early influence on Kenny.

Fig. 93. Kenny Burrell and Tommy Flanagan, Club 666, ca. 1946. *Photographer Bob Douglas, who was friendly with the club owner, engineered this shot.* (Photo: Bob Douglas ©.)

When I started playing he was very encouraging and at one point he said: "Man, there's nothing I could teach you, I can see that you're going to surpass me." . . . There was no jealousy; he was happy for me. . . . Then he switched to bass, not because of that, but because there was more work as a bass player.[123]

At Miller High School he was guided by Louis Cabrera, as Milt Jackson and Yusef Lateef had been a decade earlier. Burrell credits Cabrera with teaching him not only musical theory but also about playing jazz and how to deal with problems faced by minority musicians.[124] While still at Miller he started gigging with Tommy Flanagan, and by 1948 they were both at the Club Sudan with Youngblood Davis's beboppers. He had offers to go on the road with both Illinois Jacquet and Dizzy Gillespie but stayed in Detroit to attend Wayne.[125] At Wayne he majored in music and also kept very busy playing, which is why he did not graduate until 1955.[126] He described what he learned at Wayne 40 years later.

I learned something at Wayne, but also did not. In the early fifties Wayne, like others, did not want to deal with jazz at all. No jazz courses were available. I was pretty angry about that. . . . I developed an education based on my major in composition and theory. Theory applied to any kind of music. That knowledge I do apply now when I teach [at UCLA].[127]

In 1949 Burrell was a sideman in groups led by tenorist Tommy Burnette and pianist Earl "Count" Belcher.[128] Both groups played popular songs of the day, which meant a heavy dose of rhythm and blues of the jump blues variety as well as Tin Pan Alley standards. With Burnette, Burrell said, "we played some bebop too. . . . audiences were pretty hip then, particularly the younger people."[129] He continued to play with his contemporary beboppers at dances and at occasional concerts. His trio with Tommy Flanagan also performed at the Saturday night jazz series at the Broadway Capitol.[130] Their trio played in the style of Nat King Cole with Burrell as the vocalist. Cole's guitarist Oscar Moore was one of Burrell's first major influences.[131]

Dizzy Gillespie visited Club Juana for 10

123. Burrell, interview by Gallert, December 1, 1991.

124. John F. Howard, "Kenny Burrell," *Coda*, no. 169, 1979.

125. Ira Gitler, "Kenny Burrell," *Down Beat*, August 1, 1963; and "Christy to Record Burrell's Song," *Michigan Chronicle*, October 29, 1949.

126. Michael G. Nastos, *Ann Arbor News*, May 17, 1988.

127. Kenny Burrell, interview by Jim Gallert, "Meet the Artist," Montreux-Detroit Jazz Festival, September 1, 1996.

128. "Tommy Burnette Dee Dots at Lark Grill," *Michigan Chronicle*, March 5, 1949. Burrell played with Belcher at the Congo Lounge. This band also included trumpeter Clarence Shaw and tenorist Warren Hickey. *Michigan Chronicle*, August 20, 1949.

129. Burrell, interview by Gallert, December 1, 1991.

130. Alvin Jackson was usually playing bass with the trio. Advertisements, *Michigan Chronicle*, January 14, May 26, and June 9, 1950. Burrell, interview by Gallert, December 1, 1991.

131. Ibid.

days in February 1951, and Kenny Burrell was hired to round out the sextet.[132] The group went into the studio for Dee Gee Records a few days after the engagement in what was Burrell's first major recording.[133] Gillespie had started the Dee Gee record label in Detroit in 1950 in partnership with Dave Usher, and the Gillespie group was to be their first session. For economic reasons Gillespie was forced to break up his big band in 1950, and he formed a sextet. But he lacked a recording contract and decided to approach 21-year-old Usher about forming their own label. Usher already had some experience with record labels from a short-lived attempt in 1948 with Emanon Records.[134] Gillespie and Usher shared a view of what they wanted to do, as Usher recalled: "We wanted to bring non-jazz people into the jazz orbit."[135] Gillespie said that he "wanted to show that good art could be popular and make money. . . . Joe Carroll and I sang "School days." People still ask for it. But the bebop musicians, most of them stone broke, criticized us for it. They didn't even appreciate my comedy!"[136]

The March 1 recording date featured three tunes, one of which was "We Love to Boogie," which included vocals but is remembered today for being one of the first appearances of John Coltrane on record. Burrell got his chance to solo on "Birk's Works."

For much of the fall of 1951 Burrell played with Phil Hill's quintet at the Crystal Show Bar. This group was definitely in the modern jazz vein according to the *Michigan Chronicle*. It included Lamont Hamilton on tenor sax and Art Mardigan on drums. At times Leo Osebold, considered by many to be the top white tenor player in Detroit at the time, played tenor saxophone with the group. In 1952 Burrell appeared in three concerts at the Detroit Institute of Arts with an array of modern players, including Osebold, Mardigan, Frank Rosolino, and Barry Harris.

In March 1953 Burrell played a part in what was advertised as Detroit's "first all colored TV show."[137] The program was *Sunday with Surrell* on WXYZ, and Hindal Butts, who was the drummer in Burrell's quartet, remembered that

> *They needed a name and a moderator. And Jack Surrell was a deejay on WXYZ, so now it's "The Jack Surrell Show." . . . It came on late at night and later early on Sunday morning. . . . We played two or three tunes per show. . . . it was good at first, but . . . we ended up quittin' that show because Jack Surrell's wife wanted it to turn into a variety show or something. We quit. . . . Kenny said the TV show has done all the good it's gonna do us.*[138]

Detroit TV stations had sporadically shown jazz in swing style or jump band style since 1949, two years after TV was extended to a mass audience. The pioneers in 1949 were a swing group on WWJ-TV in 1949, which included tenorist Earl Striewski and guitarist George Rose.[139] WXYZ started a *Jazz Nocturne* program in late 1952 and featured among others baritonist Beans Bowles and tenorists Wild Bill Moore and Candy Johnson.[140] Burrell's group was by comparison more modern. They eventually took the name Kenny Burrell and the Four Sharps and first appeared under this name in April 1953 in the newly opened Palmetto Ballroom on Woodward Avenue.[141] The Burrell group was advertised as "sweet," which probably referred to their vocal features. Hindal Butts remembered that

> *The Four Sharps would sing and Kenny would lead and we'd have four part harmony. We did primarily ballads. The Original Four Sharps were Kenny, Harold McKinney [piano], Paul Chambers [bass] and me on drums. We recorded "The Nearness of You" and the Four Freshmen stole it. They stole the arrangement and put it out. How can we tell somebody the Four Freshmen stole the arrangement? They sat there and we did it three times at Klein's, they'd come in and ask for it and we did it. Mrs. Blair [at the West End Hotel] paid for*

132. The Gillespie group played the Club Juana from February 16 to 25, 1950. Advertisements, *Detroit Free Press*, February 13 and 23, 1951.

133. March 1, 1951. Burrell thinks his first record was with the BuBu Turner Group. Two sides ("I goofed," with a vocal by Turner, and "Cooling with Boo Boo") were recorded on Fortune 809. This 78 was not released until 1953, nearly two years later than the Gillespie date. Burrell, interview by Gallert, December 1, 1991.

134. Usher issued one record from a session recorded in Paris that included Gillespie orchestra musicians under drummer Kenny Clarke's leadership on March 2, 1948. Emanon was named after the Gillespie recording of the tune.

135. Jim Gallert, "Dizzy, Dave, and Those DeeGee Days," program booklet, Montreux-Detroit Jazz Festival, 1994.

136. The initial records by Gillespie's sextet sold well ("School Days" and "Umbrella Man" were minor hits), and Usher used the proceeds to record other groups, like Milt Jackson (the first session to reunite Gillespie's excellent 1948 rhythm section, which later became the Modern Jazz Quartet), Barry Harris, Frank Rosolino, and Billy Mitchell. In an effort to secure all-important national distribution Usher made a deal with Savoy Records. They would distribute the Dee Gee catalog and pay a royalty on each record sale. It was one of those deals that look good on paper but that invite dishonest bookkeeping, and that is what happened. There was also a problem with taxes, and the government confiscated the record masters. Dizzy Gillespie with Al Fraser, *To Be or Not to Bop* (New York: Doubleday, 1979), 370–71. Dee Gee's last recording session was in September 1952. Usher recently issued three CDs of Gillespie's 1956 South American tour on his Red Anchor label.

137. *Sunday with Surrell* was a 45-minute show. Advertisement, *Michigan Chronicle*, February 28, 1953. Surrell was a pianist turned deejay who also had a column in the *Michigan Chronicle*.

138. Butts, interview with Bjorn.

139. Ruth Gillis, "Detroit Musicians Sandwich in a Little Jazz as Video Debuts," *Down Beat*, January 14, 1949. WWJ was Detroit's first TV station on the air in June 1947.

140. *Michigan Chronicle*, November 15 and December 27, 1952.

141. Advertisement, *Michigan Chronicle*, April 25, 1953.

that recording, we did it on Hastings at a place called Joe's Record Shop. . . . Kenny sang the lead, we sang the backup and we did the bridge in unison. . . . Kenny called me one day and said: "turn the radio on." He was mad. . . . I turned the radio on and the Four Freshmen were singing the "Nearness of You" almost note for note.[142]

Hindal Butts was a childhood friend of Burrell's and they went to school together up through Miller High School. At Miller he played in Cabrera's dance band, replacing Leon "Grits" Rice on drums.

There was a basketball championship game at Olympia. I'll never forget it. The marching band played and half the guys who were in the marching band were in the dance band (the A band we called it). That big band rehearsed "Southern Fried" and "Harlem Nocturne" and they featured me on both of them. I got a heck of a write-up in the paper. . . . There were 15–16,000 people out there. . . . "Southern Fried" was a Barnet number, up-tempo, that's what I took the solo on. . . . we had no uniforms; the school could afford to buy the caps and the jackets and your parents had to buy the pants. . . . so when everybody left they left their pants there. . . . that's how poor the school was. They were sending us all over town to play, but they wouldn't buy us no uniforms. . . . Louis Cabrera, he was strict and the band was good.[143]

Harold McKinney became part of the bebop circle in the late 1940s, but unlike many of his peers continued to actively play classical music. After graduating from Northwestern in 1948 he attended Morehouse College but left before graduating.

I became disenchanted with the bias of the Music Department under Kepper Harold. He was violently opposed to anything but classical European music, and I was really interested in jazz at the time. Charlie Parker had hit like a bombshell. . . . I had been bitten by the be-bop bug; I was a rabid be-bopper . . . [back in Detroit]. I was at Wayne for about a year taking courses in 16th century counterpoint and orchestra conducting. I knew Kenny Burrell at Wayne where we had jam sessions in Webster Hall. There were many white musicians there. Pepper [Adams] . . . Marion Di Vita. We always were a black and white jazz community. I had gigged with Kenny when I was 18 or so. Then I was with Kenny on the first black TV show, "Sunday with Surrell."[144]

Paul Chambers was just about to turn 18 when he joined the Four Sharps. He had started on bass less than two years earlier, while a student at Cass Tech.[145] His first gigs were in 1951, and one of them was with drummer "the Baroness" Jean Douglas in her show band at a club featuring female impersonators.[146] In an interview with Valerie Wilmer in 1961 Chambers talked about his Cass days.

The curriculum took up a whole day of music. That's why it took a couple more years to graduate. For example, we'd have the first period chamber music, second period full orchestra, third either harmony or counterpoint and rudiments; then came piano and the academic classes. . . . I used to get together with Doug [Watkins], Donald Byrd and piano player Hugh Lawson in rest periods and we'd play. . . . I was working nights with Kenny Burrell . . . a very nice group with Yusef Lateef and Hindal Butts on drums.[147]

His association with Doug Watkins was very close. They were cousins and at some point lived together on the West Side.[148] Watkins was one year ahead of Chambers at Cass and graduated three years earlier. They spent a lot of time with Barry Harris in the early 1950s.

I remember when Paul Chambers came to a gig at the Civic Center and didn't even know a note. Doug Watkins could play ahead of Paul. Paul learned to play at my house; he was probably one of my main students.[149]

Chambers subbed for Watkins with Terry Pollard's duo at the Paradise Lounge in 1952.[150] Watkins left Detroit for the first time in 1953 to

142. Butts, interview with Bjorn. This is Burrell's first recording under his own name. The personnel vary in existing discographies, and a circa 1950 recording date is given, which would be at least three years too early. The Four Sharps recorded "Kenny's Sound" and "My Funny Valentine" for Joe Von Battle's J-V-B (58). This Burrell recording was done on a 78 and is very rare.

143. Butts's drum chair at Miller was taken over by Oliver Jackson. Butts, interview by Bjorn.

144. Harold McKinney, interview by Bjorn.

145. Chambers was born in Pittsburgh in 1935. He moved to Detroit in 1948 to live with his father, after his mother's death. Nat Hentoff, "Detroit Producing Big Stars: Paul Chambers Big One," *Down Beat,* January 11, 1956.

146. The Douglas group with Chambers played at Emmet "Pistol" Fuller's Cotton Club in Ecorse, a western suburb of Detroit with a significant black population. Douglas had been a drummer since World War II, and her quartets or quintets around 1950 specialized in jump tunes. *Michigan Chronicle,* November 26, 1949; December 15, 1951.

147. "Paul Chambers Talks to Valerie Wilmer," *Jazz Journal* 19, no. 3 (1961).

148. Gant, interview by Gallert.

149. Barry Harris, interview by Bjorn.

150. "Terry Pollard Jazz Duo Displays Facile Technique at Paradise Lounge," *Michigan Chronicle,* September 27, 1952. "Paul Chambers Talks Valerie Wilmer," *Jazz Journal.*

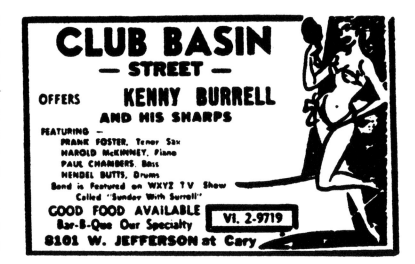

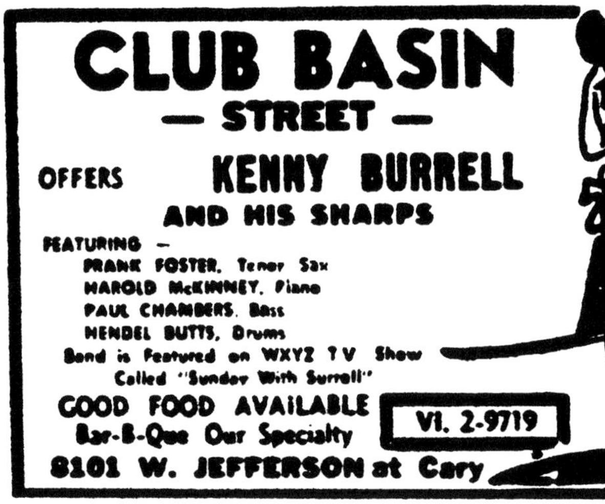

Fig. 94. Advertisement for Club Basin Street. Hindal Butt's name is misspelled. (From *Michigan Chronicle*, August 29, 1953.)

tour with James Moody and finally left for good in early 1954 to join Art Blakey's first Jazz Messengers. Chambers left the same year with Paul Quinichette and got his big break when he joined Miles Davis in July 1955. In the last half of the 1950s the two were among the most sought after bassists for hard bop sessions in New York recording studios. Both died early: Watkins at 27 in 1962 and Chambers at 33 in 1969.[151]

Chambers was a formidable walker [accompanist] on bass, but his solo playing made him unique. Hindal Butts remembered this from his days with the Four Sharps.

> *Paul was determined to make the bass a solo instrument and he practiced and practiced, hour upon hour. I waited on Paul to take a couple of girls out, and he wouldn't stop practicing! He loved to bow and he mastered the bow. . . . at Klein's he was doing all the things you heard him do [later]. . . . he might have gotten a little smoother. . . . He liked Pettiford. . . . I can remember Paul playing "Softly in the Morning Sunrise." . . . When Paul was considering leaving Detroit I told him: "How the hell are you going to make it on $125 a week with a family?" He said: "Well it's something I got to do." . . . Paul Quinichette, that's who he left with. . . . We were making almost that much at Klein's, not at first but we ended up making that much money. It was good money back then. But to travel and be away from home, how can you? . . . How he made it I don't know but he did. His wife Annie was from here, North East Detroit.*[152]

Fellow bassist Ray McKinney had the following analysis of Chambers's bowing.

> *Both Paul and Doug impressed me, but Paul became the one because he bowed a lot. He was very original. So was Doug, but he didn't pursue it as much as Paul did. He was a great admirer of Paul. There is more of [Major] "Mule" Holley's influence than Slam Stewart's [in Paul's playing]. "Mule" Holley was a guy he used to watch locally, and Ali Jackson.*[153]

The Four Sharps played several West Side spots during 1953: the Oriole Show Bar, Club Basin Street, and Klein's.[154] In November they replaced the Rudy Rutherford group at Klein's for at least a month, and they returned to Klein's a year later.[155] In November 1953 Burrell also started working at the Rouge Lounge, first with Harold McKinney, to fill in between the national acts, and later with his trio and quartet.[156] By late 1954 the Four Sharps were heading Monday night jam sessions at the Rouge.[157] The engagement was interrupted when Burrell finally took up an offer from a name band. He joined the Oscar Peterson trio from about April through June 1955, including an engagement at the Rouge Lounge.[158] This must have been a very busy time for Burrell because he also spent after hours at the West End Hotel. Hindal Butts remembered that the band "worked six nights at Klein's and three nights at the West End." Burrell had a special connection to the West End because he ended up marrying the owner's daughter.[159]

The personnel of the Four Sharps changed intermittently, and they were not always a quartet. McKinney was drafted in early 1954 and was replaced by Tommy Flanagan.[160] Elvin Jones eventually took over the drum chair in the group, some time after he had left the Blue Bird.[161] The group also at times included a saxophonist. These were, in consecutive order,

151. "Paul Chambers," "Doug Watkins," *New Grove Dictionary of Jazz*.

152. Butts, interview by Bjorn.

153. Ray McKinney, interview by Gallert.

154. Advertisements, *Michigan Chronicle*, July 18, August 22, August 29, September 19, November 21, and December 19, 1953.

155. *Detroit Free Press*, November 30, 1954; and *Down Beat*, February 9, 1955.

156. The quartet also worked at the Parrot Lounge in July and August 1954. Advertisements, *Michigan Chronicle*, July 17 and August 28, 1954. The trio also worked in the Wal-Ha Room of the Garfield Hotel with Billy Burrell on electric bass and Hindal Butts on drums. This was possibly the first trio ever with this composition. Burrell, interview by Gallert, December 1, 1991; advertisement, *Detroit Free Press*, September 28, 1954.

157. Rouge Lounge, advertisements, *Michigan Chronicle*, November 14, 1953; October 16 and November 27, 1954; June 24, 1955. *Down Beat*, September 7, 1955.

158. "Detroit Guitarist Joins Peterson," *Down Beat*, April 18, 1955. *Michigan Chronicle*, July 23, 1955.

159. Butts, interview by Bjorn.

160. Harold McKinney, interview by Bjorn.

161. Danson, "Pepper Adams."

Fig. 95. Pepper Adams in Beans Richardson's apartment, late 1950s. (Photo: James Richardson ©.)

Frank Foster (mid-1953), Yusef Lateef, and Pepper Adams.

Adams remembered joining the "wailing little band" that Burrell led at Klein's after he left the Blue Bird house band.[162] This was Adams's last regular gig in Detroit before his departure for New York in early 1956. Once in New York he recorded, but he probably became more widely known by joining the Stan Kenton orchestra in November.[163] The next year Adams was chosen the New Star on baritone in the *Down Beat* critics' poll. In 1958 he and Donald Byrd formed the first of several quintets together for an engagement at the Five Spot in New York. This quintet featured "some of the many exceptional young musicians who have in recent years migrated to New York from Detroit, [and] is notably hard-swinging, spirited and close-knit."[164] The other Detroiters in this first Adams/Byrd quintet were Doug Watkins and Elvin Jones. The quintet can be heard at its best on *10 to 4 at the 5-Spot,* which includes "Hastings Street Bounce," the first of Adams's compositions paying homage to the Detroit jazz scene.[165]

For a few weeks at Klein's in early December

162. Ibid.

163. Lee, *Stan Kenton,* 220.

164. Orrin Keepnews, liner notes, Pepper Adams Quintet, *10 to 4 at the 5-Spot,* Riverside OJC-031 (LP). Recorded April 15, 1958.

165. Another is "Twelfth and Pingree," referring to Klein's address. It is available on Pepper Adams, *Pepper,* Enja ENJ-90792 (CD).

1954, the Four Sharps included Australian saxophonist and bassoonist Errol Buddle.[166] Buddle was one of the founding members of the Australian Jazz Quartet that month.[167]

One of the last engagements for Burrell outside of the Rouge was at the Rustic Cabin in suburban Grosse Pointe in the early fall of 1955.[168] The group included Flanagan and Jones plus Beans Richardson on bass, who remembered it well because Clifford Brown sat in with the group.[169] Elvin Jones did not play the whole gig at the Rustic Cabin as he joined the Bud Powell trio for an engagement in Toronto. By early the following year Jones had moved to New York to play with Powell.[170] In January 1956 the Kenny Burrell quartet backed up Sonny Stitt at the Rouge Lounge,[171] and the following month Burrell and his old "running buddy" Flanagan moved together to New York City. Flanagan remembered that

> *The first week we lived with Kenny's aunt in Harlem. I had heard so much about Harlem. It was really exciting: a huge community, all black, a city within itself! . . . We were convinced that after playing all the clubs in Detroit, there was hardly anywhere to advance in Detroit. The next move was to go to New York to be heard by a bigger audience and to record. After one month I had recorded with Thad, Billy Mitchell, Oscar Pettiford, Kenny Burrell and Shadow Wilson. One month later [I recorded] with Miles and Sonny Rollins.*[172]

Yusef Lateef

Lateef played with the Alvin Jackson group at the Blue Bird into early 1956. In April 1956 he formed his own quintet to play Klein's Show Bar. As he was to stay until his departure for New York more than three years later, it turned into an exceptionally long residency.[173] While at Klein's the band also replaced Kenny Burrell's group as the after-hours house band at the West End.[174] These long engagements created a true ensemble feeling and allowed Lateef's artistry to express itself in new ways. There were changes in personnel over these years, but Lateef's vision dominated the performances of the group. The group was also the first Detroit group since McKinney's Cotton Pickers that created a phonographic record of its work over an extended period of time. As was true for the Cotton Pickers, this feat was only accomplished by traveling out of town.

Lateef's first quintet included a number of young and talented musicians who, like the leader, would all eventually leave for New York. The oldest was bassist Ernie Farrow, who had gone to Northeastern High School with Barry Harris. Harris remembered Farrow as "the cat I really grew up with musically all the way."[175] An early collaboration was in a band that won a Paradise Theatre amateur contest in 1946.[176] Harris remembered the contest.

> *Ernie started out as an alto player. We were going to play an amateur show at the Paradise Theatre and he didn't play alto as good as James Thompson, so he played the bass. That's how he started on bass. All he did was say "I'll play the bass" and he played it.*[177]

Farrow came from a musical family, and his sister Alice (nine years his junior) became a jazz pianist and eventually married John Coltrane.[178] In 1953 he led his own band and also played with Terry Gibbs at the Crystal.[179] The following year he joined Dave Heard's Progressive Jazz Quintet.[180] He played Klein's with this group

166. *Detroit Free Press,* November 30, 1954.

167. Vibraphonist and drummer Jack Brokensha was another member of the group. He stayed in Detroit and became an important figure in the 1960s. The personal manager of the Australian Jazz Quartet was Ed Sarkesian, and the group played frequently at Sarkesian's Rouge Lounge in the late 1950s. Sarkesian gave the group its name at their first performance at the Rouge as a backup group to Chris Connor. The quartet spent most of their time on the road in a package tour with Miles Davis, Dave Brubeck, Carmen McRae, and others but also recorded for Bethlehem Records. The group broke up in Australia in 1959, and Brokensha settled in Detroit when he became a member of the house band on *Soupy's On* on WXYZ in 1960. This band was led by Hal Gordon and included Joe Messina on guitar. Brokensha also worked nightly as a deejay on WQRS and from 1966 to 1968 ran "Brokensha's," a restaurant–jazz club in the New Center area. Brokensha, interview with Bjorn. *Down Beat,* April 7, 1966; August 8, 1968.

168. *Down Beat,* October 19, 1955.

169. Beans Richardson, interview by Bjorn and Gallert. The Clifford Brown–Max Roach group played the Rouge Lounge September 20–25, 1955. Advertisement, *Detroit Free Press,* September 19, 1955.

170. *Down Beat,* October 19, 1955. Jones played with vibraphonist Teddy Charles in Toronto a month earlier, after having played with him at the Crystal. *Down Beat,* September 7 and September 21, 1955. Flanagan, interview by Bjorn.

171. Advertisement, *Detroit Free Press,* January 13, 1956.

172. Flanagan, interview by Bjorn. The recording with Thad Jones et al. was *Detroit–New York Junction* and is discussed subsequently. The Davis recording was *Collector's Items,* Prestige LP7044, from March 16, 1956; and the Rollins recording was *Saxophone Colossus,* Prestige PRLP 7095, from June 22, 1956.

173. There are a number of conflicting stories about when the group started at Klein's. I put most credence in the first *Michigan Chronicle* reference to the group in April 1957. The 1956 date is also found in the following: Hirsch, "Jazz Goes Uptown"; and Jack Cooke, "Yusef Lateef," *Jazz Monthly,* July 1963. In 1955 the known house bands at Klein's were led by Kenny Burrell, Dave Heard, and Levi Mann. *Down Beat,* February 9, August 24, and October 30, 1955.

174. Some of the more memorable moments at the West End occurred when Sonny Rollins visited town with the Max Roach Quintet in 1956 and/or 1957. According to Frank Gant and Roy Brooks, Lateef and Rollins carried on a tenor sax duel until midmorning. Gant, interview by Gallert; Brooks, interview by Bjorn and Gallert.

175. Farrow was born in 1928 and played alto sax at the Paradise. Lowe, "Barry Harris."

176. *Michigan Chronicle,* November 16, 1946.

177. Barry Harris, interview by Bjorn.

178. Her name before marrying Coltrane was Alice McLeod. Bill McLarney, "Obituary to Ernie Farrow, 1928–1969," *Michigan Chronicle,* August 2, 1969. Farrow died tragically in a drowning accident in 1969.

179. He led his Music Makers at Murphy's Cocktail Lounge in the spring of 1953. Advertisement, *Michigan Chronicle,* May 30, 1953. According to a May 18, 1953, column in the *Detroit Free Press* he played for two weeks with Terry Gibbs at the Crystal. This band also included Terry Pollard.

180. This group opened the Cotton Club in November. Advertisement, *Michigan Chronicle,* November 20, 1954.

and one led by Hindal Butts not long before Lateef started there.[181]

Trombonist Curtis Fuller was also briefly a member of the Heard quintet. He was born in Detroit in 1934 but raised in an orphanage in the western suburb of Inkster.[182] One day a social worker took him to see the premier bop trombonist J. J. Johnson, who was playing with Illinois Jacquet at the Paradise Theatre. Fuller was impressed with Johnson's dignity in contrast to the crowd-pleasing Jacquet. He developed further musically for three years in an army band led by Cannonball Adderley. One of his major Detroit influences was Barry Harris: "He told me the RIGHT way, even though he didn't play trombone."[183] In Detroit in 1955 he gigged at the Blue Bird and took part in a recording with Paul Chambers and John Coltrane in November.[184] He was also a member of Hindal Butts's band at Klein's, as Butts remembered.

> *I had Curtis Fuller, Pepper Adams, Hugh Lawson, Ernie Farrow . . . that was a nut-cutting band, whew! . . . Curtis had just got out of the army when I hired him. Haven't seen him since he left Detroit. Curtis used to drink nothing but milk, man. He drank so much of George Klein's milk, George used to send him across the street to the Cream of Michigan to buy a quarter or half-gallon of milk and put it behind the bar. . . . He [Fuller] didn't smoke cigarettes, he didn't drink whisky, he just drank milk!*[185]

Fuller enrolled briefly at Wayne in 1956, where he roomed with tenorist Joe Henderson. He was part of the Lateef band until May 1957, when he moved to New York to join Miles Davis.[186]

Pianist Hugh Lawson was 21 when he joined the Lateef group. He had a thorough musical training and first learned from his father, who was also a jazz musician. Later he attended Cass Tech, where he studied several instruments, and Wayne, where he was a composition student.[187]

The youngest member of the group was 18-year-old drummer Louis Hayes. He also had an early start in music and was leading a band at 13.

> *My father had these instruments in the house and I started to play the piano. He taught me how to read music. My cousin, Clarence Stamps, he actually taught me how to play drums. He gave me a foundation that I could use forever. I practiced a lot when I was coming up. I had drums, vibraphone, and piano in the basement on Philadelphia. I would wake up in the morning, go down in the basement and stay there all day. Charlie Parker was my biggest influence in music coming up, definitely. I listened to him so much till I knew all the solos by heart. I still can sing them. I played with my compadres Eli Fountaine and Eddie Chambliss at Club Sudan and at club Tropicano, a teenage club on John R., near the Flame. Ernie Farrow and I became friends, [although] he was older. I don't know how I met him, but the World Stage was happening, so he got me involved in that. And that was a very unique place for me, because people understood this art form. I was very nervous about playing there. But after I played there a few times, these guys who I felt were my heroes really accepted me. That put me in another environment than with my friends I had played with all the time.*[188]

Hayes remembered how he joined Lateef's group while playing at Klein's with organist Levi Mann.

> *The club owner [George Klein] and I had a relationship going on; he really liked me. Yusef Lateef wanted a job there. The club owner told Yusef he could have the job, but he had to take me with it. So Yusef came over to my house—he didn't know me at all, naturally, because he was so much older—and he said, "Okay, you've got the job, but you're on a six-week trial." I stayed there for at least six months before they found out that I was a little youngster.*[189]

Hayes felt that he was at the top of the heap in Detroit when he played with Lateef.

181. Advertisements, *Michigan Chronicle*, July 30 and August 13, 1955. Butts, interview by Bjorn.

182. Kenn Cox, "Curtis Fuller," program booklet, *Detroit's Jazz Heritage Reunion 6*, Detroit, 1996.

183. Andrew Sussman, liner notes, Curtis Fuller, *All-Star Sextets*, Savoy 2239 (LP).

184. *Down Beat*, February 8, 1956. The Paul Chambers Sextet recorded one tune for Transition (LP30). The group also included Pepper Adams, Roland Alexander on piano, and Philly Joe Jones.

185. Butts, interview by Bjorn.

186. Sussman, liner notes, Fuller, *All-Star Sextets*.

187. Kenn Cox, "Hugh Lawson," program booklet, *Bluebird Reunion 3* (Detroit: Societie of the Culturally Concerned, 1993).

188. Hayes, interview by Bjorn. Fountaine and Chambliss were both tenorists who were one year older than Hayes. Fountaine was one of the major saxophonists with Motown in the 1960s. Chambliss should not be confused with another tenorist, Eddie Chamblee from Chicago. See also Lee Jeske, "Louis Hayes," *Modern Drummer*, July 1984.

189. Jeske, "Louis Hayes." The organist Levi Mann was the leader of the house band in the fall of 1955. Charles King was the drummer in October, and Hayes could have joined any time until the Lateef group took over in the spring of the following year. *Down Beat*, October 30, 1955.

When I was at Klein's with Yusef that place was packed every night. I never got to know Yusef as a young person. I got to know him when he came in the Cannonball [Adderley] band [in 1962]. I remember the theme song, "Yusef's Mood." I also remember the approach that we had, with Ernie playing the rabat, an instrument King David used to say his prayers, that's what Yusef used to say. We had many unusual instruments. It was a challenge to find rhythms that would fit this approach. I used mallets a lot. Yusef had a very strong presence. He was a person who for that time was into his religion and his blackness as a man. In Detroit, people were not really on that level, so he really impressed people. Yusef Lateef was the biggest thing in Detroit at the time, for sure. I was never thinking about Detroit; I was thinking about New York since I was a little kid.[190]

Hayes moved to New York in August 1956 to join the recently formed Horace Silver Quintet. This job at the center of the hard bop movement lasted three years. He got it on the recommendation of two ex-Detroiters: Kenny Burrell and Doug Watkins, the latter already a member of Silver's group.[191] On a visit to their hometown, the two had played with Hayes after hours at the West End.[192] Hayes rejoined the Lateef quintet for their first recording in New York in April 1957.

Frank Gant, who had most recently played with Lateef in Alvin Jackson's group, replaced Hayes at Klein's. He remained with Lateef until they both left for New York in 1960. Not long before leaving an incident with the Detroit police force happened that to Gant showed Lateef's personal strengths.

One night we were on our way to work [at Club 12]. . . . I was parking my car, and Yusef was riding with me. The Big Four, the Cruiser, cut me off and they jumped out of the car and started for Yusef. He was standing on the curb watching me park, had his horn and everything. One of these policemen said: "Come here I want to check you out!" and Yusef just stood there. The dude reached for his gun, it looked like, but couldn't get it, so he got his flashlight. He was coming at Yusef and Yusef blocked him. By that time two more jumped out of the car and tried to rough the man up, you know, threw him in the Cruiser. By the time they had me in there, they'd turn around to Yusef and said: "Jesus Christ hater, we'll make you spit all your teeth down your throat!" They took us into the station and lied and said the man was resisting arrest, was inciting a riot and all the rest. It was a bad scene. I couldn't even play the rest of the night, I was messed up. It messed me up in my stomach and everything, but Yusef went on and played man, just played! But he was so soulful anyway, man. He could play a ballad and play a ballad to death, and then to go through that kind of scene and get up on the bandstand [illegible] wow! . . . Next thing we tried to file a civil suit against the police department. We had John Conyers as our lawyer, but the suit never materialized. It would take about 10 years before a suit like that got through.[193]

For a period in the fall of 1957 Oliver Jackson took over the drum seat in the group. Oliver Jackson was 24 when he joined Lateef but had many years of experience playing drums in all kinds of bands.

I got my first union card in 1949 and was playing in 1947. . . . In the late forties and early fifties there were a lot of musicians around Detroit, it was the Mecca for musicians at that period. . . . I went out on the road when I was 14 with an old-time blues singer from Memphis. Then I worked with Gaye Cross who had a band similar to Louis Jordan's. . . . We had . . . John Coltrane on tenor sax. . . . a lot of people don't know that Coltrane was a very fine blues player, a real honky-tonk blues man. Just like a lot of people don't know that Tommy Flanagan was a boogie-woogie player, a top class one—I worked with them both.[194]

Jackson was part of Billy Mitchell's Blue Bird group in 1951 and played with Rudy

190. Hayes, interview by Bjorn.

191. Donald Byrd was another Detroiter in the group. He was a more occasional member of the group and appears on the first Silver quintet album, *Six Pieces of Silver,* Blue Note 1539 (LP).

192. Jeske, "Louis Hayes"; and Kenn Cox, "Louis Hayes," program booklet, *Detroit's Jazz Heritage Reunion 6,* Detroit, 1996.

193. Gant, interview by Gallert. Will Austin was also present and tells a similar story of the incident. Austin, interview by Gallert.

194. Sinclair Traill, "On the Beat," *Jazz Journal International* (January 1981). Cross was based in Sinclair, Ohio.

Fig. 96. Yusef Lateef Quintet, Klein's Show Bar, ca. 1958.
Lateef, ts/flt; Frank Morelli, bar; Frank Gant, dms; Will Austin, bs; (Terry Pollard, pno; not shown).
(Courtesy Rose Morelli.)

Rutherford for several years. Around 1953 he formed a dance/drum act with Eddie Locke, a friend from Miller High School. They called themselves "Bop and Locke," as Jackson's nickname was "Bops Jr." The two moved to New York around 1955 and performed at the Apollo Theatre. Locke remained in New York and became a sought after drummer among mainstream jazz players. Jackson returned to Detroit for about a year in the early fall of 1957 and took part in Lateef's recordings in October. On returning to New York he played and recorded with mainstream and modern jazz players.

When Curtis Fuller left for New York he was replaced by trumpeter Wilbur Harden. Harden had just arrived in Detroit in 1957 and had experience playing in rhythm and blues bands.[195] His career as a jazzman lasted no more than two years, but he was appreciated by many, including Frank Gant.

> *Another player in the band who I* LOVED, *man, was Wilbur Harden. You talk about some cornet-playing! When anybody of those cornet players, like Chet Baker, would come through Wilbur would eat them up! I mean it was pathetic when Wilbur got through with them. Now he was a beautiful cat, from Birmingham, Alabama. He wrote some very nice stuff. When*

195. Before joining Lateef, Harden played with Cuban Pete and his Progressive Calypso Band at Hajji Baba, which included several Detroit modernists: pianist Will Davis, bassist Beans Richardson, and drummer Roy Brooks. Advertisement, *Michigan Chronicle*, April 6, 1957.

he went to New York, that's the last I heard of him. I think he lasted about six months in New York, which is a drag, you know. I don't know what happened to him, but I understand he flipped out. I can't imagine how or why. 'Cause I knew him; I'd go by his house and hang out with him.[196]

Harden's main recorded legacies are the October 1957 recordings with Lateef and several albums done in 1958 with John Coltrane. At the end of the year he was hospitalized and never returned to music.

In 1958 Lateef reorganized his quintet at Klein's and brought in Frank Morelli on baritone and flute, Terry Pollard on piano, and Will Austin on bass. Pollard was the most experienced of the three new faces, having gotten off the road with Terry Gibbs in the middle of 1957. In the fall she played a long engagement with Sonny Stitt at the Frolic Show Bar and with Canadian vibraphonist Peter Appleyard at the Rouge Lounge.[197] Prior to playing with Lateef, Morelli was one of the Down Beats at the Hajji Baba.[198] Austin was a student at Wayne State, and 1958 proved to be a busy year for him. Apart from recording with Lateef, he and Frank Gant were on Barry Harris's first trio album. He recalled Lateef's group and the music they made.

Terry and I joined Yusef at the same time. . . . I would play this little thing called a "rabat"; . . . a little African instrument with one string. I had to do everything on that one string. Yusef had different rhythm things, not only 5/4, but 7/4 or 9/4. . . . 9/4 was hard! It made you think, and Yusef kept you thinking constantly. At that time, Yusef was SWINGIN'. *We'd get a groove going that was out of sight.*[199]

Pollard had a slightly different view of Lateef.

Yusef wanted to build. He wanted us to play, to be in the music. He'd say: "Terry, don't you want to play a different solo on this tune?" Yusef used to build—he'd start the music soft . . . then grow it. He sometimes had me blow into a pop bottle. He'd fill it with water . . . to get different sounds, to make the song sound like Yusef wanted it to be. And so I ended up blowing into these pop bottles. I didn't know how, and I would get dizzy every night. Yusef was an experience. When Yusef and Frank Morelli would get together, it was always so much fun.[200]

This new quintet recorded a concert at the Cranbrook Academy of Art in suburban Detroit in April 1958 and stayed together until the summer of 1959. In April 1959 Klein's changed its name to Club 12, and the new manager started a big name jazz policy in August, which meant that the Lateef quintet had to find other work after three years of steady employment.[201] There were a number of personnel changes during the fall as work became hard to find. In the front line Bernard McKinney replaced Morelli for a recording in Chicago and was followed by trumpeter Lonnie Hillyer.[202] Terry Pollard and Austin left and were replaced by Hugh Lawson and Herman Wright just in time for the last recording of Lateef's Detroit quintet in October.[203] Herman Wright had been on the road with James Moody in the early 1950s, and between 1955 and 1957 he joined Terry Pollard in Terry Gibbs's quartet.[204]

The Lateef quintet found work at the Hungry Eye and the Minor Key in the fall, and Lateef was back at Club 12 with a quartet to back Sonny Stitt in November.[205] In early 1960 Lateef decided to move to New York. He explained his decision in an interview five years later: "The music scene in Detroit became so slow that I had no choice but to go to New York."[206] Lateef traveled with his band as Frank Gant remembered it.

So we went to New York with the band. . . . We packed in Yusef's wagon. . . . Herman Wright was the bass player. Herman and I were living in Brooklyn with Yusef. Yusef had his wife there

196. Gant, interview by Gallert.

197. Terry Gibbs broke up his combo around late June 1957. *Michigan Chronicle,* July 6, 1957. Stitt and Pollard were at the Frolic for at least two weeks in October–November. *Detroit Free Press,* October 22, 1957; and *Down Beat,* November 28, 1957. The Terry Pollard Trio backed Appleyard in December. Advertisement, *Michigan Chronicle,* December 12, 1957.

198. The Down Beats were led by drummer Bill Culp and also included pianist Charles Boles. Advertisements, *Michigan Chronicle,* May 18 and August 24, 1957. Morelli was one of the few members of the Lateef group who never left Detroit. He continued to play until his death in 1987.

199. Austin, interview by Gallert.

200. Pollard, interview by Gallert.

201. The first act was the Chico Hamilton Quintet in late August. Advertisement, *Michigan Chronicle,* August 29, 1959.

202. McKinney recorded with the group in Chicago on September 11, 1959. Hillyer was part of the group at the Minor Key in early October. *Down Beat,* October 12, 1959.

203. Pollard and Austin went on to play at the Blue Bird with Joe Henderson in December. *Down Beat,* December 10, 1959. Austin became a member of Pollard's trio, which started a long engagement at the Hobby Bar in the spring of 1960. Advertisement, *Michigan Chronicle,* April 16, 1960. Will Austin recalls that "a lot of musicians would come and sit in. Sometimes Alice McLeod would come in. . . . she was something! She played almost exactly like Bud [Powell]. When Terry and Alice got up there, very few horn players wanted to get up there with them. They played up tempos constantly. . . . that was something to hear! Alice on piano and Terry on vibes." Austin, interview by Gallert. Pollard remained in Detroit for the rest of her career, with occasional recordings in New York. One recording was with the highly respected Detroit harpist Dorothy Ashby, *Soft Winds: The Swinging Harp of Dorothy Ashby,* Jazzland JLP 961, in 1961.

204. Wright was a member of Moody's group some time before October 1952, when he joined Terry Pollard's duo. "Jazz Duo Exciting at Lounge," *Michigan Chronicle,* October 4, 1952. Wright also recorded with Gibbs from 1955 to 1957. Jepsen, *Jazz Records.* Wright also played with harpist Dorothy Ashby at the Blue Note Room in 1958. *Michigan Chronicle,* June 14, 1958.

205. *Down Beat,* October 1 and 12, 1959. Advertisement, *Michigan Chronicle,* November 21, 1959.

206. Welding, "Music as Color."

Fig. 97. Yusef Lateef Quintet, Klein's Show Bar, ca. 1958. *Lateef, ts/flt; Frank Morelli, bar; Frank Gant, dms; Terry Pollard, pno; (Will Austin, bs; not shown).* (Courtesy Rose Morelli.)

207. Gant, interview by Gallert. Red Garland was the pianist in Miles Davis's quintet from 1955 to 1958 and formed his own trio thereafter.

and we were saving on meals. . . . Saida would put the pots on every day and boy, we would eat like mad! . . . We were so far out in Brooklyn that in order to get in to Manhattan we had to take three trains. That was a lot. . . . I couldn't stand it. One of the reasons I went with Red Garland was so I could get out of that kind of a trap. . . . We [the quintet] worked around New York for a while and then the gigs started getting a little slow and I jumped up and went out to California with Red Garland.[207]

Although work for the quintet was sparse in New York, within a few months Lateef was a member of the pacesetting Charles Mingus ensemble. Soon after leaving the Mingus ensemble, Lateef recommended his former trumpeter Lonnie Hillyer and Hillyer's Detroit sidekick

Charles McPherson to Mingus.[208] McPherson remembered that

Lonnie Hillyer and I went together to New York. We were living downtown, on the East Side. We used to session at a coffee house that had jam sessions in the afternoon. We would go every afternoon to the jazz sessions. Mingus came by one afternoon to hear us because he was in need of a trumpet player and an alto player and we had been recommended by Yusef. Lonnie had played with Yusef. Eric Dolphy and Ted Curson were going to quit the band and start their own respective groups. Yusef told him: "If you check out these young guys I think they'll be able to play your music." So then we started working with Mingus. First gig I made with him was a club called the Showplace. . . . that was the beginning of an association that lasted on and off for about 12 years.[209]

Lateef also stepped up his recording activity once he moved to New York and was a sideman on many dates, including some with Mingus. In 1960 alone he recorded three albums under his own name. In 1962 he received even wider exposure when he joined the Cannonball Adderley Sextet.

The Yusef Lateef Quintet Recordings. The first recordings of the Lateef quintet were done in April 1957 for Savoy Records in New York. Three more sessions in September and October resulted in six LPs.[210] The second of these was *Jazz for Thinkers*, with a cover featuring the group in front of Rodin's statue "the Thinker" at the Detroit Institute of Arts.[211] Later albums, like *Jazz and the Sounds of Nature* and *Prayer to the East*, were more likely to emphasize the exotic in Lateef's music. By the time of the first recordings the group had been together for a year, and the subsequent years at Klein's led to more recordings as Lateef remembered.

I worked at . . . Klein's Showbar for five years, 6 nights a week. We rehearsed every week so we had so much material that had been rehearsed and exercised. We were so tight we were able to go to New York on off-nights and do two albums, easily. . . . We got off Sunday night and jumped in the . . . station wagon, and we would drive all the way to Hackensack, New Jersey, and record on Monday and we'd turn right back to Detroit and open up again on Tuesday.[212]

The result was a cohesive group sound noticed by the British critic Jack Cooke in a 1963 review of Lateef's artistry.

Lateef seems to have taken considerable trouble to surround himself with men who could work well together and, by their individuality, add to the attractiveness of the music. . . . The combination of trombone and tenor produced a rich, mellow sound, and backed by the well organized rhythm section this first quintet appeared on record as a relaxed, thoroughly integrated unit encompassing a wide range of expression. From the first its dedication to original material was apparent, and this attitude helped the group achieve a real identity. Lateef's writing, like his playing, shows a flair for melody and strong rhythmic construction.[213]

Lateef's range of expression was indeed wide: he moved from slow blues to jump tunes and from modern jazz to Latin/African/Eastern moods. His use of non-Western elements was the most innovative aspect of his music at this time. By the 1960s Middle Eastern and Indian rhythms, scales, instruments, and time signatures were making wide inroads in modern jazz, but in 1957 Lateef was clearly a pioneer in this regard.[214]

He became interested in Middle Eastern music while working at Chrysler.

I realized I had to widen my canvas of expression. I spent many hours in the library on Woodward studying the music of other cultures. At this time I was also working at Chrysler's. I met a man from Syria and he asked me if I knew about the rabat. He made me a rabat and Ernie Farrow played it on the

208. Brian Priestley, *Mingus: A Critical Biography* (London: Quartet Books, 1982), 111, 120. Other Detroiters had been part of earlier Mingus groups in the 1950s. Tenorist Curtis Porter (later Shafi Hadi) joined Mingus in 1956. He played with Emitt Slay and Mathew Rucker in 1952 and 1953 and later that year led his own group at the Crystal. He is remembered by Ray McKinney and Phil Lasley as a gifted musician living a troubled life. Ray McKinney, interview by Gallert. Phil Lasley, interview by Jim Gallert, Detroit, Michigan, May 25, 2000. Trumpeter Clarence Shaw played with Gene Nero in 1949 and recorded with BuBu Turner for Fortune in 1953. He joined Mingus in 1955.

209. McPherson, interview by Bjorn. McPherson followed closely in Lateef's footsteps in those years. When Lateef left Detroit he handed the baton to the house band at the West End to McPherson. This was McPherson's first professional job in Detroit, but he soon left for New York with Hillyer.

210. *Jazz Moods*, Savoy MG12103; *Jazz for Thinkers*, Savoy MG12109; *Stablemates*, Savoy MG12115; *Jazz and the Sounds of Nature*, Savoy MG12120; and *Prayer to the East*, Savoy MG12117 (all LPs). A September session for Verve resulted in *Before Dawn*, Verve 314 557 097-2 (CD).

211. A detail no doubt noticed by few was that Louis Hayes was replaced on the cover by his brother Gerald since Hayes at the time lived in New York. Gerald is an alto saxophonist. Hayes, interview by Bjorn.

212. Lateef is mistaken about the length of the engagement at Klein's, as noted earlier. Rusch, "Interview with Yusef Lateef." This rushed schedule was not always the case. In October 1957 Barry Harris's group replaced Lateef's while they recorded for three days in New York. *Down Beat*, October 31, 1957.

213. Cooke, "Yusef Lateef."

214. Alan Groves, "Consistent Craftsman Yusef Lateef," *Jazz Journal* (September 1980).

recording. I was looking to widen my expression and made bamboo flutes on my own.[215]

The non-Western influences are already apparent on his 1957 recording dates. "The Beginning" is in 7/4 time, and "Happyology" mixes Latin and African rhythms, while "Before Dawn" employs a modal harmonic approach. Lateef also uses unusual instrumentation. On "Morning," Farrow plays the rabat, and a number of percussion instruments from around the world are also used. Most significantly, Lateef had begun to use other instruments besides the saxophone, starting with the flute. In 1956 fellow member of the New Music Society Kenny Burrell suggested Lateef take up the flute, and he followed the advice.

> *I thought it was a good idea. It just hadn't dawned on me. . . . I think he was aware of the possibilities in musical textures and the innate beauty of the flute. He had this insight and he passed it on to me.*[216]

Within a year, Lateef had a distinctive personal flute sound, acquired after much practice. Hindal Butts remembered a fishing trip with Lateef at the time that he was still starting out on the flute.

> *There was a stream and it was early in the morning and I hear this sound. . . . What the hell is that? I go around the bend in the stream and Yusef is sitting out on a big rock running the scales on the flute. . . . You will never duplicate that sound in the studio! . . . The outdoors and the water . . . The Moslem religion influenced his playing tremendously. . . . He had a way of moaning on the saxophone and the flute. . . . I've seen Yusef on a prayer rug in the basement at Klein's. . . . he was serious. . . . The religion changed his personality and his horn. . . . He'd moan when he played the blues.*[217]

Lateef's accomplishments on the flute should be put in the context of what was usually done on the instrument at the time. Cooke thought that

> *Lateef has become practically the only musician in the jazz field to bring to the flute anything other than pure technical facility. Using his tenor style, with its sweeping, highly melodic phrases, as a base, he has found a clarity of expression and a sense of the dramatic in his work on this instrument which sets him apart from other jazz flautists.*[218]

The slow blues "G.Bouk" from the April session is a good example of Lateef's flute playing. He also plays flute on "Metaphor" but starts off on an Egyptian oboelike instrument called the argol. Within a year Lateef further expanded his palatte, using a conventional oboe for the first time. His oboe playing has not, however, received as much critical acclaim as has his work on tenor and flute.

The first recording sessions also include a staple in Lateef's repertoire: "Yusef's Mood." This is a tour de force for his tenor saxophone, where he integrates modern jazz and rhythm and blues into a complete whole. After a statement of the rollicking theme by tenor and trombone, Lawson delivers a swinging piano solo. Toward the end of his solo, the horns riff in the background, increasing the rhythmic tension. Fuller follows with an elegant trombone solo after which Lateef enters. Lateef's solo is the longest and builds slowly from swinging melodic statements to more frequent honks and slurs. He is backed expertly by Lawson's chords, Fuller's riffs, and Hayes's driving cymbals. Anyone who has ever heard Lateef play this number knows it inevitably leads the audience to clap, shout, or dance.[219] While this first recording of "Yusef's Mood" was done in a studio, without an audience, a 1975 club version attests to this form of audience participation.[220] Frank Gant remembered the reaction of the audience in the late 1950s: "Yusef had a thing: he would save it until the last number: 'Yusef's Mood.' People would be up there screaming when he got through with that."[221]

By the October session Wilbur Harden's flügelhorn replaced Fuller's trombone, giving

215. Yusef Lateef, interview by Jim Gallert, "Meet the Artist," Montreux-Detroit Jazz Festival, September 6, 1999.

216. Welding, "Music as Color."

217. Butts, interview by Bjorn.

218. Cooke, "Yusef Lateef."

219. I had the privilege at Baker's Keyboard Lounge in 1976.

220. Yusef Lateef, *Ten Years Hence: Recorded Live at the Keystone Korner, San Francisco,* Atlantic SD 2-1001 (LP).

221. Gant, interview by Gallert.

the ensembles a lighter sound. He also displays his soulful Miles Davis influenced playing, even though Lateef clearly is the main soloist. This session includes a tune dedicated to Klein's, "8540 12th Street," which is based on "I Got Rhythm" changes.

Though a recording at Cranbrook in 1958 is marred by poor sound, several sessions in 1959 are memorable.[222] The last Savoy recordings in June allow for more solo space than the 1957 sessions and are probably closer to what the group sounded like in a club. Aside from the ever-impressive Lateef, Terry Pollard is consistently the most engaging soloist on these sessions. She plays with great verve and melodic inventiveness, especially in her solo on Abe Woodley's swinging blues "Arjuna."[223]

The last sessions in October produced the *Cry!-Tender* LP, a title that is an apt description of Lateef's playing.[224] The title tune is a contemplative tone poem, where Lateef leads off on the oboe, followed by some nice trumpet work by Hillyer. After an ensemble passage and Gant's mallets, Lateef returns with a soulful statement on tenor. Hugh Lawson also gets a chance to show his elegant and relaxed piano style before Lateef's dark oboe returns. The LP also features some impressive bass work by Herman Wright, particularly on a minor blues, "Dolopous."

Cool Detroit

There was another smaller modern jazz scene in Detroit that partly overlapped with the one around the Blue Bird. All players were white, in contrast to the Blue Bird–centered scene, which was predominantly black. They were adherents of the cool school of modern jazz, often associated with West Coast jazz and the music of Stan Getz, Lee Konitz, and Lennie Tristano. As has often been pointed out, there were few strict musical divisions between cool and hard bop varieties of modern jazz. Cool players certainly had more in common with, and often played with, beboppers, more so than they played with swing or dixieland players. But particularly in the formative years of these schools in the 1950s, many adherents drew the lines more clearly. The fact that these lines overlapped with racial distinctions no doubt solidified the sense that the differences were hard and fast.

Pepper Adams often talked about the white cool players in Detroit.

> *In the late 40s and early 50s there was a very active and working white jazz scene in Detroit, with white players with names like Leo Osebold or Frank Morelli or Red Ray. Who had gigs . . . many of the rest of us were not working that regularly. But they were the white jazz scene. And the interesting thing was that I would have enjoyed being able to play a gig with them or something. But I was just totally not accepted . . . because they did not like the way I played. Like all of the tenor players played exactly like Stan Getz. Leo Osebold was a remarkably fine player: played excellently, just like Stan Getz. There were several others that were good players. And they had quite a thriving jazz scene. At the Bowl-O-Drome, which was like six nights a week of jazz . . . they tried to explain to me: "If you want to play jazz, you've got to stop playing that old-fashioned stuff with that big sound." It was on the black scene that I had the recognition.*[225]

Adams's view of the cool players should be tempered to allow for more interactions with other modernists. The Bowl-O-Drome did feature some of these artists, but it also featured Willie Anderson and Art Mardigan. As we have seen previously, Osebold played a lot with Art Mardigan at the Bowl-O-Drome or in concerts in the late 1940s and early 1950s. Like Mardigan, he often played in interracial groups and does not fit Adams's depiction of the isolated cool player. For example, Mardigan and Osebold played with Phil Hill and Kenny Burrell at the Crystal in 1951, and in 1953–54 Osebold was a regular with Dave Heard's group.[226] Bess Bonnier played her first jazz gig with the Heard

222. *Yusef Lateef at Cranbrook,* Argo LP634. Recorded April 8, 1958.

223. Yusef Lateef, *The Fabric of Jazz,* Savoy MG12139. Recorded June 11, 1959. *The Dreamer,* Savoy MG12140, was recorded on the same date (LPs).

224. New Jazz 8234. Recorded October 16, 1959.

225. Hanson, "Pepper Adams: Detroit Roots." See also Tynan, "Doctor Pepper." Red Ray (Raymond Babula) played tenor and alto sax. He took part in a Bill Randle concert at the DIA in 1945 and played with Art Mardigan's jam group at the Bowl-O-Drome in the late 1940s. *Michigan Chronicle,* January 20, 1945; *Down Beat,* March 11, 1949. In the late 1940s Ray was described by *Down Beat's* Detroit correspondent as "a Parkerish alto" and a "veteran of the Rodd Raffell band which was later taken over by Charlie Spivak." *Down Beat,* March 11, 1949. Red Ray reappeared on the Detroit scene in 1958 when he played with Bess Bonnier at Little Wally's. *Down Beat,* October 2, 1958.

226. *Michigan Chronicle,* January 3, 1953; June 12, 1954.

Fig. 98. Unidentified setting, Detroit, ca. 1946. *Art Jordan, dms; Marion Di Vita, ts; Johnny Di Vita, tp.* (Courtesy Lou Cramton.)

group in 1954 but had met Osebold earlier.

The Chatterbox was a little place on Park Grove and Morang [on Detroit's East Side], a soda pop place. I met Leo Osebold there about 1947 along with Bill Spencer (a carbon copy of Bird) and Johnny and Marion Di Vita, and Art Mardigan. Osebold and the group [were] impressive. They played excellent solos but in hindsight I think they listened too much to records. Osebold sounded warm and delicious . . . not a big Ben Webster tone—he was heading towards that Lester sound but not quite there.

That Lester sound was Marion Di Vita, who was the most gorgeous tenor player as well. Art Mardigan was a great drummer and a funny guy.[227]

Trumpeter/arranger Eddie Nuccilli played with Osebold in the late 1940s.

Leo sounded like himself. Almost an advance notice of Coltrane. Not quite as technical, but Leo had great technique. I have a recording we did in 1949. I think he played on "What's New," this soulful solo.[228]

Saxophonist Jim Stefanson got to know Osebold in the 1950s and saw him as a Detroit-style bebopper.

Leo was a stone-pure, Detroit melodic bebopper. He spoke Detroit with his horn. Leo had it down so nice—he should have recorded. No matter what gig it was he was always so lyrical, in the way he would phrase his tune and the solos he would play. He had a nice round tone, but he did not have a real big resonant tone. He talked softly all the time. Just like he always said the right thing, he would play the right thing. He was highly respected with the white and black cats. I said to Leo once at the Drome: "Why don't you go to New York, man, and let them hear you? I like you more than Stan Getz and look how famous he is." He replied: "I have no desire to become famous." He was very religious and was an accountant. I don't think he was making a living at music .... Back in those days nobody could make a living on music. Leo Osebold is one of the diamonds, one of the jewels.[229]

Osebold was still an impressive player in 1960 when *Down Beat*'s Ira Gitler heard him at the American Jazz Festival. On this occasion Osebold performed with Jack Brokensha and Bess Bonnier, and in Gitler's opinion it was some of the "best jazz I heard all weekend."[230] Osebold eventually left music to become a full-time accountant. Barry Harris considered Osebold "important to my development. He was a very good player. He just decided to raise his family as opposed to becoming a musician and go to New York."[231] Two Detroit drummers played important parts in the cool movement.[232] Art Mardigan left Detroit in 1952 and played for some time with Woody Herman. In 1954 he recorded with Stan Getz.[233] He returned to Detroit in the late 1950s but only worked irregularly. Mardigan was the preferred drummer of the Di Vita brothers and Leo Osebold, according to Jim Stefanson, who said that playing with Mardigan was like "playing with a big ear, because he would put in all the punctuations, all the quotation marks, everything you need."[234] Mardigan later played with Brokensha in the 1960s and still had a very good sense of time, even though he was not well.[235] Another Detroit drummer, Frank Isola, had a similar career pattern but spent less time in Detroit in his early years. Isola played with Getz around the same time as Mardigan (1952–55) and also with Gerry Mulligan. Isola had left his hometown as a young man for military service (1943) and did not return until the late 1950s.[236]

In short, Detroit did make some contributions to the cool jazz movement in modern jazz. They are, however, less significant in comparison with those to the hard bop school.

Detroit Jazzmen in New York City

The migration of Detroit jazzmen to New York was the heaviest around 1956 and did not go unnoticed. Although their individual talents soon landed them in the recording studio, the record companies also recognized that a collective migration was taking place. Two recording sessions organized that year announce to the world that the Detroiters had arrived in the Big Apple.

Thad Jones, Detroit–New York Junction

Alfred Lion of Blue Note Records got the idea to feature Thad Jones with some fellow Detroiters (Billy Mitchell, Kenny Burrell and Tommy Flanagan) in March 1956. The LP was called *Detroit–New York Junction,* and Leonard

227. Bonnier, interview by Bjorn. Marion Di Vita was considered a good player in the 1940s, but his substance abuse seems to have severely impaired his career in music by the 1950s. His brother Johnny Di Vita was a modernist trumpeter. Eddie Nuccilli was a good friend of John Di Vita. He knew the family with five children quite well: "His father had grapevines, grew his own grapes. . . . John was naturally talented. . . . Had good knowledge of chords, great ear. . . . The whole family was equally talented. Art Di Vita was the first baritone player that I ever heard that sounded like a tenor. It was a gorgeous sound. Frank Morelli had that sound." Eddie Nuccilli, interview by Jim Gallert, Southfield, Michigan, July 25, 2000.

228. Nuccilli (born 1925), interview by Gallert. Nuccilli wrote his first arrangements at Cass Tech. After the war he wrote for a big band led by altoist John Rajeski, which also included Marion and John Di Vita and Osebold.

229. Jim Stefanson, interview by Lars Bjorn, Pontiac, Michigan, July 22, 1998.

230. Ira Gitler, "Second American Jazz Festival in Detroit," *Down Beat,* September 29, 1960. Brokensha frequently hired Osebold for studio work and characterized him as a lyrical bebop player. Brokensha, interview by Bjorn.

231. Barry Harris, interview by Bjorn.

232. A lesser role was played by altoist and tenorist Kenny Pinson, who was known as a superb lead player and a Parker stylist. He recorded with Gene Krupa in 1949 and Woody Herman in 1951 (Tom Lord, *The Jazz Discography,* vol. 9 [Methuen, N.J.: Cadence, 1994]). By the mid-1950s he was back in Detroit and played often at the Crest Lounge. Stefanson, interview by Bjorn.

233. "Art Mardigan," *New Grove Dictionary of Jazz.*

234. Stefanson, interview by Bjorn.

235. Brokensha, interview by Bjorn.

236. Gordon Jack, "The Forgotten Ones: Frank Isola," *Jazz Journal International* (December 1993). On returning to Detroit Isola played with Bess Bonnier's trio at Little Wally's. *Down Beat,* October 2, 1958.

Feather explained why in his liner notes.[237] New York, Chicago, and Los Angeles held a virtual monopoly on recording studios and

> *It is not until a musician or group migrates to one of these three that he has a chance for international recognition nowadays. Thus the title "Detroit–New York Junction" signifies a happy marriage between the rapidly growing musical produce of the Motor City and the magnetic tape of the Big Apple.*

Down Beat's reviewer Nat Hentoff was also enthusiastic.

> *Thad, potentially one of the most creative modern trumpeters, has almost no room to stretch during his nightly work with the Basie band, so that it has mainly been recordings like his two LPs on Debut and now this one that have indicated his growing value. Thad, first of all, plays with a welcome brassiness in contrast to some of his younger contemporaries' choked and or pinched tones. Thad swings with ease and his solos always sustain interest because of his care for construction. A high track is the singing "Little Girl Blue," played just by Thad, Kenny and Oscar [Pettiford]. . . . Impressive are the relatively new (outside of Detroit) talents of Burrell and Flanagan. Flanagan is also a very good comper. Billy Mitchell plays a hard-bop tenor that also has, however, an emotional fullness and a big beat. As a blowing session the solos here aren't always incandescent though very good.*[238]

What was not mentioned was the history of these Detroiters at the Blue Bird. Two of the tunes, "Blue Room" and "Zec," can be found on the EP with the Blue Bird house band three years earlier. Now they were recorded for a major jazz label.

Lion was enthusiastic enough to organize another session with Jones and some of the same Detroiters in July, resulting in *The Magnificent Thad Jones*.[239] Further motivation was provided when Jones was awarded the New Star on trumpet in *Down Beat*'s critics' poll during the summer. For this session Barry Harris replaced Tommy Flanagan, as he did at the Blue Bird. It so happened that Harris was in New York temporarily with Max Roach's quintet. Nat Hentoff's review in *Down Beat* was even more enthusiastic, and the album was just half a point off a five star rating.

> *Thad . . . has an individuality, maturity and continuity of conception that marks him as one of the most important contributors on his horn. . . . Barry Harris solos with attractive fluidity, but could dig in more emotionally. . . . Billy Mitchell, tenor with the Gillespie band, may not be a major stylist, but he plays hot, unaffected, intelligent horn that complement's Thad's more imaginative forays well. . . . The writing is minimal, this being a blowing session among experienced jazzmen with the heart and skill for collective freedom.*[240]

Kenny Clarke Meets the Detroit Jazzmen

Veteran bebop drummer Kenny Clarke had been present on a Thad Jones Debut label album in 1954, and in April 1956 he led another blowing session with a group of Detroiters on Savoy Records.[241] Newly arrived Kenny Burrell, Tommy Flanagan, and Pepper Adams were on this session, as well as their previous Detroit band mate Paul Chambers. Nat Hentoff's review in *Down Beat* was very positive.

> *The only ringer in "Jazzmen: Detroit" is the invaluable Kenny Clarke. The others are all indices of how productive a spawning ground Detroit has become for modern jazz. . . . Their blowing here is primarily of a low-flame, conversational kind. They fuse and pulse well together with the rhythm section a finely knit, flowing texture of full-sounding but not overbearing momentum. Flanagan solos with customary unhurried, functional taste and sensitive touch; Chambers, with his large-boned sound, continues to be an impressive soloist, and Burrell, as has been cited here before, is one of the most important young guitarists. Adams indicates he may well be the best relatively new baritone saxist since Jack Nimitz.*[242]

237. Blue Note BLP 1513 was recorded on March 13, 1956. Jepsen, *Jazz Records*. It is available in a Japanese release: BN Club TOCJ-1513 (CD).

238. *Down Beat*, July 25, 1956. A day earlier Lions recorded "My Heart Stood Still" under Kenny Burrell's name with the same rhythm section plus Frank Foster. This is available on *Burrell's Swingin'* in a Japanese Blue Note release, GXK8155. This group was invited back to record a complete LP in December (BLP 1543). On May 29 Lions recorded Burrell's first album under his own name, *Introducing Kenny Burrell* (BLP1523) with Flanagan, Chambers, Kenny Clarke, and percussionist Candido.

239. Blue Note BLP 1537, recorded on July 14, 1956. It has been rereleased in a CD version as CDP 7 46814 2 with two additional tracks.

240. *Down Beat*, February 6, 1957.

241. Savoy LP MG-12083. Reissued in 1977 as Savoy SJL1111.

242. *Down Beat*, January 9, 1957.

When the record was rereleased in 1977 Bob Blumenthal commented that

> *Few cities have been as talent-rich as Detroit proved to be in the 1940s and 1950s . . . the era when bebop dominated jazz. . . . the real find of this session was Pepper Adams. Here was a baritone saxophonist who had everything covered, from technique and harmonic sophistication ("Cottontail") to lyrical ease ("Your Host") and exemplary sense of pace ("Tom's Thumb"). Adams moves through all registers and, like Gerry Mulligan, occasionally suggests the flowing lines of a tenor sax, but he also brings some of the guttiness back to the big horn. Rhythmically, he never lumbers along; even at a relaxed tempo like that of "You Turned the Tables on Me" he sounds like an earth mover in low gear.*[243]

Around 1960 two additional recording dates gathered together some of the same players on two LPs with the same name: *Motor City Scene.* One was under the leadership of Pepper Adams, and the other was led by Thad Jones.[244] However, by then all the participants were well-known names with several recordings of their own. A virtual flood of "blowing sessions" in the late 1950s featured various combinations of this generation of Detroit players on the Blue Note, Savoy, and Prestige record labels. To illustrate, Kenny Burrell was the leader on seven such LPs recorded in 1956 and 1957 alone.[245] There was no doubt that this generation of Detroiters had hit the ground in New York running.

Why Was Detroit So Important in the 1950s?

What explains the creative explosion in Detroit jazz during the decade? A definitive answer to this question would require a comparative study of jazz centers, but I can offer some tentative answers. The Detroit public school system had very high standards of music education, and this provided a solid basis for future players and listeners alike. Many jazz musicians of note attended Cass Technical and Miller High Schools, the top schools for music in the city. Other schools, like Northwestern and Northern, also provided a basic music education to a smaller number of musicians.

The postwar economic boom also worked in Detroit's favor by providing challenging jobs for jazz musicians. Jobs in music result from the joint activities of audiences and musical entrepreneurs. Detroit had an audience for modern jazz from the mid-1940s, and there were businesspeople with an interest in catering to that audience. From the latter half of the 1940s to the mid-1950s there was a steady growth of jobs for modernists in nightclubs, dance halls, after-hours spots, and concerts. Numerous jump bands provided jobs for aspiring players, who could hone their craft while earning a living playing music.

When there are no challenging jobs, talented and well-trained musicians will leave for larger jazz centers, like New York, once they have completed high school. Detroit in the 1940s and 1950s was a place where jazz artists stayed around until their mid-twenties. A modernist circle of musicians developed in the latter half of the 1940s and provided a support network for aspiring youngsters. The more experienced in this network passed on information about instrumental techniques, the secrets of improvisation, the latest musical innovations, and job opportunities. Since the 1920s Detroit had been connected with what went on at the center of jazz, and these ties were solidified in the postwar years.

At the center of the modernist network were several extraordinary individuals who served as teachers-mentors-bandleaders for an extended period: Thad Jones in the early 1950s and Barry Harris and Yusef Lateef throughout the 1950s. These three stayed in the city longer than most. Jones was 31, Harris 30, and Lateef 40 years of age when they left for New York. Jones and Lateef had spent several years on the road earlier

243. Bob Blumenthal, liner notes, *Kenny Clarke Meets the Detroit Jazzmen*, Savoy SJL 1111 (LP).

244. Pepper Adams, *Motor City Scene* (Bethlehem Records, rereleased in Japan as YP-7117), featured Donald Byrd, Kenny Burrell, Tommy Flanagan, and Paul Chambers. The drummer, "Hey" Lewis, is Louis Hayes. Thad Jones, *Motor City Scene* (United Artists UAL 4025) featured Billy Mitchell, Flanagan, Chambers, and Elvin Jones. Trombonist Al Grey from the Basie band was the non-Detroiter on this LP.

245. The seven are *Introducing Kenny Burrell* (Blue Note 1523), *Kenny Burrell*, vol. 2 (Blue Note 1543), *All Night Long* (Prestige PRLP7073), *All Day Long* (Prestige PRLP7081), *Blue Moods* (Prestige LP7088), *K.B. Blues* (Japanese Blue Note GXF3052), and *Two Guitars* (Prestige LP7119).

in their careers but decided to return to Detroit before taking the leap to the Big Apple.

Is There a Detroit Jazz Style?

EVER SINCE DETROIT JAZZMEN were noticed in New York as a collective entity, the question has been raised whether Detroit has a jazz style of its own. Even though jazz players are expected to develop their own individual approaches to their instruments, there are also shared stylistic elements. It is an open question whether such elements were shared in local jazz communities, like Detroit, in the post–World War II era. Some jazz historians have argued that music from Kansas City in the 1930s was the last regional jazz style, but others argue for a West Coast jazz tradition in the postwar period.

The most commonly made argument is that there is a Detroit piano school, which is not surprising given the large number of influential Detroit pianists. When asked about a Detroit style some Detroit pianists are unwilling to identify one, and it is not easy to find agreement on exactly what would make up the style.[246]

The perceptive jazz critic Whitney Balliett has portrayed "four remarkable pianists" that came out of Detroit in the 1940s and 1950s: Hank Jones, Barry Harris, Tommy Flanagan, and Roland Hanna.

> *All have leaned on each other and on generally shared idols. Jones and Flanagan admired Fats Waller, Art Tatum, Teddy Wilson, Nat Cole and Bud Powell. Flanagan also learned from Jones, and Jones in later years probably listened to Flanagan. Harris admired Powell and Flanagan, while Hanna admired Flanagan and Erroll Garner. . . . Jones is their doyen. His touch is pearled, and improvisations are spun out of willowy single-note melodic lines that reflect Wilson's fluidity and Powell's harmonic advances. His single notes are polite and his harmonies cast soft light. Homogeneity itself is his style. Harris must have passed through Jones' benign influence, but . . . he fell under the spell of Powell and Charlie Parker, for he constantly applauds their wheeling, irregular, slightly acidulous melodic lines. . . . Hanna is a buoyant, resplendent pianist. . . . His melodic surges continually ascend and descend, and as each breasts a hill Hanna celebrates with a crescendo. Jones, Harris and Flanagan are cool players, but Hanna toils at his large, domed structures.*[247]

Balliett only hints at the similarities between the four pianists, possibly telling us that such a summation would do violence to the variety he describes. David Rosenthal in *Hard Bop* is bolder and sees the Detroit trio of Jones, Flanagan, and Harris playing a central role among "hard bop lyricists." In his view the three "all are 'musicians' musicians'—that is, masters of nuance who appeal to educated tastes, to listeners who can get beneath the surface of jazz, its overall 'sound,' and savor the dynamics and imaginative eccentricities of specific solos."[248]

Hanna is not mentioned by Rosenthal, and to Balliett his approach stands somewhat apart from the other three. Hanna's own definition of what constitutes the Detroit style is also a very broad one and would seem to go beyond pianists.

> *Detroit tells a story. You hear other pianists running notes and changes. But a musician from Detroit makes an effort to arrive at his own story and tell it in his music. You'll hear a kind of similarity in approach, in emphasis. But when Tommy or Barry or Bess [Bonnier] or I stretch out, you have to be right in the music. Many pianists don't grab your attention. But we do.*[249]

To tell a story could of course also be seen as a general criterion for any great jazz solo, and it would not be hard to find examples from the work of the masters.

Kirk Lightsey belongs to the next generation, and it is interesting that he sees himself as a Detroit pianist. He defines such a pianist as one with "a Bud Powell awareness, an Art Tatum styling, a bebop feeling, and a pianistic

246. Harris agrees that there is a Detroit piano style starting with Hank Jones but is reluctant to specify what defines it. Harris, interview by Bjorn. Flanagan is less willing to acknowledge the existence of a Detroit piano style.

247. Whitney Balliett, "Tommy Flanagan," *New Yorker*, November 20, 1978.

248. Rosenthal, *Hard Bop*, 99

249. Wilson, "Old Friends Bring Detroit Style to Series at Heavenly Restaurant." Wilson's article was written on the occasion of a Detroit piano concert in New York with Flanagan, Harris, Hanna, and Bonnier.

approach." Among his many influences, Lightsey mentions Detroiters Willie Anderson and Abe Woodley, and he says that "because I thought I'd like to think creatively, with fluid piano lines, I chose to be most influenced by Hank Jones and Tommy Flanagan."[250]

Both Balliett and Lightsey are right if one acknowledges that there is a modern Detroit piano tradition that reaches across generations. The first generation would be Hank Jones and Willie Anderson during the war years, followed by Tommy Flanagan, Barry Harris, and Roland Hanna in the second generation after the war. To this generation we could also add Hugh Lawson. A third generation would include Kirk Lightsey and his contemporaries who were active in the city in the 1960s. A general stylistic characteristic of this branch of modern jazz piano is its lyricism: fluid melodic lines, a light touch, rhythmic elegance, and harmonic sophistication.

If this lyrical style is shared by an influential line of pianists, can it also be extended to other Detroit instrumentalists? Kenny Burrell comes immediately to mind, and his affinity with Tommy Flanagan and Willie Anderson has been noted earlier. Thad Jones would be another influential Detroit stylist whose strengths clearly include this kind of lyricism. On the other hand, several important Detroit players of the period, such as Yusef Lateef, Billy Mitchell, and Pepper Adams, would more easily be fit into the "down-home" or "experimental" side of hard bop. We are not talking about differences in musical approach that led to divisions among the musicians mentioned, however, since the "lyricists" were clearly part of the same circle of modernists as the others.

I conclude that Detroit did contribute significantly to the hard bop movement in modern jazz and in particular to its lyrical side. With the exception of its pianists, the lyrical aspect of hard bop did not dominate Detroit jazz as a whole.

250. Leslie Gourse, "Profile: Kirk Lightsey," *Down Beat,* December 1984.

Lee's

Detroit Rhythm and Blues: From Jump Blues to Motown

George Favors, Walter Bragg, and Lou Barnett at Lee's Sensation Lounge, 1947.

The blues tradition in African-American music went through a number of transformations in the 1940s, and by the end of the decade three strands of blues music could be found in most large urban areas. These three strands—urban blues, jump blues, and rhythm and blues—will be discussed separately in this chapter, which does not contradict the fact that they were in constant interaction with each other.

The urban blues tradition from the interwar years evolved and underwent several changes in the 1940s. Most important were the increased use of amplified guitar as pioneered by T-Bone Walker, a heavier beat, and vocalists who turned into shouters.

Jump blues combos first appeared on record in the late 1930s on the Decca label. Their popularity both on record and in person grew steadily during the 1940s, and they were seen by promoters as a cost-effective alternative to big bands. Indeed, the rise of jump blues accelerated the decline of big bands during the latter half of the 1940s. Some of these combos were bebop oriented and eventually played more for listening audiences in jazz clubs, as discussed in earlier chapters. Although other groups recorded music in a similar vein, it was alto saxophonist and vocalist Louis Jordan and His Tympany Five who brought this style of music to the attention of the record buying public.[1] Jordan's success was due to many factors. His music combined vocals, swing riffs, blues, boogie, and shuffle into a mix that was both entertaining and spoke directly to black audiences. Jordan was a fine singer and was a master of the "blues ballad." According to Arnold Shaw, Jordan "demonstrated that, not only was there a market for black-oriented material and black-styled music, but it was a big market, white as well as black."[2]

Jordan recorded extensively for Decca

1. Trumpeter Oran "Hot Lips" Page, trombonist Leo "Snub" Mosley, and pianist Sammy Price recorded similar music for Decca around the same time.

2. Arnold Shaw, *Honkers and Shouters* (New York: Collier, 1978), 64.

Records from 1938 to 1954. Decca, formed in 1934, was a relatively new player in the record industry and focused on recording black singers and bands. In addition to recording well-known big bands such as those of Count Basie, Buddy Johnson, and Chick Webb, Decca pioneered small combo novelty/jump recordings, largely through the efforts of black recording director and talent scout J. Mayo Williams.[3]

Another part of the jump blues tradition was the honking saxophones. Jordan's alto was one example of it, but tenorists like Illinois Jacquet were even more influential. Jacquet's solo on Lionel Hampton's Decca recording of "Flying Home" in 1942 "served to launch a school of booming, demonstrative, and erotic tenor sax stylists" according to Shaw.[4]

When the honkers joined forces with the blues shouters in the mid-1940s the result was a new popular musical form, the third strand of blues music, dubbed "rhythm and blues" by *Billboard* magazine in 1949.[5] It replaced the term *race records,* which *Billboard* had used from 1945 to 1949 and which had been in use as a descriptive term for recordings of black artists since the early 1920s.[6]

Not all R & B vocalists shouted, and many had a smooth, sexy style of ballad singing, exemplified by Charles Brown, Cecil Gant, and other "sepia Sinatras." By the early 1950s vocal groups also became increasingly important as R & B vocalists.[7]

Shaw has provided the following capsule description of rhythm and blues in its social context.

> *R & B was liberated music, which in its pristine form represented a break with white, mainstream pop. Developing from black sources, it embodied the fervor of gospel music, the throbbing vigor of boogie woogie, the jump beat of swing, and the gutsiness and sexuality of life in the black ghetto.*[8]

The emergence of new African-American musical forms in the 1940s and 1950s was also accompanied by changes in the record industry. The real beginning of R & B, according to Grendysa, was in 1948: "for the first time a bunch of new acts on new labels began to dominate the R & B tallies at the same time black artists were vanishing from the Pop charts."[9] Without the new labels, R & B would not have ascended as quickly nor would it have had the same impact on the United States' music scene.

The plethora of new record labels was formed in the aftermath of the American Federation of Musicians' recording ban (1942–44). They were dubbed "independents" by the music press to differentiate them from subsidiary labels controlled by the major ("Big Three") labels.[10] They concentrated on music the major labels ignored: hillbilly, gospel, bebop, and R & B.[11] The strike, and the easing of wartime restrictions on civilian use of shellac (essential for record manufacture), broke the stranglehold of the major labels.

Most of the newcomers only distributed records locally, and minimal sales soon put them out of business. In an effort to increase sales, many independents leased their masters to a nationally distributed independent label. These deals invariably soured, and charges of unreported sales, unpaid bills, and infringement into the leasing label's territory were the end result. Many small labels were run on a shoestring budget, and lack of money forced them to use primitive recording facilities and poor quality shellac. This had a negative impact on the sound of their records and also affected sales.

Detroit had its share of independent record labels in the late 1940s and 1950s: Sensation, Staff, Fortune, and JVB.[12] The story of Sensation, in particular, shows the pitfalls involved in establishing a foothold in the marketplace for blues music. Not until 1959, when Berry Gordy started Tamla/Motown, did a Detroit independent label successfully penetrate the national market.

3. According to researcher Nigel Haslewood, the first "jump" recording session took place on March 10, 1938, under the leadership of Hot Lips Page. Nigel Haslewood, "The Jump Bands," *Storyville* 30. Jordan and Williams met through bandleader Chick Webb, in whose band Jordan worked from 1936 to 1938.

4. Shaw, *Honkers and Shouters,*173.

5. Pianist Joe Liggins's Exclusive record *The Honeydripper* in 1945 is generally acknowledged as the first R & B million seller.

6. *Billboard* tracked the popularity of black recordings under the heading "Harlem Hit Parade" from 1942 to 1945; prior to that time they were not tracked.

7. For a musical analysis see Milton Lee Stewart, "Development of Rhythm and Blues and Its Styles," *Jazz Research* 20 (1988).

8. Shaw, *Honkers and Shouters,* xvii.

9. Peter Grendysa, "Louis Jordan," (booklet), October 1990, 16.

10. RCA Victor, Decca, and Columbia. There were also specialist labels aimed at the jazz connoisseur (Commodore, Blue Note, and, after the ban, Keynote). Over 350 independents were licensed by the union by the end of 1945.

11. The ban resulted from the refusal of record companies to pay a fee to the AFM for each record sold if AFM members played on it. The fee would go into a fund to create jobs for musicians. AFM president Petrillo believed that records and, especially, jukebox play of records eliminated potential jobs for musicians, and he decreed that record companies must compensate AFM members. The labels thought they could wait the union out, but Decca ran out of stockpiled sides first and agreed to union terms in September 1943. RCA Victor and Columbia, fearful of losing ground, followed suit in 1944. For a detailed technical discussion of the ban centered around the AFM, see Robert D. Leiter, *The Musicians and Petrillo* (New York: Bookman Associates, 1953), 132–41. The strike and its aftermath are discussed in DeVeaux, *Birth of BeBop,* 295–305.

12. Another independent Detroit label was Paradise, which was briefly discussed in the third chapter, note 100.

Detroit Record Labels

Sensation Records

SENSATION RECORDS WAS FORMED in Detroit in 1947. It was an outgrowth of Pan-American Distributing Company, a record distribution company owned by John Kaplan and Bernie Besman.[13] Pan-American grew into a prosperous business that at its peak handled over 100 labels and had a regional office in Cleveland.[14] The partners formed Sensation after hearing the Todd Rhodes band at Lee's Sensation Lounge. Besman, a pianist and former dance band leader (under the name Dean Dennis), handled the artistic end, while Kaplan, an accountant, handled the money. "My partner and I named the label after Lee's [club], but there was no business connection," Kaplan remembered.[15]

The first Sensation session took place in July 1947 at United Sound Studios in Detroit. Once word got around that Sensation was recording Detroit talent, a steady flow of managers, agents, and would-be recording artists came to the Sensation office at 3747 Woodward.[16] "I think I got the best of the crop," said Besman.[17] Sensation also recorded blues singer John Lee Hooker, pianist T. J. Fowler, vibraphonist Milt Jackson, country blues singer Sylvester Cotton, and many other Detroit-based musicians of various music persuasions.[18]

Sensation's production costs were about 21–24 cents per record. This included mechanical, artist, and publishing royalties, as well as label and sleeve costs. They would be sold to a wholesale distributor for around 41 cents, a markup of around 85 percent. The records retailed for about 89 cents.[19] Sales of about 5,000 records were considered good.[20]

In Detroit as in other northern cities, R & B discs sold better than country-style blues. The market for blues and R & B records was confined to black-owned or black-operated outlets; white stores would not carry them.[21] Besman recalled that

> *Most of the stores were located in the Hastings Street area. They would come and pick up the records. [It would] always be cash. Didn't buy in large quantities—$25, $50 orders.*[22]

Radio was an important avenue for marketing recordings, but black music was only aired in Detroit at certain times. Bill Randle, a Detroit radio deejay and jazz promoter from 1942 to 1949, recalled the scene during those years.

> *There were no black disc jockeys when I started. I used to play jazz, blues, R & B and gospel records. Nobody played music that was obviously black music during the day. I could play "big band" music by Count Basie, because the station management didn't have a clue who Basie was. I could never have played "Drifting Blues" by Charles Brown, in the daytime. Only at night.*[23]

Randle's shows, *The Interracial Goodwill Hour* and *Strictly Jive*, were popular with supporters of black music, but his popularity was eclipsed by that of Ed McKenzie (Jack the Bellboy) on WJBK. McKenzie tailored his daytime show for white listeners by playing "pop" music, but he also played jazz, R & B, and blues. According to David Carson, McKenzie "became the first white deejay in town to play an abundance of black music on what was essentially a pop show."[24]

McKenzie recalled his format.

> *I just picked records I happened to like and we found an audience. I played a lot of jazz and then I'd slip in a little T-Bone Walker too.*[25]

McKenzie and WJBK were criticized for playing too much black music, but McKenzie's show was so popular and generated so much money that the station brushed aside the complaints.[26]

For entrepreneurs like Besman, this meant he would get some local air play for his jazz and R & B records, but his blues records didn't get the same exposure.

13. Besman claims that "We were the first independent distributor in Detroit. There were only four distributors at that time—Capitol, RCA, Decca and Columbia." Bernie Besman, interview by Jim Gallert, *Jazz Yesterday,* WDET-FM, Detroit, Michigan, June 23, 1990.

14. Bernie Besman, interview by Lars Bjorn and Jim Gallert, Novi, Michigan, May 14, 1991.

15. John Kaplan, interview by Martin Gross and Jim Gallert, Farmington Hills, Michigan, March 26, 1989.

16. Sensation moved to 3731 Woodward, a few doors away, in 1950.

17. Besman, interview by Gallert.

18. John Lee Hooker convinced Besman to record two of his pals: Andrew Dunham and Sylvester Cotton. Besman compared them to Hooker: "Same primitive style. Dunham had an electric guitar. He had money, didn't need to work. He was older than Hooker was. I never heard them or Hooker play in a club." Besman, interview by Gallert.

19. Ibid.

20. Sensation's biggest seller was "Bell Boy Boogie."

21. Besman, interview by Gallert.

22. Ibid.

23. Randle, interview by Gallert. Randle says he was fired "dozens" of times for a wide variety of infractions, including playing black music on a daytime show, but was always rehired because of his skill as an announcer.

24. David Carson, *Rockin' down the Dial* (Troy, Mich.: Momentum Books, 2000), 2–3.

25. Ibid., 3.

26. According to Carson, "The music and comments made Ed, as 'Jack the Bellboy,' the most talked about air personality in Detroit and definitely, *the* disc jockey of the late 1940's." Ibid., 3.

The first guy that gave me a break . . . was Ed McKenzie, Jack the Bellboy. He would play these R & B records, not all of them, but whatever he thought he could squeeze in his show. And Bill Randle . . . he was a walking encyclopedia of jazz. He would play it if it fitted the jazz picture. When I recorded John Lee Hooker, I couldn't have it [his record] played here. I had to lease the record to Modern Records. They had pretty good connections down South. That's where they really played it [on radio stations].[27]

National distribution was always a problem for regional labels, and Sensation leased some of its Rhodes masters to Chicago-based Vitacoustic Records in hopes of improving sales. Vitacoustic went under soon afterward, and Sensation then made a deal with Syd Nathan, president of Cincinnati-based King Records, which proved to be a fatal mistake.[28] King had national distribution and in-house recording capability. King would record Rhodes and distribute his records, and the other Sensation records they leased, outside of the Detroit area after local release by Sensation. Unfortunately, King did not always wait for local release by Sensation and also used some masters without permission. A series of legal actions ensued that finally killed the deal in 1952.[29] The relationship between the partners also deteriorated. Besman sold his interest to Kaplan in 1952 and moved to Los Angeles.[30]

Staff/Dessa Records

Staff was owned and operated by Idessa Malone, a forthright and savvy African-American woman who was probably born in Arkansas. Dave Usher, who formed his first record label in 1948, recalled Malone.

She worked out of Detroit on East Vernor. She called her company Idessa Malone Distributors. She was maybe 28 at the time . . . efficient, outgoing, assertive, commanding . . . not an ass-kicker, [but] knew what the hell she was doing. Baby, I looked up to her.[31]

Staff had its greatest hit with Johnny "Red" Miller's "Bewildered," which the company claimed sold 200,000 copies nationwide.[32] Miller was a Detroit blues-oriented singer and pianist who later recorded with Tiny Bradshaw. Staff also recorded several other local jazz and blues figures, including Ted Buckner, Paul Bascomb, and Baby Boy Warren, between 1947 and 1950. Malone also owned the Dessa record label, which issued a small number of gospel recordings. Neither label released any titles after 1950.

Fortune Records

Devora and Jack Brown started Fortune Records in 1947. Devora was a songwriter, and owning a record label was a guaranteed way to get her songs recorded. The Fortune offices were first located in the Brown family home on Twelfth Street in Detroit.[33] Their early recording sessions were held at various studios in Detroit. In 1951, the Browns moved their operation to a storefront at 11629 Linwood and built a small recording studio in the back. In 1956 or 1957 they moved to their present location at 3942 Third Avenue.

Fortune at first concentrated on the white pop and hillbilly record markets. Once the owners became aware of the wealth of black talent in the city, they put their resources into that area. By 1954, their catalog was heavily weighted with blues, R & B, gospel music, and some jazz. They recorded several doo-wop groups that were popular in the 1950s, including the Five Dollars, the Don Juans, Nolan Strong and the Diablos, and eccentric R & B performer Andre "Bacon Fat" Williams.

Pianist Joe Weaver and his group, the Blue Notes, often accompanied the doo-wop groups. Johnnie Bassett played guitar in Weaver's band and recalled how things worked.

27. Besman, interview by Gallert. Besman named one of Todd Rhodes's recordings ("Bell Boy Boogie") for McKenzie.

28. King acquired 64 Sensation masters, the cream of the crop, on June 19, 1948. Anthony Rotante and Paul Sheatsley, "Detroit Research," *Blues Record* 30.

29. Both labels had recording licenses from the AFM, and their case was heard by AFM boss Petrillo. According to Besman, King paid $10,000 to Sensation and returned to them all masters used without permission and records made from those masters. By the time King finally complied with the union ruling, Sensation was no longer making records.

30. Besman is still involved in the music business. Kaplan stayed in the record distribution business and rose to vice president at M. S. Handleman, a respected Detroit distribution company.

31. The business was located at 606 East Vernor Highway. Staff had a separate address next door (608). Dave Usher, interview by Jim Gallert, Detroit, Michigan, December 27, 1989.

32. "Manager of Record Distribution Company Charged with Concealing $22,000," *Michigan Chronicle*, February 5, 1949.

33. Fortune Records is listed at 11839 Twelfth Street starting in October 1946 and at 12005 Twelfth Street beginning in January 1949. Galen Gart, *ARLD* (Milford, New Hampshire: Big Nickel, 1989), 197.

It was a little, boxy place. Just a storefront. It was a record shop and a little studio in back. Five microphones. Little booth.[34]

They [Fortune] had [vocal] quartets. They needed guitar players and bands. We were the house band. Jack would call and say, "I got a new group I want you to rehearse," and we'd go down there. They would sing something, and we would sit there and listen, and they would tell us, "OK, put some music to that." No charts, no nothin'. Nobody read any music. They would sing it two or three times and say, "What do you feel? What can you do? Put some music to this thing." Joe was very talented at things like that.[35]

Fortune also recorded bluesmen like John Lee Hooker and jazz pianists Willie Anderson and Otis "BuBu" Turner.[36] Unlike the majority of Detroit record labels, Fortune leased only two of its masters. Fortune is unusual in that the label has always been family owned, and although they have not recorded anyone in decades, Devora Brown and her son Sheldon still own the label.

JVB/Gone/Von/Viceroy

Joe Von Battle owned this family of labels and operated out of Joe's Records at 3530 Hastings Street, which was a center of the Detroit blues scene in the 1950s. Von Battle put a makeshift recording studio in the back of his shop, and he recorded all kinds of music.

Johnnie Bassett went to high school with Von Battle's son, and this led to an opportunity for the Blue Notes.

He told his dad about us after he saw us at an amateur show. His dad had a studio in the back of the shop. He used to ask us to come by and rehearse.[37]

The Blue Notes rehearsed there frequently. Unbeknownst to the musicians, Von Battle ran tape during rehearsals, netting several numbers at no cost. "A lot of that stuff, they didn't tell us they was recording," said Bassett.[38] Von Battle leased four of the titles to DeLuxe Records in Cincinnati.[39] "He was a businessman interested in making money," saxophonist George Benson recalled.[40]

In addition to pioneer Detroit vocal and R&B groups, Von Battle recorded many sermons by Reverend C. L. Franklin, father of singer Aretha Franklin, and a few jazz groups, including pianist Ted Sheely, Kenny Burrell and the Four Sharps, and saxophonist George Benson.

The urban renewal of the Paradise Valley area in the late 1950s destroyed Von Battle's shop, and he relocated to Twelfth Street. He continued to issue 45 rpm singles on his Von label through the 1960s.[41]

While none of the Detroit independents managed to break onto the national market, they were part of a thriving local blues music scene.

Urban Blues

Detroit urban blues are mainly known through the artistry of guitarist John Lee Hooker. Other urban blues artists played piano in the style developed in the city in the interwar years. Like Hooker, these pianists could be heard in bars along Hastings Street and the Near East Side in the 1940s. Big Maceo, the greatest pianist in this style, had a hit in 1945 with his rousing boogie "Chicago Breakdown." Unfortunately he suffered a stroke the following year, and his later recordings never equaled his early achievements. He had a number of local followers, among whom the most prominent were Detroit Count and Boogie Woogie Red.

Detroit Count

Detroit Count was the stage name of Bob White, who arrived in Detroit in 1938.[42] He played and sang as a single in bars and clubs in Paradise Valley throughout the 1940s and in 1953 changed from piano to the Hammond organ.[43] At that time he recorded some rhythm

34. Johnnie Bassett, interview by Jim Gallert, Detroit, Michigan, January 2, 1996.

35. Jim Gallert, "Johnnie Bassett: A Blues 'Man for All Seasons,'" *Detroit Blues Magazine*, summer 1996.

36. Johnnie Bassett claims that Miles Davis recorded with the Weaver group for Fortune. Johnnie Bassett, interview by Gallert, January 2, 1996.

37. Ibid.

38. Johnnie Bassett, interview by Jim Gallert, Detroit, Michigan, September 17, 1994.

39. "1540 Special," "Soft Pillow," "J. B. Boogie," and "Baby, I'm in Love with You." Two other titles ("Do You Wanna Work Now" and "The Lazy Susan"), which were likely recorded in Von Battle's studio, were released on Jaguar, a New York based label, in 1955.

40. Benson, interview by Gallert.

41. Mike Rowe, letter to Jim Gallert, May 12, 2000. The Viceroy label recorded bandleader Sax Kari, among others.

42. White was born in Chattanooga in 1920 and attended Knoxville College for two years. *Michigan Chronicle*, October 8, 1949.

43. White played the piano at the B & C, the Paradise Club, and the Rex Bar, among others. He played the organ at Uncle Tom's Plantation, the 606 Horseshoe Lounge, and Club Juana. Advertisements, *Michigan Chronicle*, January 12, 1946; May 31, 1947; January 10 and October 10, 1953; July 10, 1954.

and blues sides with Emitt Slay for Savoy Records.[44]

Detroit Count made his name locally by recording "Hastings Street Opera" in 1948. This is a humorous description of life on Hastings Street delivered as a talking blues with piano accompaniment.

> Forest and Hastings! Sunnie Wilson's, the longest bar in town. That's the onliest bar you can walk in when you get ready to buy a bottle of beer you have to walk a mile after you get in the joint!
>
> Silver Grill! That's the only place you have to make the bartender and owner drunk before you can get a drink!
>
> Joe's Record Shop! He's got everybody in there 'cept a T-bone steak![45]

Detroit Count's other recorded work is more interesting from a musical point of view. "Hastings Street Woogie Man" is a driving barrelhouse piano blues, and "I'm Crazy about You" is close to a blues ballad in feeling.

Boogie Woogie Red

Born Vernon Harrison in Rayville, Louisiana, Boogie Woogie Red moved to Detroit with his family in 1927. He learned much from Big Maceo at rent parties in the 1930s and performed publicly for the first time in 1945. In the 1940s and 1950s Red cycled between Detroit and Chicago, where he played with the Chicago-based harmonica player and singer Sonny Boy Williamson (Rice Miller) and Detroiters like Washboard Willie and guitarist Baby Boy Warren.[46] Warren, like Red, was born in Louisiana, but he spent most of his career in Detroit. The two recorded together for Staff Records in 1950.[47] In 1953 Boogie Woogie Red recorded his first record with John Lee Hooker, who by then had established a national reputation.

John Lee Hooker

Singer and guitarist John Lee Hooker's music is an arresting and individual amalgam of country and urban blues, which he recorded for the first time in Detroit in the 1940s and 1950s. In contrast to most artists discussed in this book, Hooker made his name with recordings in Detroit. Hooker was born in Clarksdale, Mississippi, in 1917. Clarksdale is in the heart of the Mississippi Delta, the premier source of blues artists. He told *Down Beat*'s Pete Welding his story in 1968.

> *I remember Blind Blake, Blind Lemon [Jefferson], and Charlie Patton; they used to come by my stepfather's because he was a musician. . . . I didn't grow up in Clarksdale, I left there when I was 14 years old. I went to Memphis. My auntie lived there. . . . I would play a few honky-tonk joints, get a quarter, nickel or a dime here and there. . . . On my little time off I went to school when I could. . . . I didn't go far—fifth grade. . . . I stayed in Memphis two years. Then I came to Cincinnati with my other auntie, and I got a job there in a factory four months. After that I started back doing the same thing I'd done in Memphis—an usher at a downtown theater seating people. . . . And then I came to Detroit in 1943. I was 26, and I married in Detroit. I had saved up a few coins here and there; I had planned to come there. At that time jobs weren't hard to get—it was during the war. Good money too. You could go anywhere any day and get a job. . . . So I started working as an orderly at the receiving hospital . . . and then I got a job at the Dodge Main plant as a janitor . . . then . . . Comco Steel. I worked there until I got this break.*[48]

Hooker's "break" was a record date that came about after meeting Sensation Records co-owner Bernie Besman. According to Besman, record shop owner Elmer Barbee brought Hooker and Hooker's demonstration (demo) record into the Sensation office.[49]

> *He [Hooker] made a record in a booth. . . . in those days you could put twenty-five cents in the slot and make a record. That's the record he brought to me. He really didn't impress me too much, from the record.*[50]

44. Six sides were released with Slay's trio, which included drummer Lawrence Jackson. One of them was the hit "My Kind of Woman." Michel Ruppli with Bob Porter, *The Savoy Label: A Discography* (Westport, Conn.: 1980), 78.

45. "Hastings Street Opera," Various Artists, *Detroit Blues: The Early 1950s*, Blues Classics 12 (LP).

46. Boogie Woogie Red was born in 1925. Mike Joyce and Bob Rusch, "Boogie Woogie Red: Oral History," *Cadence*, September 1977, 7–9. Robert Warren was born in 1919 and came to Detroit in 1944. Mike Joyce and Bob Rusch, "Robert Baby Boy Warren: Oral History," *Cadence*, September 1977, 3–6.

47. Sheldon Harris, "Vernon Harrison," in *Blues Who's Who* (New York: Da-Capo, 1981), 216.

48. Pete Welding, "John Lee Hooker: Me and the Blues," *Down Beat*, October 3, 1968.

49. Barbee owned a record shop at 679 East Lafayette. He bought records from Pan-American.

50. Besman, interview by Gallert. Other sources claim the demo was recorded in the back room of Barbee's record shop. Phil McNeil, "Boom Boom Year," *Wire*, July 1991.

Besman's first impression of Hooker in person wasn't positive either. Hooker stuttered when he spoke but not when he sang, and at first Besman didn't believe it was Hooker on the demo.

Despite the poor quality of the recording, Besman heard something interesting in Hooker's playing and invited him to make another demo under better conditions.

> *I said, "well, next time I record Todd Rhodes you come down to the studio [United Sound Studios] and I'll make a demo to see how you really sound." Sure enough, he came down, and he sounded pretty good. He had sort of an original style. . . . I saw the possibilities.*[51]

"Boogie Chillen" from Hooker's first session for Besman in November 1948 became a number one hit on the R & B charts in early 1949. Besman, a trained musician, was puzzled by Hooker's sense of form.

> *He didn't seem to play his music the way the blues should be played. He didn't have a 12 bar situation. . . . he would end up with 15 bars, 16 bars, 36 bars. No matter how I tried to have him . . . conforming to the blues, he couldn't play it. He never sang the same song twice the same way. He started out the song, there'd be certain words. He played it for me again to make another take, it'd be a different song, different words. Finally I found out he couldn't read or write. That was the problem.*[52]

Critic Robert Palmer presents another perspective on Hooker's seminal recording.

> *Hooker wasn't copying piano boogie. He was playing something else—a rocking one-chord ostinato with accents that fell fractionally ahead of the beat. . . . Essentially it was a back-country, pre-blues sort of music—a droning open-ended stomp without a fixed verse form that lent itself to building up a cumulative, trancelike effect. On later records, Hooker would use his boogie form to build moods that suggested dark, sudden violence, but "Boogie Chillen," despite its undertone of danger, was a Detroit ghetto travelogue. . . . [Twenty] years [later] . . . the rock group Canned Heat popularized the same guitar boogie, amplified to thunderous volume, all over again. It's been a standard rock and roll rhythm pattern ever since.*[53]

The lyrics to "Boogie Chillen" are delivered in a talking blues style and give us an idea of where the Detroit blues scene was in the 1940s.

> When I first came to town, people, I was walking down
> Hastings Street,
> I heard everybody talking about Henry's Swing Club,
> I decided I'd drop in there that night and when I got there
> I said,
> Yes, people, yes they was really having a ball (Yes I know)
> Boogie, chillen![54]

Hooker recorded over 200 titles between 1948 and 1956, and all but a few were recorded in Detroit. They were issued on at least 12 different labels under nearly as many names.[55] Several of his Sensation/Modern recordings were national hits, but his biggest seller was "In the Mood" in 1951. Whereas Hooker performed alone on his first recordings, he was accompanied by guitarist Eddie Kirkland on "In the Mood," and later recordings added more musicians, including tenor sax and piano.[56] Kirkland was part of the quartet that Hooker normally used to back him in club performances in Detroit in the first half of the 1950s.[57]

Another one of his sidemen was guitarist and singer Johnnie Bassett. Bassett was just beginning his career as a blues musician and was a regular at Joe's Record Shop on Hastings. Hooker needed a second guitar for a job that night and sought him out, as Bassett recalled.

> *Someone on Hastings Street told him about me. He asked me if I would wanna play with him. I said, "sure." I didn't know who he was at that time. I was only 18. I asked him, "Won't there be a problem? I'm not old enough." He said, "there won't be a problem." We worked in a storefront bar down in Black Bottom. The*

51. Ibid. Besman published all of the music he recorded by Hooker. This was a lucrative arrangement for Besman.

52. Ibid.

53. Palmer, *Deep Blues*, 244.

54. Welding, "John Lee Hooker: Me and the Blues."

55. Including Chess, Modern, DeLuxe, Sensation, JVB, Fortune.

56. Kirkland was born in Jamaica in 1928 and came to Detroit in 1943. He settled in Georgia in 1962.

57. Some of his regulars at this time were John Hooks and Otis Finch on tenor, Boogie Woogie Red on piano, and Tom Whitehead on drums. Finch was a veteran big band saxophonist who was born in 1912 and came to Detroit in 1930. In Detroit he became the main soloist with Mathew Rucker's orchestra in the late 1930s. He was part of the Fletcher Henderson orchestra at Club De Lisa in Chicago after World War II, played with Lucky Millinder, and recorded with singer Joe Turner in 1947. In the 1950s he played with a number of Detroit bands, including Earl "Count" Belcher and Landis Brady.

> *bandstand was in a little corner; all it had was an old upright piano and drums. I was a little nervous. I asked him what kind of stuff he was gonna play. He said, "just blues." I got through the night OK and a couple of weeks later I worked with him again at the same place.*[58]

The other clubs where Hooker performed in Detroit were similar to the one described by Bassett. They allowed dancing and were within the black community, most often on the East Side: Harlem Club, Club Carribee, Town Casino, and Club Prince Royale.[59] It is interesting to note that the Flame Show Bar auditioned Hooker in the fall of 1949 but decided that "the Flame crowd liked things jumpy and that the Hooker offerings were good but 'too sad.'"[60]

Saxophonist Beans Bowles, who worked at the Flame for the first half of the 1950s, had a slightly different explanation for Hooker's failed audition.

> *John Lee Hooker was the laughingstock at that time. Everybody laughed at him because he could never play nothing. We did not consider him an artist—a musician—because he never changed, and he didn't play the form. He did his thing, but he did not know but two changes or three. . . . He sang, he'd strum, squawk or holler or something—they later called it folk music! We laughed at it, because what did this dude do? Nobody wanted to play with him because every time he played, it was the same song, but different. You had no pattern to follow, no form. That was the only prejudice we had in music: you needed to study. You were just washed over if you did not.*[61]

Bowles's view was representative of those of jazzmen. Jazz musicians prided themselves on being professional and well-trained musicians and therefore distanced themselves from country/urban blues. In contrast jazzmen were more open to rhythm and blues. To most jazz musicians the blues are constantly reinterpreted in new musical forms, and rhythm and blues was one of the new forms in the 1940s and 1950s. These perceptions resulted in more jazzmen in rhythm and blues bands than in urban blues bands.

While Hooker's music had little appeal to the show-oriented audience at the Flame, or the jazz world, the popularity of his recordings catapulted him onto the emerging folk music scene in the early 1950s. To this largely white audience Hooker alone with his guitar was "authentic black folk music." Bill Lane of the *Detroit Tribune* announced in the fall of 1951 that "John Lee Hooker, Bernie Besman's wonderful blues-singing discovery, [would] be soared across the country a la Josh White or Leadbelly shortly. He's getting praises from of all places—top universities in the U.S."[62] Hooker was not always comfortable in this new setting, but when Pete Welding heard him in 1964 he reported that he had "a good idea of what to play for each of his audiences. He plays his old blues hits for the coffee-house and concert audiences, and he's appreciative of the genuine interest these new fans show for his blues playing and singing."[63]

In 1955 Hooker began recording for Vee Jay in Chicago and produced another hit in 1962 with "Boom Boom." Palmer says this was a "sexy stop-time number that was done to death by English and American rock groups for the next ten years."[64] In the 1960s his backup groups became increasingly rock oriented as Hooker captured another segment of the white audience. In 1970 he settled in San Francisco.

While Hooker was an inspiration for white rock and roll bands he was not part of an identifiable Detroit blues style. This is in contrast to what happened in Chicago, where a distinctive urban style of blues had developed out of the migration of Delta blues musicians (like Muddy Waters). Blues scholar Mike Rowe has offered a succinct explanation.

> *While Muddy's updated Mississippi blues were a readily identifiable model for younger bluesmen to copy and develop from, Hooker's maverick style was a one-off. In its purest form its*

58. Bassett was born in Marianna, Florida in 1935. His family moved to Detroit in 1944. The Bar in Black Bottom was the Monte Carlo Inn, 7901 Mack Avenue. Johnnie Bassett, interview by Jim Gallert, Detroit, Michigan, March 19, 1995.

59. The Harlem Club was located on East Congress, near Mount Elliott. Advertisement, *Michigan Chronicle*, July 18, 1953. Club Caribee was on East Jefferson. Advertisement, *Michigan Chronicle*, August 22, 1953. Town Casino was on East Congress at Lieb. *Michigan Chronicle*, January 13, 1955. Club Prince Royale was on Gratiot. Advertisement, *Michigan Chronicle*, April 30, 1955. Hooker also played in Detroit theaters: the Duke and the Broadway Capitol. In 1956 he played Club Basin Street on West Jefferson (advertisement, *Michigan Chronicle*, February 18, 1956) and in 1957 the Apex Bar on Oakland (advertisement, *Michigan Chronicle*, July 20, 1957).

60. *Michigan Chronicle*, November 12, 1949.

61. Bowles, interview by Bjorn.

62. Bill Lane column, *Detroit Tribune*, October 6, 1951.

63. Pete Welding, "John Lee Hooker: Blues Is My Business," *Down Beat*, May 7, 1964.

64. Palmer, *Deep Blues*, 245.

impossibility to adapt to a band style was another deterrent. Hooker's blues were archaic and primitive and quite simply defied imitation.[65]

Hooker was undoubtedly an inspiration to other Detroit blues artists, even though none of them came close to Hooker's originality. Among his accompanists Eddie Kirkland and pianist Boogie Woogie Red became important figures on the Detroit blues scene in the 1950s. Other figures on this scene were guitarists Eddie Burns, Bo Bo Jenkins, Baby Boy Warren, Calvin Frazier, and Washboard Willie. The urban blues of these players were performed almost exclusively within the black community in the 1940s and 1950s.

Detroit also had several women blues singers in the postwar period. Some were all-round vocalists who incorporated some blues into their acts, just as women singers in the 1920s did during the "blues craze." Others, such as Alberta Adams and Olive Brown, moved firmly into the blues arena and remained there.

Alberta Adams

Alberta Adams was born in Indianapolis, Indiana, around 1921 or 1922 but relocated to Detroit at age three.[66] She became interested in music at an early age and frequented the Castle, Dunbar, and Koppin theaters. She started out as a tap dancer in the late 1930s and married dancer Billy Adams. Gradually she turned to singing, and, while at Club B & C from 1942 to 1945, she was billed as "the greatest blues singer since Bessie Smith." In fact, her repertoire was mainly made up of jazz standards as she recalled.

I used to pick the material I sang. I did jazz. "A Foggy Day," "Pennies from Heaven," "Who Shall I Turn To?" Had to keep the blues in there, 'cause that's what [manager Warren LaRue] wanted.[67]

In 1945 she went on her first tour of the Midwest and East Coast and was by then advertised as Detroit's Blues Queen. She worked with the city's top jazz and jump bands: Lorenzo Lawson, Todd Rhodes, King Porter, T. J. Fowler, Maurice King and the Wolverines, and Howard Bunts.

In 1953 Adams and New Orleans vocalist Velma "Chubby" Newsome formed a duo that was billed as the Bluezettes that lasted until 1955. Adams recalled their partnership.

We was the baddest thing out there. We did blues and blues ballads. We was shaped alike, like bricks, with small waistlines. We dressed alike, same hair, and we sounded like one voice.[68]

Adams first recorded in June 1953 for Chess Records at United Sound Systems in Detroit.[69] The Chess session came about while Adams was performing at the Flame Show Bar, where she was approached by Leonard Chess and his label manager Dave Clark. Unfortunately, the band backing her was brought in from Chicago, while Adams would have preferred Maurice King's band from the Flame. The two sides show Adams's strong voice and confident delivery, but Chess did little to promote the record, and it quickly died. Adams, a lifelong Detroit resident, recently recorded a CD.

Another woman blues singer of note in the city in this period was Olive Brown. She was born in St. Louis in 1922 but moved to Detroit at a young age and started her career in Detroit in the early 1940s. Brown was christened "Princess of the blues" in the black press and worked with Todd Rhodes, T. J. Fowler, Paul Williams, Sonny Stitt, and Gene Ammons. She was a fine singer whose repertoire was centered in blues, show tunes, and novelty "talking" songs of the type that Ethel Waters performed two decades earlier. Brown moved to Buffalo, New York, in the mid-1950s but returned to Detroit in the early 1970s.

65. Mike Rowe, liner notes, John Lee Hooker/Eddie Burns, *Detroit Blues 1950–1951*, Krazy Kat 816.

66. She was christened Roberta Louise Osborn.

67. Adams, interview by Gallert.

68. Ibid.

69. Four titles, all written by Adams, were waxed: "Messin' around with the Blues," "This Morning," "Remember," and "No Good Man."

Jump Blues Bands

JUMP BLUES BANDS grew out of the world of swing, so it is not surprising that the typical repertoire of these bands was a mixture of blues, swing standards, bebop, and jump numbers.[70] These bands were horn-powered outfits that were rhythmically agile and included in their repertoire blues at different tempos and sometimes frantic saxophone solos like those at late 1940s Jazz at the Philharmonic concerts. In club settings the saxophone soloist would sometimes "walk the bar." The soloist (usually the tenor saxophonist) would get on top of the bar while blowing and walk or slide on his knees, pausing so customers could stuff cash into the bell of his instrument. Sometimes the saxophonist would slide up and down the bar on his back, although this was riskier than walking and sometimes resulted in stains and/or burns on his clothing. The prevalence of saxophones and trumpets in these combos is not surprising, because there were numerous musicians trained in their use to meet the demand created by big bands. The tenor saxophone also holds a special place in African American music, a place that saxophonist Ornette Coleman, who as a young man played tenor sax in Texas R & B bands in the late 1940s, argues for:

> *The tenor is a rhythm instrument, and the best statements Negroes have made, of what their soul is, have been on tenor saxophone. Now you think about it and you see I'm right. The tenor's got that thing, that honk, you can get to people with. Sometimes you can be playing that tenor, and I'm telling you, the people want to jump across the rail. Especially that D-flat blues. You can really reach their souls with that D-flat blues.*[71]

Jump blues bands were the link between big band blues and early rock and roll, when guitars began their rise to prominence, replacing saxophones (and brass instruments) as the instrument of choice.

Detroit in the 1940s and 1950s had five major leaders of jump blues bands: Todd Rhodes, King Porter, Paul Williams, T. J. Fowler, and Candy Johnson. Tenorist Paul Bascomb led a band for many years at the El Sino but judging by the recorded evidence remained closer to swing traditions than the other bands.[72]

Todd Rhodes, the oldest bandleader (born in 1900), had a career that spans the reach of this book. Like most jump bandleaders he had his musical roots in the swing era. He came of age during the 1920s as the pianist with McKinney's Cotton Pickers. After leaving the band in 1934, Rhodes played with assorted groups in Detroit before becoming a leader in 1943. He became well known to the public, won local polls, and worked at prestigious nightspots. Changing musical tastes and the rise of television in the 1950s robbed Rhodes of his audience and of venues in which to play, and he limped through the remainder of his career. Rhodes spent his last years working as a solo pianist or leading quartets for occasional jobs.

Todd Rhodes

IN THE FALL OF 1934, following McKinney's Cotton Pickers' western states tour, Todd Rhodes quit the band.[73] As Rhodes recalled, "I returned home to Detroit and worked with local bands for a number of years."[74] After a spell with the short-lived Chic Carter orchestra, a McKinney offshoot, Rhodes spent the remainder of the decade as a member of alto saxophonist Cecil Lee's orchestra and played various venues around Paradise Valley.[75] He also worked occasionally with McKinney and Don Redman.[76]

Following the U.S. entry into World War II, Rhodes, who was 41 and too old for active military duty, opted for war work, as his widow Annie Mae recalled.

> *He said, "Well, to do something, I'll go and start working in a factory," which he'd never done before . . . 'cause his hands . . . he didn't*

70. The diverse repertoire makes it difficult to draw hard and fast lines between jump bands and other bands.

71. A. B. Spellman, *Four Lives in the Bebop Business* (New York: Pantheon, 1966), 102.

72. Bascomb led a band at the El Sino almost without interruption from 1948 until 1955 (advertisements, *Michigan Chronicle,* May 22, 1948; September 17, 1955). Bascomb was a former member of the Erskine Hawkins band and led a big band with his brother Dud before coming to Detroit in 1948. In 1956 he moved to Chicago and led an organ trio. Bascomb's Detroit group recorded in Chicago for United Records and its subsidiary States in 1952, later released on the *Bad Bascomb* LP by Delmark (DL-431). The repertoire consisted mainly of swing standards and blues, often from Hawkins days. The heavy backbeats that characterized jump blues bands were generally absent. Bascomb's tenor is the main feature throughout, and he has an outstanding solo on "Nona." Bascomb often argued that he was the writer of "After Hours," the biggest hit of the Hawkins band, and "Liza's Blues" is a reminiscent tune. Bascomb's band included several Detroit jazzmen of note, like veteran saxophonist Harold Wallace. Charlie Parker's pianist Duke Jordan (from New York) also played with the band around the time of the recording.

73. Rilla Buckner, interview by Jim Gallert, Detroit, Michigan, August 30, 1988. Rhodes was not in the band when Ted and Rilla Buckner married on November 22, 1934, during an East Coast tour.

74. Thurman Grove and Mary Grove,"Todd Rhodes: Then and Now," *Jazz Journal* (February 1953): 19.

75. Claudia Morrison, interview by Jim Gallert, Detroit, Michigan, February 27, 1989. Mrs. Morrison has in her possession Cecil Lee's scrapbook.

76. Annie Mae Rhodes (née Brown), interview by Jim Gallert, Detroit, Michigan, February 14, 1988. Redman left the Cotton Pickers in 1931.

want to hit them or nothing. So he went to work at Fisher Body. He was a maintenance man, but they knew who he was. He'd go there in the morning and clean up. . . . he'd take a suit and white shirt with him, and he played for all the people in the office . . . and then at night he'd go play music.[77]

Rhodes's move from sideman to leader began not long after his marriage, when promoter/personal manager Wilson "Stutz" Anderson entered the picture. Rhodes made the move to bandleader out of economic necessity, according to Annie Mae.

He [Anderson] asked Todd to organize a band for some little place out on Michigan Avenue. And Todd said, "Oh, it's too much responsibility. I don't wanna do that."[78]

Annie Mae, concerned with having sufficient funds to provide for their family, insisted, and Rhodes started leading a four-piece band at the Triangle Bar on Michigan and Third on the Near West Side of Detroit in 1943. In an interview 10 years later Rhodes recalled that

I formed a four piece band at the Triangle Bar on Michigan Avenue. We had a successful run of seven months. I started thinking maybe I could make a success on my own, so I hired a manager and agent and enlarged the band to seven pieces.[79]

Rhodes still took jobs as a sideman, including one with veteran bandleader Howard Bunts in June 1944. Rhodes's next job as a bandleader was at Broad's Club Zombie in June 1945. Anderson organized the booking, and Rhodes put together a six-piece outfit. Rhodes continued to build his book of band specialties, although there was little rhythm and blues content at this point. Broad's benefited from the glut of returning servicemen after the war and quickly expanded its hours of operation and the floor show as well. The shows went to seven nights a week, and a chorus line was added. The job ended two days before Christmas 1945.[80]

Rhodes's next gig was a further step upward: six months at Club Three Sixes. The job began in April 1946 and ran seven nights a week, and the pay was good.[81] Rhodes could hire the musicians he wanted, and after a few personnel changes he had a band that could run down show or production numbers and could swing out on hot jazz or blues numbers. By the time the Three Sixes gig ended, Rhodes's band was established as one of the best small groups in Detroit. For his next gig, at Lee's Sensation Lounge in late 1946, Rhodes shifted his repertoire to rhythm and blues. The sound of his band was now fully formed, as private recordings made in 1947 confirm.[82] Anderson "sold" the band to Sensation Records. The sound of Rhodes's band, especially their performance of "Dance of the Redskins," impressed the Sensation Records owners, as co-owner John Kaplan recalled.

It was a hot number, no question about it. They would leave the stand and march around the place and everyone would get up and follow them! That's what convinced me to record Todd's band.[83]

The first sessions took place at United Sound Studios in Detroit in July 1947. The four numbers recorded are a microcosm of the Rhodes band book: "Dance of the Redskins," a high-energy version of "Redskin Rhumba," which in turn is the last eight bars of "Cherokee" as recorded by Charlie Barnet's orchestra.[84] "Flying Disc" is an up-tempo boppish original credited to Rhodes, and "Blue Sensation" and "Bell Boy Boogie" (named after Ed McKenzie) and "Blues for the Red Boy" (actually "Jeep's Blues") are blues. Rhodes also recorded jazz/popular standards ("Annie Laurie," "Yesterdays") and classical pieces, including Rachmaninoff's "Prelude in C–Minor" as well as "Rhapsody in Blue," on which he had been featured while with Cecil Lee. In general, Rhodes did not write for the band. "Brenda," named for his daughter, and "Blue Sensation" are exceptions.[85] Although there were written arrange-

77. Rhodes, interview by Gallert. Todd Rhodes and Annie Mae married in 1940 and promptly started a family. Brenda was born in 1940, Elden in 1942, and Sherman in 1947.

78. Ibid.

79. In this interview Rhodes incorrectly placed this engagement after the war. Grove and Grove,"Todd Rhodes."

80. Walter Bragg, interview by Jim Gallert, Detroit, Michigan, November 25, 1988. Bragg played bass with Rhodes off and on until early 1947. He kept a diary of the band's activities.

81. Ibid.

82. Four titles were cut on February 28 and March 4 using a portable machine: "On the Sunny Side of the Street," "Squeeze Me," "Intermission Riff," and "Flying Disc."

83. Kaplan, interview by Gross and Gallert.

84. "Cherokee," Bluebird B-10373; "Redskin Rhumba," Bluebird B-10944.

85. The Rhodes band "book" contained sheet music for waltzes, pop tunes, jazz and pop standards, and many of Rhodes's blues hits. Most of the book was destroyed during a basement flood in the 1950s.

Fig. 99. Todd Rhodes band, Lee's Sensation Lounge, 1947.
George Favors, bar/as; Walter Bragg, bs; Lou Barnett, ts/cl; Huestell Talley, dms; Hallie Dismukes, as; Howard Thompson, cnt.
(Courtesy Mrs. Annie Mae Rhodes, Gallert Collection.)

ments in the book, Joe Williams remembered that

> *Most of our tunes were head tunes. There were no written arrangements. A guy would start playing a riff, and the rest of us would just fall in and play our respective parts to it. That's how we arrived at new songs.*[86]

The blues-based material proved to be the most popular, and it dominated the band's repertoire. Rhodes's records sold well locally, and, once the sides were distributed nationally by King Records (beginning in 1948), some copies were sold in the South. However, the Todd Rhodes band remained a largely regional attraction, making only occasional trips to both coasts and into Canada. In between tours, the Rhodes band was parked at Detroit nighteries (Sportree's, Lee's Sensation, the Victory Supper Club, and the Flame).

Rhodes's band personnel remained stable for nearly two years. He had some standout musicians, like alto saxophonist Hallie Dismukes, whose wailing solos added much to Rhodes's records. His style reflects his love of Johnny Hodges and Charlie Parker.[87] Dismukes is featured on most of Rhodes's recordings, and "Toddlin' Boogie" in particular contains a freewheeling solo by Dismukes that really swings. The best-known soloist to work with Rhodes was saxophonist Ted Buckner, who played baritone sax alongside Hallie Dismukes. Dismukes's reputation was such that although Buckner was

86. Joe Williams, interview by Jim Gallert, Detroit, Michigan, May 5, 1987.

87. Dismukes (born 1910) claimed he was named for Halley's comet, although he spelled his name "Hallie" on his AFM Local 5 application. He had perfect pitch and played piano well enough to sub for Rhodes on occasion. Ibid.

better known on the alto, Rhodes appreciated the former's playing and asked Buckner to take up the baritone, which he handled with the same ease and assurance as the smaller saxophone. The two occasionally duetted on alto sax and created wild and spontaneous energy that inspired the band and the audience.

Louis Barnett first filled the band's tenor sax chair. Barnett had established a very positive reputation on the Detroit jazz scene during his stay with Cecil Lee's orchestra in 1943–44. He was a "hot get-off tenor man" with a Lester Young–inspired tone who worked from a bag of hot licks and sparked the crowds with his solos on Rhodes specialties like "Dance of the Redskins," "Flying Disc," and "Page Boy Shuffle," which show Lou at his best. Barnett went on to work with Maurice King's band after his stay with Rhodes.[88] Charles "Lefty" Edwards was in the band during the early 1950s. Edwards's work is full of hallmarks of R & B tenor: a broad, sweeping tone with a rough edge, a sense of drama, and a reserve of creative horsepower to push the whole solo along ("Rocket 69," "Gin Gin Gin").[89] Bassist Joe Williams was with Rhodes for nearly a decade.[90] Williams was a "foundation" player with a big sound, and he provided plenty of support on the band's records. William "Benny" Benjamin, a fine drummer whose skills were utilized by other R & B outfits after his stay with Todd Rhodes, held the drum chair for a time.[91]

Rhodes did not have a regular vocalist with the band. The club would usually hire a singer to complement either the band or the floor show. Some, like Louie Saunders, recorded with the band. Known locally as the "Singing Waiter," he was a kind of factotum at Lee's Sensation who performed with the band in between serving entrées. Louie's versions of "Oh Baby" and "Walkie Talkie" were favorites with the crowd at Lee's. He impressed the gentlemen from Sensation Records, who thought he sounded like Frankie Laine.[92]

Rhodes usually carried a singer or vocal group on tours, who often recorded with the band if there was favorable audience response. Kitty Stevenson was the first vocalist to tour with the band. She appeared at their Apollo Theater debut in May 1951 but left shortly afterward due to illness. Stevenson was a fine singer with a solid local reputation around Detroit who is heard to advantage on "I Shouldn't Cry but I Do" and "Good Man."[93] Her replacement was Connie Allen, a hefty woman with a powerful voice ("Rocket 69") who also worked with saxophonist Paul Williams. LaVern Baker (billed as "Little Miss Sharecropper") replaced Kitty Stevenson as Rhodes's vocalist in 1952 and recorded with his band for King in July and October that year.[94] Her recordings with Rhodes include "Pig Latin Blues," which showcases her strong voice, scat singing ability, and excellent rhythmic sense. Midway through the number Baker growls, howls, and performs vocal gymnastics like Screamin' Jay Hawkins. Rhodes's rhythm section gives solid, on-the-beat support, and the performance is a blend of rock and roll and R & B horn licks. Ballads like the torchy "Lost Child" remind one of Dinah Washington. Baker, a regular at the Flame Show Bar, was the best vocalist to work with the Rhodes band.

Other singers were added for the band's later recording sessions for King, but none of them were in the same class as Stevenson or Baker. Cornelius "Pinocchio" James shouts his way through "Your Mouth Got a Hole in It," and Sadie Madison, a local singer with a small voice, sings on "Let-Down Blues."

Despite his initial reluctance, Todd Rhodes easily assumed the mantle of leadership. Like his early keyboard idol, James P. Johnson, Rhodes was low keyed, easygoing, and totally involved with music. He stood six foot two, weighed around 210 pounds, and was solidly built. He smoked cigarettes but drank very little. Claudia Morrison, the wife of bassist

88. Barnett (born 1919) played with many fine bands, including Gloster Current's Nightingales and Leroy Smith. He later worked at Motown Records for many years. Barnett is the only musician who worked for extended periods with both Rhodes (1946–51) and King (1951–59). Louis's sister Ocie was a highly regarded pianist/bandleader, and his brother Hans played tenor and was a sometime bandleader.

89. Edwards (born 1927) began his career as a trumpeter and changed to tenor saxophone in 1945. He also worked with King Porter and spent years as a Motown sideman.

90. Williams was signed to a personal management contract by Stutz Anderson, who then placed him in Rhodes's band. Williams (born 1922) went back to school after leaving Rhodes and retired as principal of Ferndale High School. He never stopped playing bass, and he worked in King Porter's band and, later, Motown Records.

91. Benjamin (born 1925) became a Motown studio drummer and was a major part of the Motown sound.

92. There are at least three unissued titles featuring Saunders in the Sensation vaults.

93. There are at least four unissued titles featuring Stevenson in the Sensation vaults.

94. Baker was from Chicago, where she was born in 1929.

Fig. 100. Todd Rhodes Quartet, Flamingo Club, Idlewild, Michigan, ca. 1960–61.
Rhodes, pno/ldr; James Jamerson, el bs; Alex Campbell, ts; unidentified, tp; Benny Benjamin, dms. In his later years, Rhodes did not have his own band, and he assembled groups for specific engagements like this one at the black resort area of Idlewild.
(Courtesy Mrs. Annie Mae Rhodes, Gallert Collection.)

Leonard Morrison, described him as follows: "He was a big man, but he had such a soft voice. He was so quiet, you didn't expect him to be a musician."[95]

Although he admired Johnson's playing and enjoyed Bud Powell and Thelonious Monk, Rhodes's real hero was Art Tatum. Rhodes did not have Tatum's command of the keyboard, but he expressed himself clearly and confidently, with an especially nice touch on ballads. And he could really play the blues. His forte was playing in a rhythm section, where his left hand helped provide a solid foundation.[96]

Rhodes won a local poll of favorite bands in 1947, and he continued to record for Sensation and later (1951–54) for King Records. His band backed many King artists, including Wynonie "Mr. Blues" Harris and pioneer blues guitarist Lonnie Johnson. King stopped recording Rhodes in 1954, when popular taste in music shifted from R & B to rock and roll.[97] It is ironic that bands such as Rhodes's pioneered rock and roll but reaped none of the financial rewards.

The loss of his record deal signaled the end of the Todd Rhodes band and, indeed, of an era. The Rhodes band had three "legs" on which it stood: records (promotion), a home base, and tours. Tours were the most important because there was better money on the road, but all three factors played a critical role in keeping the band healthy. The musicians preferred location jobs over tours because, as Joe Williams said,

> *In a club for several days, we would play some of the hits, then we'd play what we wanted to play [jazz]. On one nighters—all garbage. When the band began to wane, we would go out on occasional jobs, but we weren't on those long tours anymore, where you go out and stay for three months, six months. We were workin' more in this area [Detroit].*[98]

There was also tension within the band over the material that was featured, and when the pay went down, the tension went up. By 1957, the salaries for Rhodes's musicians were minimal, and tours were few.

The musicians had no choice but to leave, as Joe Williams sadly recalled.

The band finally fell apart. The guys went else-

95. Morrison, interview by Gallert.

96. According to Lefty Edwards: "Todd's playing wasn't modern, but the feeling was there. . . . he and T. J. Fowler played a similar piano style." Lefty Edwards, interview by Jim Gallert, Detroit, Michigan, November 1987.

97. Rhodes's final records were with R & B vocalist Andre "Bacon Fat" Williams in 1957 for Detroit based Fortune Records: "You Are My Sunshine" and "Mean Jean" (Fortune 45-834).

98. Williams, interview by Gallert.

where. We had families to support. There was always someone interested in Todd Rhodes, but the money wasn't happening. Todd continued to work without us, but he got little jobs that weren't paying anything.[99]

Rhodes and his family moved to Flint in the spring of 1958, and he attempted to establish himself on the music scene there. But the pickings were slim. "It was as bad as Detroit," Annie Mae recalled. "And the money was less."[100] Rhodes's health began to deteriorate as well; he suspected he had diabetes, but his mistrust of the medical profession stood in the way of his getting treatment.

The Rhodes family moved back to Detroit in 1960. There was new life on the Motor City music scene: Motown Records had arrived, and Detroit was jumping again. Many of Rhodes's former bandsmen worked for Motown, but he was nearly 60 years old and not current with the pop music scene. He continued to find gigs around Detroit but turned down many jobs because he felt the pay offered was too low.[101] Todd and Annie Mae separated, and he got a room at the Carver Hotel across from the Flame Show Bar.

Rhodes's career and his health continued on a downward spiral. He suffered a stroke in the autumn of 1964 while working a solo job in Canada. He never fully recovered from its effects. Todd Rhodes died on June 4, 1965, at the age of 64.[102]

King Porter

King Porter was an Alabama-born trumpeter who came to Detroit during World War II and spent a decade in the city before returning to Alabama.[103] In his late twenties when he arrived in Detroit in 1943, he was soon the leader of a big band at dance gigs.[104] He must have seen the bleak future for big bands, because by the spring of 1945 he switched over to a five-piece combo and stuck with it for the remainder of his time in Detroit.[105] In the fall he landed a job as the leader of the house band at the Three Sixes in Paradise Valley, where they played for shows and dancing. One of the singers the band backed at the Three Sixes was Olive Brown.[106] In late 1946 Porter did his first stint at the Royal Blue Bar in the North End and stayed there more or less permanently for the next seven years.[107] One significant interruption of the stay at the Royal Blue was the group's engagement at Sportree's Music Bar for several months in 1947. At Sportree's they functioned as the house band for the show, which included T-Bone Walker for several weeks and later Billy Eckstine.[108] For a month the band also played the Bizerte with Detroit's blues queen Alberta Adams.[109]

But the King Porter band became most closely identified with the Royal Blue, where Porter was advertised as a king on his throne. The Royal Blue was a neighborhood bar with an almost exclusively black clientele. The music was the only entertainment, and according to Beans Bowles "if they danced there it was between the chairs; it was just a bar. People would come in, drink a beer, listen, dance, and they would appreciate the guys playing."[110]

Al Martin replaced Millard Glover on bass during the band's stay at the Royal Blue and recalled it fondly.

The Royal Blue was just a neighborhood bar, probably the grooviest every-night place I've ever seen. . . . Seven nights a week it was filled up, overflowing with enjoyment.[111]

The early part of an evening's performance was often devoted to jazz standards, with hints of bebop. For example, "Stompin' at the Savoy" was played "with an unusual interpolation of the theme of 'Stuffy' before returning to the basic melody" according to a *Michigan Chronicle* review.[112] As the night wore on and the Royal Blue filled up with patrons, the band turned increasingly to blues and jump blues numbers.[113] It was this part of the repertoire that the band recorded in 1947–49. Roy Stephens showed his

99. Ibid.

100. Rhodes, interview by Gallert.

101. Bobby Cousar, interview by Jim Gallert, Detroit, Michigan, February 14, 1989. Cousar was with Maurice King at the Flame Show Bar around 1961 and worked with Rhodes until 1964, when he left Detroit. Rhodes worked occasionally at Idlewild.

102. *Michigan Chronicle,* June 12, 1965. Rhodes lost a leg to diabetes and never recovered enough to leave Wayne County Hospital (located near Detroit).

103. Porter was born James A. Pope in Bessemer, Alabama, in 1916 and probably moved to Detroit in 1943, since that is the year he became a member of Local 5. He moved back to Alabama in 1954. Membership files, Detroit Federation of Musicians, Local No. 5, American Federation of Musicians, Southfield, Michigan.

104. "James (King) Porter, 260 pounds, solid swing and his trumpet" and a new 16-piece band performed at the Mirror Ballroom in 1944. Advertisement, *Michigan Chronicle,* February 12, 1944. See also advertisements in *Michigan Chronicle,* March 25 and September 16, 1944.

105. Advertisement, *Michigan Chronicle,* March 24, 1945.

106. *Michigan Chronicle,* December 15, 1945.

107. Advertisement, *Michigan Chronicle,* November 30, 1946.

108. Advertisements, *Michigan Chronicle,* May 3, May 17, and August 2, 1947.

109. Advertisement, *Michigan Chronicle,* September 13, 1947.

110. Bowles, interview by Bjorn.

111. Al Martin, interview by Jim Gallert, Detroit, Michigan, July 29, 1989. Al Martin was only 19 when he accompanied Billie Holiday at the Club Congo in 1941. He played with the Mathew Rucker and Joe Norris bands before joining King Porter. In the 1950s he toured briefly with Louis Jordan.

112. "Eckstine Hit at Club," *Michigan Chronicle,* August 23, 1947.

113. Benson, interview by Bjorn and Gallert.

Fig. 101. King Porter band and others, Sportree's Music Bar, March 1948. *Alberta Adams (seated in foreground of left booth), Honey Brown (behind Adams), Ted Sheely (against the mirror), Al Martin (next to Sheely), King Porter, Joe Turner (with his arm on Porter's shoulder), Billy Mitchell (next to Turner), Joe Askew (wearing cap in center foreground), Sportree Jackson (holding cigar). Turner, Adams, and Brown were appearing with Porter's band.* (Courtesy Al Martin, Gallert Collection.)

jazz bias in a *Michigan Chronicle* review: "It was a pity the group has not recorded some of its most progressive instrumentals. . . . [They are] better than 'Russell Street Hussel.' "[114]

Bassist Gene Taylor, who also worked with Candy Johnson and T. J. Fowler, compared the three bands.

> *King Porter was a hard stomping band. To me, he was the hardest hitting. When you went to see King Porter, you was going to hear some heavy hitting rhythm and blues.*[115]

The "Russell Street Hustle" was one of the group's showpieces. Named after the location of the Royal Blue, it was their first recording and was recorded twice (with two different spellings of "Hustle"). An up-tempo 12-bar blues, it starts out with three choruses of hot tenor sax, backed by riffing horns and a pounding rhythm section. The driving rhythm is created by Millard Glover's powerful bass, Paul Moore's boogie piano, and Reethan Mallett's bass drum.[116] After more riffs, the baritone and tenor take solos. The second version has a similar loose structure favoring blowing but in this case battling tenorists. The first version is graced by the presence of Billy Mitchell, who generally avoids the cliché-ridden honking that is found on the sec-

114. Roy Stephens, "Ted Sheeley, Edwards Spark Unit," *Michigan Chronicle*, August 28, 1948.

115. Gene Taylor, interview by Lars Bjorn and Jim Gallert, Southfield, Michigan, November 28, 1999.

116. Millard Glover was one of the four Glover brothers who played bass. The other three were James, Pete, and Dedrick. Nothing is known about Paul Moore. Rethan Mallett was born in Goodman, Mississippi, in 1921; attended Miller High; and had played with Mathew Rucker. He later played with the traditional jazz bands, like the Gabriel Brothers New Orleans Jazz Band. Bob Byler, liner notes, *Gabriel Brothers New Orleans Jazz Band*, Jim Taylor Presents, JTP 108.

ond version. On the latter version tenorists Wild Bill Moore and Lefty Edwards are the main soloists, and one of them, probably Moore, is more prone to clichés. On the second version pianist Detroit Count shows how he earned his nickname.

The recipe of blues, wild saxophones, riffs, and boogie piano recurs in most of the other tunes recorded by the Porter band, sometimes with the added feature of band vocals and hand clapping. "Porter's Ball" is reminiscent of Louis Jordan and is one of the few featuring the leader's trumpet. Mitchell takes his most imaginative solo on this song.

The recordings back up altoist George Benson's recollection of how the band worked. "Our arrangements were a lot of head arrangements. [The] Todd Rhodes band [in contrast] did a lot more reading of music than we did." Benson also voiced a common view of Porter as more of an entertainer than an improviser: "I would not consider King Porter a jazz player; he did more of the commercial type thing, Louis [Armstrong] type thing."[117] Although most of the players in the band "would rather play Parker songs," "we played a lot of blues because we had to do it, you know, it was just one of those things you had to do."[118]

Porter voiced his views on modern jazz and what audiences wanted in an interview in the *Michigan Chronicle* in 1950.

> *"Bop," said the roly-poly and jovial music meister, "is deader than a doornail now."... Bop died because... "it was hoisted on the public in the wrong way".... The antics of some boppers did not help.... "All that beret-wearing, goatee-growing stuff slapped the fad stigma on bop before it could get on its feet. The public associated the music with idiocy, and just tolerated it for a time.... Bop is a feeling existing for the most part in the musicians themselves. Not in the general public. The public has one idea of the type of music it likes, while the musician has another. He tries to play 'to' the people instead of 'for' the people and his music fails to catch on." Porter said many bands will continue to play bop tunes but only occasionally. For the most part, he prophesied, swing music will be the music played. "That's what the public wants, and bands will have to give the people what the people desire."*[119]

It seems that in Porter's mind his music was a continuation of the popular tradition that the big bands had started. Like many big band musicians, musicians in jump blues bands sometimes experienced a conflict between what they were asked to play and what they would like to play. Some of Porter's musicians did go on to careers in modern jazz; others moved on to more prominent jump bands.

Billy Mitchell was the most prominent of the modern jazzmen in the band, as we have seen in earlier chapters. Another modernist with a national career was baritonist Tate Houston, but others mainly played a role in the local modern jazz scene. Pianist Ted Sheely occasionally replaced Terry Pollard in Mitchell's Blue Bird group but spent most of the late 1940s and early 1950s in Porter's band. In 1953 he formed his own organ trio. Another long-term member of the band was Lefty Edwards, who modeled himself on Lester Young and was singled out by the *Michigan Chronicle* as "beyond a doubt, the sharpest musician in the lineup . . . a tenor sax artist of great virtuosity." After Porter left Detroit Edwards played frequently at the Royal Blue with his own organ combo.

Altoist George Benson spent about a year in the Porter band and learned a lot about improvisation. He left in early 1951 to form a band that included Tommy Flanagan and guitarist Calvin Frazier. Like the Porter band, Benson's group started the evening with jazz and ended with rhythm and blues, topped by Frazier's singing and playing. Benson shifted to tenor sax in the mid-1950s and played with organ groups. He led the last house band at the Flame in the early 1960s with Earl Van Dyke at the organ.

117. See also Billy Mitchell's comments in Gitler, *Swing to Bop*, 262.

118. Benson, interview by Bjorn and Gallert.

119. "Royal Blue Trumpet Man King Porter Tells Why Bop Is Gone with the Wind," *Michigan Chronicle*, March 18, 1950.

Among the Porter musicians who made a career in rhythm and blues the most well-known was Paul Williams.

Paul Williams

ALTOIST PAUL WILLIAMS joined the Porter band in 1946 and stayed until he started his own band in late 1947. He had started on the saxophone at Northeastern and Cass and played his first job with trumpeter Lloyd "Chainey" Henderson, a high school friend. Paul Williams and his Kings of Rhythm played for five years at the Morris Café on Michigan Avenue. Williams remembered the war years in an interview with Peter Grendysa.

> *The band broke up during the war, because they said "work or fight." I was gigging during the war and I played in the band at the Ford plant, for War Bond drives and what not. I worked at the plant all day and gigged all night.... When the war ended I was working with Clarence Dorsey's band at the Sensation Club.... That was the first black audience I played for. The war work was tapering off, but I had gotten fired from Ford for sleeping on the job. Too much playing all night!* [120]

Clarence Dorsey was a veteran trumpeter who had played with Billy Minor's Melodians in the 1920s and the Cotton Pickers in the 1930s.[121] In 1943 he led his Sensational Five at Lee's Sensation in the North End, where they backed the floor show and played for dancing.[122] This included local blues singers like Olive Brown and Honey Brown and nationally known Victoria Spivey.[123] The job lasted until late summer 1945 when the band, now the Sensational Six, went on a national tour.[124] Once back in Detroit they were the first black band to play at Mickey's Show Bar.[125] In addition to Williams, the Dorsey band included another future jump band leader: pianist T. J. Fowler, who was also a frequent contributor of songs for the group.[126]

When Williams joined the Porter group he became known for his showmanship as well as his playing. The *Michigan Chronicle* felt that "Paul Williams, alto sax artist, sets the musical pace with his sax wizardry and his clowning steps which the patrons seem to appreciate."[127] This also caught the attention of Savoy Records talent scout Teddy Reig from New York, when he heard the band live in Detroit in 1947.

> *Porter was a big, husky cat, and he had a funny voice. He had a little something going on that people liked. Paul Williams was the glamorpuss. He'd play his solos and make the broads happy.*[128]

Reig approached Williams with the idea of recording him, as Williams remembered.

> *He didn't want the band, he wanted me. I don't know why—it was a very good band.... At that time I was playing mostly alto and sometimes clarinet. Teddy wanted me to play baritone. I had a baritone, but I very seldom played it. And he had a very definite idea of what I should do. He wanted me to honk. He kept telling me not to play a whole lot of notes. He kept saying, "Honk! Honk! Honk!"... He kept bugging me so much, I almost blew the date.* [129]

In fact, Williams never included Louis Jordan among his models on alto sax and instead preferred the swing era alto greats like Johnny Hodges. Reig wanted Williams to sound more like Leo Parker, whom Reig had recorded a few days earlier in Detroit. Reig described how he put together Williams's first recording session, starting in Joe Von Battle's record shop on Hastings.

> *We used to sit in the back of the store, buy a bottle and drink it up and play records. Then we'd take all the records that we wanted and go back to the house. And to be very honest, we stole. We took patterns and changed the notes. We rehearsed a band during the day in an after-hours joint called the Brown Derby and we made Paul's first records in the living room of a two-family house where a guy named Joe Syracuse had his studio, United Sounds.* [130]

For his first session on September 5, 1947,

120. Peter Grendysa, liner notes, Paul Williams and His Orchestra, *The Hucklebuck*, Saxophonograph Records, BP-500 (LP).

121. Dorsey was born in Maryland in 1894. Membership files, Detroit Federation of Musicians, Local No. 5, American Federation of Musicians, Southfield, Michigan.

122. Advertisement, *Michigan Chronicle*, December 25, 1943.

123. Advertisements, *Michigan Chronicle*, January 29, March 11; November 4, 1944.

124. The band played in New Orleans, and there were plans to play at the Café de Society in Chicago and Café Society in New York, but it is unclear if the latter two engagements came about. *Michigan Chronicle*, September 1, 1945.

125. Advertisement, *Detroit Free Press*, September 28, 1945.

126. *Michigan Chronicle*, April 14, 1945. Another member of the band was veteran drummer Samuel "Babe" Borders. Born in Alabama in 1907 and educated at Tuskegee, he played with the Black Birds of Paradise band in 1927 and later with Erskine Hawkins and many others. McCarthy, *Big Band Jazz*, 89–90. Boyd and Sinclair, *Detroit Jazz Who's Who*, 15.

127. "T-Bone Now at Sportree's Bar," *Michigan Chronicle*, May 17, 1947.

128. Reig, quoted in Robert Palmer, liner notes, Various Artists, *Honkers and Screamers, Roots of Rock 'n' Roll*, vol. 6, Savoy 2234 (LP).

129. Teddy Reig with Edward Berger, *Reminiscing in Tempo: The Life and Times of a Jazz Hustler* (Metuchen, N.J.: Scarecrow Press and the Institute of Jazz Studies, Rutgers University, 1990), 96–98.

130. Palmer, liner notes, Various Artists, *Honkers and Screamers*.

Fig. 102. Clarence Dorsey Orchestra, unidentified location, ca. 1944–45. *Samuel "Babe" Borders, dms; T. J. Fowler, pno; Duke Coates, ts; Paul Williams, as; Dorsey, tp/ldr.*
(Courtesy Mattie Fowler, Gallert Collection.)

Williams gathered a sextet made up of most of the band now led by T. J. Fowler, his old mate from the Clarence Dorsey band. A second session in October included "35-30" (the address of Joe Von Battle's store on Hastings), which soon became an R & B hit. In November Williams broke out on his own with an engagement for his "Recording Sextette" at Leto's New Villa Club on the North End that lasted for about three months. A couple of shows were organized in January 1948 at the Duke Theater, which was located further north in the black community on Eight Mile Road at Wyoming. A record crowd came out to see Paul Williams and his Recording Orchestra, plus Wild Bill Moore and a show. The *Michigan Chronicle* reported

> *Paul Williams has been a local favorite for many years and just recently became an overnight sensation with his recordings, including "Hastings St Bounce" and "35-30." Juke box operators report the Paul Williams records are the most played throughout Detroit . . . will introduce for the first time "All the Boys for the Ride," "Paradise Valley Walk," which will be released this year. . . . featured will be Moore (who recently recorded "Swinging with Pappy" and "Bubbles"); Philip Guilbeau, trumpet ace; Herman Hopkins, bass; Floyd Taylor, piano; Reethan Mallet, drums.* [131]

Williams had recorded with this sextet in November and December under Moore's name, and Williams's increasing success with "35-30" eventually led to the national stage. In February, Reig took Williams's band to the Royal Theater in Baltimore. Reig went to work on Williams's stage act and by combining knee bends and blowing a microphone into the stage with a single baritone honk Williams became

131. *Michigan Chronicle*, January 17, 1948. Guilbeau seems to have come to Detroit to play with Williams. He was born in Louisiana and later played with Ray Charles. Taylor led his own band at the Old Time Café in 1951 and 1952. The band at one time included Yusef Lateef. Advertisement, *Michigan Chronicle*, March 24, 1951.

an instant success. Williams remembered that

> *The word got out, Maan, that saxophone player down there blowed the mike into the* FLOOR*! And that was it. We started doing dances and we had lines, both ways, as far as the eye could see. Fire department, police department, everybody was there.*[132]

Williams's popularity led to a national tour of black communities with a package show including a big band. The tour also brought him back to Detroit, where he played the Paradise and the Duke. "The nation's number one sax star" was welcomed back to the Duke by a fan club made up of "girls from the Eight Mile Road section."[133]

In December 1948 Williams recorded what became his greatest hit, "The Hucklebuck," the second million dollar instrumental R & B hit since Joe Liggins's "The Honeydripper" three years earlier.[134] Williams claims he lived off this hit for the following 10 years.[135] Williams remembered how he came up with his hit.

> *It happened during our second or third trip to the Royal Theater. We were always opposite a big band, and this time we were with Lucky Millinder's great band. I was sitting in the audience with a few of the fellows from my band listening to Lucky rehearse. They had a number called "D-Natural Blues." When they began to play it, I looked at one of the cats, and he looked at me. We kept it in mind . . . [at] our next gig . . . in Devons, Pennsylvania. . . . I decided to try the new tune, and the people started doing a dance I had never seen. . . . I called out, "What is that dance?" "This is the Hucklebuck," they answered. So that's what we called it. As soon as we got to New York, Teddy recorded us doing it.*[136]

During 1949 Williams made his last recordings in Detroit with a septet including the horns from the King Porter band and played a few Detroit engagements, including Club Valley. His time was increasingly spent on the road, and his last recordings with Detroit musicians were done in 1950 in New York.[137] He led his own band on tours until 1964 and accompanied many well-known rhythm and blues singers, including Fats Domino, Lloyd Price, and James Brown.[138]

The main feature in all of Williams's recordings is his baritone, which is increasingly played with honking abandon. The early recording of "Paradise Valley Walk" is one of the few where his supple, yet soulful, alto playing can be heard. The formula for most of Williams's recordings is similar to that of King Porter: honking saxophones, riffing ensembles, boogie piano, and rhythm. In contrast to the loosely organized Porter recordings, Williams spends more time on developing catchy riffs to serve as the melodic framework to the soloing. Williams's particular strength is at medium tempo, where he produces gently rocking and very danceable music, as on "The Hucklebuck," "Pop-Corn," "Waxey Maxie," "House Rockin,'" and "Turtle Rock."

T. J. Fowler

T. J. Fowler was born in Columbus, Georgia, on September 18, 1910.[139] His parents had four children, all boys: T. J., E. J., K. C., and F. C. The Fowler family moved to Michigan in 1916. His father owned a poolroom in River Rouge, and T. J. spent his first years as a professional musician playing piano on weekends. T. J.'s widow, Mattie, recalled that

> *His father was the first black deputy sheriff in River Rouge. He was an enterprisin' fella. He had a poolroom, and under the place where they lived was a dance hall; it was empty and they used it for a dance hall. T. J. played there on Friday, Saturday and Sunday for all the young people.*[140]

T. J. got the idea to play piano while shooting pool at his father's poolroom. He heard musicians come in and play, and one evening after a pianist had performed, he remarked to his friends, "You know, I think I could play that

132. Palmer, liner notes, Various Artists, *Honkers and Screamers.*

133. *Michigan Chronicle,* April 17, 1948.

134. Shaw, *Honkers and Shouters,* 130.

135. Williams only received artist's royalties for his hit, and complicated deals were struck between the others involved as described by Reig in his biography, *Reminiscing in Tempo,* 32–33, 100–101.

136. Reig with Berger, *Reminiscing in Tempo,* 100. Millinder recorded "D-Natural Blues" on January 3, 1949, for RCA Victor, slightly ahead of Williams, who waxed "The Hucklebuck" for Savoy on December 15, 1948. The numbers are identical and incorporate Charlie Parker's seminal blues line "Now's the Time," which Parker recorded for Savoy in 1945 but unfortunately did not copyright. Both versions were big hits. Bob Porter, phone interview with Jim Gallert, October 1, 2000. Bassist Al Martin remembers playing the number at the Royal Blue when Williams was in the band. Al Martin, interview by Gallert.

137. This recording for Savoy included Guilbeau, Miller Sam, and Joe Alexander (tenors); Lee Anderson (piano); John Murphy (bass); and Benny Benjamin (drums). Ruppli with Porter, *The Savoy Label,* 44.

138. Grendysa, liner notes, Paul Williams and His Orchestra: *The Hucklebuck,* Williams settled in New York in 1960.

139. Membership files, Detroit Federation of Musicians, Local No. 5, American Federation of Musicians, Southfield, Michigan.

140. Mattie Fowler, interview by Jim Gallert, Ecorse, Michigan, July 29, 1990.

Fig. 103. T. J. Fowler band, publicity still, unidentified location, ca. 1953.
L to R: Frank Taylor, as; Walter Cox, ts; Fowler, pno/ldr; Dezi McCullers, tp; Floyd "Bubbles" McVay, dms; Gene Taylor, bs.
(Courtesy Gallert Collection.)

song. . . . it was a blues." Challenged by his buddies, Fowler sat down at the piano and played the number, or enough of it to impress them. T. J. was around 16 years old at the time, and he began taking piano lessons after school.

Fowler and Mattie were married in 1931, and he began his career in earnest. He had learned enough to work solo at his father's poolroom on weekends and did so until he was around 24 years old. He joined a band led by alto saxophonist Guy Walters, which included his pals from the neighborhood, saxophonist Julius "Duke" Coates, trombonist Ted Merriweather, and drummer Samuel "Babe" Borders. Mattie Fowler recalled: "There was a club out here on West Jefferson called the Rendezvous. That was the first gig they ever had. They worked over there about two or three years."[141]

Fowler, Coates, and Borders left Walters for Clarence Dorsey's orchestra in 1944. At the time Fowler was considered one of the best boogie pianists in the city by the *Michigan Chronicle.*

> *T. J. Fowler might well lay claim to being one of the town's sendingest boogie beat pianists. Of course Bob (Count Basie) White might also lay claim to the title. . . . Wade Boykin might wonder where he stands too. . . . all three are boogie specialists so take your choice.*[142]

Fowler left Dorsey to start his own band in 1947, and their first job was at the Club Vogue in Inkster. Unlike Todd Rhodes's band, T. J. Fowler's combo spent most of its time working around Detroit.[143] Fowler's band went to Cleveland occasionally for two- or three-week stays, and they later worked a lot in Canada. Fowler had many business interests in addition to his band, and he had to stay in town to cultivate them. In addition his wife disliked him traveling.[144]

141. Ibid.

142. *Michigan Chronicle,* August 5, 1944.

143. Fowler's band had longer stays at some of the same Detroit clubs that also featured Todd Rhodes: Club Sensation, Sportree's, Club Juana, the Royal Blue Bar, and the Eagle Show Bar. Advertisements, *Michigan Chronicle,* 1948–59.

144. Fowler had a landscaping business for many years. Fowler, interview by Gallert.

Fig. 104. Saxophone players were not the only musicians who walked the bar, as shown in this photo of Frank Taylor and Gene Taylor at Alvito's, ca. 1953. Owner Joe Alvito is behind the bar.
(Courtesy Gene Taylor, Gallert Collection.)

Fowler was a fine boogie-woogie pianist, but he also succeeded in other aspects of music. He was a composer; he owned a music publishing company and a record label; and he was well regarded as a recording engineer.[145] Dezi McCullers, who played trumpet with Fowler, remembered that

> *He was a boogie-woogie piano player . . . a good one. He played any kind of boogie-woogie, all of them intricate numbers. Most of it [the material we played] he wrote. The standard tunes that we did, he arranged 'em.*[146]

Fowler was an even-tempered person with a positive outlook. He was ambitious and was always looking for new challenges or opportunities. Dezi McCullers looked up to him.

> *He was like a father to me. He used to cool this hot head down. He didn't drink. He didn't smoke. His biggest kick was orange juice.*[147]

Fowler was a more assertive and less sophisticated pianist than Todd Rhodes, and his playing had more of a "country" feel to it. This can be heard on the band's recordings from 1948 to

145. "He was the one that set up the Motown studio. . . . he was an arranger for them." Dezi McCullers, interview by Jim Gallert, Detroit, Michigan, June 17, 1990.

146. McCullers (born 1928) worked with Fowler as a trumpeter, replacing Elliot Escoe in 1952. He later switched to tenor sax and worked in the Motown studios. Ibid.

147. Ibid.

1953, where Fowler's boogie piano is an almost constant presence. "T. J. Boogie" and "Night Crawler" feature Fowler's piano, but the predominant soloist on other tunes is tenorist Walter Cox.[148] Dezi McCullers remembered the impact of Fowler's playing.

> *Most of his things had a bluesy feel. If he did a ballad, it had a bluesy feelin' or swing to it. When you do that, you reach the "gut" of people.*[149]

Fowler always wanted to improve his musical skills. Once the band was working at a club in Canada, and one of the acts had intricate music that the drummer couldn't cut. He was replaced for the duration of the gig, and McCullers and Frank Taylor, both of whom were good readers, carried the show. Fowler had some difficulties as well. Dezi McCullers recalled the situation.

> *He could not play the part. He told her that the stuff [music] was not right. She told him it was right, and played it for him. After she played it, he got through it enough. But he . . . went back to the Institute of Music and took lessons. He studied there for years. He was never caught like that again.*[150]

One of Fowler's bassists was Gene Taylor, who was present on the band's last recordings in late 1953.[151] Taylor had recently returned from a stint in the army, where he played in the army band.[152] He recalled his time with Fowler's band.

> *[After the army] I stepped up to T. J. Fowler and the Backbiters. T. J. just ignored us and did his thing. . . . he was older [than we were]. Good blues player. It used to be a point of honor, you had to play "Flying Home" before you got out of the club. Walter Cox would walk out of the bar, and if there was a bus coming around, he would take the bus up to the next block playing "Flying Home," get out of the bus, walk back down the block back into the bar playing "Flying Home."*[153]

Walter Cox's singing was an important part of the band's presentation, although he does not sing on record. Cox's tenor saxophone is at its best on "Midnight Clipper: Part 1," where his mellow tone can be heard to full advantage.[154] On recordings, Fowler's band was augmented by blues singer/guitarist Calvin Frazier.[155] Although he worked regularly with many excellent Detroit-based blues singers, Fowler recorded only with Alberta Adams. Bassist Hank Ivory, who did his best to sound like Billy Eckstine, waxed several vocals.

The decline of jump blues bands, and the use of smaller bands in general in nightclubs, forced Fowler to cut back his group first to a quartet and finally, in the early 1960s, to a trio that featured Fowler on the ubiquitous Hammond B-3 organ.[156]

Candy Johnson

Tenorist Candy Johnson has already been introduced in the fourth chapter as someone who went from big band swing and into jump band music in the 1940s. His style of playing with his own band in the late 1940s was often likened to that of Illinois Jacquet. He was not always appreciated by jazz listeners, who found his playing too clichéd and his stage antics too much. *Down Beat*'s George Hoefer saw Johnson's Peppermint Sticks on a *Jazz in Detroit* show in 1949.

> *The bewildering part of the show, which went on twice a day for two days at the Alvin Theatre, was the antic-filled performance of Candy Johnson on the sax. This cat even played the sax with one arm behind his back and both hands on the keys. His original, called "Candy's Mood," not only included all the better known bop phrases on records, but also snatches of "Mary Had a Little Lamb," "Jingle Bells," and "The Wedding March."*[157]

On the other hand, Johnson's show was very popular with audiences, and some musicians saw it in different terms than Hoefer. Beans Bowles heard Johnson a lot around this time

148. T. J. Fowler and His Band, *Early Detroit R & B* (Official 6044) includes recordings on the National, Sensation, Gotham, Savoy, and States labels. Fowler recorded 17 titles for Sensation, most of which remain unissued.

149. McCullers, interview by Gallert.

150. Ibid.

151. Taylor was born in Toledo in 1929 but moved to Detroit in 1936 ("Gene Taylor," *New Grove Dictionary of Jazz*). One of his first gigs was at 13 with Roland Hanna and tenorist Robert Barnes. Hanna, interview by Bjorn.

152. Taylor, interview by Bjorn and Gallert.

153. Gene Taylor, interview by Bjorn and Gallert. Taylor played with the Fowler band and then backed cocktail pianist Lillette Harris at the Wal-Ha Room in 1956. In 1958, Taylor joined Harris in New York State. During his stay he was set up by Louis Hayes to audition for pianist Horace Silver, who was looking for a replacement for Teddy Kotick. Taylor successfully auditioned for Horace Silver's hard bop quintet, one of the most popular jazz groups. He remained with Silver for six years.

154. Cox was born in Nashville on September 23, 1912. Membership files, Detroit Federation of Musicians, Local No. 5, American Federation of Musicians, Southfield, Michigan.

155. Released on T. J. Fowler, *T. J. Fowler and His Rockin' Jump Band Featuring Calvin Frazier,* Savoy SJL 1187 (LP).

156. Lou Barnett on tenor saxophone and drummer Dave Burks were in Fowler's trio.

157. George Hoefer, "In Detroit Dixie Is Pure and Mary's Lamb Bopped," *Down Beat*, January 28, 1949.

Fig. 105. Candy Johnson Quartet, unidentified location and time. *Lawrence "Jacktown" Jackson, dms; Johnson, ts/bar/ldr; Levi Mann, bs; Fred Braceful, pno.* (Courtesy Gallert Collection.)

and later played with him in Bill Doggett's group.

> *Candy did commercial things. He could play good. He was not an astute chord progression man, he was a lyrical melodic man. That was one of the things he told me: "Always learn the melody and you'll never get lost. Play around the melody and no matter what the chords are you'll be all right." He was not the kind of guy who would take a chord and interpolate it and do all kinds of different things with it. He was a lyricist. Most of the musicians around that time were trying to be far out [playing] bebop. Candy was still legitimate and he made money. He worked all the time because he played for the people who liked to hear honky-tonk music, only it was "Flying Home" at that time or "In the Dark" with Lil Green, or "Salty Poppa" (sings) or "Candy's Mood," the same thing that Yusef [Lateef] uses; in fact Yusef did it after Candy.*[158]

Johnson led his Peppermint Sticks in Detroit from 1947 until 1951, when he joined Count Basie's big band. This must have been the high point of his jazz career, but he spent a little less than a year with Basie and returned to Detroit to lead his own band.[159] This band had long stays at the Chesterfield, the Oriole, the El Sino, and the Frolic and also went on several national tours.[160] In 1958 Johnson rejoined a national name band, but this time it was one of the hottest R & B groups, led by organist Bill Doggett. Beans Bowles had joined Doggett a half year earlier and remembered what the job was like.

> *Candy followed me, and during the transition we were together. That was a good paying job, and we got paid against lay-offs. I think I got $125–150, plus room and board and uniforms. We played everything: theaters, clubs, and vaudeville joints. Doggett bought a new bus, specially made for him, and everybody had a seat to sleep and eat in. We played most of the*

158. Bowles, interview by Bjorn.

159. Johnson recorded with Basie in two sessions in January 1952. He solos on "Fawncy Meeting You."

160. Advertisements, *Michigan Chronicle*, November 22, 1952; June 20, 1953; April 3 and October 9, 1954. *Detroit Free Press*, February 15, 1958.

time for black audiences. . . . "Honky Tonk" was a black hit. We did not have too many crossovers back then.[161]

Gene Taylor worked with Johnson in 1949–50 and remembered Johnson as

A great showman. We wore jackets with candy-stripes on them. . . . During the course of his performance, he would just throw peppermint sticks out there in the audience. His fortes were "The Man with the Horn" and "Rhapsody in Blue." Those were a couple of the songs that would get people's attention. Other than that, he would just play straight rhythm 'n' blues. We used to tour the Midwest. Candy was the only horn. [He played] baritone and tenor.[162]

Doggett's biggest hit was "Honky Tonk" in 1956, which featured tenorist Clifford Scott and guitarist Billy Butler. Doggett featured both Scott and Johnson on tenor on many recordings, like "Night Train," and on others Johnson soloed on baritone. He also wrote "Blip Blop," which was an R & B hit in 1958. Johnson recorded with Doggett until 1960.[163]

Rhythm and Blues

THE JUMP BLUES BANDS were an important component of a new form of black popular music that emerged in the latter half of the 1940s and became commonly known as rhythm and blues by the 1950s. When the instrumental style of jump bands was added to new popular vocal styles, the result was R & B. Detroit had its share of vocalists in this style, and we will take a brief look at some of them in their club settings.

Detroit's premier venue in the 1940s for black musical entertainment had been the Paradise Theatre, but with the opening of the Flame in 1949 and the closing of the Paradise in November 1951, the action moved over to the Flame. The Flame did differ from the Paradise in having a whiter, older, and more affluent audience.[164] It was a solid testing ground for black entertainers who wanted to cross over to an adult mass audience. The Flame was similar to the Paradise in presenting the top national acts, but it also gave some room for local talent. For younger audiences interested in dancing to top national bands and vocalists, the Graystone and the Madison were alternative downtown venues in the 1950s. For a couple of years the Club Valley in Paradise Valley was also popular. By 1954–55 two downtown theaters started to include top-flight R & B in their offerings: the Fox and the Broadway Capitol.

The Flame: House Bands and Vocalists

THE FLAME HAD A HOUSE BAND that backed most acts and also played some numbers of their own. For the first 10 months the Flame was open, three bands filled this job, before Maurice King was asked to take over band-leading duties. The Snooky Young band from Ohio opened up the club in June and was replaced by Todd Rhodes in August. Rhodes favored the jazz side of his repertoire for the band's own selections at the Flame, but the band also backed a variety of artists during the fall. These included Dinah Washington, Wynonie Harris, and Detroiter Kitty Stevenson. Stevenson was a very talented singer whose life ended abruptly in 1952. Beans Bowles remembered how impressive Stevenson was and how the outspoken Dinah Washington reacted when Stevenson was on the same bill.

Kitty Stevenson was bad! Dinah Washington was the star and they put Kitty in front of her and Dinah pissed and bitched: "Don't ever put no children, dogs and Kitty Stevenson in front of me, 'fore I gotta go on!"[165]

Stevenson had recorded with Rhodes in 1948–49 and sang both blues and ballads with great feeling but was typically billed as a "blues bombshell."[166] In January 1950 she left the Flame to tour with Rhodes, after which she worked as a single.

The Rhodes band was replaced by T. J. Fowler's band until April 1950, when Maurice

161. Bowles, interview by Bjorn. Bowles left the Flame in 1956 to join the Illinois Jacquet band. After playing in Baltimore with Erskine Hawkins for a few months he joined Doggett in June 1957 and stayed until April 1958. This stay included several recordings. Ziggy Johnson column, *Michigan Chronicle*, June 8, 1957; and Bill Lane column, *Michigan Chronicle*, April 12, 1958.

162. Gene Taylor, interview by Bjorn and Gallert.

163. Hugues Pannasie, "Candy Johnson," *Bulletin du Hot Club de France*, no. 237, 1974. Other Detroiters who recorded with Doggett were bassist Jimmy Glover in 1954–55 and guitarist John Faire in 1952 and 1956.

164. The shift from the Paradise to the Flame also reflected the decline of big bands in popular entertainment in the late 1940s.

165. Bowles, interview by Bjorn.

166. Stevenson was born in Thompson, Georgia, around 1918 and came to Detroit in 1929. She started out as a dancer and had her first singing job in Detroit with Lorenzo Lawson at Lee's Sensation. Under the management of Al Green she toured widely in 1950 and 1951. (Roy Stephens, "Kitty Stevenson," *Michigan Chronicle*, August 6, 1949; Bill Lane column, *Michigan Chronicle*, July 1, 1950; "Kitty Stevenson: Night Club Singer Succumbs," *Michigan Chronicle*, June 7, 1952.) Kitty Stevenson is the mother of Mickey Stevenson, one of Motown's main producers in the 1960s.

Fig. 106. Flame Show Bar, 1950s.
Seated, L to R: Bobby "Mumbles" Lewis, Ida Clarke, Roy Hamilton, Morris Wasserman, Ziggy Johnson, unidentified dancer, Todd Rhodes. Standing: Unidentified, Al Green.
(Courtesy Mrs. Annie Mae Rhodes, Gallert Collection.)

King settled into the job. Rhodes's band returned on a regular schedule to replace the King band when they got a break every eighth week, and Fowler came in when Rhodes was not available.

Maurice King had come to Detroit in the late 1930s and played with Leroy Smith, whose musicianship and deportment greatly impressed King. In late 1944 he became the music director for the International Sweethearts of Rhythm, the foremost "all-girl" band at the time. King left the band in 1948 and returned to Detroit.[167] He was contacted by Flame owner Morris Wasserman in 1950, as King recalled.

> *He asked if I could put together a band to accompany national acts which would work every night of the week. I told him I could, but the caliber of musicians I had in mind might cost a little more. He said, "do it." I agreed on the condition that I would have control over the music and band personnel. I named the band after the state animal.*[168]

King took the job and led his seven Wolverines at the Flame for 11 years. The Flame offered three or four shows Sunday through Thursday and five on Friday and Saturday. The shows were about one hour long and followed a standard formula, as Beans Bowles recalled.

> *We'd hit at nine o'clock. Our theme was "My Old Flame." Every show had local singers, dancers, a comedian and the headliner. We had a new headliner every week.*[169]

King assembled a group of musicians with the necessary skills to play anything from jazz to rhythm and blues. After some juggling the first year, King settled on experienced players in their thirties: tenorist Louis Barnett (formerly with Todd Rhodes and also with King in Leroy Smith's WPA band), trumpeter Russell Green (formerly with King in Leroy Smith's WPA band, later with Jimmie Lunceford), pianist Neal "Ghandi" Robinson (with Ted Buckner), and drummer Elbert "Dagwood" Langford (with Rudy Rutherford). Two younger players

167. Maurice King, interview by Jim Gallert, Oak Park, Michigan, June 6, 1986. King was born in 1911 in Greenwood, Mississippi, where he started on clarinet in elementary school. He switched to alto saxophone after hearing one in a minstrel show. King studied music performance and arranging at Tennessee State University in Nashville, where some of his fellow students were bassist Jimmy Blanton and trumpeter Sammy Lowe.

168. Ibid.

169. Bowles, interview by Gallert.

Fig. 107. Maurice King orchestra and others, Flame Show Bar, June 1949.
L to R: Russell Green, tp; King, as/arr/ldr; Beans Bowles, bar; Anita O'Day, vcl; possibly Carl Hoff (Anita O'Day's husband); Wendell Jenkins, bs; Lou Barnett, ts; Edward "Chips" Grant, dms; Ghandi Robinson, pno.
(Courtesy Mrs. Russell Green, Gallert Collection.)

rounded out the septet, bassist Clarence Sherrill and baritonist Beans Bowles.[170] King himself played the alto sax, but his main task was as musical leader of the band, and he always credited Leroy Smith with teaching him leadership skills that King, in turn, passed on to younger musicians. He put his goals for the band this way.

> *"I wanted a big band sound, with as few horns as I could get! I'm blessed with the knowledge . . . of being able to orchestrate in such a manner that a band sounds bigger than you would expect. When I rehearse a band, I insist that every man plays his note with the fullest and roundest sound he can deliver in order to bring out the blend I have created."*[171]

Trumpeter Johnny Trudell met King in 1957, subbed for Al Aarons a couple of times at the Flame, and later worked with King at the Metropole. The two men became close friends, and Trudell, 20 years old at the time, learned much from King.

> *He was an elegant bandleader, more like Duke Ellington. Excellent leader. Everything was meticulous, his dress, his custom made shoes, his custom made everything. Total class, man. I learned a lot about my approach to bandleading from him. He was almost like a father to me. He was a great arranger, an orchestrator in the same sense as Benny Carter, (Fletcher) Henderson. He didn't need a piano, he just wrote the scores. . . . as a saxophonist he was somewhere in the mix with Teddy Buckner, Earl Bostic, Johnny Hodges, Louis Jordan. Good saxophone player, great intonation. He could play everything he wrote.*[172]

King always regretted that he "couldn't sell any of this stuff to the commercial record companies," but the Wolverines did wax several

170. Wendell Jenkins on bass and Ed "Chips" Grant on drums were members of the first band but were soon replaced. "Maurice King Set to Debut His New Band at Flame," *Michigan Chronicle*, April 15, 1950.

171. King, interview by Gallert.

172. Johnny Trudell, interview by Jim Gallert, Sterling Heights, Michigan, February 25, 2000.

titles for Okeh Records in 1951. "Nightfall" (not the Benny Carter composition) is an attractive melody with a soulful solo by King that shows his spiritual link to the swing-era alto masters. "Make Love to Me" is a pop tune that incorporates "Tin Roof Blues." This is a really exciting number; the band does indeed sound larger than seven pieces. The arrangement is excellent, there is a prominent backbeat, and the icing on the cake is Putney Nails, a singer with a gravelly, driving voice who jumps in on the last chorus. This is a good example of early rock and roll before guitars supplanted horns. Vocalist Lavern Baker recorded with King in 1951, and she's a good match for King's band on "Good Daddy," a red-hot number.

Several singers at the Flame were important figures in the rapidly developing R & B field during the 1950s. One of the first was Johnnie Ray, who started at the Flame in early 1951.[173] In a 1974 interview with Arnold Shaw, Ray looked back on his days at the Flame.

> *The Flame was a continuous show, right through the night. And I was the only white guy; as far as the show was concerned it was a black and tan club. . . . I became a Billie Holiday collector. . . . I lived to see the day she came into the Flame and saw me in person. . . . [I was] invited to her hotel for drinks . . . started a friendship. . . . I recorded "Whiskey and Gin/Tell the Lady I Said Goodbye" for Okeh. Oddly enough I was signed on Okeh for Rhythm and Blues. . . . I came to Detroit from Cleveland, . . . Al Green auditioned me and signed me for about $125 a week. One night Robin Seymour, a local disc jockey, happened to catch me. He got hold of Danny Kessler [president of Columbia] who offered me a contract with Okeh. . . . [We] recorded in Detroit. The record became a hit in many cities and I got a gig at Capitol Lounge in Chicago . . . then Cleveland where Bill Randle had driven my record right up to the top.*[174]

It was the Maurice King band that backed Ray on his first two sides for Okeh, and they were not happy with their lack of recognition for it.[175] Ray's next record, "Cry," was a number one hit on both R & B and pop charts. Kessler has told the story of how the Columbia sales force thought Ray was a black female on first hearing, and many record buyers obviously agreed.[176] Ray never repeated his "reverse crossover" hit.

In 1952, Chicago-born LaVern Baker spent several months at the Flame and made her first R & B recordings with Todd Rhodes.[177] Baker had earlier fashioned herself as a jazz singer in the style of Sarah Vaughan and Dinah Washington. In Detroit she was, like Ray, managed by Al Green, who got her a Columbia recording contract. The following year she left Detroit, joined Atlantic Records, and produced her first hit with "Tweedle Dee," which has been called "the poppiest ever recording by Atlantic by a black act."[178]

Della Reese was another singer who had the talent to perform well in many styles. She was born in Detroit and was a featured gospel singer in weekly radio broadcasts at six years of age.[179] As a teenager she toured with the Mahalia Jackson gospel choir for five summers and eventually formed her own gospel group. She was forced to leave Wayne University to find work, due to family misfortunes, and eventually ended up at the Flame. This turned into her first professional job as a singer.

> *I stayed there for 18 weeks. The pay was sensational—$85 a week. And that was my start in show business. . . . At the Flame I sang three jazz songs. I thought they were jazz songs but later found out that they were standards. "Fine and Dandy" was one. But I considered myself a great jazz singer, this departure from "Jesus Keep Me Near the Cross." . . . When I went into the Flame I had had an opportunity to hear Ella Fitzgerald. I was the opening act. I worked with Dinah Washington, Billie Holiday, Billy Eckstine, Count Basie, Garner, and just everyone who came to town. The Flame was the place*

173. *Michigan Chronicle*, April 14, 1951. Ray was managed by Al Green, but Danny Kessler took the position away from him, with some eventual compensation. Shaw, *Honkers and Shouters*, 367.

174. Arnold Shaw, *The Rockin' 50s* (New York: Hawthorne Books, 1974), 54–56.

175. Ziggy Johnson column, *Michigan Chronicle*, March 22, 1952.

176. Shaw, *Honkers and Shouters*, 448. Reese worked as a hostess/singer at the Oriole Show Bar on Linwood in 1953 and sang at the Flame for the first time mid-year. She returned to the Flame in March 1954. "From the Choir to the Bright Lights: That's Della Reese," *Michigan Chronicle*, March 27, 1954.

177. At the Flame, Baker was billed as "LaVern Baker, Little Miss Sharecropper." She had adopted the Little Miss Sharecropper name in the late 1940s. Advertisements, *Michigan Chronicle*, March 8 through June 21, 1952.

178. Phil Hardy and Dave Laing, *The Faber Companion to 20th-Century Popular Music* (Winchester, MA: Faber and Faber, 1990), 36.

179. Reese was born Delloreese Patricia Early in 1931 and grew up on Vernor Highway on the East Side. She graduated from Northeastern in 1947 and changed her name some time in late 1952 or early 1953. She had just started performing secular songs, and the marquee at a local club could not handle her long name. Della Reese, *Angels along the Way: My Life with Help from Above* (New York: Putnam, 1997).

to be.... In Detroit, in an area of 5 or 6 blocks, there wasn't one without spots of live entertainment.... Friday and Saturday night were get-up-and-go nights, get dressed and go out. Wayne University was [near] and so a lot of the young people came in, particularly on Saturday nights. But every night was nightclub night. The Flame was the hottest spot in town and we had a mixed audience.... The Flame was letting your hair down. Maurice King... had the house band. He made me arrangements on "April in Paris" and "With These Hands." My program consisted entirely of standards. I recorded on a label called Great Lakes Records... owned by Tony Vance.[180]

Reese's next change of musical direction came when she was heard by record producer and manager Lee Magid.

Al Green called me. Said, "There's a chick out here can go white. Nobody knows what to do with her." And he sent the girl in. She borrowed twenty-five bucks to come meet me in New York. So in comes this girl. Nipsey Russell was the emcee. So I says, "Nipsey, put her on the stage for me."... And this chick got up there, and I'll never forget it. She sang "There'll Never Be Another You" as a ballad and up-tempo the second chorus. And then "Birth of the Blues"—and forget it! The house came down! She was the prettiest thing I'd seen—her hands, her diction. I says, "Female Hibbler! No question! She could be the greatest!"[181]

Magid got bandleader Erskine Hawkins to hire Reese, after which she went on to make hit recordings on both R & B and pop lists.[182] In her recent autobiography Reese remarks that "In time, I was to gain a reputation as a versatile singer who could swing from pop to jazz to blues to gospel. And to this day, I don't see myself in any one category; nor do I care to be pigeonholed."[183]

Jackie Wilson was another Detroit singer who crossed over, but he was more clearly in the R & B fold than was Della Reese. Like Reese, Wilson started out singing in church, and he led his own gospel group, the Falcons, in the early 1950s.[184] He won amateur contests at the Paradise several times, and at one of them, in 1951, he impressed R & B pioneer and talent scout Johnny Otis. Otis was playing the Paradise and arranged a talent show, as he told Arnold Shaw.

A one-hour show stretched into an hour-and-a-half, and there was still another hour-and-a-half of kids waiting. In later years, when I thought of what Berry Gordy did in Detroit, I was not surprised. For some reason, Detroit was loaded with talent; it just needed the vision and creative power of Gordy to help it mature. A tremendous percentage of the young people heard at the Paradise were talented. Three of them made a strong impression. They were Little Willie John, Jackie Wilson, and a group called The Royals.[185]

At a subsequent audition, Billy Ward of the vocal group the Dominoes also heard Wilson, which in 1953 led to his becoming the group's new lead singer, replacing Clyde McPhatter. In the intervening years Wilson sang at the Sensation and showed off his vocal chops in a recording of "Danny Boy" for Dee Gee.[186] As a member of the Dominoes, Wilson helped shape the doo-wop vocal group tradition, in which McPhatter was a pioneer. Apart from McPhatter, Wilson credited gospel singers as the main influences on his style. He left the Dominoes in 1956 and returned to Detroit, as he told Arnold Shaw.

Then I went solo into the Flame Show Bar. Al Green ran it... and he had La Vern Baker and Johnnie Ray... Della Reese.... He knew talent. Detroit was the Paradise Theatre, the Flame Bar, and Al Green. Berry Gordy came later. But he hung around the Flame and his sister worked in the club. I made some demos for Al, and he took them into New York. "Reet Petite" was one, a song by Berry Gordy. That's how I got with Brunswick Records.... "Reet Petite" was my first record. It never showed on

180. Shaw, *Rockin' 50s*, 201.

181. Shaw, *Honkers and Shouters*, 368.

182. Her first big hits were with Jubilee Records: "In the Still of the Night" in 1954, which sold about half a million records, and "And That Reminds Me" in 1957, which was the first of her five million record hits.

183. Reese, *Angels along the Way*, 143.

184. Wilson was born in Detroit in 1934.

185. Shaw, *Honkers and Shouters*, 168. Otis was a talent scout for King Records, but King was not interested in Wilson, nor in Little Willie John, but picked up a vocal group, the Royals, later called Hank Ballard and the Midnighters.

186. Shaw, *Honkers and Shouters*, 442. Wilson recorded for Dee Gee under the name Sonny Wilson. Wilson rerecorded "Danny Boy" twice. One of the later versions is found on Jackie Wilson, *Higher and Higher*, Charly CPCD 8005 (CD).

R & B charts. It went pop and sold a quarter of a million. "To Be Loved" was my first R & B chart-song. . . . It was by Berry Gordy, his sister Gwen, and Tyran Carlo.[187]

The same song team also wrote Wilson's first number one hit, "Lonely Teardrops," in 1958 when he moved to New York.

Ballrooms and Theatres

SINCE MUCH OF THE AUDIENCE for R & B was under 21, ballrooms and theaters were more welcoming to R & B than nightclubs. Many of Detroit's vocal groups and solo vocalists got their start in neighborhood theaters, like the Gold Coast Theatre on Twelfth Street. The top rung of venues was located downtown: the Graystone, the Madison, the Fox, and the Broadway Capitol.

One of the many local doo-wop groups was the Royals, led by Hank Ballard, who was born in Detroit in 1936. After being discovered by Johnny Otis at the Paradise in 1951, the group got a King recording contract and had a number eight R & B hit with "Get It" in 1953.[188] By the fall they were performing frequently at the Graystone.[189] The group was renamed Hank Ballard and the Midnighters when they hit the top of the chart with "Work with Me, Annie" and the sequel "Annie Had a Baby" in 1954. Ballard also wrote and recorded "The Twist" in 1959, which was covered (recorded) by Chubby Checker the following year.[190]

Little Willie John was discovered at the Paradise at the same time as the Royals. John was born in Arkansas in 1939 and came to Detroit at age four. He made his first recordings at fourteen for the local Prize label, but it was his contract with King in 1955 that made him a household name in R & B.[191] In 1956 he had a hit with "All around the World" and performed locally at the Graystone, Club Vogue, and the Madison.[192] John is probably best known for "Fever," which was his first crossover hit in 1956. In 1958 Peggy Lee had her biggest hit with a cover version of John's recording. Arnold Shaw sees John's singing on "Fever" as crossing the dividing line between R & B and soul, the latter a term not yet invented to describe a popular genre of music.[193]

Motown

A MAJOR STUMBLING BLOCK for Detroit musical talent was the lack of sizable local recording companies. Motown changed all that in the 1960s, but we must go back to the 1950s and the life of Berry Gordy to understand its emergence.

Berry Gordy

BERRY GORDY TRIED HIS HANDS at several aspects of the music business before he came up with a winning formula. Born in Detroit in 1932 into a family grounded in the small-business ethos of Booker T. Washington, Gordy's first venture was the 3-D Record Mart in the family's building on Farnsworth and St. Antoine in 1953. Gordy had become a jazz fan in the 1940s, and at first that was all he sold in his store. When his customers proved more interested in blues records he added these to his wares, but it was too late, as Gordy told in his autobiography.

> *The more I heard the Blues the more I liked it. I finally had to admit to myself that Blues was in my soul, probably stemming from my early exposure to Gospel. There was an honesty about it; it was just as pure and real as jazz. In fact, jazz had its roots in the Blues. Ironically, the same simplicity that I'd rejected in the Blues was the very thing that people related to. This important lesson came too late to save the store, but would not be too late to make a difference in my songwriting.*[194]

After working as a salesman and as an assembly-line worker at Lincoln-Mercury, Gordy turned to full-time songwriting in 1957. At night he hung around the clubs on John R., in particular the Flame, where his favorites were Dinah Washington, Sarah Vaughan, and Billie

187. Shaw, *Honkers and Shouters*, 443.

188. Jay Warner, *The Billboard Book of American Singing Groups: A History 1940–1990* (New York: Billboard Books, 1992), 73.

189. Advertisements, *Michigan Chronicle*, August 11, September 5, and October 10, 1953.

190. Liner notes, Hank Ballard and the Midnighters, *20 Hits*, King-5003X (LP).

191. "Willie John Captures City's Fancy," *Michigan Chronicle*, December 12, 1953.

192. Advertisements, *Michigan Chronicle*, March 10 and May 19, 1956.

193. Shaw, *Honkers and Shouters*, 287.

194. Berry Gordy, *To Be Loved* (New York: Warner Books, 1995), 64–65.

Holiday. His sister Gwen had the photo concession at the Flame with camera assistance from her sister Anna and two other brothers in the darkroom. After being introduced to Al Green by Gwen, Gordy started writing songs for Green's artists, in particular Jackie Wilson. Pianist/saxophonist Teddy Harris Jr. was a childhood friend of both Gordy and Wilson, and he played on Wilson's recordings of "Reet Petite" and "To Be Loved."

> *He [Gordy] was crazy about music. . . . he was always around music. Jackie Wilson was a friend of ours. We all used to box at Brewster Center. Jackie and I were like brothers. We used to sing; we had a little quartet, used to sing in churches. Berry got this idea, that he wanted to make this record. It was made at his sister's little studio on Farnsworth and St. Antoine. And, he hired all jazz musicians. . . . we didn't charge him anything. And the record became popular and made money. And that's how Motown actually started.*[195]

Wilson's recordings of "Reet Petite" and "To Be Loved" gave Gordy a name, and singers started to come to him for material. One of them was singer/songwriter Smokey Robinson, who was the 17-year-old leader of the Matadors (later the Miracles). Gordy started to manage the group and produced their first record, "Got a Job," for the End label. It became a local hit record in early 1958, but Gordy made only $3.19 for songwriting and production.[196]

With economic returns such as these, Gordy decided to form his own record company, and with a $800 loan from his family, Tamla was born in January 1959. He produced "Come to Me" with Marv Johnson at United Sound, where he took increased control over sound balancing. "With Marv's inspired performance and the great flute solo by Beans Bowles, one of Detroit's best jazz musicians, I felt I had what I needed for a big hit," Gordy said, and he was right.[197] "Come to Me" got airplay on local radio stations and became a national hit after being picked up by United Artists.[198] In the summer of 1959, Gordy became "the first Negro in the city to open a recording studio of any noticeable consequence" when he purchased the former Gene LeVett photo building on West Grand Boulevard.[199] Gordy christened the new headquarters Hitsville USA, and his increased control over the production, distribution, and marketing of music led to a steady flow of hits. Motown's first number one R & B hit was the Miracles' "Shop Around" in 1960, and the first number one pop hit was the Marvelettes' "Please Mr Postman" in 1961. The Motown organization grew rapidly and eventually became the largest black-owned enterprise in the nation. For the first time black music was successfully brought to the mass white market by a company that was in black hands. It was also a remarkable achievement from a local perspective, since for the first time a Detroit record company became a national competitor.

What explains the success of Motown? A complete answer is clearly beyond the scope of this book. However, we can examine the creative process that brought about what is commonly called the Motown Sound.

The Motown Sound

The Motown Sound was fully developed by 1964 and has been described by Simon Frith as "the rhythmic sound of a beat, a compulsion which depended not on one instrument but emerged from the blend of many—bass, drums, voices, jabs of horn and strings and organ; the gospel-derived sound of a beseeching lead singer and her answering chorus. The sounds of soul music."[200] The production of this sound required the cooperation and creativity of a number of participants: producers, songwriters, arrangers, vocalists, and instrumentalists. The role of the producer was to coordinate and guide the process as a whole, but he was clearly dependent on the creativity of the others. Gordy described what he did as a producer.

195. Teddy Harris, interview by Jim Gallert, Detroit, Michigan, May 12, 1999. Harris was born in Detroit in 1934 and began to study music at age nine. His father was a respected pianist/bandleader around Detroit. For a time Harris Sr. led the pit band at the Paradise Theatre, where young Harris sat in with Lionel Hampton's orchestra. He attended Northern High School and began to work jobs as a tenorist. During his army service (1956–60), Harris met Eddie Harris, then playing piano in the Seventh Army band. They traded lessons on their instruments, and Teddy remained in Paris after his discharge from the army to study composition with Nadia Boulanger before returning to Detroit. Harris worked in the arranging department for Motown, touring with tenorist Choker Campbell's band. Harris worked for Motown for 16 years and served as music director for the Supremes. Teddy Harris, interview by Jim Gallert, Detroit, Michigan, August 24, 1992.

196. Gordy, *To Be Loved*, chaps. 4 and 5. Smokey Robinson with David Ritz, *Inside My Life* (New York: McGraw Hill, 1989), 78.

197. Gordy, *To Be Loved*, 115.

198. The third record with Johnson, *You Got What It Takes*, put Tamla in the black. Don Waller, *The Motown Story* (New York: Scribner's, 1984), 31.

199. Bill Lane column, *Michigan Chronicle*, November 7, 1959.

200. Simon Frith, "You Can Make It If You Try: The Motown Story," in *The Soul Book*, ed. Ian Hore et al. (New York: Dell, 1975), 47.

Fig. 108. Joe Hunter band, publicity still, ca. 1959. *Benny Benjamin, dms; James Jamerson, el bs; Hunter, pno/ldr; Larry Veeder, gtr; Hank Cosby, ts; Mike Terry, bar.* (Courtesy Joe Hunter, Gallert Collection.)

On my sessions we'd work from handwritten chord sheets. The "feel" was usually the first thing I'd go for. After locking in the drumbeat, I'd hum a line for each musician to start. Once we got going, we'd usually ad lib all over the place until we got the groove I wanted. Many of these guys came from a jazz background. I understood their instincts to turn things around to their liking, but I also knew what I wanted to hear—commercially. So when they went too far, I'd stop them and stress, "We gotta get back to the funk—stay in that groove." . . . They did all kinds of stuff—always pushing me to the limit and beyond.[201]

Jazz musicians were most creative under these conditions, as Beans Bowles explained.

Motown didn't have any "sound"—they had

201. Gordy, *To Be Loved*, 130.

ideas, and when they brought the music to us it was all lead sheets. We did the arranging on the spot. We're all jazz players, so we did it on the spot. It was like having a jam session. The producer said: "Play something for me man!" "What do you want to hear?" "We don't know what we want to hear, ya'll just play!" And then they'd hear something: "Hey man, what's that you just played?" "You mean this?" "Yeah, let me hear that again, that's what I want, right there!" Now who's writing this thing? That's how production started. Smokey and Berry were the only guys who had a general idea of what they wanted; all the rest of the producers were doing what I just told you. They learned how to be producers from that and watching Berry. That's the way it started. Berry might hum something to you. "Can you play [hums]?" "No that's too much man, just play [hums]." . . . and then you'd fool around until you get something closer to it. We could be there all day to do one song. And we're getting five dollars per "Song!"[202]

Drummer Pistol Allen was one of the three drummers used by Motown. He described the same experience with producers as did Bowles and concluded that the producers were "picking our brains." Allen also described how open-ended the creative process was by holding up a chord sheet from one of the sessions he played.

Try to find Joe Messina, Pistol Allen, or James Jamerson on that sheet of paper! Who wrote the arrangement? Not listed. . . . [It is] just a list of chords. Try to get the Motown Sound off that sheet of music! They went to California and used different personnel out there. Did they come up with the same sound? Have you heard anything after '72? . . . They got other great drummers out there but they play different from me.

One of Allen's specialties at Motown was playing shuffle rhythms.

I played the shuffle better than Benny [Benjamin]. He could play it too, but they liked the way I played it. . . . I couldn't play what he or Uriel [Jones] played, because they thought differently. . . . Everybody was important down there. . . . As far as we were concerned, as a group we did everything together. . . . It took three guitar players, bass and three drummers to create this. So everybody was important, but we never were recognized. . . . We were versatile. We could do everything. . . . We learned from each other—we were like a family at Motown.[203]

Allen's versatility was a function of his experience playing jazz, blues, and R & B in Detroit and in his hometown, Memphis. His jazz credentials included gigs with Sonny Stitt, recording for Riverside in New York, and jam sessions at the Blue Bird and the West End. In the years immediately before starting at Motown in 1961, he played with Maurice King at the Flame and toured with the Idlewild Revue. The Revue featured among others Jackie Wilson and future Motown artists the Four Tops.[204]

This versatility was present in the earliest Motown studio band, pianist Joe Hunter's group. Teddy Harris remembered the band.

Joe Hunter had [bassist] James Jamerson, [drummer] Benny Benjamin, [baritonist] Mike Terry, [tenorist] Hank Cosby, [guitarist] Larry Veeder. That was actually the first Motown band that recorded as a band. They did a lot of shows around town.[205]

Gordy engineered the formation of Hunter's band, as Hunter recalled.

Berry introduced me to Smokey [Robinson]. He took me to Claudette's house [Smokey's girlfriend] for a rehearsal. Benny Benjamin was there. So was Beans Bowles and Joe Messina. Originally, Ernie Farrow was playing bass, but he didn't want to play this kind of music. So Berry told me to get a band together. I brought in Hank Cosby, and [bassist] Joe Williams, then Joe left and Tweed Beard was in for a minute. Then I got Jamerson.[206]

Hunter's band contained two musicians most identified with the Motown sound: James Jamerson and William "Benny" Benjamin.

202. Bowles, interview by Bjorn.

203. Pistol Allen, interview by Lars Bjorn, Detroit, Michigan, July 22, 1998.

204. After finishing high school Allen moved from Memphis to Flint, Michigan, in 1950. In 1958 he played with Sonny Stitt in Saginaw and played Birdland in New York with pianist Evans Bradshaw's trio. Bradshaw was another musician from Memphis who had moved to Flint. Allen and bassist Alvin Jackson recorded with the trio for Riverside in January 1959. Ibid. Tom Lord, *The Jazz Discography*, vol. 3 (Redwood, N.Y.: Cadence, 1992), 725.

205. Teddy Harris, interview by Jim Gallert, Detroit, Michigan, May 12, 1997.

206. Joe Hunter, interview by Jim Gallert, Detroit, Michigan, February 23, 2000. Hunter (born 1927) came to Detroit from his hometown of Jackson, Tennessee, in 1939. He studied piano and clarinet off and on at Northern High School. He co-led a band with Cosby in 1944 and moved into music following his discharge from the service in 1949. Hunter toured with Hank Ballard and the Midnighters in the 1950s before joining Gordy in 1958. Joe Hunter, *Musicians, Motown, and Myself* (Detroit: Global Sound Publications, 1996).

These two, along with pianist/organist Earl Van Dyke and guitarist Robert White, were part of a small group dubbed the "Funk Brothers" by Benjamin.[207]

Van Dyke started out as a jazz pianist in the 1940s and switched to organ in the 1950s, when he spent several years in New York with rhythm and blues bands.[208] He returned to Detroit in late 1961 to play at Motown and in the last house band at the Flame with tenorist George Benson.[209]

Trumpeter Johnny Trudell worked with Van Dyke during and after Motown, and he recalled the pianist.

> *Earl was one of the greatest piano players I ever worked with. Great accompanist, great sense of time. Earl had a gospel background. Great jazz background too.*[210]

Benny Benjamin was another veteran player by the time he joined Motown at its inception. Beans Bowles remembered that "Candy Johnson brought him here from the Danville—St. Louis area and Candy helped develop him in swing, because Candy was a strong swing man."[211] Benjamin's jump band experience was made richer by playing with Paul Williams, Floyd Taylor, Todd Rhodes, and King Porter. His most notable straight jazz job in the 1950s was with Roland Hanna's trio in 1954–55.[212] Bassist Ray McKinney was the third member of Hanna's trio, and he recalled Benjamin.

> *Benny was the kind of guy that every lick he hit was the greatest thing he ever did. He used to play his ass off, real rhythm drummer. Had a whole lotta stuff going for him rhythmically.*[213]

According to Joe Hunter, "Benny Benjamin was made out of rhythm; he could play drunk or sober. I think he knew what Berry wanted before Berry did."[214]

James Jamerson is often singled out as a key innovator of the Motown Sound. He was younger than Van Dyke and Benjamin and started on bass at Northwestern High School in 1954, playing in a jazz band with Roy Brooks. His first regular job was with his father-in-law, blues singer Washboard Willie, in 1958, the same year he made his first rhythm and blues recording. By the next year he recorded his first Motown hit with the Miracles' "Way over There." Teddy Harris remembered Jamerson.

> *Jamerson was originally a upright bass player. He used to carry that little Fender thing around as an accessory. I don't think there was ever any music written for Jamerson. They just told him what they wanted and he did it.*[215]

In 1961 he switched to the electric (Fender) bass and became a pioneer on the instrument. Jamerson's bass playing was a departure from what other R & B bassists had done, according to his biographer, Dr. Licks.

> *James had the ability to incorporate his jazz background into Berry Gordy's R & B influenced pop format. . . . Gone were the stagnant two beat, root-fifth patterns and post- "Under the Boardwalk" clichéd bass lines. . . . Jamerson had modified or replaced them with chromatic passing tones, Ray Brown style walking bass lines, syncopated 8th note figures, previously unheard of in pop music.*[216]

Joe Hunter offered an insight into Jamerson's unmatched rhythmic flexibility.

> *When I first heard him, he was with Washboard Willie. Washboard had a type of rhythm . . . . he'd stay on one chord for ten bars, then change for one bar, then go back to the first chord. You had to follow him and "turn him around." James had to find his way through that. At Motown, he fit right in. He'd get his part and throw it on the floor and play his own stuff. He had a better conception [of the material] than the arrangers.*[217]

This core group of musicians, led by Van Dyke, created the distinctive sound that Gordy wanted, as Teddy Harris recalled.

> *Earl was able to fit that music . . . with these lyricists that came in there . . . nobody was a professional song writer. Once he [Gordy] found out that Earl and these guys could do*

207. Hunter, *Musicians, Motown, and Myself*, 46. Hunter was an original "Funk Brother" until he left Motown in 1963.

208. Van Dyke was born in Detroit in 1929 and won an amateur contest with his band at the Paradise Theatre in 1946. *Michigan Chronicle*, May 18, 1946. Obituary, *Detroit Free Press*, September 21, 1992.

209. Benson, interview by Bjorn and Gallert.

210. Trudell, interview by Gallert. Trudell was born in Detroit in 1939 and played his first job at 13. He formed a singing group, the Four Holidays, and toured nationally. He has led a band in Detroit since the early 1960s.

211. Bowles, interview by Bjorn.

212. Hanna, interview by Bjorn.

213. Ray McKinney, interview by Gallert.

214. Hunter, interview by Gallert.

215. Teddy Harris, interview by Gallert, May 12, 1999.

216. Dr. Licks, *Standing in the Shadows of Motown: The Life and Music of Legendary Bassist James Jamerson* (Wynnewood, Pa.: Dr. Licks Publishing, 1989), 12.

217. Hunter, interview by Gallert.

that, he stuck with that. And everything else was just embellishment. We got to the point where they were using arrangers. As the sound became more popular, they began to embellish it with strings and hire outside musicians.[218]

Johnny Trudell summed up the Funk Brothers this way.

If you [wanted] soul music, there was nothing like the Funk Brothers. They knew gospel music and they knew jazz, had a jazz influence. Put it together with some great tunes and great arrangers, now you got something.[219]

Just outside the Funk Brothers core was a circle of 10 musicians, many with extensive jazz backgrounds. This circle had two pianists (including Johnny Griffith), two guitarists (including Joe Messina), two drummers (including Pistol Allen), three percussionists (including Jack Brokensha), and saxophonist Beans Bowles. Johnny Griffith had played with Joe Henderson and other jazzmen in the late 1950s.[220] Joe Messina and Jack Brokensha were both on the Soupy Sales TV show and had a background in jazz going back to the 1940s. Messina had been a member of one of the early jazz house bands on Detroit television in the early 1950s, and by the time he got to Motown he was responsible for the backbeats and any difficult written parts.[221]

Given the lack of musical training among Motown producers a crucial role was played by Motown's staff of arrangers.[222] Jack Brokensha put it this way.

Motown also needed jazz musicians, the arrangers came out of that, and the players. . . . Motown was a funny mix of things. The producers could not even count up to four, you know, when you start the band off. . . . It was that combination of street smarts and the arrangers who would come in and clean up this thing onto some kind of sheet we could all hang on to. . . . Then the rhythm section would add their thing to it, because you could not write most of that stuff.[223]

The arrangers included veteran jazz and rhythm and blues players like Johnny Allen, Willis "Willie" Shorter, and Maurice King. Allen had played piano and arranged for the jump blues bands of Lucky Millinder and Bull Moose Jackson in the late 1940s. In the 1950s he returned to Detroit and led his own, mostly jazz-oriented groups, notably for a long stay at LaVert's. He joined Motown in 1962 and worked as an arranger, a conductor, and sometimes a pianist.[224] Shorter was a pianist in Mathew Rucker's band and an admirer of Milt Buckner's skills as an arranger. King joined Motown about a year after leaving his job as leader of the band at the Flame. Like Allen he took care of tasks at Motown other than arranging, including teaching the acts how to phrase.[225] According to Johnny Trudell, "Maurice brought discipline and sophistication to Motown."[226]

By the time Motown left Detroit for Los Angeles in 1972, Gordy had made stars out of many Detroit singers. The musicians, however, remained in the background, according to Johnny Trudell.

That's the biggest thing with Motown Records, bothered the guys more than anything. Not the money so much, it was that we never got any album credits. And, the reason they [Motown] didn't want that, they didn't want anybody to steal [the musicians]. Especially that rhythm section. So, if they aren't going to put the rhythm section's names on the records, they certainly weren't going to put the horns and strings [on the records].[227]

The Motown Sound would not have been possible without the creativity, skills, and experiences of the jazz and R & B musicians mentioned. Once they had done their job the Gordy production system took over to make hit records. It is often tempting to liken this to an assembly-line process, since it took place in Detroit, but this is too facile an analogy. While cars are produced in a process minutely planned by industrial engineers, the creation of

218. Teddy Harris, interview by Gallert, May 12, 1999.

219. Trudell, interview by Gallert.

220. *Down Beat,* April 4, 1957; and *Michigan Chronicle,* May 31, 1958.

221. Dr. Licks, *Standing in the Shadows of Motown,* 31. Jack Brokensha's view is that "Joe Messina taught everyone how to play; there would be no Motown without him." Brokensha, interview by Bjorn.

222. This is willingly admitted by Gordy (*To Be Loved,* 132).

223. Brokensha, interview by Bjorn.

224. Jim Gallert, "Piano Man: Johnny Allen," *Metropolitan Entertainment Plus Magazine,* May 1992.

225. King, interview by Gallert.

226. Trudell, interview by Gallert.

227. Ibid.

new musical sounds requires a more interactive process. Gordy realized this and did not interfere with the musicians. As Jack Brokensha put it, "We saw Gordy once in a while, he was a smart cookie; he knew to stay away most of the time."[228] Gordy's genius came into play after the tracks were laid down, as Teddy Harris recalled: "Once he found the sound he wanted, nothing went out of there unless it passed Berry's ear."[229]

Before Motown there was jazz in Detroit, and jazz was more than a footnote in its development. We leave it to scholars of popular music to fully explain the rise of the Motown Sound and how it came to stand for Detroit in the popular mind.

228. Brokensha, interview by Bjorn.

229. Teddy Harris, interview by Gallert, May 12, 1999.

The Social History of Detroit Jazz: A Summary

Beyond the details of who played when and where in Detroit over four decades, I have also examined two aspects of the social context of music making. On the one hand we have the relationship between musicians and their audiences, while on the other hand we have the wider context of race relations. How have these relationships changed over the four decades covered?

With regard to the relationship between jazz musicians and their audiences the major change was that from jazz for dancing to jazz for listening. This change roughly coincided with the change from swing to bebop. Jazz became a popular music to dance to as Detroit ballrooms mushroomed in the downtown area in the later years of the second decade of the twentieth century and in the 1920s. Ballroom dancing was a strictly segregated affair, and there was limited access for black Detroiters. This did not mean that black bands were idle, for in fact they were very busy playing for white audiences. In Detroit, black society bands had been very popular with white dancers since before jazz emerged, and these bands were important forerunners of jazz big bands. The other influence on big band jazz was from the blues end of the spectrum of African-American music, which was a classic case of subcultural music, performed by and for African Americans. Classic blues was found at the Koppin Theatre, and there were a number of country blues artists in Detroit as well. The genius of the creators of big band jazz, like Don Redman of McKinney's Cotton Pickers, was to recombine society band music and the blues tradition into a new vital musical form. The new music functioned primarily as dance music for the masses, but it was also seen as art music by the musicians and a smaller group of listeners. It was in the after-hours clubs that grew up in Paradise Valley in the 1930s that big band musicians relaxed and exchanged musical ideas in jam sessions.

Bebop was an outgrowth of this musicians' subculture and was taken to the public in clubs and concert halls in the mid-1940s. The bebop audience was smaller than that of the ballroom dancers, but it was large enough to sustain the further development of the music. The case of Detroit also shows that bebop maintained some commercial viability with a very gradual transition from dancers to listeners. Well into the first half of the 1950s, modern jazz functioned as dance music in downtown ballrooms. Modern jazz musicians also survived by playing more popular kinds of music, like jump blues. Black audiences were by the latter half of the 1940s increasingly favoring jump blues, as we can see by the number of venues in Detroit's black community devoted to it. In the 1950s, the full development of rhythm and blues further bifurcated the black audience by attracting a larger and younger audience, while a smaller audience heard jazz in what became known as jazz clubs.

The center for the modernist circle of musicians was the Blue Bird Inn and a handful of other clubs, mainly downtown and on the West Side. A large majority of musicians were African American, but the audiences were more evenly split along racial lines. I also found that the emergence of these clubs was associated with a lowering of racial barriers among musicians and audiences alike in the 1940s. In the prewar years white and black musicians only played together during informal jam sessions; now they played together in the same bands in front of mixed audiences. Jazz had come a long way in the 20 years that passed between the Cotton Pickers at the Graystone and the beboppers at the Blue Bird.

Jazz in Detroit since 1960

If the 1950s were the golden age of jazz in Detroit what followed must have been something less magnificent. There is some truth in this sweeping generalization, but it needs to be qualified by noting that Detroit has continued to make substantial contributions to the world of jazz up to today. A number of talented musicians have started their musical careers in Detroit and moved on to New York in the last 40 years. Some recent examples of Detroiters who have joined the forefront of the development of the music are pianist Geri Allen and saxophone marvel James Carter.

One of Allen's most important mentors in Detroit was trumpeter Marcus Belgrave, who in the 1970s started the Jazz Development Workshop. Belgrave was one of several musicians who had been attracted to Detroit in the early 1960s by the presence of Motown and a vital jazz tradition. In the 1970s his Jazz Workshop was one of several educational projects organized by local musicians. Carter was also importantly influenced in his early years by the activities of jazz educators: in his case it was the Trane-Sco-Now band organized by Donald Washington.

In spite of the accomplishments of players like Allen and Carter, it is safe to say that the flow of talent from Detroit has slowed down in the last 40 years. Many factors have contributed to this. Nationally there were serious problems for jazz musicians in finding work in the late 1960s and 1970s. In Detroit the departure of Motown in 1972 and a steady outflow of population made conditions more difficult. The city of Detroit has steadily lost population since 1952, so that by the turn of the century it will have half of the population it had 50 years earlier. Much of this population has moved to the suburbs, and so has some of the jazz activity, which today can be found throughout the Metro Detroit area.

Still, there are many signs of resilience. New jazz venues still pop up in the city, and some old-timers like Baker's and the Blue Bird are still around. Jazz festivals have blossomed since the 1970s, particularly the Montreux-Detroit (now the Ford Detroit International) Jazz Festival, which is the largest free jazz festival in the nation. Every Labor Day weekend a healthy mixture of local and national jazz talent draws half a million listeners to Hart Plaza on Detroit's beautiful riverfront. The national jazz talent often includes former Detroiters, who revel at these homecomings bringing them back in touch with local musicians and audiences. They are all proud to be part of a living and continually evolving Detroit jazz tradition.

The jazz tradition that was born in Detroit before Motown is still alive and well long after the departure of the city's most widely known musical institution and namesake. Just as there was jazz in Detroit before Motown, there is jazz in the city after Motown.

Appendix A
List of Interviews

THE FOLLOWING INDIVIDUALS in the Detroit jazz world were interviewed by Lars Bjorn and/or Jim Gallert. Most of the interviews were at the respondents' homes; some were on the air (Jim Gallert's *Jazz Yesterday,* WDET-FM, Detroit); a few were in clubs; and a few were over the telephone.

Adams, Alberta
Allen, Johnny
Allen, Pistol
Anderson, Stutz
Austin, Will
Baker, Clarence
Bassett, Johnnie
Benson, George
Besman, Bernie
Bonnier, Bess
Bowles, Beans
Boykin, Ulysses
Boykin, Wade
Bragg, Walter
Brokensha, Jack
Brooks, Roy
Buckner, Rilla
Burrell, Kenny
Butts, Hindal
Campau, Ann
Campau, Jack
Cornfoot, Bob
Cousar, Bobby
Cox, Kenn
Cramton, Lou
Crutcher, Porter
Duquette, Jack
Edwards, Lefty
Edwards, Teddy
Flanagan, Tommy
Foster, Frank
Foster, Paul
Fowler, Mattie
Gabriel, Charlie
Gant, Frank
Gray, Jeri
Green, Russell
Hanna, Roland
Harris, Barry
Harris, Teddy
Hayes, Louis
Hill, Carl
Hunter, Joe
Jackson, Alvin
Jordan, Sheila
Kahn, Marvin
Kalb, Irv
Kaplan, John

Kenyon, Reuel
King, Maurice
LaGassé, Oscar
Lasley, Phil
Lateef, Yusef
Mann, Lawrence
Martin, Al
Martin, Kelly
McCray, Malvin
McCullers, Dezi
McKibbon, Al
McKinney, Harold
McKinney, Ray
McPherson, Charles
Mitchell, Billy
Moore, Charles Victor
Morrison, Claudia
Nero, Gene
Norris, Joe
Nuccilli, Eddie
Perkins, Jack
Perry, Ditto
Pierce, Reade
Plovan, Mike
Pollard, Terry
Powell, Preston
Randle, Bill
Rhodes, Annie Mae
Richardson, Beans
Ritten, Eddie
Rodgers, Ernie
Rucker, Mathew
Smith, Alma
Stefanson, Jim
Taylor, Frank
Taylor, Gene
Trafton, Johnny
Trudell, Johnny
Tucich, Rudy
Usher, Dave
Van Riper, Earl
Warren, Wilson "Junior"
Wilborn, Dave
Williams, Joe
Wilson, Gerald

Appendix B
Library Resources Used

Local libraries are essential for writing a book like this, mainly because of their vast collections of local newspapers. I took advantage of the collections of the Detroit Public Library, Wayne State University Library, and the University of Michigan libraries in Ann Arbor and Dearborn. I systematically searched the entertainment pages of several local newspapers from 1920 to 1960.

The African-American papers yielded most items of jazz interest, since they included not only advertisements for jazz spots but also columns and general feature articles on jazz musicians and spots. The most relevant information was found in the *Michigan Chronicle* (1936–60), closely followed by the *Detroit Tribune* (1933–53). Other Detroit African-American papers were less useful since they had less coverage, were published less frequently, or were not available: the *Paradise Valley News* (1937) and the *Detroit People's News* (1930). I also examined the entertainment pages of the *Chicago Defender* from 1917 to 1933.

I also looked at the entertainment pages of the two major dailies, the *Detroit Free Press* and the *Detroit News* for 1920–60 and the *Detroit Times* for a few years in the mid-1950s. The coverage of jazz in these papers was sparser, as it consisted of ads for mainstream venues and occasional entertainment columns. A weekly entertainment publication, *Detroit Saturday Night*, proved useful for researching the white dance band world from 1920 to 1933.

Polk's *Detroit City Directory* was a valuable resource for locating jazz venues and some musicians in time and space. It was available for almost all years of the period studied. The Burton Historical Collection at the Detroit Public Library also has the personal papers of Fred Hart Williams. The same library's E. Azalia Hackley Memorial Collection has many high quality photos and clipping files for a few jazz artists.

Specialized jazz periodicals provided another important source. I searched *Down Beat* magazine from 1940 to 1960 for interviews with local musicians and columns about the Detroit jazz scene. *Metronome* also had a few articles of interest in the 1940s.

The Institute of Jazz Studies at the Rutgers State University campus in Newark, New Jersey, is the world's premier jazz research facility. It has some useful oral history interviews with Detroit musicians and a wealth of jazz periodicals.

Appendix C
List of Recommended CDs

This is a list of recommended and currently available CDs with the work of the major artists covered in this book. Only CDs recorded at the time the artists lived in Detroit, or soon after their departure, are included. For a select few records or out-of-print CDs have been included. Be warned that CDs go rapidly out of print. However, reissues are also frequent.

Pepper Adams. *The Cool Sound of Pepper Adams.* Savoy 198 (1957, includes Bernard McKinney, Hank Jones, and Elvin Jones).

———. *10 to 4 at the 5-Spot.* OJC-31 (1958, includes Donald Byrd, Doug Watkins, and Elvin Jones).

Big Maceo. *Bluebird Recordings 1941–1942.* RCA 66715.

———. *Victor/Bluebird Recordings 1945–1947.* RCA 66716.

Kenny Burrell. *Introducing Kenny Burrell.* Blue Note 1523 (1956, includes Tommy Flanagan and Paul Chambers).

———. *Blue Moods.* OJC-019 (1957, includes Tommy Flanagan, Doug Watkins, and Elvin Jones).

———. *All Day Long.* OJC-456 (1957, includes Tommy Flanagan, Doug Watkins, Donald Byrd, and Frank Foster).

Donald Byrd. *Byrd's Word.* Savoy 132 (1955, includes Frank Foster, Hank Jones, and Paul Chambers).

———. *First Flight: Yusef Lateef with Donald Byrd.* Delmark DD-407 (1955, includes Yusef Lateef, Frank Foster, Bernard McKinney, Barry Harris, Hank Jones, Paul Chambers, Alvin Jackson, and Frank Gant).

Betty Carter. *Meet Betty Carter and Ray Bryant.* Columbia/Legacy 64936 (1955–56).

Paul Chambers. *Whims of Chambers.* Blue Note 37647 (1956, includes Donald Byrd and Kenny Burrell).

———. *Bass on Top.* Blue Note B2-46533 (1957, includes Kenny Burrell and Hank Jones).

Teddy Edwards. *Steady with Teddy.* Cool and Blue 115 (1946–48, with Howard McGhee).

Tommy Flanagan. *Overseas.* OJC-1033 (1957, includes Elvin Jones).

T. J. Fowler. *T. J. Fowler and His Rockin' Jump Band.* Savoy ZDS-1187 (1948, 1952–53, includes Calvin Frazier, Alberta Adams, Dezi McCullers, Walter Cox, John Lawton, and Lee Gross).

Curtis Fuller. *New Trombone.* OJC-77 (1957, includes Sonny Red, Hank Jones, Doug Watkins, and Louis Hayes).

———. *Curtis Fuller with Red Garland.* OJC-1862 (1957, includes Sonny Red, Paul Chambers, and Louis Hayes).

Jean Goldkette Orchestra. On Bix Beiderbecke, *The Indispensable.* RCA 66540 (1925–30, includes Beiderbecke, Frank Trumbauer, and Tommy Dorsey).

Wardell Gray. *Wardell Gray Memorial Volume Two.* Prestige, OJCCD-051-2 (1950–52).

Barry Harris. *Breakin' It Up.* Argo LPS-644 (1958, LP, includes Will Austin and Frank Gant).

Joe Henderson. *Page One.* Blue Note B2-84140 (1963).

John Lee Hooker. *Legendary Modern Recordings.* Capitol 39658 (1948–54).

Milt Jackson/Sonny Stitt. *In the Beginning.* OJC-1771 (1948, includes Alvin Jackson).

Thad Jones. *The Fabulous Thad Jones.* OJC-625 (1954–55, includes Hank Jones).

———. *Detroit–New York Junction.* Blue Note 1513 (1956, includes Tommy Flanagan, Billy Mitchell, and Kenny Burrell).

———. *The Magnificent Thad Jones.* Blue Note 46814 (1956, includes Barry Harris, Billy Mitchell, and Kenny Burrell).

Yusef Lateef. *Jazz for the Thinker.* Savoy SJC 404 (1957, LP, includes Curtis Fuller, Hugh Lawson, Ernie Farrow, and Louis Hayes).

———. *Before Dawn.* Verve 314 557 097-2 (1957, includes Curtis Fuller, Hugh Lawson, Ernie Farrow, and Louis Hayes).

———. *The Last Savoy Sessions.* Savoy 92881 (1957–59, includes Bernard McKinney, Wilbur Harden, Terry Pollard, Hugh Lawson, Will Austin, Ernie Farrow, Oliver Jackson, and Frank Gant).

Howard McGhee. *Howard McGhee 1946–1948.* Classics 1089 (includes Teddy Edwards, Milt Jackson, Hank Jones, and J. C. Heard).

McKinney's Cotton Pickers. *McKinney's Cotton Pickers 1928–1929.* Classics 609.

———. *McKinney's Cotton Pickers 1929–1930.* Classics 625.

———. *McKinney's Cotton Pickers 1930.* Classics 649.

Billy Mitchell Quintet. On Various Artists, *Swing Not Spring.* Savoy SV-0188 (1953, Japanese, includes Thad Jones, Terry Pollard, Beans Richardson, and Elvin Jones).

King Porter. *Special Request.* Official 6056 (1947–52, Danish LP, includes Billy Mitchell, Wild Bill Moore, and Lefty Edwards).

Sonny Red. *Out of the Blue.* BN 52440 (1959–60, includes Paul Chambers and Roy Brooks).

Todd Rhodes. *Dance Music That Hits the Spot.* Contact ST 1020 (1949–54, Danish LP, includes Louis Barnett, Holley Dismukes, and Ted Buckner).

Frank Rosolino Quartet (with Barry Harris). On Various Artists, *Swing Not Spring.* Savoy SV-0188 (1952, Japanese).

Sonny Stitt. *Burnin'.* Argo LP(S)661 (1958, LP).

———. *Sonny Stitt.* MCA 9317 (1958, includes Barry Harris, Will Austin, and Frank Gant).

Lucky Thompson. *The Beginning Years.* IAJRC CD 1001 (1945–47, includes Rudy Rutherford and Karl George).

Paul Williams. *Complete Recordings,* vol. 1. Blue Moon 6020 (1947–49, includes King Porter, Billy Mitchell, Walter Cox, and John Lawton).

Appendix D
Detroit Jazz Spots 1920–60

Ace Bar, 3678 Hastings
Addison Hotel, 3001 Woodward
Alvito's Bar, 3600 Russell
Arcadia, 3527 Woodward
Band Box, 602 E. Adams
B & C, 1730 St. Antoine
Bizerte, 9006 Oakland
Blossom Heath, 24800 Jefferson, St. Clair Shores
Blue Bird Inn, 5021 Tireman
Blue Note Room, 2931 John R.
Bowl-O-Drome, 12707 Dexter
Brown Bomber Chicken Shack, 424 E. Vernor
Buffalo's, 606 E. Adams
Carribee, 6811 E. Jefferson
Chesterfield Lounge, 4721 John R.
Chic's Show Bar, 8441 Hamilton
Chocolate Bar, 632 Livingstone
Civic Center, 114 Erskine
Club Congo, 550 E. Adams
Club Deliese, 2406 E. Davison
Club Harlem, 281 E. Vernor
Club Juana, 2725 Woodward
Club Owens, 1730 St. Antoine
Club Paradise, 1933 St. Antoine
Club Plantation, 550 E. Adams
Club Sudan, 550 E. Adams
Club Three 666, 666 E. Adams
Club Zombie, 8825 Oakland
Congo Lounge, 2337 Gratiot
Cotton Club, 632 Livingstone
Cozy Corner, 4100 Hastings
Crest Lounge, 12707 Fullerton
Crystal, 2769 Woodward
Crystal, 5612 Grand River
Denny's, 8417 Linwood
Double V, 17910 Conant
Dunbar Theatre, 2814 Hastings
Eagle Show Bar, 8737 Twelfth
El Sino, 1730 St. Antoine

Enrico's Theatre Cabaret, 3062 Rivard
Falcon Show Bar, 19901 Van Dyke
Flame Show Bar, 4264 John R.
Forest Club, 700 E. Forest
Frolic Show Bar, 4450 John R.
Garden Terrace, 301 E. Warren
Grande, 8952 Grand River
Grand Terrace, 3067 Grand Blvd.
Graystone, 4235 Woodward
Hajji Baba, 3775 Gratiot
Harlem Cave, Brush/Canfield
Henry's Swing Club, 1700 Orleans
Hobby Bar, 13106 Linwood
House of Joy, 4701 W. Warren
Jefferson Beach, E. Jefferson at Grand
Jess Faithful's Rhythm Club, 1701 St. Antoine
Klein's, 8540 Twelfth
Koppin Theatre, 528 Gratiot
Larry's Show Bar, 6911 Gratiot
Latin Quarter, 3067 Grand Blvd.
LaVert's, 8521 Linwood
Lee's Sensation, 1300 Owen
Little Wally's, Mack at Maryland
Madison, Woodward at Forest
Majestic, 3116 Woodward
MDL Club, Livingstone/St. Antoine
Melody Club, 1933 St. Antoine
Mickey's Show Bar, 623 E. Seven Mile
Minor Key, 11541 Dexter
Mirror, 2940 Woodward
Monticello, 14421 E. Jefferson
New Bohemia, Woodward at Mack
Oriole Show Bar, 8521 Linwood
Oriole Terrace, 3067 Grand Blvd.
Palais de Danse, 7336 E. Jefferson
Palm Garden Café, Warren/Russell
Palms, 1935 1/2 St. Antoine
Paradise Theatre, 3711 Woodward
Parrot Lounge, 504 E. Canfield
Pier, 7300 E. Jefferson
Rage Show Bar, 2210 Davison
Rhythm Club, 301 E. Warren
Roosevelt Lounge, 10813 Mack
Rose Bud Inn, 2337 Hastings
Rouge Lounge, 1937 Coolidge Hwy.
Royal Blue Bar, 8401 Russell
Royal Garden Cabaret, Gratiot at St. Antoine
Russell House, 615 E. Adams
Shangri-La, 8715 Harper
Sportree's Music Bar, 2014 Hastings
Spot Bar, 8606 Twelfth
Three Star Bar, Hastings at Brewster
Tuxedo Grill/Club Tuxedo, 4758 Hastings
Twenty Grand, 5020 Fourteenth
Vanity, 14301 E. Jefferson
Vaudette Theatre, 764 Gratiot
Wal-Ha Room, 4457 John R.
West End, 515 S. West End Ave.
World Stage, 13525 Woodward
Wyoming Show Bar, 14834 Wyoming
Young's Cocktail Lounge, 10810 Plymouth

Appendix E
Abbreviations Used in Photo Captions

arr	arranger
as	alto saxophone
bar	baritone saxophone
bbs	brass bass (sousaphone or tuba)
bjo	banjo
bs	string bass
bsn	bassoon
cl	clarinet
cnt	cornet
C-m	C-melody saxophone
dir	director
dms	drums
el bs	electric bass
flt	flute
gtr	guitar
ldr	leader
o	oboe
pno	piano
ss	soprano saxophone
tb	trombone
tp	trumpet
ts	tenor saxophone
vbs	vibraphone
vcl	vocalist
vln	violin
x	xylophone

Name Index

Subject Index